Topics in Advanced Language Implementation

Topics in Advanced Language Implementation

Edited by

PETER LEE

The MIT Press
Cambridge, Massachusetts
London, England

This book was printed and bound in the United States of America.

Library of Congress Cataloging-in-Publication Data

Topics in advanced language implementation / edited by Peter Lee.
    p. cm.
    Includes bibliographical references and index.
    ISBN 0-262-12151-4
    1. Programming languages (Electronic computers) I. Lee, Peter, 1960– .
QA76.7.T65 1991
005.13—dc20
                                                91-9709
                                                CIP

Contents

Preface

The subject of compiler construction has been an active area of research for over thirty years, and for nearly the same period it has been an important part of the curriculum in computer science. It is remarkable, then, to see how little our teaching of this subject has changed over this period. Of course, we now teach better parsing techniques, attribute grammars are commonplace, and oftentimes one sees that much more is taught about flow analysis and optimization now than was the case ten years ago. But the emphasis is still on "conventional" programming languages such as Pascal and C, despite the fact that increasingly, many "advanced" languages are being used in practical applications.

So, it seems a good time to consider a move to newer and more interesting horizons in language implementation. I propose the following: advanced techniques for implementing advanced programming languages, or *advanced language implementation techniques* (ALIT). By "advanced languages," I mean general programming languages such as Lisp, Scheme, Standard ML, Prolog, Smalltalk, Haskell, and many others, which could conceivably be called "practical," or at least nearly so, but are still widely regarded as unconventional. By "advanced implementation techniques," I mean techniques that address the special challenges posed by advanced languages, for example: techniques for automatic garbage collection, design considerations for compiling to unconventional architectures, methods for utilizing special hardware devices such as caches and memory-management units, semantics-based optimization, type analysis for type-safe separate compilation, and so on.

Only the passage of time will tell whether a "discipline" of ALIT will ever really exist. But I firmly believe that it will, and imagine that it will consist of at least the following major subject areas:

- *Type checking and separate compilation.* The static analysis of programs in order to check their well-formedness, even across module boundaries.

  The language Standard ML supports polymorphic types and a powerful language of modules that permits type-safe separate compilation. These features make special demands on the analysis component of a compiler. Even languages such as Lisp, Scheme, and Prolog, which are dynamically typed, can often benefit from static type analyses which can be used to enable certain code optimizations.

- *Compile-time structures.* The structures built and maintained by the compiler in order to support analysis and efficient compilation.

The internal form of the source program can have a major effect on the complexity of the compiler. For example, Scheme compilers (as well as some compilers for Lisp and Standard ML) use an internal representation called "continuation-passing style." This representation allows most of the analyses and optimizations to be carried out on a remarkably simple and semantically well-understood language, thereby greatly simplifying issues of the correctness of optimizations. Some important kinds of information can be lost in such representations, however, and so other internal forms, or variations on the continuation-passing-style representation, must also be considered.

- *Static analysis and optimization.* The static analysis of programs in order to enable optimizations that improve run-time efficiency.

  Programs written in advanced languages can exhibit extremely complicated flow of control. In Lisp and Scheme programs, for example, there are usually many more procedure calls than in corresponding Pascal or C programs. Static analysis of control flow is thus very important, but also much more difficult to carry out. Standard optimizations that depend on control-flow information, for example register allocation and dataflow analysis, must be adjusted to reflect these special circumstances.

- *Data representations and memory management.* Strategies for keeping to a minimum the overhead involved in the allocation, retrieval, and disposal of program data objects.

  Advanced language implementations typically must allocate and dispose of data structures automatically. So, fast garbage collection is crucial for a practical system. This can become quite difficult on a multiprocessor system. Features such as dynamic or polymorphic typing mean that accesses to data may involve the handling of stored run-time type information. Type-tagging schemes can have a major impact on the amount of overhead involved in data accesses.

- *Run-time system organization.* The organization of the run-time system to support interactive development and debugging in an efficient and portable manner.

  Advanced languages typically have sophisticated run-time systems that support highly interactive program development and debugging. The portability and efficiency of the run-time system can have a significant effect on the design of other aspects of the implementation, for example on data representations.

- *Parallelization.* Strategies for optimal utilization of multiple processors, arranged in various topologies.

  Some advanced languages can be extended in a straightforward way with constructs for expressing parallel computation. Examples include the addition of "futures" to

Scheme, or "xappings" to Lisp. The importance of many implementation issues become magnified by the presence of parallelism.

I have no doubt that I have missed many important topics. But at any rate, this list reflects my current understanding of what might comprise a "discipline" of advanced language implementation. In essence, I view ALIT as the next logical step beyond the conventional compiler construction of today.

In the fall of 1989 I conducted my first graduate seminar on ALIT in the School of Computer Science at Carnegie Mellon. The seminar featured a large number of guest lectures, and so Alessandro Forin (also the author of Chapter 9) suggested that I collect together and publish the lecture notes so that future courses could benefit from them. This, then, is how we began this project.

However, once we got started, a number of contributing authors chose to present the results of more recent research, in a way that could still fit in with the general scope and theme of the book. Some authors joined the project long after the seminar was over, in order to help fill in a few key missing topics. In the end, we ended up with fifteen writings by eighteen contributing authors. (All of this, of course, also greatly extended the amount of time it took to finish this book!) But I hope that we have also created a more useful book – one that can serve at least partially two purposes. The first is to help provide a basis for a more formal course on advanced language implementation techniques. Such a course certainly seems necessary. The practice of language implementation, both in the research community and in industry, already confronts issues in advanced language implementation on a daily basis. Issues such as run-time tagging of data, garbage collection, polymorphic type checking, and so forth, are becoming increasingly commonplace. The second purpose is to provide a reference for practitioners. Hopefully, this book can fill some of the void between books like the venerable "dragon" book and the widely scattered literature in advanced language implementation.

In organizing the book, I have divided the contributions into four parts:

I: *Advanced Implementation Techniques.* Basic implementation techniques common to most advanced languages, such as run-time tagging and garbage collection.

II: *Practice and Experience with Advanced Implementations.* Descriptions of the design considerations in actual implementations of advanced languages.

III: *Languages for Parallel and Distributed Systems.* The special issues that pertain to parallel and distributed languages.

IV: *New and Unconventional Languages and Techniques.* A survey of issues and implementation techniques for very unusual languages and systems.

Parts I and II contain material which is directly applicable to most Lisp, Scheme, and ML implementations. This collection is by no means complete, and so there are many important topics which would be covered in a textbook on advanced language implementation, but are missing in this book. These include conversion to continuation-passing style, separate compilation and modules, polymorphic type checking, trace scheduling, the Warren abstract machine, and case studies of compilers such as ORBIT and Standard ML of New Jersey. The bibliography contains references to papers covering some of these topics, so the interested reader is encouraged to study these in order to get a complete picture of the basic issues.

Part III contains three chapters on implementing three very different styles of parallel/distributed computation. Again, there are many important topics missing here, in particular with regard to architecture and operating system issues. Finally, Part IV presents a collection of chapters on more "fringe" techniques and languages. These are given in part for contrast, but also to give what may be a glimpse of some of future implementation techniques.

In reading this book, one may notice the preponderance of run-time over compile-time concerns. I believe this to be a reflection of the current state of knowledge of practical techniques, which turn out mostly to be applicable only at run time. It is far from clear that the best or most interesting techniques ultimately will be run-time based. In fact, the intense research activity today in the areas of logic, semantics, and type theory are almost certain to have a significant effect on the importance of static analysis issues in advanced language implementation. The future of ALIT seems very exciting indeed.

Before closing, I would like to express my deepest thanks to all of the contributing authors. It is because of their enthusiasm for the idea of ALIT that this book has become much more than just a collection of lecture notes. They really put me to work! There were also many active participants in the seminar, which contributed greatly to the exciting atmosphere in the seminar and, I am certain, also helped to provide the necessary momentum to make this book possible. IEEE allowed me to reprint Chapter 11 by Detlefs, Herlihy, and Wing. (This chapter appeared originally in *IEEE Computer*, December 1988, pp. 57–69.) Mike Blackwell did a wonderful job typesetting this book, making sure that every contribution is formatted uniformly, right down to the figures and code listings. Mark Leone and David Tarditi carefully proofread several drafts. Michelle Jackson helped out by making the index. Chester on several occassions deleted entire paragraphs by putting his paws on my keyboard. Finally, I would like to thank Bob Prior at the MIT Press for his sound advice and patience during this project.

Peter Lee

Contributing Authors

Andrew W. Appel, Princeton University.

Joseph Bates, Carnegie Mellon University.

David L. Detlefs, Carnegie Mellon University.

Conal Elliott, Sun Microsystems, Mountain View.

Scott E. Fahlman, Carnegie Mellon University.

Alessandro Forin, Carnegie Mellon University.

Maurice P. Herlihy, DEC Cambridge Research Laboratory, Cambridge.

Philip J. Koopman, Jr., Harris Semiconductor, Melbourne.

Kevin J. Lang, NEC Research Laboratories, Princeton.

Peter Lee, Carnegie Mellon University.

Barak A. Pearlmutter, Carnegie Mellon University.

Frank Pfenning, Carnegie Mellon University.

Uwe F. Pleban, Applied Dynamics International, Ann Arbor.

Eugene J. Rollins, Carnegie Mellon University.

Olin Shivers, Carnegie Mellon University.

Peter A. Steenkiste, Carnegie Mellon University.

Skef Wholey, Carnegie Mellon University.

Jeannette M. Wing, Carnegie Mellon University.

Part I
Advanced Implementation Techniques

The first part of this book is concerned with implementation techniques that are applicable to most advanced languages. These include techniques for tagging and run-time type checking, register allocation, dataflow analysis, and garbage collection. The common theme is the efficient handling of data – its creation, retrieval, and removal.

One of the distinguishing characteristics of an advanced language is the need to carry type information with data objects at run time. This need arises in dynamically typed languages such as Lisp and Scheme so that proper dispatching can be made on calls to primitive generic operations. For example, the addition operation in Lisp must check the types of its arguments at run time, so that a decision can be made as to what kind of addition operation should be used – integer, floating-point, bignum, rational, and so on – and what kinds of type conversions should be applied. Although not strictly necessary, run-time type information is also generally used in statically typed languages such as Standard ML in order to facilitate garbage collection. (The garbage collector must be able to distinguish pointers from other data.) Chapter 1 by Peter A. Steenkiste (*The Implementation of Tags and Run-time Type Checking*), provides an excellent survey and comparison of various techniques for implementing run-time type checking. He identifies the basic elements of type-tag handling and presents benchmark data that shows exactly the sources of high overhead.

Another characteristic of advanced languages is the complexity of control flow. Programs written in advanced languages typically have large numbers of transfers of control, primarily via procedure call. In fact, in Scheme and Standard ML, procedure call is essentially the only control-flow mechanism (excepting first-class continuations and exceptions). This places special demands on the register allocator since it must therefore perform global allocation if it is to make any significant improvement in the efficiency of the object code. Chapter 2 by Peter A. Steenkiste (*Advanced Register Allocation*) describes many of the issues in register allocation for Lisp and presents a survey of several major techniques. He concentrates on a technique that he co-developed called "bottom-up allocation." The effectiveness of this technique on Lisp programs is described.

A serious obstacle to carrying out any kind of compile-time analysis of programs in advanced languages, including register allocation, is the undecidability of the problem of obtaining a control-flow graph for a program. This is due to having procedures as first-class objects; determining the control-flow graph of a program thus is tantamount to determining the program's run-time values. Thus, one must compute safe approximations to the control-flow graph. Chapter 3 by Olin Shivers (*Dataflow Analysis and Type Recovery in Scheme*) describes a semantics-based approach to control-flow analysis and discusses some of the issues involved in using such control-flow information to carry out classical dataflow analysis for Scheme. As a concrete example, he shows how the types of references to variables may be partially recovered at compile-time, thereby allowing the compiler to elide some run-time type checks.

The final two chapters in this part, Chapter 4 by Andrew W. Appel (*Garbage Collection*) and Chapter 5 by David L. Detlefs (*Concurrent Garbage Collection for C++*), are concerned with the problem of fast garbage collection for advanced languages. Appel presents an excellent survey of the major techniques used for "friendly" languages such as Lisp, Scheme, and Standard ML. Garbage collection algorithms have advanced quite a bit since the mark-and-sweep technique used in the original Lisp. In modern implementations, the cost of garbage collection in principle can be made arbitrarily small. For "hostile" languages (i.e., languages that allow pointer arithmetic), special considerations and approximations must be made. The chapter by Detlefs details how this is done for a concurrent version of the language C++.

There are many other important topics missing from this part of the book that certainly belong here. These include instruction scheduling and code generation, trace scheduling, conversion to continuation-passing style, separate compilation and modules, and polymorphic type checking. For introductions to these topics, I refer the reader to the papers listed below.

References

[1] L. Cardelli. Basic polymorphic type checking. *Science of Computer Programming.*, Vol. 8, No. 2, April 1987, 147–172.

[2] J. A. Fisher. Trace scheduling: a technique for global microcode compaction. *IEEE Transactions on Computers*, Vol. C-30, No. 7, July 1981, 478–490.

[3] J. Hennessy and T. Gross. Postpass code optimization of pipeline constraints. *ACM Transactions on Programming Languages and Systems*, Vol. 5, No. 3, July 1983, 422–448.

[4] R. Kelsey and P. Hudak. Realistic compilation by program transformation. *Conference Record of the 16th Annual ACM Symposium on Principles of Programming Languages*, January 1989, 281–292.

[5] D. Kranz, R. Kelsey, J. Rees, P. Hudak, J. Philbin, and N. Adams. Orbit: an optimizing compiler for Scheme. In *Proceedings of the SIGPLAN'86 Symposium on Compiler Construction*, Palo Alto, June 1986, 219–233.

[6] D. MacQueen. An implementation of Standard ML modules. In *Proceedings of the 1988 ACM Conference on Lisp and Functional Programming*, Snowbird, Utah, July 1988, 212–223.

1 The Implementation of Tags and Run-Time Type Checking

Peter A. Steenkiste

In statically typed languages like Pascal, type checking is done at compile-time. Languages like LISP do not require the user to specify the type of each data item and *run-time type checking* is required in such cases. Run-time type checking is implemented by adding a *tag* to each data item to encode the type of that item; operations on the data can then be type checked using the tag. Operations on tags are a significant component of the execution time of dynamically-typed programs on general-purpose processors. A study on the run-time behavior of LISP, for example, showed that programs spent 22% of their time on tag handling [27]. To reduce the cost of tag handling, architectures sometimes provide architectural support for tags. LISP machines, for example, often operate on the tag and data item in parallel, thus hiding the cost of tag handling.

In this chapter we describe a number of ways to implement tags. We will concentrate on software implementations that can be used on general-purpose processors, but we also look at strategies that require architectural support. We first discuss the problem of runtime type checking and we look at how it is address with type tags. The main body of the chapter is a study of a LISP system: we evaluate how much time is spent on tag handling and we look at a wide range of tag implementations and how well they perform. We also evaluate the payoff of different degrees of hardware support for tags. All the measurements were done for Portable Standard Lisp on MIPS-X, but the results should apply to a wide range of language implementations.

1.1 Run-time Type Checking

In dynamically typed languages, each data object contains besides the data an encoding of the type of the data. The tag-data combination is called a *data item*. Tag handling operations are primitive operations that operate on tags. Run-time type checking and type dispatching are higher level operations that are implemented in terms of tag operations. We discuss both groups of operations in this section.

1.1.1 Tags

Tags can be associated with data objects in a number of ways on general-purpose processors. A first approach is to store a pointer to the data and an *immediate tag* in the same word: a number of bits encode the type, and the remaining bits contain the pointer. The tag is usually located in either the most or the least significant bits of the word. An alternative is to use an *indirect tag*: the type information is not stored with the pointer, but with the data. Indirect tags have the disadvantage that a memory reference is required to get the type of an object, but they have the advantage that they allow the use of longer tags without reducing the address space. Another disadvantage is that indirect tags consume more space, often an extra word per data object. Many implementations of dynamically typed languages combine immediate and indirect tags: frequently needed type information is stored in the pointer using an immediate tag, and more detailed type information is stored with the data as an indirect tags.

For some data types, it is possible to store the data, instead of a pointer to the data, in the data item. Typical examples are symbols and "short" integers. This representation has the advantage that it is compact, and that both the (immediate) tag and the data can be accessed without dereferencing a pointer. Integers that do not fit in the data item are put in one or more separate words, and the item contains a pointer. These "long" integers have a different tag value. In this chapter, "integer" stands for "short integer."

We can distinguish four primitive operations on tags and items:

- *tag insertion*: given a piece of data, or a pointer, and its type (tag) value, construct the data item.

- *tag extraction*: given an item, extract the tag value.

- *tag removal*: given an item, extract the data item, that is, create a valid pointer or data object that can be used in an operation.

- *tag checking*: given an item, check whether the tag has a specific value; it consists of a tag extraction followed by an equality test.

The cost of the tag operations depends on both the tag implementation and on the architecture of system. Several implementations are described later in the chapter.

1.1.2 Types

A *type-dispatching* function uses the types of its operands to determine what operation should be executed. Type dispatching is used for method selection in object-oriented systems [23], and in a more restricted form to implement generic operations, for example generic arithmetic in LISP. The difference between the two uses is that in the case of generic operations, the range of types and operations is restricted and determined by the language implementation. In object-oriented systems, the range of types and operations is program-dependent, and some systems even allow operations and types to be added or changed at run time.

All these flavors of type dispatching can be implemented using one basic mechanism based on table lookup [23]. A type dispatching operation uses the type of the operand, identified by a *tag*, and the operation specified in the program, identified by a *key*, to select the actual operation to be executed. One of the values, the tag or the key, is used to select a table, while the other value is used as an index in the table. The selected table entry identifies the required operation, usually as a code pointer or as code that should be executed. The value (key or tag) that is used as an index should be a short integer. The value used for table selection can either be the address of the table itself, or an identifier that can be used to load the base of the table. A more in-depth discussion of various type-dispatch mechanisms and their efficiency can be found in [23]. Although all type dispatching operations can be implemented using a table lookup, simpler implementations that are optimized for specific dispatching operations are very common.

Run-time type checking verifies whether operands are of the right type. It can be viewed as a degenerate form of type dispatching: the type is either correct, in which case the operation can proceed, or incorrect, in which case an error should be reported. In its simplest form, run-time type checking corresponds to a simple tag-checking operation, but in some cases, several tag values can be valid, depending on the tag implementation and the choice of tag values. We will look at a number of examples later in the chapter.

Tagged architectures have special instructions that can use the tag and the data part of an item without taking the item apart with separate instructions. They usually support tag checking operations in parallel with other operations, and often also have hardware support for type checking and type dispatching, often in the form of microcode. An example is a typed integer addition: the integer addition and the type check on the two operands would be done in parallel, and a trap would be generated if a type error or overflow occurs. LISP machines [21,30] are the most widely used tagged architectures, but people have also built architectures for Smalltalk [32]. Some architectures provide more limited support: they are basically general-purpose systems which have a limited number of instructions that directly support common tag-handling operations.

1.2 Case Study: LISP on a RISC

In the remainder of the chapter we look at a specific dynamically typed language (LISP) and we use a specific implementation of the language to evaluate the run-time cost of tag handling and run-time type checking. We then analyze how changes in the tag implementation influence program execution time [28]. The system used is Portable Standard Lisp (PSL), and our evaluation is based on ten programs that were executed on an instruction-level simulator for the MIPS-X microprocessor. Architectural support for type tags was evaluated by modifying the MIPS-X simulator and PSL compiler. MIPS-X [8] is a high-performance processor, and it is used as a typical example of a reduced-instruction-set processor. An advantage of using a RISC architecture in this type of study is that one can measure both instruction counts and execution time easily, since the latter depends directly on the former (ignoring cache misses). The ten programs used in the study include a compiler frontend, a garbage collector, and a rational function evaluator, and three of the larger Gabriel benchmarks [12]; together they contain about 11,000 lines of LISP code, not including comments (see Section 1.8). Portable Standard Lisp [14,13] is a small, efficient LISP dialect that has been ported to a large number of architectures. In the remainder of this section we discuss the PSL implementation on the MIPS-X.

1.2.1   The Implementation of Tags in PSL

The PSL implementation on MIPS-X [8] uses immediate tags that are stored in the five most significant bits of the word. For a number of data types, the value or the order of the tag values has been chosen in a special way. Three cases are important:

1. Positive integers have the tag 0, and negative integers have the tag 31 (all 1's).

2. The tag values of all number types, except for negative integers, are in the range 0 to 3.

3. All types where the item contains a pointer, not a value, are in a continuous range to allow fast checking by the garbage collector.

As a result of the special tag values for integers, the LISP representation for a short integer is the same as the two's complement machine representation of an integer ([13], cf [6]). This means that the arithmetic instruction of the processor can be used on integer items without any reformatting (if no overflow occurs). Note that if we add two LISP integer items, and overflow occurs, the result will not be a LISP integer, so overflow checking for addition (and subtraction) can be implemented as a type-checking operation.

Because the MIPS-X processor does not allow immediate operands in conditional branches, each tag checking operation would normally include an instruction to load the constant comparison tag value, into a register. To avoid this overhead, our PSL implementation keeps the tag values for pairs and symbols, the most frequently used data types, in designated registers. Without this optimization our set of ten programs would on average run 3.6% slower.

1.2.2   Run-Time Checking and Generic Operations in PSL

Because we wanted our measurements to be representative for a large class of currently used LISP systems, we first optimized PSL run-time checking [26] to make its performance comparable to that of some newer, optimized LISP systems [5,17]. In this section, we describe the optimized implementation of type checking for the data types that are used in our test programs.

For many operations, run-time checking is equivalent to checking the tag of the operand. An important example is type checking on *list operations* such as *car* and *cdr*: the operand must be a list; otherwise the operation is illegal. Type checking for a symbol also consists of a single tag check.

Because of the special assignment of tag values, type checking for some data types becomes more complicated. Examples are (short) integers and numbers:

- *check tag for short integer*: an integer can be either a positive or a negative integer, and both have a different tag value. The simplest way to test for an integer is to sign extend the least significant bit of the tag, which is also the sign bit of the integer; the item is an integer if the original item is equal to the item with the sign-extended sign bit. Other implementations are discussed in Section 1.4.1.

- *check tag for number*: an item is an integer if it has the tag 31, or if it has a tag in the range 0 to 3. Two tests are required: one to test if the tag is smaller than 4 (tags are always positive), and if this fails, a test for equality with 31.

Because the type of the operands of an *arithmetic operation* is not known at compile time, the LISP run-time system has to deal with type conversion and has to pick an operator that matches the type of the operands. Generic arithmetic in PSL is implemented using type dispatching through a branch table: the operation determines the location of the table and the operand types provide the index. The branch table dispatches control to a routine that does the proper type conversion and addition. In the standard PSL implementation, all generic arithmetic is done through procedure calls that do a general type-dispatching operation. In practice, integers are by far the most common type of numbers in LISP, and generic arithmetic can be sped up by first specifically testing for integer operands, thus giving a fast result for the most common integer case. The expensive general sequence is only used if non-integers are involved. The integer tests and the integer operation can be done inline. This optimization of generic arithmetic for integers is very common.

Run-time checking for *vector accesses* is relatively complicated. Compilers for statically typed language like Pascal and C sometimes allow the programmer to specify run-time bounds checking. In LISP, vector accesses with full run-time checking will not only do bounds checking, but will also check that the indexed object is a vector and that the indexing type is legal.

Most LISP dialects define more data types than are used on our programs, but the data objects most actively used will be of the above types (numbers, symbols, lists, or vectors). Many other data types are also modeled after or implemented using one of the above data types; examples are *structures*, *strings*, and *bit-vectors* [25]. Because the data types used in our programs, and their implementation, are similar to those used in other LISP systems, the numbers presented in this paper should be representative for a large number of LISP implementations.

1.2.3   Compile-time versus Run-time Checking

Even though LISP does not require type declarations, it is sometimes possible for the compiler to determine the type of an operand. The compiler can then generate code that does not do run-time checking, while still guaranteeing the correctness of the operation. A typical example occurs when the programmer inserts an explicit type-checking operation before a *car* operation; additional run-time type checking on the *car* is clearly redundant. In some cases it is possible to eliminate part of the run-time testing. For example, if several vector elements are accessed in the same basic block, it might be possible to do the type checking on the vector operand only once, or it might be possible to move the type checking for vector accesses inside loops to loop headers and to eliminate bounds checking, if the index is a simple function of the loop counter. The elimination of run-time checking by the compiler requires type deduction [19] and range analysis on vector and loop indices [31,15], both of which have been studied in the literature. (See, for instance, Chapter 3 for an in-depth treatment of this subject.)

Run-time type checking can also be avoided by allowing programmers to use variable declarations and type-specific operators [24,20,5]. The compiler can use these hints to generate faster code. Note that wrong type declarations can result in hard to find run-time errors. Some LISP compilers actually have a switch that can be set by the programmer to indicate whether the compiler should give priority to speed or to safety [25]. Adding a type system to object-oriented languages can similarly eliminate some of the overhead associated with run-time method lookup.

In the following sections we describe the cost of tag handling for various tag implementation strategies. We will present results for programs that do no type checking and for programs that do full run-time checking. The results for a specific implementation will lie somewhere between these two extremes. The exact values will depend on how much type deduction is done in the compiler and whether the compiler has been tuned to compile "for safety," in which case all operations will do full run-time checking, or "for speed," in

	arith	vector	list	total
inter	0.6	0.0	19.0	19.7
deduce	0.1	0.0	12.3	12.4
dedgc	0.0	0.0	6.6	6.6
rat	4.9	0.0	13.7	18.5
comp	0.1	0.0	10.3	10.4
opt	2.7	11.8	28.0	42.4
frl	0.5	0.0	9.7	10.2
boyer	0.0	0.0	17.5	17.5
brow	0.0	0.0	19.9	19.9
trav	3.1	72.0	13.2	88.3
average	1.2	8.4	15.0	24.6

Table 1.1: Percentage increase in execution time when run-time checking is added.

which case run-time checking will be avoided. No run-time checking on primitive LISP operations does not mean that the tags have been eliminated; the tags are still necessary for garbage collection and to implement tests that are explicitly present in the source code.

1.3   Time Spent on Tag Operations

In this section we look at how much time ten PSL programs spend on tag operations. The tags are kept in the five most significant bits of the word (Section 1.2.1), but small changes in the implementation, like putting the tags in the low order bits, should not influence our results significantly. Radically different tag implementations, and their effect on performance, are discussed later. The tag values for the most frequently used data types are kept in registers, and run-time checking is done as is described in the previous section. For each group of measurements we present data for programs both with and without run-time checking; these costs are expressed as a percentage of the execution time with and without run-time checking respectively. Table 1.1 shows the increase in execution time if we add run-time type checking to arithmetic, vector and list operations; on average the programs run 25% slower, but the numbers vary strongly from program to program.

1.3.1   Tag Insertion

A tag has to be inserted each time when a new item is created. Because of our choice of tag values, no tag insertion is necessary when an integer is created, for example as the

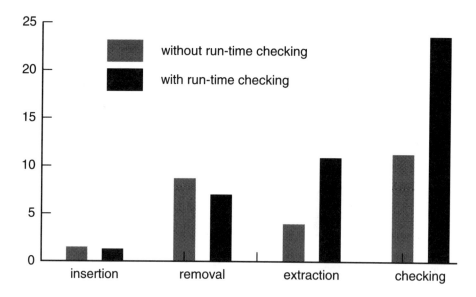

Figure 1.1: Summary of the cost of tag handling.

result of an arithmetic operation. Inserting a tag in a data item when both the tag and the item are in a register costs two cycles: one to shift the tag to the most significant bits, and one to "or" the tag and the item together. The tag is originally in the low order bits of the word, where it is placed by a load-immediate instruction. Figure 1.1 shows that the ten programs spend on average 1.3% of their time on the insertion of tags.

We will not discuss tag insertion any further, both because there is little possibility for improvement by simple changes in software or hardware, and because it is not time-critical. For example, keeping a *preshifted* list tag in a register, thus reducing the cost of tag insertion for list cells to one cycle, would speed up our programs 0.5%.

1.3.2   Tag Removal

On the MIPS-X, the tag has to be removed before the data part of an item can be used. Integers are an exception. Removing the tag can be done in one cycle by masking it out with a mask kept in a designated register. Figure 1.1 shows that the programs without run-time checking spend 8.7% of their time on masking out tags. With run-time checking, the cost drops to 7%, because the total execution time increases (due to time spent on extracting and checking tags) while the time spent on tag removal stays the same.

1.3.3 Tag Extraction

On the MIPS-X, it is necessary to extract the tag of a data item before it can be compared with a known tag value to check the type of the item. Tag extraction can be done in a single cycle with a logical shift that places the tag in the low-order part of the word. Figure 1.1 shows that 4% of the execution time is spent on tag extraction when no run-time checking is done. These tag-extraction operations are part of type tests that are explicitly specified in the source program.

The dark bars in Figure 1.1 show the cost of tag extraction in programs with full run-time checking. It has two components: operations that were already present in the programs without run-time checking (corresponding to the light bars), and operations that were added as part of the run-time checking. Adding full run-time checking sharply increases the extraction cost; checking list operations is responsible for 80% of this increase. When we add run-time checking, the increase in the number of tag extraction operations, and thus in the number of tag checking operations, is approximately equal to the number of tag-removal operations. This is what one would expect: with full run-time checking the type of each data item is checked before the item is used, and using a data item requires the removal of its tag.

1.3.4 Tag Checking

Figure 1.1 shows that programs without run-time checking spend 11% of their time on tag checking. The cost of tag checking includes one cycle for extracting the tag, one cycle for a comparison, and possibly one or two cycles for unused branch-delay slots. With full run-time checking almost 24% of the execution time is used for tag checking. Both with and without run-time testing, 95% of the tag checking operations are of the simple type (tag extraction followed by a comparison with a constant); the remaining tag checking operations are related to testing for integers and numbers.

1.3.5 Summary

In this section we saw that the total cost of tag handling is between 22% and 32% (Figure 1.1), depending on how much run-time checking is done. This cost is fairly constant across all programs – the standard deviations are 5.6% and 7.5% respectively – although the programs are widely different. In the following sections we will look at different tag implementations that reduce the cost of tag handling: in Section 1.4 we discuss software tag implementations that speed up integer testing, and in Sections 1.5 and 1.6 we look at schemes that can be used to reduce the cost of tag removal and tag checking.

1.4   Integer Testing and Software Optimization of Generic Arithmetic

On general-purpose processors a short integer and its tag share the same word. This section first describes tag checking for integers and then demonstrates how a special encoding of the tags makes it possible to reduce the number of test-for-integer operations required for integer-biased generic arithmetic.

1.4.1   Integer Tags and Integer Testing

PSL uses immediate tags that are placed in the most significant part of the word. In Section 1.2.1 we discussed how tag removal for arithmetic operations can be avoided by making the tag the sign extension of the sign bit. Since integer arithmetic is relatively common, this is an important optimization, but the disadvantage is that integer tests are no longer simple tag-checking operations. They can be implemented in a number of ways (assume 5 tag bits):

- Extract the tag, then check for a positive integer; if that fails, check for a negative integer.

- Sign-extend the least significant 28 bits; the item is an integer if the result is equal to the original item. This implementation is used in PSL.

- Assuming that an arithmetic-shift-left gives a trap on overflow, doing an arithmetic-shift-left over 4 bits will trap if the item is not an integer.

With the last method, checking for an integer can be done in a single cycle, and a generic add of two integers can be done in 4 cycles, with 4 lines of code (remember that testing for overflow is basically a check for integer on the result). This is clearly the fastest method, but the problem is that most architectures do not have a true arithmetic shift left. Another disadvantage is that recovering from a trap is expensive on most systems, so the non-integer case will be slow. This might be acceptable for error recovery, but it is not an attractive way to implement generic arithmetic. Neither the first nor the second method require special hardware. Their relative speed depends on the sign of the number and on the architecture. On MIPS-X, the second method always costs 3 cycles, and the first method is faster for positive and slower for negative numbers.

An alternative is to place the immediate tags in the least significant part of the word. In that case it is attractive to use the tag value 0 for short integers, since it again allows many common arithmetic operations to be performed without tag manipulation. The integer type-checking operation is now a single tag check, as it is for other data types. Some LISP implementations [2,35] use the addresses in system space for integers, and all arithmetic operations require the conversion of integers between their LISP and their machine representation. The same is true for LISP implementations that do not have short integers [24].

The SPARC microprocessor is a general-purpose processor, but it has add and subtract instructions that trap if the bottom two bits of the operands are not zero [11]. These instructions directly support the tag implementation described in the previous paragraph, but they are only useful in LISP systems that follow this tag implementation. LISP machines have more extensive hardware support, and they typically do all integer checking in hardware in parallel with the operation (Section 1.6.2).

1.4.2 Reducing the Cost of Generic Arithmetic

Generic arithmetic operations are relatively expensive because several tag checking operations are needed. For example, for a generic add, two tests are needed to check the type of the operands, and one to check the result for overflow. It is possible to assign tag values in such a way that the sum of two tag values can never result in the tag value of a short integer, unless both are short-integer tag values, and there is no overflow. With this tag assignment we can add the numbers, and do all the type and overflow checking with one single type checking operation on the result. The requirement on tag values can be met by using an extra tag bit, or by reducing the number of tag values that are required by putting some of the typing information in indirect tags. For a generic add on a MIPS-X, for example, the cost for an integer add drops from 10 cycles to 4. For relational and unary operations, the number of tests is reduced from 2 to 1. Multiplication and division still require separate type tests on the operands and on the result and subtraction requires two tests. With the special encoding of tags, the time spent on generic arithmetic is roughly divided by two. For our test programs, the gain is minimal: a drop from 2% to 1%.

This tag implementation has the disadvantage that it requires an extra tag bit. Not only does this reduce the address size by one bit, but it also means that this scheme cannot be used with tag implementation schemes that allow only 2 or 3 tag bits (see Section 1.5). Since these tag implementation strategies have a potentially higher payoff, at least for our set of programs, we will not use the encoding described in this section.

1.5 Support for Tag Removal

In Section 1.3.2 we found that our set of LISP programs spend around 9% of their time masking out the tag of a data item in order to be able to use the data part. In this section we look at why tag removal is needed and at what can be gained by avoiding tag removal. Finally, we describe a number of tag implementations that allow most data types to be used without removing the tag explicitly.

1.5.1   The Need for Tag Removal

The data part of most LISP objects contains a pointer to the data, so it will always be used as an address. Two important exceptions are integers and symbols. We saw earlier that no tag removal is necessary for integers, and symbols are either compared with other symbols, without removing the tag, or they are used as an index in a symbol table, in which case the data part of the item is again used for the purpose of addressing a memory location. On a processor that drops the top 5 bits of 32 bit addresses before accessing memory, it is not necessary to mask the tag of an item explicitly when the data part of the item is used to access memory, which is, as we just argued, usually the case.

We changed the PSL compiler so that no masking of the tag is done for items that are used as addresses, and we changed the MIPS-X simulator, so that it only uses the bottom 27 bits of an address when accessing memory. Figure 1.2 shows, for programs with no run-time checking, the decrease in instruction frequencies resulting from this optimization. When we compare the "and" entry in Figure 1.2 with the "removal" entry in Figure 1.1, we see that almost all masking operations have been removed. Part of the gain is undone by an increase in move instructions which is a consequence of the requirement that all load instructions have to be idempotent (repeatable) on the MIPS-X. The increase in wasted cycles (no-ops and squashed instructions) results from the fact that fewer ALU instructions are available to fill delay slots after branches, loads and stores. Not having to mask the tag speeds up the test programs by about 6%.

1.5.2   Implementation

Tag masking can be avoided on general-purpose architectures by placing a short immediate tag in the bottom bits of the word. On the MIPS-X, for example, most tag removals for addresses can be eliminated by using the two low-order bits of a word as a tag. The MIPS-X uses byte addresses, but all memory accesses are word aligned, hence, the bottom two bits of an address are dropped before the (word-addressed) memory is accessed. With two tag bits, three combinations are used to encode the most frequently used data types, leaving one combination as an escape for an indirect tag, and thus eliminating tag masking for most memory accesses. Several architectures use word aligned memory accesses, but they do look at the whole address and generate a trap when it is not word aligned. On these architectures, the two bottom bits can still be used for the tag without requiring tag removal, but the compiler now has to adjust the offset that is used to access the object so that the tag is eliminated [22,33]. An advantage of placing the tag in the bottom bits is that the full address space is available, which is important for large LISP systems. A disadvantage is that an extra memory access is needed to retrieve detailed type information.

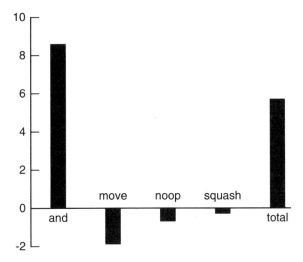

Figure 1.2: Percentage reduction in instruction frequencies due to the elimination of tag removal.

Screme [33] (see Chapter 7 in this book), the Scheme implementation on the 88000, places the tag in the two least significant bits. The tag value 00 is used for short integers to provide fast integer arithmetic (Section 1.4.1), and the tag values 01 for immediates and 10 for pointers. The tag value 11 is illegal. The implementation uses the fact that the 88000 traps on misaligned memory access to get tag checking for pointers for free: if the tag does not have the expected value (01) an unaligned address will be generated and a trap will occur. By making the tag value 11 illegal the Screme implementation can also check for a symbol or a pointer without doing tag extraction using the 88000 "branch on bit" instruction.

It is possible to avoid tag removal for more LISP types by using the *three bottom bits* for tag encoding. Even and odd integers get the tag values 000 and 100, so that integer arithmetic and indexing in word vectors will be fast. Four tag values can be used for frequently used data types, and the values 011 and 111 (two bottom bits 1) are reserved as an escape. For data types with 3 bit tags, data objects will always be aligned on even or odd word boundaries. This is not a problem since list cells always require two words, and other types such as vectors and structures often come in larger blocks, so wasting a word to ensure the alignment is relatively cheap. Aligning list cells on double word boundaries might also be beneficial for caches with block sizes larger than two. The

Lucid compiler uses the three bottom bits as tag bits for some architectures.

Another way to avoid tag masking is to put the tag in the most-significant bits, and to make the tag an integral part of the address. The effect is that data items of a different type will end up in different parts of the address space. Making the tag part of the address has the disadvantage that data are scattered throughout the virtual address space, which can have a negative influence on virtual memory management. CMU Common Lisp [18] (See Chapter 6 in this book) uses this implementation with 5 tag bits. It runs under Mach, an operating system that supports large virtual address spaces efficiently [1].

On machines where the address length is shorter than the word length, tag removal can be avoided by placing the tag in the upper bits of the word. Several architectures with this property exist (68000 [29], IBM/370 [34]), but most architectures that are designed today have a full 32 bit address space.

LISP machines typically treat the tag and the data part of a data item as separate entities, so it is natural that the tag is automatically dropped when memory is accessed [3,21]. Given a general-purpose processor like the MIPS-X it would be possible to add special hardware that would blank out the 5 most significant bits of each address, before it is put on the address bus. This hardware could be controlled by a bit in the processor status word or special load and store instructions could be added to the instruction set. If the tag were kept in least significant bits of the item, the address would be shifted when the processor is in "LISP mode." These tagged architectures make it possible to avoid tag removal while using a full range of immediate tag values.

1.6 Support for Tag Extraction and Tag Checking

Our programs spend between 11% and 24% of their time on tag checking (Figure 1.1), depending on how much run-time checking is done, so tag checking is an attractive candidate for optimization. Tag-checking operations and type dispatching are required in a number of situations:

1. *run-time error checking*, for example type checking as part of a *car* operation,

2. *generic operations*, for example generic arithmetic, and

3. *checking operations specified at the source level*, for example the function *atom*, which verifies whether an object is a list cell.

Ignoring efforts to eliminate type and tag checking at compile time using type deduction, the cost of tag checking can be reduced in two ways. First, eliminate the need for tag extraction, thus reducing the cost of tag checking operations in all of the above categories. Second, eliminate one or more tag checking operations completely in some of the categories using special-purpose hardware.

1.6.1 Eliminating Tag Extraction

We saw in Section 1.3.4 that the most common form of type checking is to test whether the tag is equal to a specific tag value. The implementation of tag checking on general-purpose processors depends on the details of the instruction set. On most RISC architectures such as MIPS-X, tag checking is typically implemented using two instructions: an explicit tag extraction followed by an eq/neq comparison. On CISC architectures such as the Vax-11 architecture [10], the explicit tag extraction operation can often be avoided by implementing tag checking using bit-field comparison instructions that are part of the regular instruction set. However, tag checking using a single instruction is not necessarily faster than using a sequence of simpler instructions, since the complex bit comparison instructions usually take several cycles to complete. On some architectures it is possible to implement fast tag checking by using unusual instructions and an appropriate tag encoding. An example is the Scheme implementation for the 88000 [33] described in the previous section: tag checking is done using the bit comparison instruction.

Tag extraction can be avoided with hardware support in the form of a special conditional eq/neq branch that only tests the part of the word that contains the tag. Such an instruction would be more restricted, and potentially faster, than the general-purpose bit comparison instructions. The special conditional branches can be implemented in a number of ways, with different tradeoffs between simplicity and flexibility. First, the bits used in the comparison can be hardwired into the processor. This is not very flexible, because the architecture, and not the software, determines where the tag bits should be placed in the word. Second, the special conditional branch can take a mask as a third argument. This solution is more flexible, but it is expensive to implement because it introduces an instruction with 3 source registers. This makes the register file more complicated, and it reduces the branch offset. Third, the bits can be specified by a special mask register that is set under program control. Note that an eq/neq comparison on part of a word, specified by a mask, is easy to implement and very fast.

For PSL on the MIPS-X, not having to do an explicit type extraction would eliminate about 4% of the instructions without run-time checking, and about 10% of the instructions with full run-time checking. The speedup would depend on the implementation (cost of bit-field comparison instruction and the impact of its implementation on the cycle time).

1.6.2 Hardware Tag Checking

The cost of tag checking can be substantially reduced by providing special hardware that does some tag-checking operations in parallel with other operations. LISP machines such as the Symbolics 3600 [21], TI Explorer [9] and SPUR [30] always provide some hardware support for error checking on primitive operations and for generic operations (categories one and two of page 14). It is in general not possible to eliminate tag-checking operations that are specified in the source code (category three), although they can be optimized, as was described in the previous section. In this section we briefly describe some hardware schemes that were designed to eliminate tag checking operations that are executed as part of error checking or as part of generic operations.

Error Checking   Software tag checking used for error testing on primitive LISP operations can be eliminated with special instructions that do the tag checking in parallel with the operation, and that trap if a type error occurs. An example is a special memory instruction that checks the tag of the address during address calculation, and traps if the tag does not have the expected value; the tag to be expected could be specified in a register, as an immediate value, or in the opcode. An important point is that the hardware support is limited to a simple tag check. In the case of vector accessing for example, range checking would still have to be done in software. Hardware error checking assumes that the tag is not removed before the data part of the item is used, so no tag removal will be required for these memory accesses (Section 1.5).

Run-time checking on list operations is the most expensive group of error checking in our set of programs. Adding hardware to do this test in parallel with the address calculation would give a speedup of between 0% and 12%, plus an extra 0%–4% because no tag removal would be required for memory accesses to lists. Extending the hardware to allow parallel tag checking for other data types (vectors and structures), would slightly increase the speedup. This hardware would be simple and fast if the tag location and the tag values can be built into the hardware, but it would be much harder to implement if the tag implementation were left to software. Fixing the tag implementation in hardware is no problem for LISP machines, but on general-purpose processors it incurs the risk that some LISP implementations will not use the tag support because it does not fit their exact needs.

Note that the MIPS-X architecture naturally allows some overlap between an operation and its corresponding tag checking operation. In a *squashed delayed branch*, two instructions are executed while the branch condition is calculated and while the next instruction is fetched, and the effect of both instructions is canceled if the the branch is not taken [16]. An operation and its tag check will happen concurrently, if the branch condition is "tag equal to expected tag" and if the operation is moved in a delayed slot of the branch. Figure 1.3 illustrates this for run-time checking on a *cdr* operation. The first code segment is the assembly code that is generated by the PSL compiler, and the second code segment is the code after reorganization. The *cdr* operation (the *and* and the *ld*) has been moved in the delayed slot of the conditional branch, and the branch has been changed into a squashed branch. If the type test succeeds, as is almost always

```
        lsr     r1,#27,r22
        beq     r22,r18,L1   ; r18: tag value for a list
        ; error handling
L1:     and     r1,r19,r21   ; r19: mask to mask out tag
        ld      4[r21],r2
        ...


        lsr     r1,#27,r22
        beqsq       r22,r18,L1
        and     r1,r19,r21
        ld      4[r21],r2
        ; error handling
L1:     ...
```

Figure 1.3: The use of delayed branches for run-time type checking.

the case, the conditional branch for the tag checking operation does not create any idle cycles, but if the test fails, the effect of the *cdr* operation will be undone, which is what should happen.

This optimization is automatically done by the reorganizer. The only requirement is that a successful test corresponds to a taken branch, something that can easily be arranged by the compiler. As a result, we get an overlap between an operation and the corresponding tag checking operation (the operation can start before tag checking is finished). This is similar to what happens on LISP machines, but they use special hardware to overlap tag checking with other operations.

Generic Operations   Generic operations are operations that can handle data of different types. On general-purpose architectures, they can be implemented using the general type dispatching mechanism of Section 1.1.2, but as has been discussed for generic arithmetic, it is often advantageous to first test explicitly for the common data type, and to use the more expensive type dispatch only if this test fails. This biased implementation is only effective if the guess about the data type is right most of the time. If the "common" data type is not really very common, this implementation will be slower than an unbiased implementation based on dispatching through a branch table.

Hardware support for generic operations can be provided at various levels. A first possibility is to use a strategy similar to what was described for error checking in the previous section: the operation is executed in hardware assuming that the operands are of the most common type, while the operand types are tested in parallel. If the test fails, a trap is generated, and the operation is aborted; less common data types can then be handled in software, similar to error conditions. The implementation of arithmetic operations on SPUR [30] follow this strategy. The effectiveness of this scheme will depend on how often the "less common" occurs and how expensive it is to handle. The first factor depends on the program; for example, a floating-point program that uses integer-biased generic arithmetic could be very slow. The second factor depends on how expensive traps are, and how hard it is to retrieve the operands. By also providing hardware support for dispatching on the type of operands, it is possible to further speed up generic operations. The VLSI chip used in the TI Explorer II [4], for example, has a special on-chip memory for dispatch tables that can be used by the micro-code.

Compile-time analysis can be used to reduce the cost of using the wrong bias (see Chapter 3). If compile-time analysis indicates that the operands are probably not integers, the compiler can generate code that immediately invokes the general dispatch routine, or that has a different bias. As the compiler is more and more successful at deducing data types, the "less common" case will become more and more an exception.

It is hard to evaluate the payoff of hardware support for generic operations, because the benefit depends strongly on the frequency and the exact implementation of the generic operations, the usage frequency of "less common" data types, and the implementation details of the hardware. A key issue is whether the tag implementation can be made part of the processor architecture. If this is acceptable, as in a LISP machine, then a small amount of extra hardware can eliminate up to two thirds of the tag checking operations; for PSL on MIPS-X this corresponds to a 3% to 17% speedup. The hardware to reduce the cost of tag checking becomes more complicated, if the implementation of the tags must be left open for the software.

1.7 Conclusion

In this chapter we described a number of tag implementations and we evaluated them using measurements for a LISP implementation on a RISC processor. We found that tag checking, which includes the cost of extracting the tag, is the most expensive tag operation, certainly if full checking at run-time is required (11%–24%). Tag removal, which is done before using the data, uses about 8% of the execution time, and tag insertion uses 1.5%.

We then looked at how the cost of tag handling can be reduced with different software and hardware tag implementations. Software schemes that place the tag in the bottom two or three bits are very attractive: they avoid tag removal for almost all memory accesses without requiring special hardware, and they have the added advantage that the address space is not limited, which is important for large LISP systems. They also allow fast integer arithmetic if the tag value 0 is used for short integers.

Speeding up tag checking often requires special hardware. A first optimization is to eliminate the need for tag extraction before a tag check. This is simple to implement, and it gives a speedup of 4% to 10%, depending on how many tag checking operations can be eliminated by the compiler. Another possibility is to have special hardware that does tag checking in parallel with memory access operations. This, together with the previous features, gives a speedup of between 9% and 22%. It corresponds to implementing a tagged architecture: it requires more complicated hardware, and the tag implementation has to be built into the architecture.

1.8 Description of Programs

The following set of 10 LISP programs were used to collect data:

- *inter*: a simple interpreter for a subset of LISP is used to calculate the Fibbonaci number 10, and to sort a list of numbers; adapted from "Lisp in Lisp" [36].

- *deduce*: a deductive information retriever for a database organized as a discrimination tree; adapted from [7].

- *dedgc*: the same program as *deduce*, but a copying garbage collector is invoked. The program spends about 50% of its time in the garbage collector.

- *rat*: a rational function evaluator that comes with the PSL system.

- *comp*: the first pass of the frontend of the PSL compiler.

- *opt*: the optimizer that was added to the compiler. It uses lists and vectors.

- *frl*: a simple inventory system using the *frame representation language*.

- *boyer*: the boyer benchmark; a rewrite-rule-based simplifier combined with a dumb tautology-checker; benchmark published by Gabriel [12].

- *brow*: a short version of the browse benchmark; creates and browses through an AI-like database of units; benchmark published by Gabriel [12].

- *trav*: a short version of the traverse benchmark; creates and traverses a tree structure; uses structures which are implemented as vectors; benchmark published by Gabriel [12].

Table 1.2 gives the number of procedures, the number of lines of source code (without comments), and the number of MIPS-X machine instructions after compilation, for each program. Each program includes besides the user program, the LISP system modules, or parts of modules, that are used by the program.

	number of procedures	lines source code	words object code
inter	64	710	1533
deduce	100	900	3419
dedgc	116	1100	4112
rat	148	1900	6315
comp	220	2400	9466
opt	226	3500	11121
frl	198	2500	11802
boyer	84	1200	1793
brow	91	1000	2296
trav	78	810	1673

Table 1.2: Information on the 10 test programs.

References

[1] M. J. Accetta, R. V. Baron, W. Bolosky, D. B. Golub, R. F. Rashid, A. Tevanian, Jr., and M. W. Young. Mach: A new kernel foundation for UNIX development. In *Proceedings of the Summer 1986 USENIX Conference*, July 1986.

[2] R. L. Bates, D. Dyer, and J. Koomen. Implementation of Interlisp on the VAX. In *Proceedings of the 1982 Symposium on LISP and Functional Programming*, pages 81–87, Pittsburgh, August 1982. ACM.

[3] A. Bawden, R. Greenblatt, J. Holloway, T. Knight, D. Moon, and D. Weinreb. Lisp machine progress report. Technical Report Memo No 444, MIT Artificial Intelligence Laboratory, August 1977.

[4] P. Bosshart, C. Hewes, M. Chang, and K. Chau. A 553K-transistor LISP processor chip. In *Digest 1987 International Solid-State Circuits Conference*, pages 202–203, New York, February 1987. IEEE.

[5] R. Brooks, D. Posner, J. McDonald, J. White, E. Benson, and R. Gabriel. Design of an optimizing, dynamically retargetable compiler for Common Lisp. In *Proceedings of the 1986 Conference on LISP and Functional Programming*, pages 67–85, Boston, August 1986. ACM.

[6] R. A. Brooks, R. P. Gabriel, and G. L. Steele Jr. S-1 Common Lisp implementation. In *Proceedings of the 1982 Symposium on LISP and Functional Programming*, pages 108–113. ACM, August 1982.

[7] E. Charniak, C. K. Riesbeck, and D. V. McDermott. *Artificial Intelligence Programming*. Lawrence Erlbaum Associates, Hillsdale, New Jersey, 1980.

[8] P. Chow and M. Horowitz. Architectural tradeoffs in the design of MIPS-X. In *Proceedings of the 14th Annual International Symposium on Computer Architecture*, pages 300–308. ACM, June 1987.

[9] C. J. Corley and J. A. Statz. LISP workstation brings AI power to a user's desk. *Computer Design*, 24(1), January 1985.

[10] DEC. *VAX11 Architecture Handbook*. Digital Equipment Corporation, Maynard, MA, 1979.

[11] Fujitsu. *MB86900 RISC Processor - Architecture Manual*, 1987.

[12] R. P. Gabriel. *Performance and evaluation of LISP systems*. Computer Systems Series. The MIT Press, 1985.

[13] M. L. Griss, E. Benson, and G. Q. Maguire. PSL: A portable LISP system. In *Proceedings of the 1982 Symposium on LISP and Functional Programming*, pages 88–97, Pittsburgh, August 1982. ACM.

[14] M. L. Griss and A. C. Hearn. A portable LISP compiler. *Software - Practice and Experience*, 11(6):541–605, June 1981.

[15] W. Harrison. Compiler analysis of the value ranges for variables. Technical Report RC 5544, IBM Thomas J. Watson Research Center, 1975.

[16] M. Horowitz and P. Chow. The MIPS-X microprocessor. In *Westcon 1985*, November 1985.

[17] D. Kranz, R. Kelsey, R. Rees, P. Hudak, J. Philbin, and N. Adams. Orbit: An optimizing compiler for Scheme. In *Proceedings of the SIGPLAN '86 Symposium on Compiler Construction*, pages 219–233, Palo Alto, June 1986. ACM.

[18] David B. McDonald, Scott E. Fahlman, and Skef Wholey. Internal design of CMU Common Lisp on the IBM RT PC. Technical Report CMU-CS-87-157, Carnegie Mellon University, April 1987.

[19] R. Milner. A theory of type polymorphism in programming. *Journal of Computer and System Science*, 17(3):348–375, December 1978.

[20] D. A. Moon. *Maclisp Reference Manual*. MIT, Laboratory of Computer Science, 1983.

[21] D. A. Moon. Architecture of the Symbolics 3600. In *Proceedings of the 12th Annual International Symposium on Computer Architecture*, pages 76–83, Boston, June 1985. ACM. Also in SIGARCH Newsletter 13(3).

[22] J. Rees and N. Adams. T: A dialect of LISP, or LAMBDA: The ultimate software tool. In *Proceedings of the 1982 Symposium on LISP and Functional Programming*, pages 114–122, Pittsburgh, August 1982. ACM.

[23] J. Rose. Fast dispatch mechanisms for stock hardware. In *Proceedings of the Object-Oriented Programming Systems, Languages and Applications Conference*, pages 27–35, San Diego, CA, September 1988. ACM. Also in SIGPLAN Notices, Volume 23, No 11, November 1988.

[24] G. L. Steele Jr. Fast arithmetic in Maclisp. In *Proceedings of the 1977 MACSYMA Users' Conference*. NASA Technical Information Office, July 1977.

[25] G. L. Steele Jr. *Common Lisp - The Language*. Digital Press, 1984.

[26] P. Steenkiste. *LISP on a Reduced-Instruction-Set Processor: Characterization and Optimization*. PhD thesis, Stanford University, March 1987.

[27] P. Steenkiste and J. Hennessy. Lisp on a reduced-instruction-set-processor. In *Proceedings of the 1986 Conference on LISP and Functional Programming*, pages 192–201, Boston, August 1986. ACM.

[28] P. Steenkiste and J. Hennessy. Tags and type checking in LISP: Hardware and software approaches. In *Proceedings of the Second International Conference on Architectural Support for Programming Languages and Operating Systems*, pages 50–59, Palo Alto, October 1987. ACM/IEEE.

[29] E. Stritter and T. Gunter. A microprocessor architecture for a changing world: The Motorola 68000. *IEEE Computer*, 12(2):43–52, February 1979.

[30] G. S. Taylor, J. Hillfinger, P. N. Larus, et al. Evaluation of the SPUR LISP architecture. In *Proceedings of the 13th Annual International Symposium on Computer Architecture*, pages 444–452, Tokyo, June 1986. ACM.

[31] A. Tenenbaum. Type determination for very high level languages. Technical Report 3, Courant Computer Science Report, 1974.

[32] D. Ungar, R. Blau, P. Foley, D. Samples, and D. Patterson. Architecture of SOAR: Smalltalk on a RISC. In *Proceedings of the 11th Annual International Symposium on Computer Architecture*, pages 188–197, Ann-Arbor, June 1984. IEEE. Also in SIGARCH Newsletter, Vol 12, No 3.

[33] Steven R. Vegdahl and Uwe F. Pleban. The runtime environment for Screme, a Scheme implementation on the 88000. In *Proceedings of the Third International Conference on Architectural Support for Programming Languages and Operating Systems*, pages 172–182, Boston, April 1989. ACM/IEEE.

[34] J. White. Lisp/370: A short technical description of the implementation. *SIGSAM*, 12(4):23–27, November 1978.

[35] S. Wholey and S. Fahlman. The design of an instruction set for Common Lisp. In *Proc. 1984 Lisp Conference*, pages 150–157, Austin,TX, Aug 1984. ACM.

[36] P. Winston and B Horn. *Lisp*. Addison-Wesley Publishing Company, 1981.

2   Advanced Register Allocation

Peter A. Steenkiste

Register allocation is an important optimization in many compilers, and global register allocators have been developed for many languages: PL.8 [5], C [8], Pascal and Fortran [9], and LISP [22]. The large register sets available in many recent architectures have further increased the expectations from register allocation. However, several studies [19,27,29] found that after register allocation, a lot of the executed instructions are stack references suitable for register allocation, while at the same time most of the registers remain unused. These measurements suggest that improvements in the register allocation strategy can give a substantial speedup.

The task of the register allocator is to allocate the variables of the program to registers in such a way that program execution time is minimized. "Variables of the program" includes not only user-defined local and global variables, but also objects such as compiler-generated temporaries, parameters and return addresses. The register allocation problem is an instance of the knapsack problem, an NP-complete problem. Programs typically have several thousand variables, i.e. the problem size is very large, and unless efficient heuristics are used, register allocation will be unacceptably slow.

Most compilers do not do register allocation on the program as a whole, but on a per-procedure basis. The problem remains the same, allocate the variables of a procedure while minimizing execution time, but the problem size is much smaller. Per-procedure register allocation is a natural way to do register allocation. First, compilation is done one procedure at the time, so per-procedure register allocation can be done as part of the regular optimization phase. Second, the number of variables in a procedure is small enough that good register allocation can be achieved using efficient heuristics. Furthermore, for many architectures there is also a good match between the number of registers (8 or 16) and the number of variables in a procedure.

In most computer systems, memory references are expensive relative to ALU instructions, making good register allocation important. Newer architectures try to help the register allocator by providing large register files (32 or more registers). Unfortunately, for most programs, this in itself does not reduce memory traffic [19,27,29]. The reason is that per-procedure register allocators cannot use the additional registers because procedures typically only have a few variables. Moreover, in most compilers, procedure calls result in the saving of all live registers in memory, making procedure calls expensive, even on architectures where the basic call/return mechanism is cheap. The high frequency of procedure calls in many languages [27,30] is a major reason for the limited success of global register allocation. A further reduction in memory traffic requires more sophisticated register allocation strategies that reduce the memory traffic caused by procedure calls. This requires that we move away from the traditional per-procedure register allocation.

In the remainder of the chapter we first review traditional per-procedure register allocation algorithms (Section 2.1); we will refer to them as *intraprocedural register allocation*. Section 2.2 gives an overview of two different approaches to *interprocedural register allocation*. A first strategy is *program-wide* register allocation: register allocation is done for all variables in the program at the same time. Another approach is to do register allocation on a per-procedure basis, but to use program-wide (or interprocedural) information to reduce the overhead associated with calls and returns. In Section 2.3 we look at some issues that make interprocedural register allocation hard: recursion, indirect procedure calls and separate compilation. Section 2.4 views interprocedural register allocation as a graph coloring problem, and Section 2.5 summarizes the chapter.

Several architectures provide support to keep local variables in a processor register set across procedure calls. The schemes include top-of-stack or stack caching approaches [14,24,4], multiple register sets [27,3,33]. Architectural support for keeping variables in the processor will not be discussed in this chapter. A brief overview of some of these techniques can be found in [30].

2.1   Intraprocedural Register Allocation

With intraprocedural register allocation, allocation is done on a per-procedure basis, but the allocation in different procedures is not completely independent. Procedures have to agree on the locations of shared variables (e.g. parameters and globals) and non-shared variables (e.g. locals and temporaries) should be allocated so that they are not overwritten during procedure calls. This is achieved by using a *procedure call convention* that rigorously defines the behavior of the caller and callee at procedure call and return boundaries. Central to the call convention is the *call state* that specifies the locations of variables during procedure calls and returns. The per-procedure register allocator has to make sure that variables are in the locations specified by the call state at procedure call and return points.

Intraprocedural register allocation implementations have to select a register allocation algorithm and a call convention; these choices are to a large degree independent. In this section we review some of commonly used register allocation algorithms and call conventions.

2.1.1   Basic Register Allocation Algorithms

One of the simplest approaches to register allocation is *information retention* or *register tracking*: the code generator allocates registers as they are needed and it keeps track of the content of each register in a register descriptor [31,34,15]. Whenever a value is needed, the code generator first checks whether it is already in a register, and if this is not the case, it fetches it from memory. During code generation, the register descriptor is continuously updated: when two control paths join, for example after an if-then-else construct, the contents of the register descriptors at the end of the paths are intersected. Information retention schemes do not allocate registers for the duration of a loop, because when the beginning of the loop is compiled, nothing is known about the register usage before the backward loop branch at the end of the loop. When the code generator runs out of registers, a register is freed by writing its contents back to memory. This is called *spilling*.

Register allocation based on *usage counts* is a simple form of global register allocation [2]. First, the allocator determines which variables will be used most frequently, and it then places those variables into a register for the entire procedure or for some large region in the procedure (e.g. a loop). When estimating how often variables will be used, the loop structure of the program is usually taken into account.

Several refinements of the global register allocation scheme based on usage counts exist. The approach is always the same: determine what can be gained by allocating each variable to a register using some cost function, and allocate the variables that give the biggest gain. Algorithms differ in the accuracy and complexity of the cost function. Examples of register allocators using this approach are the Bliss-11 compiler [35,20], and the PQCC project [23,28]. The basic allocation unit is a *temporary name* (TN), which is a user variable, a compiler temporary, or a copy variable that represents some variable for part of its lifetime. Register allocation corresponds to packing as many TN's as possible in registers, while minimizing some cost function. The cost function tries to model the execution time of the program. Because the profit of allocating one TN to a register can depend on the location of other TN's, the more aggressive implementations sometimes revise gain estimates during register allocation [28].

The problem of global register allocation can be transformed into a graph coloring problem [5,9], which corresponds to a systematic solution of the packing problem described in the previous paragraph. An interference graph is used to represent the problem. Each variable, or live-range (a store to a variable followed by all uses of that variable where the value may have been assigned by the store) of a variable is represented by a node in a graph, and the nodes representing variables that can be live simultaneously are connected by an interference arc in the graph. The register allocation problem is now

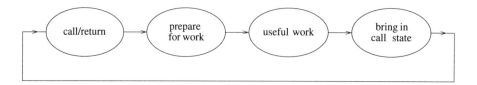

Figure 2.1: Procedure calls and program execution.

equivalent to coloring the (variable) interference graph, using a number of colors equal
to the number of available registers. When coloring the graph, no two adjacent nodes
may receive the same color, forcing separate registers to be used for interfering ranges.
Determining whether a coloring is possible is an NP-complete problem, but heuristics
have been found that give good results in time linear with the number of nodes in the
interference graph, if coloring is possible [6,22]. If the graph cannot be colored, spilling
is required. Spilling inserts a store that divides a live-range, thereby lowering the number
of neighbors for the node and hopefully making it easier to color the resultant graph.

Several recent compilers use powerful global register allocators. The HP compiler
[12], the MIPS R2000 compilers [8], and the SPUR compiler [22] use graph coloring.
The register allocator in EPIC [21] uses the temporary name binding technique [23].

2.1.2   Call/Return State Specifications

The call state specifies the location of variables at call/return boundaries so that procedures can share data and avoid overwriting each other's local variables. Because of the
high frequency of procedure calls, the definition of the call state has a big impact on
performance. From the point of view of register allocation a program cycles through
four states (Figure 2.1) – we would like to minimize the amount of time spent in the
"prepare for work" and the "bring in call state" phases. Because the CPU operates on
registers, keeping variables in registers across procedure calls reduces overhead.

Variables fall into two groups: global variables (and constants) and local variables
(and constants). Global variables are used program-wide. An intraprocedural register
allocator can allocate globals to registers, but it will not keep globals in registers across
procedure calls since other procedures would not be able to find them. System globals
or constants such as the heap pointer and commonly used tag values in LISP systems
are sometimes placed in registers for the duration of the program, but such decisions are
made by the language implementor, and not by the register allocator.

Local variables include not only user-defined locals, but also compiler-generated temporaries, parameters, function results, return addresses, etc. A common feature of local

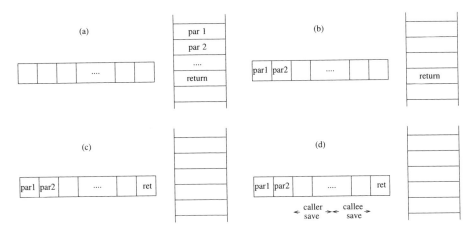

Figure 2.2: Frequently used call conventions.

variables is that new instances are created on every procedure call. A simple call convention is to have procedures allocate space in their stack frame for all their locals, and to keep all local variables on the stack during procedure calls (Figure 2.2a). This convention is simple because it avoids register conflicts. The calling convention that places arguments and the return address on the stack is often directly supported in hardware in older architectures; the VAX-11 [13] *calls* and *ret* instructions are an example.

The above convention usually generates many unnecessary memory accesses: the last action of the caller is typically calculating the parameters, while the first operations in the callee often use the parameters. It is more efficient, and more natural, for the caller to leave the parameters in registers, where they can be used directly by the callee (Figure 2.2b). During a return, the result of a function should similarly be left in a register. Using registers for parameter passing is currently widely used [17]. Also passing the return address in a register (Figure 2.2c) is attractive if procedure calls are implemented using a branch-and-bound instruction, which leaves the return address in a register [12,8]. With this convention, the return address only has to be saved on the stack if the callee itself makes procedure calls.

In any of the above cases, the saving of registers can be done using a caller-save or callee-save convention. With the caller-save convention, the caller saves all live locals on the stack before the procedure call and the callee is free to use any registers. With the callee-save convention, the saving is done by the callee; the caller can leave values in registers and the callee has to save and restore any registers it uses. Unused parameter registers fall into the caller-save group.

Procedure call overhead can be further reduced by dividing the registers in a caller-save and a callee-save group [12,8] (Figure 2.2d). The compiler assigns variables to the two groups depending on whether their live ranges overlap with procedure calls. If a variable is never live during a procedure call, it is allocated in the caller-save area, thus avoiding saving and restoring. If a variable is live across multiple calls, it is allocated in the callee-save area, since saving/restoring the register once at procedure entry/exit is better than saving and restoring it across every procedure call. Leaf procedures do not make any procedure calls and can often do all their work in the caller-save area; they never have to access the stack and no stack frame is built.

2.2   Interprocedural Register Allocation

With interprocedural register allocation the call convention gives more freedom to the register allocator, making it possible to reduce the procedure call overhead. Interprocedural strategies fall into two groups:

- With program-wide allocation, register allocation is taken out of the regular (procedure by procedure) compilation process, and it is done on all variables in the program at once in a separate phase. This approach is taken by Wall [32].

- A more incremental strategy is to still do register allocation as part of the procedure-per-procedure compilation process but to use interprocedural information to optimize the call state at individual call sites. This approach is taken by Steenkiste [30] and Chow [7].

In the remainder of this section we first look at the basic algorithms used in the different interprocedural register allocation implementations. We then look at issues that complicate the basic algorithm: recursion, indirect procedure calls, separate compilation and global variables. How these issues are addressed is largely independent from the basic allocation algorithm.

2.2.1   Bottom-up Register Allocation

The limitations of intraprocedural register allocation can best be explained with an example. Consider a procedure A that calls a procedure B. With a intraprocedural register allocator, the registers that are live at the call site in A must be saved, and later restored. However, it is unlikely that the sum of the registers required by A and B exceeds the total number of registers on the machine. An intraprocedural register allocator cannot exploit this because register allocation in A and B is done completely separately, but an interprocedural allocator might be able to avoid the saving and restoring of registers by allocating nonoverlapping sets of registers to A and B.

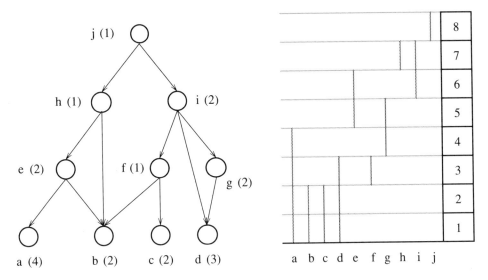

Figure 2.3: Interprocedural register allocation: an example.

The bottom-up algorithm is based on this simple idea. For programs without recursion, the call graph is a directed acyclic graph (DAG). Compilation starts with the leaf procedures at the bottom of the call DAG, and moves gradually up, only compiling a procedure after all its descendents have been compiled. Leaf procedures are assigned registers 0 through $n - 1$, where n is the maximum number required for the procedure, as determined by the intraprocedural allocator. When compiling a nonleaf procedure, the interprocedural allocator assigns the procedure registers $m + 1$ through $m + n$, where m was the highest register used by any child of the procedure. Figure 2.3 illustrates the algorithm. The key observation in this algorithm is that only the ancestors of a given procedure can be active at the same time as the procedure. This allows siblings to share registers. If the architecture has enough registers, all locals will be permanently allocated to registers and no stack accesses will occur.

The bottom-up register allocator was first implemented in the Portable Standard Lisp (PSL) compiler [18] for the MIPS-X processor [10,30]. The main motivation for the bottom-up algorithm was the observation that for a large number of LISP programs the call graph was wider at the bottom than at the top, and that the programs spend most of their time in the bottom of the call graph. With a bottom-up order of register allocation, the most promising part of call graph is guaranteed to have good register allocation. It allows both leaf procedures and a large number of non-leaf procedures to do all their

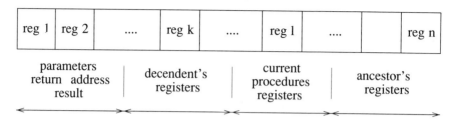

Figure 2.4: Call state with bottom-up register allocation.

work in registers and can be viewed as an extension of the split caller-save callee-save strategy of Section 2.1.2.

For most programs all registers will be committed before compilation reaches the top of the call graph. One possible strategy is to spill some registers and to continue interprocedural register allocation. The implementation of the bottom-up algorithm in PSL ignores spilling and uses intraprocedural register allocation for the procedures in the top of the call tree. This decision is clearly suboptimal, but measurements indicated that spilling would only slightly improve the results because the majority of the variable references are made at the lower levels of the call tree. For the PSL implementation, recursion is the major limiting factor on the performance (see Section 2.3.2).

With bottom-up register allocation, the call state is different from call site to call site, although it always has the same format (Figure 2.4). Procedures can use the parameter and descendent registers between call sites, but the descendent registers have to be clear at every call site. The set of descendent registers can be different for different call sites in the same procedure. For example in Figure 2.3, only the locals of "c" that are live during the call(s) to "b" interfere with the locals of "b"; "e" can keep live locals in registers three and four during calls to "b," but not during calls to "a." Information on the register usage of callees is available during bottom-up register allocation, and it sometimes makes it possible to use the same register at several levels. Differentiating between different call sites is particularly useful if the last action of a procedure is another procedure call: at the time of the call, all locals of the caller are dead, so the caller and the callee can use the same registers.

One problem with the bottom-up algorithm is that rarely executed procedures at the bottom of the call graph can ruin the register allocation for a large number of procedures in the program. Fortunately, many of these procedures are fairly easy to detect. In the LISP system, examples are the garbage collector and error routines. In the user program, these procedures can be detected by profiling or with the help from the programmer. Rarely used procedures should be compiled using a callee-save convention, and when propagating information upwards in the call graph, calls to these callee-save procedures should be processed as if they use no registers.

The bottom-up allocator for PSL on MIPS-X was evaluated using 11 LISP programs [30]. More than 70% of the stack accesses remaining after the standard register allocation were eliminated and the average speedup was 10%. The 10% speedup was made up of a 7.8% decrease in loads, a 4.5% decrease in stores, a 3.5% decrease in no-ops (due to the removal of load and store delay slots), and a 5.8% *increase* in register-to-register move instructions. This increase in move instructions results from the register-based parameter passing convention. At the entry to a nonleaf procedure, parameters have to be moved to their allocated register to free up the low-order registers for use in future procedure calls. Without interprocedural register allocation, these register-register moves were memory references. It is possible to reduce the number of moves by having the calling procedure put the parameters directly in the register they have been allocated to in the called procedure, but this makes the procedure call convention substantially more complicated since parameters have to be stored in different registers depending on what procedure is called. Moreover, this information has to be available at run-time so that indirect procedure calls work correctly. Because of this complexity, this change was not implemented.

Mulder implemented the bottom-up algorithm for Pascal [16,25] with encouraging results. Although the differences in language and programs makes a comparison difficult, the results for Mulder's five large Pascal programs are remarkably similar – with 16 globally allocated registers, he was able to remove 73% of the stack references. With 64 registers, he is able to eliminate 87% of the removable references. An implementation of the bottom-up algorithm by Chow is discussed in Section 2.2.3.

2.2.2   *Program-wide Register Allocation*

Wall implemented an interprocedural register allocator that operates on all variables in the program [32]. The register allocation phase during compilation is very limited, and the real register allocation is done at link-time when all program information is available. The compile-time register allocator operates on basic blocks: expression temporaries are allocated to a limited set of registers, and variables are loaded for the duration of the basic block if they are needed. The code is also annotated to indicate what code changes will be necessary when local variables are allocated to registers. Examples of annotations are the removal of load and store instructions when a specific variable is allocated to a register, changing of operands from a temporary register to the register to which the variable was allocated, and replacing loads and stores by register moves.

The program-wide allocator first groups variables that cannot be live concurrently into pseudo-registers; this property exists between "parallel nodes" in the call graph. Global variables each get assigned to their own pseudo-register. The usage frequencies of local and global variables are then used to determine the global usage frequency of each pseudo-register. The usage frequencies can either be based on a static program analysis or on dynamic profiling information. The pseudo-registers with the largest global usage count are assigned to registers, while the others are allocated in memory. The code is changed to reflect the allocation at link-time using the annotations.

The key observation in both the bottom-up allocator and Wall's allocator is that variables of procedures that cannot be active at the same time can be allocated to the same register. This technique makes it possible to pack a lot of variables in a limited number of registers in a simple way, and it has been used before to pack the variables of nested procedures in a single stack frame [26].

The main difference between the two allocators is that Wall uses program-specific information to choose the order of allocation, while the bottom-up strategy relies on the observation that most programs spend a lot of time in the bottom of the call graph. If the accesses to all variables are uniformly distributed, Wall's priority function will cause a bottom-up allocation, because the groups representing variables at the bottom of the call tree will contain more variables and thus have more accesses and a larger priority. Similar to the bottom-up allocator, Wall does not use spilling. When the registers are exhausted, the most important objects should be allocated, and spilling will not yield much improvement.

Using program-specific profiling information instead of general observations avoids two potential pitfalls. First, a heavily used variable high up in the call tree will never be allocated using bottom-up allocation, but might be by Wall's algorithm; this is probably a minor effect. Second, Wall's algorithm will avoid allocation of a variable or an entire procedure's worth of variables that are at the bottom of the tree but have little dynamic use. By not allocating those variables, registers are conserved, allowing the allocator to reach a higher position in the call graph. It is possible to add procedure-level profiling to the bottom-up allocator to avoid these pitfalls. The fact that the bottom-up algorithm does not use program-specific information simplifies the implementation, and makes it possible to do interprocedural register allocation using only a single pass over the program. On the other hand, a scheme based on profiling should give better results, especially in programs that do not adhere to our observations about call trees.

Wall presents performance data for his interprocedural register allocator both with and without the use of dynamic profiling information. Without profiling, but with the use of graph coloring inside a procedure, he measured speedups ranging from 3% to 8%, relative to the case of per procedure register allocation. If profiling is used, the speedup increases to between 3% and 12%. Although comparisons are difficult because the benchmarks, the underlying compiler, and the number of registers available for allocation differ, Walls' results appear to be similar to the results for the bottom-up register allocation implementations. Wall compared his scheme with the bottom-up algorithm [33]: he concludes that with profiling information, his approach is slightly more effective, but that without profiling information, the bottom-up algorithm performs better.

2.2.3 Bottom-up Allocation in the MIPS Compiler

Chow implemented interprocedural register allocation in the context of the MIPS R2000 compiler system [8,7]. His interprocedural register allocator uses the bottom-up strategy: compile the procedures in bottom-up order using a depth-first traversal of the call graph, and use knowledge about the register usage of the callee to reduce register saving and restoring across calls. Chow's implementation is on top of an intraprocedural register allocator that uses priority-based graph coloring and a split caller-save callee-save call convention. One of the requirements of the allocator was that it must be possible to link modules that were compiled with interprocedural and intraprocedural register allocation.

The basic optimization provided by the bottom-up allocator is that caller-save registers that are not used by callees do not have to be saved and restored. The per-procedure register allocator exploits this by giving registers that are not used by any of the callees of the procedure a higher priority, so the compiler will allocate variables to such registers as long as they are available. When the limited number of registers is exhausted the compiler has to allocate variables to registers that have to be saved across procedure calls. The resulting allocation in the upper regions of the call graph is similar to that obtained using intraprocedural register allocation, as was also the case in the PSL implementation of the bottom-up algorithm. Because interprocedural information can be used to avoid the saving and restoring of caller-save registers, but not for callee-save registers, callee-save registers are used in caller-save mode when interprocedural register allocation is used. Interprocedural register allocation makes the per-procedure register allocator slightly more complicated: since the save/restore cost for a variable now depends on what register it is allocated to, priorities are no longer associated with variables but with variable/register pairs. Chow reports that this extra complexity has almost no impact on compilation time.

Because only registers used in caller-save mode can be optimized, it looks like it would never be advantageous to use callee-save mode with interprocedural register allocation. This is true when there are enough register available to accommodate all variables in the program, but it is not true if the allocator runs out of registers, as will be the case for all but the smallest programs. The reason is that poor register usage can occur if variables that are used on only some of the execution paths in a procedure are allocated to a caller-save register: such variables can force the saving of the register in an ancestor of the procedure, even though the register is not necessarily used during that invocation. Chow's implementation avoids this pitfall by only using caller-save mode when a variable is used throughout the procedure and by using the callee-save mode for registers that are only used on some execution paths. Registers that are used in callee-mode show up as unused in the register-usage summary of the procedure. By restricting the use of optimizable caller-save registers to variables that have a higher probability of being used, more caller-save registers are made available for use in procedures higher in the call graph.

To avoid unnecessary saving and restoring of callee-save registers, the *shrink-wrapping* optimization is used. It moves the saving and restoring of callee-save registers away from procedure entry and exit towards the basic blocks that actually use the register [7].

In the MIPS implementation of bottom-up allocation, the caller places the parameters directly in the registers to which they were allocated in the callee, so for each procedure, the compiler also has to keep track of which registers the parameters have to be passed in. This optimization was considered in the PSL implementation of bottom-up allocation, but was deemed too complicated in the dynamic LISP environment.

Chow measured speedups ranging from -1.4% to 14.1% with a mean of 1.3% over intraprocedural register allocation. These results are not as good as those observed by Steenkiste, Mulder and Wall. The reason is that the intraprocedural register allocator employed a very efficient linkage convention using split caller-save and callee-save registers. The implementation of two classes of registers in the linkage convention lowers the overall improvement that we might see from interprocedural register allocation [7] because it already captures some of the benefit for leaf procedures. Another reason is that some of Chow's programs have a low procedure-call frequency. The LISP programs in the PSL implementation have a high procedure-call frequency, making them much better candidates for interprocedural register allocation.

2.3 Dealing With Real Programs

In the previous section we described the basic allocation algorithms used in three interprocedural register allocators, but we ignored several important program features and requirements, such as indirect and recursive procedure calls, separate compilation and the allocation of global variables. These features require special treatment, and we describe some possible strategies in this section.

2.3.1 Indirect Procedure Calls

In an indirect procedure call the called procedure is not known until run-time, so a compile-time or link-time register allocator cannot determine which registers it uses or where it expects its parameters. The three register allocators described in the previous seciton deal with this problem in a similar way.

The bottom-up allocator for PSL saves all the registers used by the procedure containing the indirect call or by its ancestors in the call tree. These are all the "active" registers at the time of the indirect call, so saving and restoring them leaves the actual procedure invoked by the indirect call with a clean set of registers. Since the PSL intraprocedural register allocator uses a caller-save convention, this corresponds to converting to the regular calling convention. Parameter passing is not a problem for the PSL interprocedural register allocator, since all functions expect their arguments in the same registers. Note that this solution only introduces overhead when a procedure is invoked indirectly. This is desirable in a language like LISP where typically a large number of procedures can be called indirectly.

Similar to the PSL implementation, Wall's implementation saves and restores all registers that might be active around indirect calls. With program-wide register allocation, parameters that are allocated to a register are directly placed in that register by the caller, and these registers are not known by the register allocator. To deal with this problem, indirect calls pass parameters in the stack, and each procedure has a preamble that loads the parameters in the right registers. The preamble is skipped by direct calls. The same technique could be used by a bottom-up allocator that places parameters directly in the registers to which they are allocated in the callee.

Chow handles the problems of indirect calls, recursion and separate compilation in a unified way by distinguishing between *open procedures* and *closed procedures*. Closed procedures are basically well behaved, so that bottom-up interprocedural register allocation can be applied. Procedures are open if some of their callers have been compiled before they are (i.e. recursive procedures) or if some of their callers are unknown (indirect calls or calls from other modules). Register usage information about an open procedure cannot be propagated to all its callers using bottom-up allocation. As a result, open procedures are called using the regular, intraprocedural call convention, i.e. split caller-save callee-save registers with fixed registers for parameters. Besides being called in a special way, open procedures also have to save and restore any callee-save registers that either they or their descendents use; shrink-wrapping is again used to avoid unnecessary saving and restoring. A disadvantage of the mechanism of open procedures is that they introduce overhead, even when open procedures are called in a regular "closed" way, for example, when a procedure that can be called indirectly is called directly. A big advantage of the mechanism of open and closed procedures is that a single concept solves the problem of recursion, indirect calls and separate compilation, and it also allows the linking of code that was compiled using both interprocedural and intraprocedural register allocation.

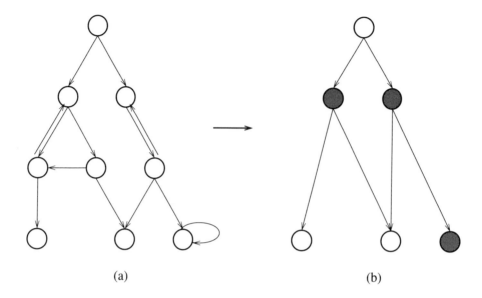

(a)   (b)

Figure 2.5: Reducing a call graph to a DAG.

2.3.2   Recursion

In recursive programs several instances of the same local variable can exist at the same time, and the instances will have to be saved between recursive calls. The three interprocedural register allocators handle this problem in different ways.

With the bottom-up algorithm the problem of recursion manifests itself through cycles in the program call graph, making a bottom-up (or depth first) compilation order impossible. To eliminate the cycles, the allocator for the PSL compiler replaces each strongly connected component [1], or *recursive procedure group*, of the call graph by a single compound node as is illustrated in Figure 2.5. This reduces the call graph (a) to a DAG (b), which we call the *reduced call graph*.

The bottom-up register allocation algorithm is then applied to the reduced call graph with one change to the algorithm – when doing interprocedural register allocation for a procedure in a recursive group, calls to procedures in the recursive group save all the registers allocated by the calling procedure (Figure 2.6b). Each procedure in the group will then reuse the same registers. Procedures from outside the group that call a procedure in a recursive group should not use any of the registers allocated by any procedure in the group (nor any register used by a descendent of a group member). Interprocedural register allocation is still used for non-recursive calls inside the recur-

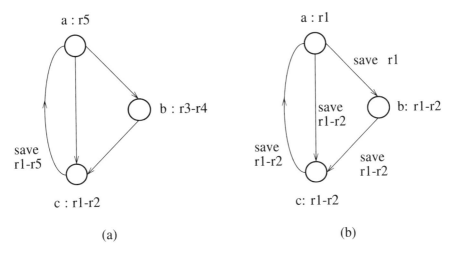

Figure 2.6: Differences in handling recursion: (a) Wall (b) Incremental saving.

sive group, i.e. when a procedure inside a recursive group calls a procedure outside the group.

Wall uses a slightly different scheme (Figure 2.6a). Program-wide register allocation is applied to a program with all calls that form a cycle in the call graph (backward arcs) removed, so the call graph has been reduced to a call tree. After register allocation, the compiler inserts save and restore instructions around the backward calls for all the register that are in use in the recursive group; no registers are saved for the other (forward) calls.

For languages with a lot of recursion, such as LISP, the incremental saving used in the bottom-up allocator (scheme b) has two advantages. First, the total number of registers used by the compound node (and hence unavailable to the ancestors) is only the largest number of registers used by any procedure in the recursive group. This is because a parent and child in a recursive group will use the same registers, since they are saved by the parent when the child is called. In contrast, Wall's algorithm allocates different registers to the parent and child, and as a result, Wall's algorithm consumes more registers for the recursive group, making fewer registers available for procedures higher up in the call graph. For the example in Figure 2.6, the recursive group uses registers r1-r5 with Wall's scheme, and r1-r2 with incremental saving. The second advantage is that saving registers on backward arcs can result in saving registers that are not in use; this can never happen with the incremental saving scheme. Figure 2.6 shows an example: using Wall's scheme, registers r1-r5 are saved on each iteration, although registers r3-r4 are not always used.

2.3.3   Separate Compilation

To achieve the full benefit of an interprocedural algorithm the entire program must be processed at once. One way of doing this is by delaying register allocation until link-time, as is done by Wall. The advantage of link-time allocation is that it allows many of the benefits of separate compilation to be retained. Of course, the cost is a slower link step when register allocation is performed. Note that the choice of compile-time versus link-time allocation is a separate issue from the choice of an allocation algorithm. Bottom-up allocation can also be implemented at link-time.

At first glance it would appear that link-time allocation is the only solution to the problem of separate compilation, but that is not true. The problem with interprocedural register allocation, or any interprocedural optimization, is that changes in one part of the program can invalidate the register allocation all over the program. The standard technique to avoid recompilation of the whole program every time it changes is to use tools such as *make* or the **R**^{n} program environment [11]: the idea is to keep track of dependencies between modules and to restrict recompilation to the modules that are affected by a program change. This technique can also be used to limit recompilation when interprocedural optimization is used.

With bottom-up allocation for example, changes to a procedure require at most the recompilation of that procedure and its ancestors in the call graph. Only the recompilation of the function is required, if the new version is restricted to use only the registers used by the old version. Because of this restriction, the new function might have to save and restore some registers so register allocation will not necessarily be optimal, but the advantage is faster recompilation. As individual functions are changed and recompiled, the benefits of the interprocedural allocator will diminish, but reallocating the registers interprocedurally will restore the benefits. An alternative is to use the same technique at the module level: when changes are made, only recompile the modules that were changed, and make sure that the register usage as it is seen at the entry points to the module remains unchanged. An environment such as the **R**^{n} programming environment [11] being developed at Rice University, would allow maintenance of sufficient information that interprocedural allocation could be done without requiring complete recompilation or linking. An advantage of bottom-up allocation is that it only propagates information upwards in the call graph; as a result, changes in the user programs do not require recompilation of libraries or the run-time system (such as for LISP).

Chow deals with separate compilation in a completely different way. Procedures that are exported by the module are open procedures and are called using the regular intraprocedural call convention. The advantage of this approach is that it is simple: no intermodule information is needed and separate compilation does not create a problem.

The disadvantage is a loss in performance, but as long as the frequency of inter-module calls is much lower than the frequency of calls inside a module, the effect should be small.

2.3.4   Global Variables

Wall's algorithm will allocate heavily used global variables to registers, while both bottom-up allocators apply interprocedural register allocation only to local variables. The reason is simple: the bottom-up allocators use only a single pass and they cannot collect the program-specific information that is needed to decide which globals should be allocated to registers. When interprocedural register allocation is applied to globals, it is not only necessary to select the most heavily used globals, but also to compare the benefit of allocating a global to the benefit of using the register for a group of locals. This is a hard problem: not only does it require program-wide information, but it is difficult to compare the usage counts of globals and locals.

  Note that allocating a global to a register for the duration of the program is relatively expensive, since it forces many locals to memory. Ideally one would like to allocate globals to registers only for the parts of the program where they are heavily used; these registers can then be used for locals or other globals in other parts of the program. This is clearly a difficult problem, and the payoff is probably very small.

2.3.5   Scoping Rules

Specific language features can further complicate interprocedural register allocation. An example is nested procedure declarations in Pascal. Since inner procedures can access the local variables of enclosing outer procedures, allocating such variables to registers would require information to flow downwards in the flow graph, from the outer procedure to the inner procedure. This would make a bottom-up register allocator more complicated. The simplest solution is not to make such variables available for interprocedural register allocation [25]. The performance impact is small since these variables are not common.

2.4   Interprocedural Register Allocation as a Graph Coloring Problem

The goal of register allocation is to allocate the variables of the program to registers in such a way that execution time is minimized. Using our experience with per-procedure allocation, we would expect graph coloring of the program-wide variable interference graph to yield good results. The interference graph contains a node for every live range of every variable in the program, and two nodes are connected with an arc if the corresponding variables can be live at the same time. A coloring of the graph with the number of colors corresponding to the physical register count would constitute an interprocedural allocation of the registers. Unfortunately, this approach is computationally unacceptable even without recursion. The interference graph for a large program would be enormous. Analysis of a LISP program with 220 procedures and 3,500 lines of source code, for example, showed that the interference graph would contain over 500 nodes (number of live ranges), and more than 50,000 arcs! A straightforward application of graph coloring to the interprocedural register allocation problem appears impractical, and more tractable coloring strategies have to be found. Bottom-up interprocedural register allocation can be viewed as such a solution.

The register allocation problem can be simplified by breaking it up into an intraprocedural part, to be handled with any register allocation algorithm, and an interprocedural part. In the interprocedural phase, we first construct the *procedure interference graph* as the transitive closure of the program call graph. Two procedures that can be active at the same time will be adjacent in the procedure interference graph; they have an ancestor-descendent relationship in the call graph. The procedure interference graph can be viewed as a simplified version of the program-wide variable interference graph where the locals of each procedure have been collapsed into a single node. The interprocedural register allocation problem can now be solved as a coloring problem on the procedure interference graph. Each node in the graph should be assigned a number of colors equal to the number of registers that are required for the locals of that procedure, as determined by an intraprocedural register allocator. The colored procedure interference graph describes the call state.

Building and coloring the procedure interference graph is a more realistic solution: it has a number of nodes equal to the number of procedures in the program (versus number of live ranges). The number of arcs in the procedure interference graph has an upper bound that is quadratic in the number of nodes. For the same LISP program mentioned above, the procedure interference graph has 220 nodes and about 7,000 arcs. Recursion still generates problems because it creates nodes in the procedure interference graph that are adjacent to themselves, making the graph not colorable. The transformation introduced in Section 2.3.2 eliminates the loops caused by recursion.

Bottom-up register allocation corresponds to a coloring of the procedure interference graph, where priority is given to procedures in the bottom of the graph. An interesting point is that when a bottom-up coloring order is used, it is not necessary to build the interference graph. A depth-first traversal of the program call graph has the same effect. For our LISP program, the call graph has 360 arcs (the number of calls), down from 7000 in the interference graph.

The graph-coloring heuristic used in interprocedural bottom-up coloring is similar to the strategy used by Chow for per-procedure coloring [9]. The critical feature of the different coloring strategies is the order of assignment (or spilling) when a register shortage exists, as is usually the case with interprocedural register allocation. Chow uses the ratio of the estimated cost savings to the size of the live range to determine the coloring order of the hard-to-color nodes. This metric reduces the priority of variables that tie up a register for a long time. The bottom-up coloring heuristic is similar to Chow's priority function: it assumes that variables in procedures near the leaves have the highest cost savings, since execution profiles are typically weighted towards those procedures [30]. Since the number of variables that can be allocated to a register decreases as we move up the call graph from the leaves towards the root (the call graph is wider at the bottom than at the top), variables in the bottom of the call graph are "less expensive" to allocate since they may share a register with more variables. By first allocating the variables of procedures near the leaves, priority is given to variables that have on average the highest ratio of benefit to cost-of-allocation, just as Chow does.

The PSL implementation of the bottom-up algorithm simply colors bottom-up and switches to intraprocedural register allocation when all colors/registers are in use. Chow's implementation uses the callee-save mode for local variables that are not used throughout their procedure. This corresponds to using spilling for less attractive nodes in the interference graph, thus freeing registers for better candidates higher in the call graph.

2.5 Conclusion

In this chapter we studied three interprocedural register allocation implementations. Steenkiste and Chow rely on a bottom-up compilation order of procedures to propagate register usage information through the program; this information is used to avoid saving registers that are not used by a callee or its descendents. Wall uses program-wide register allocation: register allocation is done for all program variables at once at link-time. The three implementations handle recursion and indirect calls in similar ways: they revert to an intraprocedural call convention for indirect calls, and they save registers across recursive calls in either an incremental way or on the backward calls. Measurements show that interprocedural register allocation can result in speedups as high as 10%, but that the performance is very sensitive to to factors such as the procedure call frequency and the the frequency of recursive calls. Chow's results show that efficient calling conventions such as split caller-callee save registers, together with good per-procedure register allocation can also capture some of the benefit of interprocedural register allocation.

Future interprocedural allocators will probably combine a number of features of the different approaches. They will almost certainly exploit the fact that sibling procedures can share the same registers. A bottom-up compilation order seems to be an attractive technique, but program-wide information will have to be used to allocate globals and to avoid allocating rarely used variables. Future implementations will probably also support spilling so that more variables can benefit from interprocedural register allocation, and they will have to solve the problem of separate compilation. The cost and complexity of interprocedural register allocation should be small enough so that it does not outweigh its benefits.

References

[1] A. Aho, J. Hopcroft, and J Ullman. *Data Structures and Algorithms*. Addison-Wesley Publishing Company, 1983.

[2] A. Aho, R. Sethi, and J Ullman. *Compilers: Principles, Techniques, and Tools*. Addison-Wesley, 1986.

[3] E. Basart and D. Folger. Ridge 32 architecture – a RISC variation. In *International Conference on Computer Design VLSI in Computers*, pages 315–318. IEEE, October 1983.

[4] A. Berenbaum, D. Ditzel, and H McLellan. Architectural innovations in the CRISP microprocessor. In *Spring 1987 COMPCON Digest of Papers*, pages 91–95, San Fransisco, February 1987. IEEE.

[5] G. Chaitin. Register allocation & spilling via graph coloring. In *Proceedings of the SIGPLAN '82 Symposium on Compiler Construction*, pages 98–105, Boston, June 1982. ACM.

[6] F. Chow. *A Portable Machine-Independent Global Optimizer - Design and Measurements*. PhD thesis, Stanford University, December 1983. Technical Note 83-254.

[7] F. Chow. Minimizing register usage penalty at procedure calls. In *Proceedings of the SIGPLAN '88 Conference on Programming Language Design and Implementation*, pages 85–94, Atlanta, June 1988. ACM.

[8] F. Chow, M. Himelstein, E. Killian, and L. Weber. Engineering a RISC compiler system. In *Spring 86 COMPCON Digest of Papers*, pages 132–137, San Fransisco, March 1986. IEEE.

[9] F. C. Chow and J. L. Hennessy. Register allocation by priority-based coloring. In *Proceedings of the SIGPLAN '84 Symposium on Compiler Construction*, pages 222–232, Montreal, Canada, June 1984. ACM.

[10] P. Chow and M. Horowitz. Architectural tradeoffs in the design of MIPS-X. In *Proceedings of the 14th Annual International Symposium on Computer Architecture*, pages 300–308. ACM, June 1987.

[11] K. Cooper, K. Kennedy, and L. Torczon. Interprocedural optimization: Eliminating unnecessary recompilation. In *Proceedings of the SIGPLAN '86 Symposium on Compiler Construction*, pages 58–67, Palo Alto, June 1986. ACM.

[12] D. Coutant, C. Hammond, and W. Kelly. Compilers for the new generation of Hewlett-Packard computers. *Hewlett-Packard Journal*, (1):4–18, January 1986.

[13] DEC. *VAX11 Architecture Handbook*. Digital Equipment Corporation, Maynard, MA, 1979.

[14] D. R. Ditzel and H. R. McLellan. Register allocation for free: The C machine stack cache. In *Proceedings of the SIGARCH/SIGPLAN Symposium on Architectural Support for Programming Languages and Operating Systems*, pages 48–56. ACM, March 1982. Published in Computer Architecture News 10(2).

[15] C. N. Fischer and R. J. LeBlanc. *Crafting a Compiler*. Benjamin/Cummings, Menlo Park, Ca., 1988.

[16] M. Flynn, C. Mitchell and H. Mulder. And now a case for more complex instruction sets. *IEEE Computer*, 20(9):71–83, September 1987.

[17] M. L. Griss, E. Benson, and A. C. Hearn. Current status of a portable LISP compiler. In *Proceedings of the SIGPLAN '82 Symposium on Compiler Construction*, pages 276–283, Boston, June 1982. SIGPLAN, ACM.

[18] M. L. Griss, E. Benson, and G. Q. Maguire. PSL: A portable LISP system. In *Proceedings of the 1982 Symposium on LISP and Functional Programming*, pages 88–97, Pittsburgh, August 1982. ACM.

[19] M. Huguet. A C-oriented register set design. Technical Report CSD-850019, UCLA, June 1985.

[20] R. Johnsson. *An Approach to Global Register Allocation*. PhD thesis, Carnegie-Mellon University, December 1975.

[21] R. Kessler, J. Peterson, H. Carr, et al. Epic - a retargetable highly optimizing LISP compiler. In *Proceedings of the SIGPLAN '86 Symposium on Compiler Construction*, pages 118–130, Palo Alto, June 1986. ACM.

[22] J. Larus and P. Hilfinger. Register allocation in the SPUR LISP compiler. In *Proceedings of the SIGPLAN '86 Symposium on Compiler Construction*, pages 255–263, Palo Alto, June 1986. ACM.

[23] B. Leverett. *Register Allocation in Optimizing Compilers*. UMI Research Press, 1981.

[24] D. A. Moon. Architecture of the Symbolics 3600. In *Proceedings of the 12th Annual International Symposium on Computer Architecture*, pages 76–83, Boston, June 1985. ACM. Also in SIGARCH Newsletter 13(3).

[25] J. Mulder. *Tradeoffs in Processor-Architecture and Data-Buffer Design*. PhD thesis, Stanford University, December 1987. Appeared as Stanford Technical Report CSL-87-345.

[26] T. Murtagh. A less dynamic register allocation scheme for Algol-like languages. In *Conference Record of the Tenth Annual ACM Symposium on Principles of Programming Languages*, pages 283–289, Austin, TX, 1983. ACM.

[27] D. A. Patterson and C. H. Sequin. A VLSI RISC. *Computer*, 15(9):8–22, September 1982.

[28] A. Reiner. Cost-minimization in register assignment for retargetable compilers. Technical Report CMU-CS-84-137, Carnegie-Mellon University, June 1985.

[29] P. Steenkiste and J. Hennessy. LISP on a reduced-instruction-set-processor. In *Proceedings of the 1986 Conference on LISP and Functional Programming*, pages 192–201, Boston, August 1986. ACM.

[30] P. Steenkiste and J. Hennessy. A simple interprocedural register allocation algorithm and its effectiveness for LISP. *ACM Transactions on Programming Languages and Systems*, 11(1):1–32, January 1989.

[31] W. Waite. Code generation. In *Compiler Construction - An Advanced Course*, chapter 3.E, pages 302–332. Springer-Verlag, 1976.

[32] D. Wall. Global register allocation at link time. In *Proceedings of the SIGPLAN '86 Symposium on Compiler Construction*, pages 264–275, Palo Alto, June 1986. ACM.

[33] D. Wall. Register windows vs. register allocation. In *Proceedings of the SIGPLAN '88 Conference on Programming Language Design and Implementation*, pages 67–78, Atlanta, June 1988. ACM.

[34] T. Wilcox. *Generating Machine Code for High-Level Programming Languages*. PhD thesis, Cornell University, September 1971.

[35] W. Wulf, R. Johnsson, C. Weinstock, S Hobbs, and C Geschke. *The Design of an Optimizing Compiler*, volume 2 of *Programming Languages Series*. American Elsevier, 1975.

3 Data-Flow Analysis and Type Recovery in Scheme

Olin Shivers

The lack of explicit type information in Scheme prevents the application of many compiler optimizations. Implicit type information can oftentimes be recovered by analyzing the flow of control through primitive operations and conditionals. Such flow analysis, however, is difficult in the presence of higher-order functions. This chapter presents a technique for recovering type information from Scheme programs using flow analysis. The algorithm used for flow analysis is semantically based, and is novel in that it correctly handles the "environment flow" problem. Several examples of a working implementation of the analysis are presented. The techniques are applicable not only to Scheme type recovery, but also to related languages, such as Common Lisp and Standard ML, and to related data-flow analyses, such as range analysis, future analysis, and copy propagation.

3.1 Introduction

Scheme is a *latently typed* language [22]. This means that unlike statically typed languages such as ML or Pascal, types are associated only with run-time values, not with variables. A variable can potentially be bound to values of any type, and type tests can be performed at run time to determine the execution path through a program. This gives the programmer an extremely powerful form of polymorphism without requiring a verbose system of type declarations.

This power and convenience is not without cost, however. Since run-time behavior can determine which values are bound to a given variable, precisely determining the type of a given reference to a variable is not decidable at compile time. For example, consider the following fragment of Scheme code:

```
(let ((x (if (oracle) 3 'three)))
  (f x))
```

The reference to **x** in the subexpression (**f x**) could have any one of the types integer, symbol, integer+symbol, or "bottom," depending on whether the oracle always returns true, always returns false, sometimes returns both, or never returns at all, respectively. Of course, determining the oracle's behavior at compile time is, in general, undecidable.

We can appeal to data-flow analysis techniques to recover a conservative approximation of the type information implicit in a program's structure. However, Scheme is a difficult language to analyse: its higher-order procedures and first-class continuations render the construction of a control-flow graph at compile time very difficult. The problem of conservatively approximating, at compile time, the types of the values associated with the references to variables in a Scheme program thus involves data-flow analysis in the presence of higher-order functions.

In this chapter, I present an algorithm for flow analysis that can correctly recover a useful amount of type information from Scheme programs, even in the presence of higher-order functions and `call/cc`. This algorithm performs a kind of type inference. Since the term "type inference" is commonly used to refer to the recovery of static type assignments for variables, I will instead refer to the type analysis performed by this algorithm as *type recovery*: the recovery of type information from the control and environment structure of a program.

3.1.1   Sources of Type Information

Type information in Scheme programs can be statically recovered from three sources: conditional branches, applications of primitive operations, and user declarations.

Conditional Branches   Consider a simple version of the Scheme `equal?` predicate:

```
(define (equal? a b)
  (cond ((number? a)
         (and (number? b) (= a b)))
        ((pair? a)
         (and (pair? b)
              (equal? (car a) (car b))
              (equal? (cdr a) (cdr b))))
        (else (eq? a b))))
```

There are three arms in the `cond` form. References to **a** in the first arm are guaranteed to have type number. Furthermore, in the numeric comparison form, `(= a b)`, an assumption can be made that **b** is also a number, since the **AND** guarantees that control reaches the comparison only if `(number? b)` is true. Similarly, we can infer that references to **a** in the second arm of the `cond` have the pair type and, less usefully, that references to **a** in the third arm of the `cond` do not have either type pair or number. It is important to realise from this example that Scheme type recovery assigns types not to variables, but to variable *references*. The references to **a** in the different arms of the `cond` all have different types.

Type recovery of this sort can be helpful to a Scheme compiler. If the compiler can determine that the `(= a b)` form is guaranteed to compare only numbers, it can compile the comparison without a run-time type check, gaining speed without sacrificing safety. Similarly, determining that the `(car a)`, `(car b)`, `(cdr a)`, and `(cdr b)` forms are all guaranteed to operate on pairs allows the compiler to safely compile the `car` and `cdr` applications without run-time type checks.

Primop Application   An obvious source of type information is the application of primitive operations (called "primops") such as `+` and `cons`. Clearly the result of `(cons a b)` is a pair. In addition, we can recover information about the type of subsequent references to primop arguments. For example, after the primop application `(cdr p)`, references to `p` along the same control path can be assumed to have the pair type.

As a simple example, consider the following Scheme expression:

```
(let* ((a (cdr b))
       (q (char->integer (vector-ref a i))))
  ... (car b) ... (+ q 2))
```

References to `b` occurring after the `(cdr b)` form are guaranteed to have the pair type – otherwise, the `cdr` application would have rendered the effect of the computation to be undefined. Hence, the subsequent `(car b)` application does not need to do a type check. Similarly, after evaluating the second clause of the `let*`, references to `a` have type vector and references to `i` and `q` are small integers, because `vector-ref` requires an integer index, and `char->integer` generates an integer result. Hence the compiler can omit all type checks in the object code for `(+ q 2)`, and simply open code the addition.

In recovering information about the arguments to primops, we are essentially using information from "hidden conditional tests" inside the primop. The semantics of a (dangerous) CPS `car` primop is:

```
(define (car p cont)
  (if (pair? p) (cont (%car p))
      ($)))
```

where the subprimitive operation `%car` is only defined over cons cells, and `$` is the "undefined effect" primop. Computation proceeds through the continuation `cont` only in the then arm of the type test, so we may assume that `p`'s value is a cons cell while executing the continuation. Recovering the type information implied by `car` reduces to recovering type information from conditional branches.

Of course, the compiler does not need to emit code for a conditional test if one arm is `$`. It can simply take the undefined effect to be whatever happens when the code compiled for the other arm is executed. This reduces the entire **car** application to the machine operation **%car**.

A safe implementation of Scheme is one that guarantees to halt the computation as soon as a type constraint is violated. This means, for example, replacing the **$** form in the else arm of the **car** definition with a call to the run-time error handler:

```
(define (car p cont)
   (if (pair? p) (cont (%car p))
       (error)))
```

Of course, type information recovered about the arguments to a particular application of **car** may allow the conditional test to be determined at compile time, again allowing the compiler to fold out the conditional test and error call, still preserving type-safety without the run-time overhead of the type check.

User Declarations   Type inference can also utilize information from judiciously placed declarations inserted by the programmer. There are essentially two types of user declarations, one requesting a run-time type check to enforce the verity of the declaration, and one simply asserting a type at compile time, in effect telling the compiler, "Trust me. This quantity will always have this type. Assume it; don't check for it."

The first kind of declaration is just T's **enforce** procedure [21], which can be defined as:

```
(define (enforce pred val) (if (pred val) val (error)))
```

Enforce simply forces a run-time type check at a point the user believes might be beneficial to the compile-time analysis, halting the program if the check is violated. For example,

```
(block (enforce number? x) ...forms...)
```

allows the compiler to assume that references to **x** in the forms following the **enforce** have the number type. **Enforce** allows execution to proceed into the body of

```
(let ((y (enforce integer? (foo 3)))) body)
```

only if **(foo 3)** returns an integer. Clearly, **enforce**-based type recovery is simply conditional-branch based type recovery.

The "trust me" sort of user declaration is expressed in Scheme via the **proclaim** procedure, which asserts that its second argument has the type specified by its first argument. For example, **(proclaim symbol? y)** tells the compiler to believe that the value of **y** has type symbol. Like **enforce**, **proclaim** can also be viewed as a kind of conditional expression:

```
(define (proclaim pred val) (if (pred val) val ($)))
```

```scheme
(define (delq elt lis)
  (letrec ((lp (λ (ans rest)
                 (if (pair? rest)
                     (let ((head (car rest)))
                       (lp (if (eq? head elt) ans
                               (cons head ans))
                           (cdr rest)))
                     (reverse! ans)))))
    (lp '() lis)))

(define (fact n)
  (letrec ((lp (λ (ans m)
                 (if (= m 0) ans
                     (lp (* ans m) (- m 1))))))
    (enforce integer? n)
    (lp 1 n)))
```

Figure 3.1: Scheme **delq** and factorial.

where **$** denotes a computation with undefined effect. Since an undefined effect means that "anything goes," the compiler is permitted to elide the conditional expression altogether and simply take note of the programmer's assertion that **val** has the declared type. Incorrect assertions will still result in undefined effects.

3.1.2   *Type Recovery from Multiple Sources*

All three sources of type information – conditional branches, primop applications, and user declarations – can be used together in recovering type information from programs, thereby enabling many optimizations. Consider the **delq** procedure of Figure 3.1. Because **ans** is only bound to the constant **'()**, itself, and the result of a **cons** application, it must always be a list. So all references to **ans** can be completely typed at compile time. Because of the conditional type test **(pair? rest)**, **car** and **cdr** are guaranteed to be applied to legitimate pair values. Thus compile-time type recovery can guarantee the full type safety of **delq** with no extra run-time type checks.

For a numerical example, consider the factorial procedure in Figure 3.1. Note the use of an explicit run-time type check, **(enforce integer? n)**, to force the subsequent reference to **n** to be of integer type. With the help of this user declaration, the analysis can determine that **m** is always bound to an integer, and therefore, that **ans** must also be bound to an integer. Thus, the factorial function written with generic arithmetic operators can have guaranteed type safety for the primop applications and also specialise the generic arithmetic operations to integer operations, at the expense of a single run-time type check per **fact** call.

If we eliminate the **enforce** form, then the type recovery can do less, because **fact** could be called on non-integer values. However, if the equality primop (**= m 0**) requires its arguments to have the same type, we can infer that references to **m** after the equality test must be integer references, and so the multiplication and subtraction operations are guaranteed to be on integer values. Hence, even in the naive, declaration-free case, type-recovery analysis is able to pick up enough information from the code to guarantee the type safety of **fact** with only a single type check per iteration, as opposed to the four type checks required in the absence of any analysis.

The implementation of the type recovery algorithm discussed in Section 3.6 can, in fact, recover enough information from the **delq** and **fact** procedures of Figure 3.1 to completely assign precise types to all variable references, as discussed above. For these examples, at least, compile-time type analysis can provide run-time safety with no execution penalty.

3.1.3   Overview of the Chapter

The remainder of this chapter will describe some of the details of the type recovery algorithm. Section 3.2 introduces the notion of quantity-based analysis, which underlies the type recovery algorithm. Section 3.3 briefly reviews CPS Scheme, the intermediate representation used by the analysis, and the non-standard abstract semantic (NSAS) interpretation approach to program analysis that is the general framework for the type recovery analysis. Section 3.4 then uses the quantity model and the NSAS framework to present a "perfect" (and hence uncomputable) type recovery analysis for CPS Scheme. Section 3.5 abstracts the perfect analysis to a computable, useful approximate type recovery analysis. Section 3.6 describes an implementation of the approximate type recovery algorithm. Section 3.7 is a collection of assorted discussions and speculations on Scheme type recovery. Finally, Section 3.8 discusses related work.

3.2   Quantity-based Analysis

Type recovery is an example of what I call a *quantity-based analysis*. Consider the Scheme expression

$$(\text{if } (< \text{ j } 0) \ (- \text{ j}) \ \text{j})$$

Whatever number `j` names, we know that it is negative in the then-arm of the `if` expression, and non-negative in the else-arm. In short, we are associating an abstract property of `j`'s value (its sign) with control points in the program. It is important to realize that we are tracking information about *quantities* (`j`'s value), not *variables* (`j` itself). For example, consider the following expression:

```
(let ((i j)) (if (< j 0) (foo i)))
```

Clearly, the test involving `j` determines information about the value of `i` since they *both name the same quantity*. In a quantity-based analysis, information is tracked for quantities, and quantities can be named by multiple variables. This information can then be associated with the variable references appearing in the program. For the purposes of keeping track of this information, we need names for quantities; variables can then be bound to these quantity names (which are called *qnames*), which in turn have associated abstract properties.

In principle, calls to primops such as `+` or **cons** create new qnames since these operations involve the creation of new computational quantities. On the other hand, lambda binding simply involves the binding of a variable to an already existing qname. In practice, extra qnames often must be introduced since it can be difficult to determine at compile-time which qname a variable is bound to. Consider, for example, the following procedure:

```
(define (foo x y) (if (integer? x) y 3))
```

It might be the case that all calls to **foo** are of the form (**foo a a**), in which case **x** and **y** can refer to the same qname. But if the analysis cannot determine this fact at compile time, **x** and **y** refer to at least two distinct qnames; hence determining information about **x**'s value will not shed light on **y**'s value.

As another example, consider the vector reference in the expression:

```
(let ((y (vector-ref vec i))) ...)
```

Now, **y** is certainly bound to an existing quantity, but it is unlikely that a compile-time analysis will be able to determine which one. So, a new qname must be assigned to **y**'s binding.

A conservative, computable, quantity-based analysis approximates the tracking of information on run-time values by introducing new qnames whenever it is unable to determine to which existing qname a variable is bound. These extra qnames limit the precision of the analysis, but force the analysis to err conservatively.

3.3 CPS and NSAS

3.3.1 CPS

The intermediate representation used for type recovery is Continuation-Passing Style Scheme, or CPS Scheme. CPS Scheme is a simple variant of Scheme in which procedures do not return, side-effects are allowed on data structures but not on variables, and all transfers of control – sequencing, conditional branching, loops, and subroutine call/return – are represented by procedure calls. This simple language is a surprisingly useful intermediate representation: variants of CPS Scheme have been used as the intermediate representation for several Scheme, Common Lisp and ML compilers [28,15,3].

CPS Scheme has the following simple syntax:

$$
\begin{array}{llll}
\text{PR} &::= & \text{LAM} \\
\text{LAM} &::= & (\lambda \ (v_1 \ldots v_n) \ c) & [v_i \in \text{VAR}, \ c \in \text{CALL}] \\
\text{CALL} &::= & (f \ a_1 \ldots a_n) & [f \in \text{FUN}, \ a_i \in \text{ARG}] \\
& & (\texttt{letrec} \ ((f_1 \ l_1)\ldots) \ c) & [f_i \in \text{VAR}, \ l_i \in \text{LAM}, \ c \in \text{CALL}] \\
\text{FUN} &::= & \text{LAM} + \text{REF} + \text{PRIM} \\
\text{ARG} &::= & \text{LAM} + \text{REF} + \text{CONST} \\
\text{REF} &::= & \text{VAR} \\
\text{VAR} &::= & \{\texttt{x}, \texttt{z}, \texttt{foo}, \ldots\} \\
\text{CONST} &::= & \{3, \texttt{false}, \ldots\} \\
\text{PRIM} &::= & \{\texttt{+}, \texttt{if}, \texttt{test} - \texttt{integer}, \ldots\}
\end{array}
$$

A program is a single lambda expression. The `letrec` form is used to define mutually recursive functions. Non-conditional primops like `+` and `cdr` take an extra continuation argument to call on their result: `(cdr x k)` calls procedure `k` on the cdr of `x`. Conditional branches are performed by special conditional primops which take multiple continuations. The `if` primop takes three arguments: `(if x c a)`. If the first argument `x` is a true value, the consequent continuation `c` is called; otherwise, the alternate continuation `a` is called. There is also a class of `test` primops that perform conditional type tests. For example, `(test-integer x c a)` branches to continuation `c` if `x` is an integer, otherwise to continuation `a`. Side effects on data structures are performed with appropriate primops, such as `set-car!`; side effects on variables are not allowed. CPS Scheme does not have the troublesome `call/cc` operator. When translating Scheme programs into their CPS Scheme representations, every occurrence of `call/cc` can be replaced with its CPS definition:

$$(\lambda \ (\texttt{f} \ \texttt{k}) \ (\texttt{f} \ (\lambda \ (\texttt{v} \ \texttt{k0}) \ (\texttt{k} \ \texttt{v})) \ \texttt{k}))$$

```
(λ (n) (letrec ((lp (λ (i sum) (if (zero? i) sum
                                    (lp (- i 1)
                                        (+ i sum)))))))
            (lp n 0)))
(λ (n k)
   (letrec ((lp (λ (i sum c)
                   (test-zero i
                      (λ () (c sum))
                      (λ ()
                         (+ sum i (λ (sum1)
                            (- i 1 (λ (i1)
                               (lp i1 sum1 c)))))))))))
            (lp n 0 k)))
```

Figure 3.2: Standard and CPS Scheme to sum 1 through n.

Figure 3.2 shows a procedure that sums the first **n** integers in both standard Scheme and its CPS Scheme representation. It bears repeating that this extremely simple language is a practical and useful intermediate representation for full Scheme. In fact, the dialect presented here is essentially identical to the one used by the optimising Scheme compiler ORBIT.

For purposes of program analysis, let us extend this grammar by assuming that all expressions in a program are tagged with labels, drawn from some suitable set LAB:

$$\ell:(\lambda \; (\mathbf{x}) \; c:(r_1:\mathbf{f} \; r_2:\mathbf{x} \; k:3 \; r_3:\mathbf{x}))$$

Each lambda, call, constant, and variable reference in this expression is tagged with a unique label. Expressions in a program that are identical receive distinct labels, so the two references to **x** have the different labels r_2 and r_3. Labels allow us to uniquely identify different pieces of a program. We will suppress them when convenient. A useful syntactic function is the *binder* function, which maps a variable to the label of its binding lambda or **letrec** construct, e.g., *binder* $[\![\mathbf{x}]\!] = \ell$.

3.3.2 NSAS

Casting our problem into CPS gives us a structure to work with; we now need a technique for analysing that structure. The method of non-standard abstract semantics (NSAS) is an elegant technique for formally describing program analyses. It is the tool we will need to solve our type recovery problem as described in the previous section. Section 3.8 gives several standard references for NSAS techniques.

Suppose we have a programming language L with a denotational semantics S, and we wish to determine some property X at compile time. Our first step is to develop an *alternate semantics* S_X for L that precisely expresses property X. That is, whereas semantics S might say the meaning of a program is a function "computing" the result value of the program given its inputs, semantics S_X would say the meaning of a program is a function "computing" the property X on its corresponding inputs.

S_X is a precise definition of the property we wish to determine, but its precision typically implies that it cannot be computed at compile time. It might be uncomputable; it might also depend on the run-time inputs. The second step, then, is to *abstract* S_X to a new semantics, $\widehat{S}_X$ which trades accuracy for compile-time computability. This sort of approximation is a typical program-analysis tradeoff – the real answers we seek are uncomputable, so we settle for computable, conservative approximations to them.

The method of abstract semantic interpretation has several benefits. Since an NSAS-based analysis is expressed in terms of a formal semantics, it is possible to prove important properties about it. In particular, we can prove that the non-standard semantics S_X correctly expresses properties of the standard semantics S, and that the abstract semantics $\widehat{S}_X$ is computable and safe with respect to S_X. Further, simply expressing an analysis in terms of abstract semantic interpretations helps to clarify it. This is due to its formal nature, and because of its relation to the standard semantics of a programming language.

The reader who is more comfortable with computer languages than denotational semantics equations should not despair. The equations presented in this chapter can quite easily be regarded as interpreters in a functional disguise. The important point is that these "interpreters" do not compute an actual value of a program, but some other property of the program – in our case, the types of all the variable references in the program. We compute this with a non-standard, abstract "interpreter" that abstractly executes the program, collecting information about references as it goes.

3.4 Perfect Type Recovery

Following the NSAS approach, the first step towards type recovery is to define a "perfect" analysis that will capture the notion of type recovery. Our perfect semantics, which we will call PTREC, does not have to be computable; we will concern ourselves with a computable approximation in Section 3.5.

Perfect type recovery gives us a *type cache*:

A *type cache* for a CPS Scheme program P is a function δ that, for each variable reference r and each context b over r, returns $\delta\langle r, b\rangle$, a type of all the values to which r could evaluate in context b.

(For now, we will be intentionally vague about what a "context" is; this will be made precise later.) Once we have computed a type cache, we can easily find the type for any variable reference $r{:}v$ in our program:

$$\text{RefType}[\![r{:}v]\!] = \bigsqcup_b \delta\langle r, b\rangle$$

3.4.1 Notation

D^* is used to indicate all vectors of finite length over the set D. Functions are updated with brackets: $e\,[a \mapsto b,\, c \mapsto d]$ is the function mapping a to b, c to d, and everywhere else identical to function e. Vectors are written $\langle a, b, c\rangle$. The ith element of vector v is written $v{\downarrow}i$. The power set of A is $\mathbf{P}(A)$. Function application is written with juxtaposition: $f\,x$. We extend the meet and join operations on a lattice to functions into the lattice in a pointwise fashion: $f \sqcap g = \lambda x.\,(f\,x) \sqcap (g\,x)$

3.4.2 Basic Domains

The PTREC semantics maps a CPS Scheme program to its type cache. Its structure, however, is very similar to a standard semantics for CPS Scheme. Let us first consider this basic structure without paying close attention to the parts of the semantics that actually track type information.

There is a basic domain, Bas, which consists of the integers and a special false value. (I will follow traditional Lisp practice in assuming no special boolean type; anything not false is a true value.) The domain of CPS Scheme procedures, Proc, has three parts: a primop is represented by its syntactic identifier ($prim \in$ PRIM), while a lambda closure is represented by a lambda/environment pair ($\langle\ell, \epsilon\rangle \in$ LAM $\times$ BEnv). The special token *stop* is the top-level continuation: in the standard semantics, calling *stop* on a value v halts the program with result v. The value domain D consists of the basic values and CPS Scheme procedures. The answer set TCache is the set of type caches.

$$
\begin{aligned}
\text{Bas} &= \mathcal{Z} + \{\text{false}\} \\
\text{Proc} &= (\text{LAM} \times \text{BEnv}) + \text{PRIM} + \{stop\} \\
\text{D} &= \text{Proc} + \text{Bas} \\
\text{TCache} &= (\text{REF} \times \text{CN}) \to \text{Type}
\end{aligned}
$$

Several items are conspicuously absent from these sets. This "toy" dialect omits I/O and a store, features that would be found in a full CPS Scheme semantics. It only provides three basic types of value: integers, false, and procedures. The run-time error checking has been left out of the semantics. These omissions are made to simplify the presentation. Extending the analysis to a more complete dialect of CPS Scheme is straightforward once the basic technique is understood. For example, the implementation described in Section 3.6 handles all of these missing features.

One of the pleasant features of CPS Scheme is the scarcity of bottom values. Most of the semantic structures are unordered sets instead of continuous partial orders. For example, the set D does not require a bottom value because all the expressions that can appear in a procedure call – constants, variable references, primops, and lambdas – are guaranteed to terminate when evaluated. In other words, the $\mathcal{A}_v$ function of Section 3.4.3 never produces a bottom value. In the standard semantics, bottom can only show up as the final value for the entire program, never at an intermediate computation. For this reason, the disjoint union constructor + is taken to be a *set* constructor, not a domain constructor – it does not introduce a new bottom value. A careful treatment of the semantics of CPS Scheme at this level is beyond the scope of this chapter [25,27].

3.4.3   *Environments and Procedures*

The PTREC semantics factors the environment into two parts: the *variable environment* ($ve \in$ VEnv), which is a global structure, and the lexical *contour environment* ($\epsilon \in$ BEnv).[1]   A contour environment ϵ maps syntactic binding constructs – lambda and **letrec** expressions – to *contours* or dynamic frames. Each time a lambda is called, a new contour is allocated for its bound variables. Contours are taken from the set CN (the integers will suffice). A variable paired with a contour is a *variable binding* $\langle v, b \rangle$, taken from VB. The variable environment *ve*, in turn, maps these variable bindings to actual values. The contour part of the variable binding pair $\langle v, b \rangle$ is what allows multiple bindings of the same identifier to coexist peacefully in the single variable environment.

$$
\begin{aligned}
\text{CN} & & \textit{Contours} \\
\text{VB} & = & \text{VAR} \times \text{CN} \\
\text{BEnv} & = & \text{LAB} \to \text{CN} \\
\text{VEnv} & = & \text{VB} \to \text{D}
\end{aligned}
$$

Lexical scoping semantics requires us to close a lambda expression with the contour environment that is present when the lambda is evaluated. We can see both the closure of lambda expressions and the lookup of variables in the $\mathcal{A}_v$ function below. $\mathcal{A}_v$ is the function that evaluates arguments in procedure calls, given the lexical contour

---

[1]The term "BEnv" stands for "binding environment."

environment ϵ and the global variable environment ve.

$$\mathcal{A}_v : \mathrm{ARG} \cup \mathrm{FUN} \rightarrow \mathrm{BEnv} \rightarrow \mathrm{VEnv} \rightarrow \mathrm{D}$$

$$
\begin{aligned}
\mathcal{A}_v [\![\ (\lambda \ (v_1 \dots v_n) \ c) \ ]\!] \ \epsilon \ ve \ &= \ \langle [\![\ (\lambda \ (v_1 \dots v_n) \ c) \ ]\!], \ \epsilon \rangle \\
\mathcal{A}_v \ [\![v]\!] \ \epsilon \ ve \ &= \ ve \ \langle v, \ \epsilon(binder \ v) \rangle \\
\mathcal{A}_v \ [\![prim]\!] \ \epsilon \ ve \ &= \ prim \\
\mathcal{A}_v \ [\![k]\!] \ \epsilon \ ve \ &= \ \mathcal{K} \ k
\end{aligned}
$$

$\mathcal{A}_v$ closes lambdas over the contour environment ϵ. Variable references are looked up in a two step process. First, the contour environment is indexed with the variable's binding lambda or **letrec** expression $binder \ v$ to find in which contour this reference occurs. The contour and the variable are then used to index into the variable environment ve, giving the actual value. Since primops are denoted by their syntactic identifiers, $\mathcal{A}_v$ maps these to themselves. Constants are handled by some appropriate meaning function $\mathcal{K}$.

New contours are created when procedures are called. Procedure calls are handled by the $\mathcal{C}$ and $\mathcal{F}$ functions.

$$\mathcal{C} : \mathrm{CALL} \rightarrow \mathrm{BEnv} \rightarrow \mathrm{VEnv} \rightarrow \mathrm{QEnv} \rightarrow \mathrm{TTab} \rightarrow \mathrm{TCache}$$

$$
\mathcal{C} [\![\ (e_0{:}f \ e_1{:}a_1 \dots e_n{:}a_n) \ ]\!] \ \epsilon \ ve \ qe \ \tau \ = \delta \sqcup (\mathcal{F} \ f') \ av \ qv \ ve \ qe \ \tau'
$$
$$
\begin{aligned}
\text{where } av{\downarrow}i &= \mathcal{A}_v \ a_i \ \epsilon \ ve \\
f' &= \mathcal{A}_v \ f \ \epsilon \ ve \\
\tau' &= \begin{cases} \tau \sqcap \top \left[\mathcal{A}_q \ f \ \epsilon \ qe \ \mapsto \mathrm{type/proc} \right] & f \in \mathrm{REF} \\ \tau & otherwise \end{cases} \\
\delta &= \left[\langle e_i, \ \epsilon \, (binder \ e_i) \, \rangle \mapsto \tau(\mathcal{A}_q \ e_i \ \epsilon \ qe) \right] \quad \forall [\![e_0{:}f]\!], [\![e_i{:}a_i]\!] \in \mathrm{REF} \\
qv{\downarrow}i &= \begin{cases} \mathcal{A}_q \ a_i \ \epsilon \ qe & a_i \in \mathrm{REF} \quad \text{(quantity)} \\ \mathcal{A}_t \ a_i & otherwise \quad \text{(type)} \end{cases}
\end{aligned}
$$

$\mathcal{C}$ takes five arguments: a call expression, the lexical contour environment ϵ, the variable environment ve, and two others used for type recovery. (We will return to the details of the type machinery – QEnv, TTab, τ', δ, and qv – in the following subsections). $\mathcal{C}$ uses the $\mathcal{A}_v$ function to determine the values for the procedure being called f' and the arguments being passed to it. The argument values are collected into a single argument vector av. CPS Scheme procedures are represented by either lambda/environment pairs or by primop identifier names; the semantic function $\mathcal{F}$ converts this denotation of procedure f' to a functional value. The resulting function provides the contribution made to the final type cache by the execution of the program from the entry of procedure f' forward.

The secondary, functional representation of CPS Scheme procedures is produced by the $\mathcal{F}$ function:

$$\mathcal{F} : \text{Proc} \rightarrow \text{D}^* \rightarrow (\text{Quant} + \text{Type})^* \rightarrow \text{VEnv} \rightarrow \text{QEnv} \rightarrow \text{TTab} \rightarrow \text{TCache}$$

$$\mathcal{F} \langle [\![\ell\!: \ (\lambda \ (v_1 \ldots v_n) \ c)]\!], \epsilon \rangle =$$
$$\lambda av \ qv \ ve \ qe \ \tau. \ \mathcal{C} \ c \ \epsilon' \ ve' \ qe'' \ \tau'$$
$$\text{where} \quad b = nb$$
$$\epsilon' = \epsilon \left[\ell \mapsto b \right]$$
$$ve' = ve \left[\langle v_i, \ b \rangle \mapsto av{\downarrow}i \right]$$
$$qe' = qe \left[\langle v_i, \ b \rangle \mapsto qv{\downarrow}i \right] \quad \forall i \ \ni \ qv{\downarrow}i \in \text{Quant} \qquad (*)$$
$$\left. \begin{array}{l} qe'' = qe' \left[\langle v_i, \ b \rangle \mapsto \langle v_i, \ b \rangle \right] \\ \tau' = \tau \left[\langle v_i, \ b \rangle \mapsto qv{\downarrow}i \right] \end{array} \right\} \forall i \ \ni \ qv{\downarrow}i \in \text{Type} \quad (**)$$

(As with QEnv and TTab, Quant and Type will be described later.) A CPS Scheme lambda procedure is represented by a function that takes five arguments: an argument vector av, the variable environment ve, and three others concerned with type recovery. Upon entry to this function, a new binding contour b is allocated for the lambda's scope. The function nb is responsible for allocating the new binding contour; it is essentially a gensym, returning a unique value each time it is called. The lexical contour environment ϵ is updated to map the current procedure's label ℓ to this new contour. The mappings $\left[\langle v_i, \ b \rangle \mapsto av{\downarrow}i \right]$ are added to the variable environment, recording the binding of ℓ's parameters to the arguments passed in av. We update the type-tracking values qe and τ, and call $\mathcal{C}$ to evaluate the lambda's internal call expression c in the new environment.

One detail glossed over in the functional definition of closures and other parts of the PTREC semantics is the handling of run-time errors, e.g., applying a two-argument procedure to three values, dividing by zero, or applying **+** to a non-number. This is simple to remedy: run-time errors are defined to terminate the program immediately and return the current type cache. The extra machinery to handle these error cases has been left out of this chapter to simplify the presentation; restoring it is straightforward.

To fully specify $\mathcal{F}$, we must also give the functional representation for each primop and the terminal *stop* continuation. We will return to this after considering the mechanics of type-tracking. We also need to specify how $\mathcal{C}$ handles call forms that are **letrec** expressions instead of simple procedure calls. This case is simple: $\mathcal{C}$ just allocates a new contour b for its scope, closes the defined procedures in the new contour environment ϵ' (thus providing the necessary circularity), and evaluates the **letrec**'s interior call form c in the new environment.

$$\mathcal{C}[\![\ell:\ (\texttt{letrec}\ ((f_1\ l_1)\ldots)\ c)]\!]\epsilon\,ve\,qe\,\tau = \mathcal{C}\,c\,\epsilon'\,ve'\,qe'\,\tau'$$
$$\text{where } b = nb$$
$$\epsilon' = \epsilon\,[\ell \mapsto b]$$
$$ve' = ve\,\big[\langle f_i,\ b\rangle \mapsto \mathcal{A}_v\,l_i\,\epsilon'\,ve\,\big]$$
$$qe' = qe\,\big[\langle f_i,\ b\rangle \mapsto \langle f_i,\ b\rangle\big]$$
$$\tau' = \tau\,\big[\langle f_i,\ b\rangle \mapsto \text{type/proc}\big]$$

It is an interesting curiosity that the definition of **letrec** presented here does not involve a recursive construction. Lambdas are closed over contour environments but not the variable environment, which is a global structure. So the actual evaluation of the **letrec**'s lambdas, $\mathcal{A}_v\,l_i\,\epsilon'\,ve = \langle l_i,\ \epsilon'\rangle$, is completely independent of the *ve* argument. The variable environment is not used because no variables are looked up in the evaluation of a lambda. We can close the lambdas over the new contour environment ϵ' without actually having the new contour's values in hand. This artifact of the factored semantics is considered in more detail elsewhere [25].

3.4.4   Quantities and Types

The semantics presented so far could easily be for a standard interpretation of CPS Scheme. We can now turn to the details of tracking type information through the PTREC interpretation. This will involve the quantity analysis model discussed in Section 3.2. The general type recovery strategy is straightforward:

- Whenever a new computational quantity is created, it is given a unique qname. Over the lifetime of a given quantity, it will be bound to a series of variables as it is passed around the program. As a quantity (from D) is bound to variables, we also bind its qname (from Quant) with these variables.

- As execution proceeds through the program, we keep track of all currently known information about quantities. This takes the form of a *type table* τ that maps qnames to type information. Program structure that determines type information about a quantity enters the information into the type table, for later reference.

- When a variable reference is evaluated, we determine the qname it is bound to, and index into the type table to discover what is known at that point in the computation about the named quantity. This tells us what we know about the variable reference in the current context. This information is entered into the answer type cache.

This amounts to instrumenting our standard semantics to track the knowledge determined by run-time type tests, recording relevant snapshots of this knowledge in the answer type cache as execution proceeds through the program.

The first representational decision is how to choose qnames. A simple choice is to name a quantity by the first variable binding $\langle v, b \rangle$ to which it is bound. Thus, the qname for the cons cell created by

$$\text{(cons 1 2 } (\lambda \text{ (x) } \dots))$$

is $\langle [\![\mathbf{x}]\!], b \rangle$, where b is the contour created upon entering **cons**'s continuation. When future variable bindings are made to this cons cell, the binding will be to the qname $\langle [\![\mathbf{x}]\!], b \rangle$. Thus, our qname set Quant is just the set of variable bindings VB:

$$\text{Quant} = \text{VB}$$

Having chosen our qnames, the rest of the type-tracking machinery falls into place. A quantity environment ($qe \in$ QEnv) is a mapping from variable bindings to qnames. The quantity environment, the qname analog of the variable environment ve, is a global structure that is augmented monotonically over the course of program execution. A type table ($\tau \in$ TTab) is a mapping from qnames to types. Our types are drawn from some standard type lattice; for this example, we use the obvious lattice over the three basic types: procedure, false, and integer.

$$
\begin{aligned}
\text{Type} &= \{ type/proc, type/int, type/false, \bot, \top \} \\
\text{QEnv} &= \text{VB} \rightarrow \text{Quant} \\
\text{TTab} &= \text{Quant} \rightarrow \text{Type}
\end{aligned}
$$

We may now consider the workings of the type-tracking machinery in the $\mathcal{F}$ and $\mathcal{C}$ functions. Looking at $\mathcal{F}$, we see that our function linkage requires three additional arguments to be passed to a procedure: the quantity vector qv, the quantity environment qe, and the current type table τ. The quantity environment and type table are as discussed above. The quantity vector gives quantity information about the arguments passed to the procedure. Each element of qv is either a qname or a type. If it is a qname, it names the quantity being passed to the procedure as its corresponding argument. However, if a computational quantity has been created by the procedure's caller, then it has yet to be named – quantities are named by the first variable binding to which they are bound, so it is the duty of the current procedure to assign a qname to the new quantity as it binds it. In this case, the corresponding element of the quantity vector gives the initial type information known about the new quantity. Consider the cons example given above. The **cons** primop creates a new quantity – a cons cell – and calls the continuation $(\lambda \text{ (x) } \dots)$ on it. Since the cons cell is a brand new quantity, it has not yet been given a qname; the continuation binding it to **x** will name it. So instead of passing the continuation a qname for the cell, the **cons** primop passes the type $type/pair$ in qv, giving the quantity's initial type information.

We can see this information being used in the $\mathcal{F}$ equation. The line marked with (*) binds qnames from the quantity vector to their new bindings $\langle v_i, b \rangle$. The lines marked with (**) handle new quantities that do not yet have qnames. A new quantity must be assigned its qname, which for the ith argument is just its variable binding $\langle v_i, b \rangle$. We record the initial type information ($qv{\downarrow}i \in$ Type) known about the new quantity in the type table τ'. The new quantity environment qe'' and type table τ' are passed to the $\mathcal{C}$ function.

$\mathcal{C}$ receives as type arguments the current quantity environment qe, and the current type table τ. Before jumping to the called procedure, $\mathcal{C}$ must perform three type-related tasks:

- Record in the final answer cache the type of each variable reference in the call. Each variable reference $e_i{:}a_i$ is evaluated to a qname by the auxiliary function $\mathcal{A}_q$, the qname analog to the $\mathcal{A}_v$ function. The qname is used to index into the type table τ, giving the type information currently known about the quantity bound to variable a_i. Call this type t. We record in the type cache that the variable reference e_i evaluated to a value of type t in context $\epsilon(binder\ e_i)$. This is the contribution δ that $\mathcal{C}$ makes to the final answer for the current call.

- Compute the quantity vector qv to be passed to the called procedure f. If a_i is a variable reference, its corresponding element in qv is the qname it is bound to in the current context; this is computed by the $\mathcal{A}_q$ auxiliary. On the other hand, if the argument a_i is a constant or a lambda, then it is considered a new, as-yet-unnamed quantity. The auxiliary $\mathcal{A}_t$ determines its type; the called procedure will be responsible for assigning this value a qname.

- Finally, note that $\mathcal{C}$ can do a bit of type recovery. If f does not evaluate to a procedure, the computation becomes undefined at this call. We may thus assume that f's quantity is a procedure in following code. We record this information in the outgoing type table τ': if f is a variable reference, we find the qname it is bound to and intersect $type/proc$ with the type information recorded for the qname in τ. If f is not a variable reference, it is not necessary to do this. (Note that in the **letrec** case, $\mathcal{C}$ performs similar type recovery, recording that the new quantities bound by the **letrec** all have type $type/proc$. This is all the type manipulation $\mathcal{C}$ does for the **letrec** case.)

$$
\begin{aligned}
\mathcal{A}_q \; [\![v]\!] \; \epsilon \; qe &= qe \; \langle v, \; \epsilon \, (binder\ v) \rangle \\
\mathcal{A}_t \; [\![\; (\lambda \; (v_1 \ldots v_n) \;\; c) \,]\!] &= type/proc \\
\mathcal{A}_t \; [\![n]\!] &= type/int \quad (\text{numeral } n) \\
\mathcal{A}_t \; [\![\mathtt{false}]\!] &= type/false
\end{aligned}
$$

Most of the type information is recovered by the semantic functions for primops, retrieved by $\mathcal{F}$. As representative examples, I will show the definitions of + and **test-integer**.

$$\mathcal{F} [\![+]\!] = \lambda\langle a, b, c\rangle \langle qa, qb, qc\rangle \, ve \, qe \, \tau. \; (\mathcal{F} \, c) \, \langle a+b\rangle \, \langle ts\rangle \, ve \, qe \, \tau''$$
$$\text{where } ta = \text{QT } qa \, \tau$$
$$tb = \text{QT } qb \, \tau$$
$$ts = \text{infer+}\langle ta, \, tb\rangle$$
$$\tau' = \text{Tu } qa \, (ta \sqcap type/int) \, \tau$$
$$\tau'' = \text{Tu } qb \, (tb \sqcap type/int) \, \tau'$$

The + primop takes three arguments: two values to be added, a and b, and a continuation c. Hence the argument vector and quantity vector have three components each. The primop assigns ta and tb to be the types that execution has constrained a and b to have. These types are computed by the auxiliary function QT:(Quant + Type) $\rightarrow$(Quant $\rightarrow$ Type) $\rightarrow$ Type:

$$\text{QT } q \, \tau = \tau \, q \qquad \text{QT } t \, \tau = t$$

QT maps an element from a quantity vector to type information. If the element is a qname q, then QT looks up its associated type information in the type table τ. If the element is a type t (because the corresponding quantity is a new, unnamed one), then t is the initial type information for the quantity, and so QT simply returns t. Having retrieved the type information for its arguments a and b, + can then compute the type ts of its result sum. This is handled by the auxiliary function infer+, whose details are not presented. Infer+ is a straightforward type computation: if both arguments are known to be integers, then the result is known to be an integer. If our language includes other types of numbers, infer+ can do the related inferences. For example, it might infer that the result of adding a floating point number to another number is a floating point number. However infer+ computes its answer, ts must be a subtype of the number type, since if control proceeds past the addition, + is guaranteed to produce a number. Further, + can make inferences about subsequent references to its arguments: they must be numbers. (Otherwise the computation becomes undefined at the addition.) The auxiliary function Tu updates the incoming type table with this inference; the result type table τ'' is passed forwards to the continuation.

$$\text{Tu } q \, t \, \tau = \begin{cases} \tau & q \in \text{Type} \\ \tau \, [q \rightarrow t] & q \in \text{Quant} \end{cases}$$

Tu takes three arguments: an element q from a quantity vector (i.e., a qname or type), a type t, and a type table τ. If q is a qname, the type table is updated to map $q \mapsto$

t. Otherwise, the type table is returned unchanged. The corresponding quantity is ephemeral, being unnamed by a qname. There is no utility in recording type information about it, as no further code can reference it. With the aid of Tu, + constrains its arguments *a* and *b* to have the number type by intersecting the incoming type information *ta* and *tb* with *type/number* and updating the outgoing type table τ'' to reflect this. The sum $a + b$, its initial type information *ts*, and the new type table τ'' are passed forward to the continuation, thus continuing the computation. As mentioned earlier, we omit the case of halting the computation if there is an error in the argument values, e.g., *a* or *b* are not numbers.

The reader may have noticed that the + primop is missing an opportunity to recover some available type information: it is not recovering type information about its continuation. For example, in code executed after the call to +'s continuation, we could assume that the quantity called has type *type/proc*. This information is not recovered because it is not necessary. Since CPS Scheme is an intermediate representation for full Scheme, the user cannot write CPS-level continuations. All the continuations, variables bound to continuations, and calls to continuations found in the CPS Scheme program are introduced by the CPS converter. It is easy for the converter to mark these forms as it introduces them. So the types of continuation variables can be inferred statically, and there's no point in tracking them in our type recovery semantics.

$$\mathcal{F} [\![\texttt{test-integer}]\!] =$$

$$\lambda \langle x, c, a \rangle \langle qx, qc, qa \rangle \, ve \, qe \, \tau. \begin{cases} (\mathcal{F} \, c) \, \langle \rangle \, \langle \rangle \, ve \, qe \, \tau_t & x \in \mathcal{Z} \\ (\mathcal{F} \, a) \, \langle \rangle \, \langle \rangle \, ve \, qe \, \tau_f & otherwise \end{cases}$$

$$\text{where } tx = \text{QT } qx \, \tau$$
$$\tau_f = \text{Tu } qx \, (tx - type/int) \, \tau$$
$$\tau_t = \text{Tu } qx \, (tx \sqcap type/int) \, \tau$$

The primop **test-integer** performs a conditional branch based on a type test. It takes as arguments some value *x*, and two continuations *c* and *a*. If *x* is an integer, control is passed to *c*, otherwise control is passed to *a*. **Test-integer** uses QT to look up *tx*, the type information recorded in the current type table τ for *x*'s qname *qx*. There are two outgoing type tables computed, one which assumes the test succeeds (τ_t), and one which assumes the test fails (τ_f). If the test succeeds, then *qx*'s type table entry is updated by Tu to constrain it to have the integer type. Similarly, if the test fails, *qx* has the integer type subtracted from its known type. The appropriate type table is passed forwards to the continuation selected by **test-integer**, producing the answer type cache.

Finally, we come to the definition of the terminal *stop* continuation, retrieved by $\mathcal{F}$. Calling the *stop* continuation halts the program; no more variables are referenced. So the semantic function for *stop* just returns the bottom type cache $\perp$:

$$\mathcal{F} [\![stop]\!] = \lambda \langle v \rangle \; qv \; ve \; qe \; \tau. \; \perp$$

The bottom type cache is the one that returns the bottom type for any reference: $\perp_{\text{TCache}} = \lambda x. \; \perp_{\text{Type}}$. Note that in most cases, the bottom type cache returned by calling *stop* is *not* the final type cache for the entire program execution. Each call executed in the course of the program execution will add its contribution to the final type cache. This contribution is the expression δ in the $\mathcal{C}$ equation for simple call expressions on page 13.

Having defined all the PTREC type tracking machinery, we can invoke it to compute the type cache δ for a program by simply closing the top-level lambda ℓ in the empty environment, and passing it the terminal *stop* continuation as its single argument:

$$\delta = (\mathcal{F} \langle \ell, \perp \rangle) \, \langle stop \rangle \, \langle type/proc \rangle \perp \perp \perp$$

3.5   Approximate Type Recovery

3.5.1   Initial Approximations

Having defined our perfect type recovery semantics, we can consider the problem of abstracting it to a computable approximation, while preserving some notion of correctness and as much precision as possible.

Conditional branches cannot, in general, be determined at compile time. So our abstract semantics must compute the type caches for both continuations of a conditional and union the results together. Note that this frees the semantics up from any dependence on the basic values Bas, since they are not actually tested by the semantics. Hence they can be dropped in the approximate semantics.

In addition, the infinite number of contours that a lambda can be closed over must be folded down to a finite set. The standard abstractions introduced in my earlier work [25] can be employed here: we can replace our variable environment with one that maps variable bindings to sets of procedures; and we can replace the contour allocation function nb with a function on lexical features of the program – e.g., the contour allocated on entry to lambda $[\![\ell: (\lambda \; (v_1 \dots v_n) \; c)]\!]$ can be the label ℓ of the lambda (what I call the "0th-order procedural approximation"). This allows multiple bindings of the same variable to be mapped together, allowing for a finite environment structure, which in turn gives a computable approximate semantics.

Earlier papers [25,26] provide a detailed treatment of these abstractions and discuss more precise alternatives to 0th-order approximation.

3.5.2 Problems with the Abstraction

It turns out that this standard set of approximations breaks the correctness of our semantics. The reason is that by folding together multiple bindings of the same variable,
information can leak across quantity boundaries. For example, consider the following
puzzle:

```
(let ((f (λ (g x) (if (integer? x) (g)
                      (λ () x))))))
  (f (f nil 3.7) 2))
```

Suppose that the procedural abstraction used by our analysis identifies together the contours created by the two calls to **f**. Consider the second execution of the **f** procedure:
the variable **x** is tested to see if its value (2) is an integer. It is, so we jump to the value of
g, which is simply (λ () **x**). Now, we have established that **x** is bound to an integer,
so we can record that this reference to **x** is an integer reference – which is an error,
since **g** = (λ () **x**) is closed over a different contour, binding **x** to a non-integer, 3.7.
We tested one binding of **x** and referred to a different binding of **x**. Our analysis got
confused because we had identified these two bindings together, so that the information
gathered at the test was erroneously applied at the reference.

This is a deep problem of the approximation. Quantity-based analyses depend upon
keeping separate the information associated with different quantities; computable procedural approximations depend upon folding multiple environments together, confounding
the separation required by a quantity-based analysis. I refer to this problem as the "environment problem" because it arises from our inability to precisely track environment
information.

Only certain data-flow analyses are affected by the environment problem. The key
property determining this is the direction in which the iterative analysis moves through
the approximation lattice. In control-flow analysis, or useless-variable elimination [26],
the analysis starts with an overly-precise value and incrementally weakens it until it
converges; all motion in the approximate lattice is in the direction of more approximate
values. So, identifying two contours together simply causes further approximation, which
is safe.

In the case of type recovery, however, our analysis moves in both directions along the
type lattice as the analysis proceeds, and this is the source of the environment problem.
When two different calls to a procedure, each passing arguments of different types, bind
a variable in the same abstract contour, the types are joined together – moving through
the type lattice in the direction of increasing approximation. However, passing through
a conditional test or a primop application causes type information to be narrowed down
– moving in the direction of increasing precision. Unfortunately, while it is legitimate to

narrow down a variable's type in a single perfect contour, it is not legitimate to narrow down its type in the corresponding abstract contour – other bindings that are identified together in the same abstract contour are not constrained by the type test or primop application. This is the heart of the problem with the above puzzle.

In general, then, the simple abstraction techniques of my earlier work yield correct, conservative, safe analyses only when the analysis moves through its answer lattice only in the direction of increasing approximation.

3.5.3   Control Flow Analysis

Before proceeding to a solution for the environment problem, we must define a necessary analysis tool, the *call context cache* provided by *control flow analysis*:

> A call context cache (*cc cache*) for a CPS Scheme program P is a function γ that, for every call site c in P and every environment ϵ over c gives $\gamma \langle c, \epsilon \rangle$, a conservative superset of the procedures called from c in environment ϵ during the execution of P.

This is a straightforward computation using the non-standard abstract semantic interpretation approach discussed above. Note that a cc cache is essentially a trace of program execution to some level of approximation – later we will exploit this property to "restart execution" at some arbitrary point in the computation. The cc cache is an approximation in two ways. First, the set it returns for a given call context is not required to be tight – it is only guaranteed to be a superset. Second, the environment structure ϵ that is the second component of a call context $\langle c, \epsilon \rangle$ and a closure $\langle l, \epsilon \rangle$ is a finite abstraction of the fully detailed environment structure.

A detailed account of control flow analysis can be found in an earlier paper [25].

3.5.4   Perfect Contours

Our central problem is that we are identifying together different contours over the same variable. We are forced to this measure by our desire to reduce an infinite number of contours down to a finite, computable set. The central trick to solving this problem is to reduce the infinite set of contours down to a finite set, *one of which corresponds to a single contour in the perfect semantics*. Flow analysis then tracks this perfect contour, whose bindings will never be identified with any other contours over the same variable scope. Information associated with quantities bound in this perfect contour cannot be confounded. The other approximate contours are used only to provide the approximate control flow information for tracing through the program's execution. We still have only a finite number of contours – the finite number of approximate contours plus the one perfect contour – so our analysis is still computable.

For example, suppose we know that procedure $p = \langle [\![\ell\!:(\lambda \ (\mathbf{x} \ \mathbf{y}) \ \dots)]\!], \epsilon \rangle$ is called from call context $\langle [\![c\!:(\mathbf{f} \ \mathbf{3} \ \mathbf{false})]\!], \epsilon' \rangle$. We can do a partial type recovery for references to $\mathbf{x}$ and $\mathbf{y}$. We perform a function call to p, creating a new perfect contour b. The variables we are tracking are bound in this contour, with variable bindings $\langle [\![\mathbf{x}]\!], b \rangle$ and $\langle [\![\mathbf{y}]\!], b \rangle$. We create new qnames for the arguments passed on this call to p, which are just the new perfect variable bindings $\langle [\![\mathbf{x}]\!], b \rangle$ and $\langle [\![\mathbf{y}]\!], b \rangle$. Our initial type table $\tau = \left[\langle [\![\mathbf{x}]\!], b \rangle \mapsto type/int, \langle [\![\mathbf{y}]\!], b \rangle \mapsto type/false \right]$ is constructed from what is known about the types of the arguments in c (this may be trivially known, if the arguments are constants, or taken from a previous iteration of this algorithm, if the arguments are variables).

We may now run our interpretation forwards, tracking the quantities bound in the perfect closure. Whenever we encounter a variable reference to $\mathbf{x}$ or $\mathbf{y}$, if the reference occurs in the perfect contour b, then we can with certainty consult the current type table τ to obtain the type of the reference. Other contours over $\mathbf{x}$ and $\mathbf{y}$ will not confuse the analysis. Note that we are only tracking type information associated with the variables $\mathbf{x}$ and $\mathbf{y}$, for a single call to ℓ. In order to completely type analyse the program, we must repeat our analysis for each lambda for each call to the lambda. This brings us to the Reflow semantics.

3.5.5 The Reflow Semantics

The abstract domains and functionalities of the Reflow semantics are given in Figure 3.3. The abstract domains are very similar to the perfect domains of the PTREC semantics and show the approximations discussed in Section 3.5.1: basic values have been dropped, the contour set $\widehat{\mathrm{CN}}$ is finite, and elements of $\widehat{\mathrm{D}}$ are sets of abstract procedures, not single values.

The idea of the Reflow semantics is to track only one closure's variables at a time. This is done by the *Reflow* function:

$$Reflow : \widehat{\mathrm{CC}} \to \widehat{\mathrm{VEnv}} \to \mathrm{Type}^* \to \widehat{\mathrm{TCache}}$$

For example, *Reflow* $\langle [\![(\mathbf{f} \ \mathbf{a} \ \mathbf{b})]\!], \epsilon \rangle \ ve \ \langle type/int, type/proc \rangle$ restarts the program at the call $(\mathbf{f} \ \mathbf{a} \ \mathbf{b})$, in the context given by the (approximate) contour environment ϵ and variable environment ve, assuming $\mathbf{a}$ has type $type/int$ and $\mathbf{b}$ has type $type/proc$. *Reflow* runs the program forward, tracking only the variables bound by the initial call to $\mathbf{f}$, returning a type cache giving information about references to these variables. This is done by allocating a single, perfect contour for the initial procedure called from $(\mathbf{f} \ \mathbf{a} \ \mathbf{b})$, and tracking the variables bound in this contour through an abstract execution of the program.

$$\widehat{\text{Proc}} = (\text{LAM} \times \widehat{\text{BEnv}}) + \text{PRIM} + \{stop\}$$
$$\widehat{\text{D}} = \mathbf{P}(\widehat{\text{Proc}})$$
$$\widehat{\text{TCache}} = (\text{REF} \times \widehat{\text{CN}}) \to \text{Type}$$
$$\widehat{\text{CC}} = \text{CALL} \times \widehat{\text{BEnv}}$$
$$\widehat{\text{CN}} = \text{LAB} \cup \{\langle perfect, l\rangle \mid l \in \text{LAB}\}$$
$$\widehat{\text{VB}} = \text{VAR} \times \widehat{\text{CN}}$$
$$\widehat{\text{BEnv}} = \text{LAB} \to \widehat{\text{CN}}$$
$$\widehat{\text{VEnv}} = \widehat{\text{VB}} \to \widehat{\text{D}}$$

$$\widehat{\text{Quant}} = \widehat{\text{VB}}$$
$$\widehat{\text{TTab}} = \widehat{\text{Quant}} \to \text{Type}$$

$$\widehat{\mathcal{C}} : \quad \text{CALL} \to \widehat{\text{BEnv}} \to \widehat{\text{VEnv}} \to \widehat{\text{TTab}} \to \widehat{\text{TCache}}$$
$$\widehat{\mathcal{F}} : \quad \widehat{\text{Proc}} \to \widehat{\text{D}}^* \to (\widehat{\text{Quant}}_\perp)^* \to \widehat{\text{VEnv}} \to \widehat{\text{TTab}} \to \widehat{\text{TCache}}$$
$$\widehat{\mathcal{F}}_p : \quad \widehat{\text{Proc}} \to \widehat{\text{D}}^* \to \text{Type}^* \to \widehat{\text{VEnv}} \to \widehat{\text{TCache}}$$

Figure 3.3: Abstract domains and functionalities.

The initial type vector given to *Reflow* comes from an auxiliary function, *TVInit*:

$$TVInit : \widehat{\text{CC}} \to \widehat{\text{TCache}} \to \text{Type}^*$$
$$TVInit \langle [\![\ (f \ a_1 \ldots a_n)]\!], \ \epsilon\rangle \ \delta = \langle t_1 \ldots t_n\rangle$$
$$\text{where } t_i = \begin{cases} \delta\langle a_i, \epsilon(binder \ a_i)\rangle & a_i \in \text{REF} \\ \mathcal{A}_t \ a_i & a_i \notin \text{REF} \end{cases}$$

TVInit takes a call context and a type cache, and returns the types of all the arguments in the call. If the argument is a variable reference, the type cache is consulted; if the argument is a constant, lambda, or primop, the auxiliary function $\mathcal{A}_t$ gives the appropriate type.

If we wish to restart our program at an arbitrary call context $\langle c, \epsilon\rangle$ with *Reflow*, we require the variable environment *ve* that pertained at this point of call. This is easy to handle: we always use the final variable environment that was present at the end of the control-flow analysis of Section 3.5.3. Since the variable environment is only augmented monotonically during the course of executing a program, the terminal environment is a superset of all intermediate variable environments. So, our initial control-flow analysis computes two items critical for the Reflow analysis: the call cache γ and terminal variable environment ve_{final}.

Given *TVInit* and *Reflow*, we can construct a series of approximate type caches, converging to a fixed point. The initial type cache δ_0 is the most precise; at each iteration, we redo the reflow analysis assuming type cache δ_i, computing a weaker type cache δ_{i+1}. The limit δ is the final result. The recomputation of each successive type cache is straightforward: for every call context $\langle c, \epsilon \rangle$ in the domain of call cache γ (that is, every call context recorded by the control-flow analysis of Section 3.5.3), we use the old type cache to compute the types of the arguments in the call, then reflow from the call, tracking the variables bound by the call's procedure, assuming the new type information. The returned type caches are joined together, yielding the new type cache. So the new type cache is the one we get by assuming the type assignments of the old type cache. A fixed point is a legitimate type assignment. Since all of our abstract domains are of finite size, and since our type lattice has finite height, the least fixed point is computable.

$$
\begin{aligned}
\delta_0 &= \lambda \langle r, b \rangle . \perp \\
\delta_{i+1} &= \delta_i \ \sqcup \bigsqcup_{\langle c, \epsilon \rangle \in Dom\ \gamma} Reflow \ \langle c, \epsilon \rangle \ ve_{final} \left(\ TVInit \ \langle c, \epsilon \rangle \ \delta_i \ \right) \\
\delta &= \bigsqcup_i \delta_i
\end{aligned}
$$

Before we get to the machinery of the *Reflow* function itself, let us define a few useful auxiliary functions and concepts (Figure 3.4). Because the Reflow semantics has a single perfect contour coexisting with the approximate contours, we need a few utility functions for manipulating the two different kinds of contours. The approximate contours are simply the labels of all the syntactic binding constructs (lambdas and **letrec**'s): in the 0th-order approximation, the contour allocated when entering lambda $[\![\ell : (\lambda \ (v_1 \ldots v_n) \ c)]\!]$ is just ℓ, so all contours over a single lambda are identified together. For every approximate contour l, we want to have a corresponding perfect contour $\langle perfect, l \rangle$. These perfect contours are pairs marked with the token *perfect*. The predicate *perfect?* distinguishes perfect contours from approximate ones. The function *ptoa* strips off the perfect token, mapping a perfect contour to its approximate counterpart. The $\widehat{\mathcal{A}_v}$ function evaluates call arguments and is the straightforward abstraction of its counterpart in the PTREC semantics. The $\widehat{\mathcal{A}_q}$ function is a little more subtle. Since we only track variables bound in perfect contours in the Reflow semantics, $\widehat{\mathcal{A}_q}$ only returns quantities for these bindings; approximate bindings are mapped to an undefined value, represented with $\perp$.

$$\widehat{\mathcal{A}_v} \; [\![\ell\colon\; (\lambda\;\; (v_1 \ldots v_n)\;\;\; c)\;]\!] \; \epsilon \; ve \; = \{\langle \ell, \, \epsilon \rangle\} \qquad \widehat{\mathcal{A}_v} \; [\![prim]\!] \; \epsilon \; ve \; = \{prim\}$$

$$\widehat{\mathcal{A}_v} \; [\![v]\!] \; \epsilon \; ve \; = ve \; \langle v, \, \epsilon(binder\; v) \rangle \qquad\qquad \widehat{\mathcal{A}_v} \; [\![k]\!] \; \epsilon \; ve \; = \emptyset$$

$$\widehat{\mathcal{A}_q} \; [\![v]\!] \; \epsilon \; = \begin{cases} \langle v, \, b \rangle & perfect?\; b \\ \bot & otherwise \end{cases} \qquad (b = \epsilon(binder\; v))$$

$$ptoa \; \langle perfect, \, b \rangle \; = b$$

$$perfect? \; \langle perfect, \, b \rangle \; = true \qquad perfect? \; b \; = false$$

Figure 3.4: Abstract auxiliary functions.

Now we are in a position to examine the machinery that triggers a single wave of perfect contour type tracking: the *Reflow* function, and its auxiliary $\widehat{\mathcal{F}_p}$ function.

$$Reflow \; \langle [\![c\colon\; (f\;\; a_1 \ldots a_n)\;]\!], \, \epsilon \rangle \; ve \; tv \quad = \bigsqcup_{f' \in F} (\widehat{\mathcal{F}_p} f') \; av \; tv \; ve$$

$$\text{where } F = \widehat{\mathcal{A}_v} \; f \; \epsilon \; ve$$

$$av{\downarrow}i = \widehat{\mathcal{A}_v} \; a_i \; \epsilon \; ve$$

Reflow simply reruns the interpretation from each possible procedure that could be called from call context $\langle c, \, \epsilon \rangle$. Each procedure is functionalised with the "perfect" functionaliser $\widehat{\mathcal{F}_p}$, who arranges for the call to the procedure to be a perfect one. The type caches resulting from each call are joined together into the result cache.

$$\widehat{\mathcal{F}_p} \; \langle [\![\ell\colon\; (\lambda\;\; (v_1 \ldots v_n)\;\;\; c)\;]\!], \, \epsilon \rangle \; = \lambda av \; tv \; ve. \; \widehat{\mathcal{C}} \; c \; \epsilon' \; ve' \; \tau$$

$$\text{where } b = \langle perfect, \, \ell \rangle$$

$$\tau = \big[\langle v_i, \, b \rangle \mapsto tv{\downarrow}i \big]$$

$$\epsilon' = \epsilon \, [\ell \mapsto b]$$

$$ve' = ve \sqcup \big[\langle v_i, \, b \rangle \mapsto av{\downarrow}i \big]$$

The perfect functionalisation of a procedure produced by $\widehat{\mathcal{F}_p}$ is called only once, at the beginning of the reflow. A new contour is allocated, whose value is marked with the special *perfect* token to designate it the one and only perfect contour in a given execution thread. The incoming values are bound in the outgoing variable environment ve' under the perfect contour. The incoming type information is used to create the initial type table τ passed forwards to track the values bound under the perfect contour. The rest of the computation is handed off to the $\widehat{\mathcal{C}}$ procedure. $\widehat{\mathcal{C}}$ is similar to $\mathcal{C}$ with the exception that it only records the type information of references that are bound in the perfect contour.

$\widehat{\mathcal{F}_p}$ must also be defined over primops. Primops do not have variables to be type-recovered, so instead primops pass the buck to their continuations. The + primop uses its initial-type vector $\langle ta, tb, tc \rangle$ to compute the initial-type vector $\langle ts \rangle$ for its continuation. The + primop then employs $\widehat{\mathcal{F}_p}$ to perform type recovery on the variable bound by its continuation. The **test-integer** primop is even simpler. Since its continuations do not bind variables, there is nothing to track, so the function just immediately returns the bottom type cache.

$$\widehat{\mathcal{F}_p} \, [\![+]\!] \quad = \quad \lambda \, \langle a, b, c \rangle \, \langle ta, tb, tc \rangle \, ve. \bigsqcup_{c' \in c} (\widehat{\mathcal{F}_p} c') \, \langle \emptyset \rangle \, \langle ts \rangle \, ve$$

$$\text{where } ts = \text{infer+} \, \langle ta, tb \rangle$$

$$\widehat{\mathcal{F}_p} \, [\![\text{test-integer}]\!] = \lambda \, \langle x, c, a \rangle \, \langle tx, tc, ta \rangle \, ve. \perp$$

Once the initial call to $\widehat{\mathcal{F}_p}$ has triggered a wave of type recovery for a particular lambda's variables, the actual tracking of type information through the rest of the program execution is handled by the $\widehat{\mathcal{F}}$ and $\widehat{\mathcal{C}}$ functions. Most of the action happens in the $\widehat{\mathcal{C}}$ function.

$$\widehat{\mathcal{C}} \, [\![\quad (e_0 {:} f \;\; e_1 {:} a_1 \ldots e_n {:} a_n) \,]\!] \, \epsilon \, ve \, \tau = \delta \sqcup \left(\bigsqcup_{f' \in F} (\widehat{\mathcal{F}} f') \, av \, qv \, ve \, \tau' \right)$$

$$\text{where } \; F = \widehat{\mathcal{A}_v} \, f \, \epsilon \, ve$$
$$b_i = \epsilon(binder \, a_i) \quad (\forall a_i \in \text{REF})$$
$$b_0 = \epsilon(binder \, f) \quad (\text{if } \; f \in \text{REF})$$
$$av{\downarrow}i = \widehat{\mathcal{A}_v} \, a_i \, \epsilon \, ve$$
$$qv{\downarrow}i = \widehat{\mathcal{A}_q} \, a_i \, \epsilon$$
$$\delta = \left[\langle e_i, \; ptoa \, b_i \rangle \mapsto \tau \, \langle a_i, b_i \rangle \right] \quad (\forall b_i \ni perfect? \, b_i)$$
$$\tau' = \begin{cases} \tau \sqcap \left[\langle f, b_0 \rangle \mapsto \text{type/proc} \right] & perfect? \, b_0 \\ \tau & otherwise \end{cases}$$

As $\widehat{\mathcal{C}}$ evaluates its arguments, it checks to see if any are variables whose types are being tracked. A variable a_i is being tracked if it is closed in a perfect contour, that is, if *perfect?* b_i is true, where $b_i = \epsilon(binder \, a_i)$. If an argument is being tracked, we look up its current type $\tau \, \langle a_i, b_i \rangle$, and record this in $\widehat{\mathcal{C}}$'s contribution δ to the type cache (recording the reference under the perfect contour b_i's abstraction *ptoa* b_i). The rest of $\widehat{\mathcal{C}}$'s stucture is similar to the perfect variant of Section 3.4. An outgoing type table τ'

is constructed, reflecting that f must be of type $type/proc$ (Again, note that this fact is only recorded in τ' if f is a variable currently being tracked).

Note also that since multiple contours are identified together in the abstract semantics, values in the approximate domain are *sets* of abstract procedures. Because of this, the call must branch to each of the possible procedures f' the function expression f could evaluate to. The result type caches are then all joined together.

The function returned by $\widehat{\mathcal{F}}$ constructs approximate contours when called. Because multiple environments are identified together by $\widehat{\mathcal{F}}$'s functionalised value, it cannot track type information for the variables bound by its procedure. Hence $\widehat{\mathcal{F}}$ has a fairly simple definition when applied to a closure, just augmenting the environment structure and passing the closure's body c off to $\widehat{\mathcal{C}}$. Note that the environment is updated by unioning a parameter's value set $av{\downarrow}i$ to the set already bound under the abstract contour.

$$\widehat{\mathcal{F}}\,\langle\llbracket \ell\colon\ (\lambda\ (v_1\ldots v_n)\ c)\rrbracket, \epsilon\rangle = \lambda av\ qv\ ve\ \tau.\ \widehat{\mathcal{C}}\ c\ \epsilon'\ ve'\ \tau$$
$$\text{where } b = l \quad \text{(0th order proc. approx.)}$$
$$\epsilon' = \epsilon\,[\ell \mapsto b]$$
$$ve' = ve \sqcup \big[\langle v_i,\ b\rangle \mapsto av{\downarrow}i\big]$$

$\widehat{\mathcal{F}}$'s definition for the terminal *stop* continuation is, again, trivial, ignoring its argument v and returning the bottom type cache:

$$\widehat{\mathcal{F}}\,\llbracket stop \rrbracket = \lambda\,\langle v\rangle\ qv\ ve\ \tau.\ \bot$$

$\widehat{\mathcal{F}}$'s behavior on primops is more interesting. If the argument x being passed to **test-integer** is being tracked (i.e., qx is a quantity, not bottom), then we intersect $type/int$ with qx's incoming type, passing the result type table τ_t to the true continuation, and we subtract $type/int$ from qx's type in τ_f the table passed to the false continuation. In other words, we do the type recovery of the PTREC semantics, but only for the values being tracked.

$$\widehat{\mathcal{F}}\,\llbracket\text{test-integer}\rrbracket = \lambda\,\langle x, c, a\rangle\ \langle qx, qc, qa\rangle\ ve\ \tau.$$
$$\left(\bigsqcup_{c' \in c}(\widehat{\mathcal{F}}c')\,\langle\rangle\,\langle\rangle\ ve\ \tau_t\right) \sqcup \left(\bigsqcup_{a' \in a}(\widehat{\mathcal{F}}a')\,\langle\rangle\,\langle\rangle\ ve\ \tau_f\right)$$
$$\text{where } \tau_f = \begin{cases} \tau\,[qx \mapsto (\tau\,qx - type/int)] & qx \neq \bot \\ \tau & otherwise \end{cases}$$
$$\tau_t = \begin{cases} \tau\,[qx \mapsto (\tau\,qx \sqcap type/int)] & qx \neq \bot \\ \tau & otherwise \end{cases}$$

The **+** primop is similar. If the arguments a and b are being tracked, then we update the type table passed forwards, otherwise we simply pass along the incoming type table

τ unchanged. Since the continuations c' are functionalised with the approximate functionaliser, $\widehat{\mathcal{F}}$, the quantity vector is $\langle \bot \rangle$ – we will not be tracking the variables bound by the call to c'.

$$\widehat{\mathcal{F}}\,[\![+]\!] \quad = \quad \lambda\,\langle a,\, b,\, c\rangle\,\langle qa,\, qb,\, qc\rangle\, ve\, \tau. \bigsqcup_{c' \in c} (\widehat{\mathcal{F}}c')\,\langle \emptyset \rangle\,\langle \bot \rangle\, ve\, \tau''$$

$$\text{where } \tau' = \begin{cases} \tau\,\big[qa \mapsto (type/number \sqcap \tau\, qa)\big] & qa \neq \bot \\ \tau & \textit{otherwise} \end{cases}$$

$$\tau'' = \begin{cases} \tau'\,\big[qb \mapsto (type/number \sqcap \tau'\, qb)\big] & qb \neq \bot \\ \tau' & \textit{otherwise} \end{cases}$$

To finish off the Reflow semantics, we must take care of `letrec`. Abstracting $\mathcal{C}$'s definition for `letrec` is simple. Evaluating the `letrec`'s bound expressions only involves closing lambdas, not referencing variables. So the `letrec` will not "touch" any of the variables we are currently tracking. Hence the `letrec` does not make any local contribution to the answer type cache, but simply augments the variable environment ve with the procedure bindings and recursively evaluates the inner call c.

$$\widehat{\mathcal{C}}[\![\ell\colon \ (\texttt{letrec} \ ((f_1 \ l_1)\ldots) \ c)]\!]\textit{eve}\tau = \widehat{\mathcal{C}}\, c\, \epsilon'\, ve'\, \tau$$
$$\text{where } b = \ell$$
$$\epsilon' = \epsilon\,[\ell \mapsto b]$$
$$ve' = ve \sqcup \Big[\langle f_i,\, b\rangle \mapsto \widehat{\mathcal{A}_v}\, l_i\, \epsilon'\, ve\Big]$$

One detail of `letrec` that we have neglected is tracking the types of the variables bound by `letrec`. There are several ways to handle this. We could add a case to the *Reflow* function to handle reflowing from `letrec` expressions, creating a perfect contour for the `letrec`'s binding. This is a fairly complex and expensive way to handle a simple case. Because `letrec` is syntactically restricted to binding only lambda procedures to its variables, we can statically analyse this case, and simply assign in advance the procedure type to all references to all `letrec` variables. The simplest place to insert this static assignment is in the initial type cache δ_0 used in the *Reflow* iteration:

$$\delta_0 = \lambda\,\langle [\![r\colon\! v]\!],\, b\rangle\,.\,\begin{cases} type/proc & binder\; v \in \text{CALL} \quad (\texttt{letrec}) \\ \bot & binder\; v \in \text{LAM} \quad (\text{lambda}) \end{cases}$$

This performs the type analysis of the `letrec` variables in one step, leaving the rest of the Reflow semantics free to concentrate on the variables bound by lambdas.

3.6 Implementation

I have a prototype implementation of the type recovery algorithm written in Scheme. It analyzes Scheme programs that have been converted into CPS Scheme by the front end of the ORBIT compiler [15]. The type-recovery code is about 900 lines of heavily commented Scheme; the control-flow analysis code is about 450 lines.

The implemented semantics features a store (allowing side-effects) and a type lattice that includes the symbol, pair, false, procedure, fixnum, bignum, flonum, vector, list, integer, and number types. Procedures are approximated using the first-order procedural abstraction (1CFA) [25]. In addition, CPS-level continuations are syntactically marked by the front-end CPS converter; this information is used to partition the procedure domain. This partition appears to greatly reduce the size of the sets propagated through the analysis, improving both the speed and precision of the analysis.

The implementation is for the most part a straightforward transcription of the approximate type recovery semantics. The variable environment, store, quantity environment, and result type cache are all kept as global data structures that are monotonically augmented as the analysis progresses.

The recursive semantic equations are realised as a terminating Scheme program by memoising the recursive $\widehat{C}$ applications; when the Scheme $\widehat{C}$ procedure is applied to a memoised set of arguments, it returns without making further contributions to the answer type cache. This is the "memoised pending analysis" technique of Hudak and Young [32].

Little effort has been made overall to optimize the implementation. Still, the current analyzer runs acceptably well for small test cases; response time has been sufficiently quick in the T interpreter that I have not felt the need to compile it. At this point in my experimentation, there is no reason to believe that efficiency of the analysis will be an overriding issue in practical application of the type recovery algorithm.

The allure of type recovery, of course, is type-safe Scheme implementations with little run-time overhead. It remains to be seen whether there is enough recoverable type information in typical code to allow extensive optimisation. The algorithm has not been tested extensively on a large body of real code. However, early results are encouraging. As an example of the algorithm's power, it is able to completely recover the types of all variable references in the `delq` and `fact` procedures given in Section 3.1.

3.7   Discussion and Speculation

This section is a collection of small discussions and speculations on various aspects of Scheme type recovery.

3.7.1   Side Effects and External Procedures

The PTREC and Reflow semantics in this chapter are toy semantics in that side-effects and external procedures have been explicitly left out to simplify the already excessively unwieldy equations. Restoring them is not difficult. We can adopt a simple model of side-effects where all procedural values placed into the store can be retrieved by any operator that accesses the store. These procedures are called "escaped procedures." We can also introduce the idea of unknown external procedures by introducing a special "external procedure" and a special "external call." Any value passed to the external procedure escapes; all escaped procedures can be called from the external call.

This model of side-effects and external procedures is discussed elsewhere [26]. More precise models, of course, are possible [12].

The implementation discussed in Section 3.6 uses this simple model of side-effects and external procedures. The store is represented as a single set of escaped procedures. Because the store is only monotonically augmented during the course of the analysis, it is represented as a global variable that is an implicit argument to the $\widehat{C}$ function. Because of the monotonic property of the store, the memoised pending analysis actually memoises a last-modified timestamp for the store, which greatly increases the efficiency of the memoising. This trick is also used for the global variable environment *ve*.

3.7.2   Safe and Unsafe Primops

A given implementation of Scheme chooses whether to provide "safe" primops, which are defined to cause a graceful error halt when applied to illegal values, or "dangerous" primops, which simply cause undefined effects when applied to illegal values. For example, most Scheme compilers efficiently open-code car as a single machine operation. Without compile-time type recovery to guarantee the type of the argument to a car application, this fast implementation is dangerous.

Type recovery can accept either safe or dangerous primops, or a combination of both. In both cases, the primop semantics allows flow-analysis based type-recovery. However, while it is possible to recover types given dangerous primops, the analysis is of limited value. The information provided by type recovery has two basic uses:

- Eliminating run-time error checks from safe primop applications.

- Specialising generic primops based on their argument types (e.g., converting a generic arithmetic operation to an integer operation).

In a dangerous implementation, the first of these uses does not apply. As we shall see below, specialising generic arithmetic is of limited utility as well.

3.7.3   Limits of the Type System

From the optimising compiler's point of view, the biggest piece of bad news in the Scheme type system is the presence of arbitrary-precision integers, or "bignums."

Scheme's bignums, an elegant convenience from the programmer's perspective, radically interfere with the ability of type recovery to assign small integer "fixnum" types to variable references. The unfortunate fact is that two's complement fixnums are not closed under any of the common arithmetic operations. Clearly adding, subtracting, and multiplying two fixnums can overflow into a bignum. Less obvious is that simple negation can overflow: the most negative fixnum overflows when negated. Because of this, not even fixnum division is safe: dividing the most negative fixnum by -1 negates it, causing overflow into bignums. Thus, the basic fixnum arithmetic operations cannot be safely implemented with their corresponding simple machine operations. This means that most integer quantities cannot be inferred to be fixnums. So, even though type recovery can guarantee that all the generic arithmetic operations in Figure 3.1's factorial function are integer operations, this does not buy us a great deal.

Not being able to efficiently implement safe arithmetic operations on fixnums is terrible news for loops, because many loops iterate over integers, particularly array-processing loops. Taking five instructions just to increment a loop counter can drastically affect the execution time of a tight inner loop.

There are a few approaches to this problem:

- *Range analysis*

  Range analysis is a data-flow analysis technique that bounds the values of numeric variables [10]. For example, range analysis can tell us that in the body of the following C loop, the value of i must always lie in the range $[0, 10)$:

  ```
  for(i=9; i>=0; i--) printf("%d ", a[i]);
  ```

  Range analysis can probably be applied to most integer loop counters. Consider the **strindex** procedure below:

  ```
  (define (strindex c str)
    (let ((len (string-length str)))
      (letrec ((lp (lambda (i)
        (cond ((>= i len) -1) ; lose
              ((char= c (string-ref str i)) i) ; win
              (else (loop (+ i 1))))))) ; loop
        (lp 0))))
  ```

  Type recovery can guarantee that **len**, being the result of the **string-length** primop, is a fixnum. Range analysis can show that **i** is bounded by 0 and a fixnum; this is enough information to guarantee that **i** is a fixnum. Range analysis is useful in its own right as well – in this example, it allows us to safely open code the character access **(string-ref str i)** with no bounds check.

- *Abstract Safe Useage Patterns*

  The poor man's alternative to range analysis is to take the usage patterns that are guaranteed to be fixnum specific, and package them up for the user as syntactic or procedural abstractions. These abstractions can be carefully decorated with **proclaim** declarations to force fixnum arithmetic. For example, a loop macro which has a **(for c in-string str)** clause can safely declare the string's index variable as a fixnum. This approach can certainly pick up string and array index variables.

- *Disable Bignums*

  Another cheap alternative to range analysis is to live dangerously and provide a compiler switch or declaration which allows the compiler to forget about bignums and assume all integers are fixnums. Throwing out bignums allows simple type recovery to proceed famously, and programs can be successfully optimised (successfully, that is, until some hapless user's program overflows a fixnum...).

- *Hardware support*

  Special tag-checking hardware, such as is provided on the SPARC, Spur and Lisp Machine architectures [8,11,18], or fine-grained parallelism, such as is provided by VLIW (very long instruction word) architectures [6,7], allow fixnum arithmetic to be performed in parallel with the bignum/fixnum tag checking. In this case, the limitations of simple type recovery are ameliorated by hardware assistance.

  VLIWs could be ideal target machines for languages that require run-time type-checking. For example, when compiling the code for a safe **car** application, the compiler can pick the trace through the type test that assumes the **car**'s argument is a legitimate pair. This will almost always be correct, the sort of frequency skew that allows trace scheduling to pay off in VLIWs. The actual type check operation can percolate down in the main trace to a convenient point where ALU and branch resources are available; the error handling code is off the main trace.

  Common cases for generic arithmetic operations are similarly amenable to trace picking. The compiler can compile a main fixnum trace (or flonum trace, as the common case may be), handling less frequent cases off-trace. The overhead for bignum, rational, and complex arithmetic ops will dominate the off-trace time in any event, whereas the lightweight fixnum or flonum case will be inlined.

  The VLIW trace-scheduling approach to run-time type safety has an interesting comparison to the automatic tag checking performed by Lisp Machines. Essentially, we have taken the tag-checking ALU and branch/trap logic, promoted it to general-purpose status, and exposed it to the compiler. These hardware resources can now be used for non-typechecking purposes when they would otherwise lay idle, providing opportunities for increased fine-grained parallelism.

The Lisp Machine approach is the smart hardware/fast compiler approach; the VLIW approach is the other way around.

3.7.4 Declarations

The dangerous **proclaim** declaration is problematic. A purist who wants to provide a guaranteed safe Scheme implementation might wish to ban **proclaim** on the grounds that it allows the user to write dangerous code. A multithreaded, single address-space PC implementation of Scheme, for example, might rely on run-time safety to prevent threads from damaging each other's data. Including **proclaim** would allow the compilation of code that could silently trash the system, or access and modify another thread's data.

On the other hand, safe declarations like **enforce** have limits. Some useful datatypes cannot be checked at run time. For example, while it is possible to test at run time if a datum is a procedure, it is *not* possible, in general, to test at run time if a datum is a procedure that maps floating-point numbers to floating-point numbers. Allowing the user to make such a declaration can speed up some critical inner loops. Consider the floating-point numeric integrator below:

```
(define (integ f x0 x1 n)
  (enforce fixnum? n)   (enforce procedure? f)
  (enforce flonum? x0) (enforce flonum? x1)
  (let ((delta (/ (- x1 x0) n)))
    (do ((i n (- i 1))
         (x x0 (+ x delta))
         (sum 0.0 (+ sum (f x))))
        ((= i 0) (* sum delta)))))
```

In some cases, analysis might be able to find all applications of the integrator, and thus discover that **f** is always bound to a floating-point function. However, if the integrator is a top level procedure in an open system, we can't guarantee at compile time that **f** is a floating-point function, and we can't enforce it at run time. This means that the sum operation must check the return value of **f** each time through the loop to ensure it is a legitimate floating-point value.

While the **proclaim** declaration does allow the user to write dangerous code, it is at least a reasonably principled loophole. **Proclaim** red-flags dangerous assumptions. If the user can be guaranteed that only code marked with **proclaim** declarations can behave in undefined ways, debugging broken programs becomes much easier.

Finally, it might be worth considering a third declaration, **probably**. (**probably flonum? x**) is a hint to the compiler that **x** is most likely a floating-point value, but could in fact be any type. Having a **probably** declaration can allow trace-scheduling compilers to pick good traces or optimistically open-code common cases.

3.7.5 *Test Hoisting*

Having one branch of a conditional test be the undefined effect $ or **error** primop opens up interesting code motion possibilities. Let us call tests with an **(error)** arm "error tests," and tests with a **$** arm "$-tests." These tests can be hoisted to earlier points in the code that are guaranteed to lead to the test. For example,

```
(block (print (+ x 3))
       (if (fixnum? x) (g x) ($)))
```

is semantically identical to

```
(if (fixnum? x) (block (print (+ x 3)) (g x))
    ($))
```

because the undefined effect operator can be defined to have any effect at all, including the effect of **(print (+ x 3))**. This can be useful, because hoisting type tests increases their coverage. In the example above, hoisting the **fixnum?** test allows the compiler to assume that **x** is a fixnum in the **(+ x 3)** code. Further, error and $-tests can be hoisted above code splits if the test is applied in both arms. For example, the type tests in

```
(if (> x 0)
    (if (pair? y) (bar) ($))
    (if (pair? y) (baz) ($)))
```

can be hoisted to a single type test:

```
(if (pair? y)
    (if (> x 0) (bar) (baz))
    ($))
```

Real savings accrue if loop invariant type tests get hoisted out of loops. For example, in a naive, declaration-free dot-product subroutine,

```
(define (dot-prod v w len)
  (do ((i (- len 1) (- i 1))
       (sum 0.0 (+ sum (* (vector-ref v i)
                          (vector-ref w i)))))
      ((< i 0) sum)))
```

each time through the inner loop we must check that **v** and **w** have type vector. Since **v** and **w** are loop invariants, we could hoist the run-time type checks out of the loop, which would speed it up considerably. (In this particular example, we would have to duplicate the termination test **(< i 0)**, so that loop invariant code pulled out of the loop would only execute if the loop was guaranteed at least one iteration. This is a standard optimising compiler technique.)

Hoisting error tests requires us to broaden our semantics to allow for early detection of run-time errors. If execution from a particular control point is guaranteed to lead to a subsequent error test, it must be allowed to perform the error test at the control point instead.

In the general case, error and $-test hoisting is a variant of very-busy expression analysis [2]. Note that hoisting $-tests has an effect similar to backwards type inferencing [14]. Finding algorithms to perform this hoisting is an open research problem.

3.7.6 Other Applications

The general Reflow approach to solving quantity-based analyses presented in this chapter can be applied to other data-flow problems in higher-order languages. The range analysis discussed in Section 3.7.3 is a possible candidate for this type of analysis. Copy propagation in Scheme is also amenable to a Reflow-based solution.

A final example very similar to type recovery is future analysis. Some parallel dialects of Scheme [16] provide *futures*, a mechanism for introducing parallelism into a program. When the form **(future <exp>)** is evaluated, a task is spawned to evaluate the expression **<exp>**. The **future** form itself immediately returns a special value, called a *future*. This future can be passed around the program, and stored into and retrieved from data structures until its actual value is finally required by a "strict" operator such as **+** or **car**. If the future's task has completed before the value is needed, the strict operation proceeds without delay; if not, the strict operator must wait for the future's task to run to completion and return a value. (See Chapter 9 for more about implementing futures.)

Futures have a heavy implementation expense on stock hardware, because all strict operators must check their operands. Future checking can add a 100% overhead to the serial run time of an algorithm on stock hardware.

"Future analysis" is simply realising that references to a variable that happen after the variable is used as an argument to a strict operator can assume the value is a non-future, because the strict operator has forced the value to resolve itself. Thus, in the lambda

$$(\lambda \ (x) \ (print \ (car \ x)) \ ... \ (f \ (cdr \ x)) \ ...)$$

the **(cdr x)** operation can be compiled without future checking. Clearly, this is identical to the type-recovery analysis presented in this chapter, and the same techniques apply.

3.8 Related Work

The method of non-standard abstract semantic interpretations has been applied to a variety of program analyses [4,20,12,9,25]. Abramsky and Hankin provide a useful collection [1]. The semantic basis for Scheme control-flow analysis [25,27] also forms the basis for the type recovery semantics described here.

Steenkiste's dissertation [29] and chapter in this book give some idea of the potential gains type recovery can provide. Steenkiste ported the PSL Lisp compiler to the Stanford MIPS-X processor. He implemented two backends for the compiler. The "careful" backend did full run-time type checking on all primitive operations, including **car**'s, **cdr**'s, vector references, and arithmetic operations. The "reckless" backend did no run-time type checking at all. Steenkiste compiled about 11,500 lines of Lisp code with the two backends, and compared the run times of the resulting executables. Full type checking added about 25% to the execution time of the program.

Clearly, the code produced by a careful backend optimised with type-recovery analysis will run somewhere between the two extremes measured by Steenkiste. This indicates that the payoff of compile-time optimisation is bounded by the 25% that Steenkiste measured. Steenkiste's data, however, must be taken only as a rough indicator. In Lisp systems, the tiny details of processor architecture, compiler technology, data representations and program application all interact in strong ways to affect final measurements. Some examples of the particulars affecting his measurements are: his Lisp system used high bits for type tags; the MIPS-X did not allow **car** and **cdr** operations to use aligned-address exceptions to detect type errors; his 25% measurement did not include time spent in the type dispatch of generic arithmetic operations; his generic arithmetic was tuned for the small integer case; none of his benchmarks were floating-point intensive applications; his measurements assumed interprocedural register allocation, a powerful compiler technology still not yet in common practice in Lisp and Scheme implementations; and Lisp requires procedural data to be called with the **funcall** primop, so simple calls can be checked at link time to ensure they are to legitimate procedures.

These particulars of language, hardware, implementation, and program can bias Steenkiste's 25% in both directions (Steenkiste is careful to discuss most of these issues himself). However, even taken as a rough measurement, Steenkiste's data do indicate that unoptimised type-checking is a significant component of program execution time, and that there is room for compile-time optimisation to provide real speed-up.

The idea of type recovery for Scheme is not new. Vegdahl and Pleban [31] discuss the possibility of "tracking" types through conditionals, although this was never pursued. The ORBIT compiler [15] is able to track the information determined by conditional branches, thus eliminating redundant tests. ORBIT, however, can only recover this information

over trees of conditional tests; more complex control and environment structures, such
as loops, recursions, and joins block the analysis.

Curtis discusses a framework for performing static type inference in a Scheme variant [5], along the lines of that done for statically typed polymorphic languages such as
ML [17] or LEAP [19]. However, his work assumes that most "reasonable" Scheme
programs use variables in a way that is consistent with a static typing discipline. In
essence, Curtis' technique types variables, whereas the type recovery presented in this
chapter types variable references, an important distinction for Scheme. Note that without
introducing type-conditional primitives that bind variables, and (perhaps automatically)
rewriting Scheme code to employ these primitives, this approach cannot recover the information determined by conditional branches on type tests, an important source of type
information.

Typical examples of applying data-flow analysis to recover type information from
latently-typed languages can be found in papers by Tenenbaum [30], and also Kaplan
and Ullman [14]. The technique is also covered in chapter 10 of the compiler textbook
by Aho, Sethi, and Ullman [2]. These approaches, based on classical data-flow analysis
techniques, differ from the technique in this chapter in several ways:

- First, they focus on side-effects as the principle way values are associated with
  variables. In Scheme, variable binding is the predominant mechanism for associating values with variables, so the Scheme type recovery analysis must focus on
  variable binding.

- Second, they assume a fixed control-flow graph. Because of Scheme's first-class
  procedures, control-flow structure is not lexically apparent at compile time. The
  use of a CPS-based internal representation only makes this problem worse, since
  all transfers of control, including sequencing, branching, and loops are represented
  with procedure calls. The analysis in this chapter handles procedure calls correctly.

- Third, they assume a single, flat environment. Scheme forces one to consider multiple bindings of the same variable. The reflow semantics of Section 3.5 correctly
  handles this complexity.

- Finally, they are not semantically based. The type recovery analysis in this chapter
  is based on the method of non-standard abstract semantic interpretations. This
  establishes a formal connection between the analysis and the base language semantics. Grounding the analysis in denotational semantics allows the possibility
  of proving various useful properties of the analysis, although such proofs are beyond the scope of this chapter.

These differences are all connected by the centrality of lambda in Scheme. The preva-
lence of lambda is what causes the high frequency of variable binding. Lambda allows

the construction of procedural data, which in turn prevent the straightforward construction of a compile-time control-flow graph. Lambda allows closures to be constructed, which in turn provide for multiple extant bindings of the same variable. And, of course, the mathematical simplicity and power of lambda makes it much easier to construct semantically-based program analyses.

In the lambda operator, all three fundamental program structures – data, control, and environment – meet and intertwine. Thus, any analysis technique for Scheme must be prepared to face the three facets of lambda. In essence, the analysis in this chapter is the application of classical data-flow type-recovery analysis in the presence of lambda.

Acknowledgements

I am very grateful to the people who helped me with this chapter. My advisor, Peter Lee, substantially improved the early drafts. Norman Adams, Peter Lee, Jonathan Rees, and Mark Shirley reviewed the penultimate draft under extreme time pressure, and provided me with detailed, thoughtful comments and suggestions. Daniel Weise and an anonymous referee suggested some valuable references.

John Reynolds helped pin down the details of the semantics. Jonathan Rees pointed out to me the idea of representing user declarations as conditional branches in 1984. Uwe Pleban pointed out to me the type constraints that safe primop applications place on their arguments.

References

[1] S. Abramsky and C. Hankin (ed.). *Abstract interpretation of declarative languages*. Ellis Horwood (1987).

[2] Aho, Sethi, and Ullman. *Compilers, Principles, Techniques and Tools*. Addison-Wesley (1986).

[3] A. Appel and J. Trevor. "Continuation-passing, Closure-passing Style." *Proceedings of the 16th Annual ACM Symposium on Principles of Programming Languages* (January 1989), pp. 293–302.

[4] P. Cousot and R. Cousot. "Abstract interpretation: a unified lattice model for static analysis of programs by construction or approximation of fixpoints." *4th ACM Symposium on Principles of Programming Languages* (1977), pp. 238–252.

[5] P. Curtis. *Constrained Quantification in Polymorphic Type Analysis*. Ph.D. dissertation, Cornell University, 1990. *(In preparation)*

[6] J. Ellis. *Bulldog: A Compiler for VLIW Architectures*. Ph.D. dissertation, Yale University. MIT Press (1986). Also available as Research Report YALEU/DCS/RR-364.

[7] J. A. Fisher, J. R. Ellis, J. C. Ruttenberg, and A. Nicolau. "Parallel Processing: A Smart Compiler and a Dumb Machine," Proceedings of the ACM SIGPLAN '84 Symposium on Compiler Construction, *SIGPLAN Notices Vol. 19, No. 6* (June, 1984), pp. 37–47.

[8] R. Garner, *et al.* "Scaleable processor architecture (SPARC)." COMPCON, IEEE (March, 1988) San Francisco, pp. 278–283.

[9]   W. L. Harrison, III. "The Interprocedural Analysis and Automatic Parallelization of Scheme Programs." *Lisp and Symbolic Computation* vol. 2(3/4) (October 1989), pp. 179–396.

[10] W. H. Harrison. "Compiler Analysis of the Value Ranges for Variables," *IEEE Transactions on Software Engineering* vol. SE-3, no. 3 (May 1977), pp. 243–250.

[11] M. Hill, *et al.* "Design Decisions in Spur." *COMPUTER* (November 1986), pp. 8–22.

[12] P. Hudak. "A Semantic Model of Reference Counting and its Abstraction." *Proceedings of the 1986 ACM Conference on Lisp and Functional Programming* (August 1986).

[13] P. Hudak and A. Bloss. "Variations on Strictness Analysis." *Proceedings of the 1986 ACM Conference on LISP and Functional Programming* (August 1986).

[14] M. A. Kaplan and J. D. Ullman. "A Scheme for the Automatic Inference of Variable Types," *JACM* 27:1 (January 1980), 128–145.

[15] D. Kranz, *et al.* "ORBIT: An Optimizing Compiler for Scheme." *Proceedings of SIGPLAN '86 Symposium on Compiler Construction* ACM (June 1986), pp. 219–233. Proceedings published as *SIGPLAN Notices* 21(7), July 1986.

[16] D. Kranz, R. Halstead, and E. Mohr. "Mul-T: A High-Performance Parallel Lisp" *Proceedings of SIGPLAN '89 Symposium on Programming Languages Design and Implementation* (June 1989).

[17] R. Milner. "The Standard ML Core Language." *Polymorphism, vol. II(2).* (October 1985). *Also* ECS-LFCS-86-2, University of Edinburgh, Edinburgh, Scotland (March 1986).

[18] D. Moon. "Architecture of the Symbolics 3600." *Proc. 12th Symp. on Computer Architecture,* Boston, MA (June 1985).

[19] F. Pfenning and P. Lee. "Metacircularity in the Polymorphic Lambda-Calculus." *Theoretical Computer Science* (1990) *(To appear).*

[20] U. Pleban. *Preexecution Analysis Based on Denotational Semantics.* Ph.D. dissertation, University of Kansas, 1981.

[21] J. Rees and N. Adams. "T: a dialect of LISP, or, Lambda: the ultimate software tool." Symposium on Lisp and Functional Programming, ACM (August 1982), pp. 114–122.

[22] J. Rees and W. Clinger, editors. "The revised[3] report on the algorithmic language Scheme." In *ACM SIGPLAN Notices* 21(12) (December 1986).

[23] J. Rees, N. Adams, and J. Meehan. *The T Manual.* 4th edition, Yale University Computer Science Department (January 1984).

[24] O. Shivers. *The Semantics of Scheme Control-Flow Analysis (Prelim).* Technical Report ERGO-90-090, CMU School of Computer Science, Pittsburgh, Penn. (November 1988).

[25] O. Shivers. *The Semantics of Scheme Control-Flow Analysis. (In preparation)*

[26] O. Shivers. "Control Flow Analysis in Scheme." *Proceedings of SIGPLAN '88 Conference on Programming Language Design and Implementation* (June 1988). (Also available as Technical Report ERGO-88-60, CMU School of Computer Science, Pittsburgh, Penn.)

[27] O. Shivers. *Control-Flow Analysis in Higher-Order Languages.* Ph.D. dissertation, CMU. *(In preparation)*

[28] G. L. Steele. *Rabbit: A Compiler for Scheme.* AI-TR-474. MIT AI Lab (Cambridge, May 1978).

[29] P. Steenkiste. *Lisp on a Reduced-Instruction-Set Processor: Characterization and Optimization.* Ph.D. dissertation, Stanford University (March, 1987). Computer Systems Laboratory, Technical report CSL-TR-87-324.

[30] A. Tenenbaum. *Type determination for very high level languages.* Rep. NSO-3, Courant Inst. Math. Sci., New York U., New York (1974).

[31] S. Vegdahl and U. Pleban. "The Runtime Environment for Screme, a Scheme Implementation on the 88000." *ASPLOS-III Proceedings* (April 1989), pp. 127–182.

[32] J. Young and P. Hudak. *Finding Fixpoints on Function Spaces.* Research Report YALEU/DCS/RR-505, Yale University (December 1986).

4   Garbage Collection

Andrew W. Appel

In McCarthy's 1960 LISP system, linked lists could be freely created by the cons operator, and accessed by the car and cdr operators. The revolutionary innovation of LISP was that the programmer did not need to tediously reclaim unneeded list cells. This made the manipulation of lists as mathematical values much easier, and as a result, LISP endures to this day.

More recent language implementations require the garbage collection not just of lists but of function activation records, function closures, executable code, strings, and other data structures. Automatic management of dynamic storage is increasingly regarded as a necessary feature of a modern programming language.

This chapter is a survey of garbage collection algorithms; Cohen's survey [11] is a comprehensive and well-organized review of the literature to 1980.

4.1 Mark and Sweep

The first LISP garbage collector used a depth-first search to mark all nodes accessible from a set of "root" locations (e.g. global variables), and then did a sweep through the address space gathering all accessible cells onto a free list. McCarthy [17] explains it concisely:

> Each register [memory location] that is accessible to the program is accessible because it can be reached from one or more of the base registers by a chain of car and cdr operations. When the contents of a base register are changed, it may happen that the register to which the base register formerly pointed cannot be reached by a car-cdr chain from any base register. Such a register may be considered abandoned by the program because its contents can no longer be found by any possible program; hence its contents are no longer of interest, and so we would like to have it back on the free-storage list. This comes about in the following way.

> Nothing happens until the program runs out of free storage. When a free register is wanted, and there is none left on the free storage list, a reclamation cycle starts. First, the program finds all registers accessible from the base

registers and makes their signs negative. This is accomplished by changing the sign of every register than can be reached from it by a car-cdr chain. If the program encounters a register in this process which already has a negative sign, it assumes that this register has already been reached.

After all the accessible registers have had their signs changed, the program goes through the area of memory reserved for the storage of list structures and puts all the registers whose signs were not changed in the previous step back on the free-storage list, and makes the signs of the accessible registers positive again.

McCarthy doesn't say what the marking algorithm is, but we can assume it might be a depth-first search. The problem with depth-first search is that it requires an auxiliary stack, which might require as much storage as all the accessible list cells. A clever technique, discovered independently by Peter Deutsch and by Herbert Schorr and W. M. Waite in 1965 and described in section 2.3.5 of Knuth [15], is known as *pointer reversal*: the stack can be kept in the graph itself, with only one bit per node extra storage. As a chain of pointers is followed from the root by the depth-first search, each already-traversed node is made to point to the previous node. At any point, the current and next nodes are remembered in registers. Then, when it's time to "pop" the stack, previous nodes can be retrieved at will.

4.2 Copying Collection

The problem with mark-and-sweep garbage collection is that each collection touches the entire memory, even if most of it is garbage. *Copying* collection avoids touching the garbage. Memory is divided into two spaces, and list cells are allocated in one space until it fills. Then all the accessible cells are copied into the other space (and the pointers within them are adjusted to point at the new copies). The copied cells don't come close to filling the new space (because there should have been some garbage in the old space). Then the program is resumed, allocating new cells in the remainder of the new space. When the new spaces fills up, the roles of the spaces are reversed and the live cells are copied back.

The accessible cells can be copied in any order. Fenichel and Yochelson [13] first presented copying collection with a depth-first search using pointer-reversal, and Cheney [10] demonstrated a breadth-first version. Cheney's algorithm has become a basis for many recent garbage collection algorithms, so we will study it in detail.

At the beginning of a garbage collection, we have a set of *root* registers (which might be machine registers or global variables); a *from-space* containing accessible list cells and garbage; and a *to-space* which is initialially empty. We will assume that each list cell occupies two consecutive memory words that are addressable separately. We will also assume that pointers are distinguishable from non-pointers (more about this later).

We wish to copy the graph of accessible cells from from-space into to-space by a breadth-first search. The classical breadth-first search algorithm requires a queue of unprocessed graph-edges, which could grow quite large. Cheney's algorithm cleverly uses a portion of to-space as the queue: there are two pointers into new space, called *scan* and *next*, which define the head and tail of the queue. Initially, *scan* and *next* point to the beginning of new-space.

In the data structure originally residing in from-space, a given node may have many pointers to it. When the node is copied to to-space, it is important to record the address of the copy, so that all the pointers can be properly updated. We record this information in the node itself, overwriting the first field with a *forwarding pointer*, after first copying all the fields to to-space (see Figure 4.1).

The fundamental operation of Cheney's algorithm is **forward**ing: converting a pointer to from-space into a pointer to to-space by following a forwarding-pointer (if the cell has already been copied) or by making a copy and installing a forwarding pointer:

```
forward(p) = IF p points into from-space
                THEN IF mem[p] points into to-space
                        THEN RETURN mem[p]
                        ELSE mem[next]   := mem[p]
                             mem[next+1] := mem[p+1]
                             mem[p] := next
                             next := next+2
                             RETURN mem[p]
             ELSE return p
```

If p doesn't point into from-space, it won't be affected by this garbage collection. If **mem**[p] already pointed into to-space, it must have been a forwarding pointer; there is no other way for such a pointer to arise inside from-space.

Now, here's Cheney's algorithm:

```
scan := next := beginning of to-space
FOR each root  p
    p := forward(p)
WHILE scan < next
    mem[scan] := forward(mem[scan])
    scan := scan+1
```

Now let us compare the efficiencies of mark-and-sweep versus copying collection [2]. The mark phase of a mark-and-sweep collection takes time linear in the amount A of

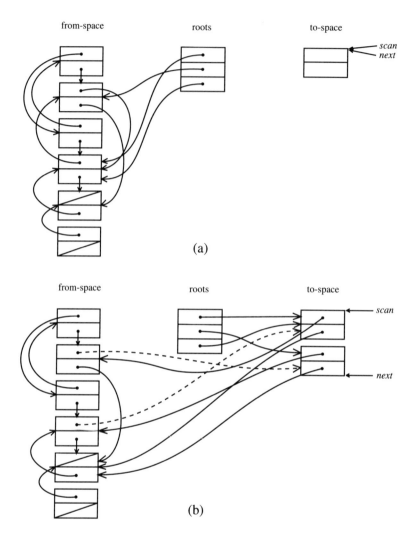

Figure 4.1: Breadth-first copying garbage collection. Initially (a) the to-space is empty. First all the roots are forwarded (b), with the forwarding pointers (dashed lines) installed in each copied cell. Then, (c) each pointer in the to-space is forwarded. The "scan" pointer advances past each forwarded cell; the "next" pointer advances past each copied cell. All cells above "scan" in the to-space point only into to-space; all cells between "scan" and "next" point into from-space. When "scan" catches up with "next," all cells have been forwarded and the algorithm terminates.

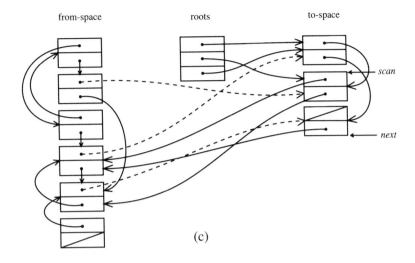

Figure 4.1: *cont.*

accessible data, and the sweep phase takes time linear in the size of memory M. So the cost of one collection is $c_1 A + c_2 M$ for some constants c_1 and c_2. After a collection, there are $M - A$ cells free before the next collection; we can calculate the amortized cost per cell allocated for mark-and-sweep collection:

$$C_{\text{mark-and-sweep}} = \frac{c_1 A + c_2 M}{M - A}$$

Similarly, for copying collection, a depth-first or breadth-first copy takes time linear in the number of cells copied. The number of cells that can be allocated before the next collection is only $M/2 - A$, however, because we have divided memory in half. Thus, the amortized cost per cell for copying collection is

$$C_{\text{copying}} = \frac{c_3 A}{\frac{M}{2} - A}$$

Since memories are becoming larger and larger, it is interesting to note what happens in the limit of very large memories. The number of accessible cells A is, independent of the memory size; it depends only on the algorithm and its input. When we take the limit as M approaches infinity, we find that the amortized cost of mark-and-sweep collection approaches c_2 per allocation, while the amortized cost of copying collection approaches zero.

Furthermore, copying collection compacts the useful data in memory, thereby reducing fragmentation; and the free memory is contiguous, which simplifies allocation of new cells. These advantages become important if records of different sizes are allocated.

For these and other reasons, copying collection is usually to be preferred. The remaining uses of mark-and-sweep collection in modern systems are usually where it is hard to distinguish pointers from integers [9], so that one cannot safely move cells from one place to another.

4.3 Reference Counts

Instead of having the garbage collector traverse the accessible memory, the allocating program can keep track of which cells are still referenced by pointers [12]. Each time a new pointer to a cell is created, the cell's *reference count* is incremented; when a pointer is destroyed, the cell's reference count is decremented. When the reference count goes to zero, the cell can be reclaimed; this can happen immediately, or there can be a periodic sweep phase that looks for zero-count cells. There are two serious problems with reference counting schemes:

1. Cyclic data structures cannot be reclaimed; an inaccessible cycle of cells will still have nonzero reference counts.

2. Maintaining the reference counts is very costly; every time a pointer is stored to memory, there must be an additional fetch, increment, and store to change the reference count (and if the stored-to destination contains a valid pointer, there must be yet another fetch, decrement, store, and test-for-zero to destroy the old pointer).

These problems can be ameliorated by using mark-and-sweep as a backup algorithm for reference counts; in this case, the size of the reference count field in each object need not be large; when it reaches the maximum value, it is never decremented [15]. The mark-and-sweep collector reclaims all cyclic objects and those unreachable objects with "stuck" reference counts.

4.4 Incremental Collection

A single garbage collection can take a long time, and in real-time or interactive applications it is undesirable to have a long pause in the computation while the collector is invoked. Baker's algorithm [7] is an example of an *incremental* garbage collector.

We consider a machine model with a finite set of registers; any value from memory must be fetched into a register before being operated upon. Now, we use Cheney's algorithm, but we let the allocating program resume execution as soon as we have forwarded all the registers. Any cells allocated by the program are put at the end of the to-space, in an area where they won't interfere with *scan* and *next*.

The following invariant will be maintained by the allocating program:

Registers never point to from-space.

This will certainly hold as soon as all the registers are forwarded. But since the unfor-warded locations in to-space can contain pointers to from-space, the allocating program has the duty to forward every pointer that it fetches from memory. In the long run (especially in large memories), most pointers fetched from memory will not point into from-space, and thus will return quickly from the *forward* procedure as shown above. However, there must be at least a comparison and branch after each fetch, which takes at least one instruction (unless special hardware is provided, as on a LISP machine). Since fetches comprise about 30% of all instructions, the overhead of Baker's algorithm is fairly high.

While the allocating program is executing, the garbage collector must also execute, trying to make *scan* catch up to *next* as in Cheney's algorithm. This can be accomplished even in a sequential system by letting the *cons* procedure also forward k pointers to advance *scan* by k. What remains are management details, like adjusting k for best performance and concurrency.

Aside from the overhead of checking the result of every fetch, Baker's algorithm has the same efficiency as Cheney's algorithm, since exactly the same set of cells will be copied from from-space to to-space.

4.5 Generational Collection

In 1983, Lieberman and Hewitt [16] made the following observations about LISP programs:

1. Newer cells tend to point to older cells.
2. Newer cells tend to be shorter-lived than older cells.

When one writes (CONS A B) in a program, one constructs a newer cell that points to two older cells. The only way that an older cell can point to a newer cell is if its car or cdr is modified after it is created, which is rare.

When a cell has been accessible for a long time, it is typically part of a global data structure that will continue to be necessary. New cells tend to contain intermediate results of computations that will soon be useless. In this respect, dynamically allocated list cells are unlike radioactive atoms, whose future lifetimes are quite unrelated to their past lifetimes.

Now, we can take advantage of these two observations. Observation 2 implies that we should concentrate our garbage collection effort on the newer cells (which have a higher proportion of garbage), and observation 1 implies that this is possible.

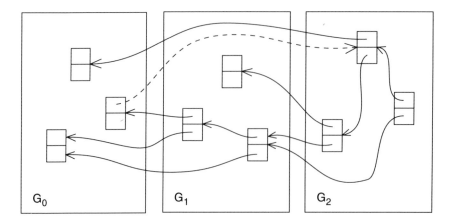

Figure 4.2: All the records in generation G_2 are newer than the records in G_1; the oldest records are in G_0. The pointer represented by the dashed line is anomalous; it must have been created by an assignment that modified an old object.

Allocated cells will be kept in several distinct areas G_i of memory, called *generations*. Cells in the same generation are of similar age, and all the records in generation G_i are older than the records in generation G_{i+1}. This implies (by observation 1 above) that for $i < j$, there are (almost) no pointers from G_i into G_j (see Figure 4.2).

Consider the newest generation, G_n. The copying garbage collector may be applied to this generation, using the global variables and runtime stack as a root set. Because (almost) no pointers in the other generations can possibly point to records in G_n, the other generations (almost) need not be considered as roots. The garbage collector may copy the reachable objects of G_n into a new generation G_n' without touching the other generations. This is advantageous because G_n is expected (by observation 2 above) to have a higher proportion of garbage than any of the other generations.

In general, the garbage collector can work on generation G_i if it also works on all the newer generations; that is, it may work on any subset $G_i, G_{i+1}, ..., G_n$ of the generations. For greatest efficiency, the garbage collector should usually copy just G_n, but occasionally copy the older generations.

This algorithm depends on the fact that cells contain pointers only to older cells. In the presence of assignments to fields of old cells, this acyclic condition will not hold. Lieberman and Hewitt [16] handle this problem by making such fields point indirectly through an "assignment table." A simpler scheme devised by Ungar [19] keeps a set of addresses of cells that point to newer cells; this set must be maintained with the help of the allocating program – whenever it assigns a pointer into an existing cell, it must add the address of that cell to the modified set. In some implementations, there is just one modified set; at the other extreme, there is a modified set for each pair (i, j), $i < j$, for pointers from G_i into G_j.

Then, when collecting generations $G_k \cdots G_n$, the modified sets of generations $G_0 \cdots G_{k-1}$ must be treated as root pointers.

The management of the memory areas for the generations, modified sets, etc. can get tedious; things can be simplified by having only two generations [4], and performance doesn't suffer much.

In practice, generational garbage collection performs extremely well; though it is typically implemented only for programming languages (like LISP, Scheme, ML, Smalltalk, etc.) where modification of older objects is relatively rare. In general, it is widely agreed that garbage collection need not take more than 5% of computation time.

4.6 Virtual Memory Hardware

The disadvantage of Baker's algorithm – the *only* thing that really causes it to be less efficient than Cheney's "stop-and-copy" algorithm – is the checking of every pointer fetched into registers to make sure it's not a from-space pointer. The disadvantage of generational collection – the *only* thing that could possibly make it slower than Cheney's algorithm – is the checking of every pointer assigned into an existing list cell.

Both of these checks can be approximated very cheaply by the virtual memory hardware available on most computers. The Appel-Ellis-Li algorithm [6] is a concurrent garbage collection algorithm (the garbage collector and the allocating program can run simultaneously, on the same processor or on different processors) with very low overhead and low latency – the allocating program is rarely suspended for more than a few dozen milliseconds. The algorithm is like Baker's algorithm, except that immediately after the registers are forwarded, the to-space is protected (by turning off the read and write accessibility bits in the virtual memory page tables). Then, as each page of to-space between *scan* and *next* is forwarded by the garbage collector, that page is made accessible.

When the allocating program fetches from a protected page of to-space, the collector immediately forwards all the pointers on that page, and makes the page accessible. The allocating program can then resume, and the only delay has been the time to forward one page, which is a few milliseconds. Newly allocated cells are put in an accessible (unprotected) region of to-space, and cause no page faults.

Thus, the chief disadvantage of Baker's algorithm – the need to spend an extra instruction on every fetch to check for a from-space pointer value – has been eliminated; it has been replaced by a cheap (practically free) hardware test that is already being performed by the hardware anyway for other reasons. Since the number of pointers that get forwarded is still the same as in Cheney's algorithm, the only extra overhead will be in the page-fault handler. And by the principle of locality, we would expect that a typical program will not touch many different pages before the collector has a chance to forward all the pages of to-space, and experience with one implementation has found the performance of this algorithm to be quite good.

Similarly, generational garbage collection can make use of virtual memory hardware [18]. Whenever a pointer is stored into an older generation, the location modified must be recorded in an "anomalous references" set. But we can mark all the older generations read-only in the page tables, and the first assignment to an older cell will cause a page fault. We handle the fault by putting the page address in an anomalous-references set, and marking the page read-write. Then, at garbage collection time, the collector must scan the entirety of each page in the set for possible roots of the newest generation(s).

In imperative programming languages like Pascal, Modula, Mesa, etc., where storing pointers into existing cells is very common, it is clear that observation 1 (about generational garbage collection) will not hold. However, there is no good evidence that there is *any* programming language that violates observations 1 and 2 over a large scale, i.e. we might modify observation 1 as follows:

1. A cell usually points to cells that are older than it, or at least not much newer.

Thus, most assignments of pointers will be into the newest generation, where there will be no page fault. If we assume that anomalous references in the older generations exhibit some locality (tend to be rare or clustered), then the number of distinct pages in the modified set will be small, and thus the number of page faults will also be small. With this scheme, assignments into the newest generation or into any recently modified cell will not incur the cost of a page fault. Thus, this scheme might work well even for imperative languages of the Algol family, where the modified observation 1 might hold.

4.7 Representation of Data

In most garbage collection schemes (but not all [9]) it is necessary for the collector to be able to distinguish pointers from non-pointers (characters, integers, reals, etc.); and to determine the length and format of each record. A language's compiler and runtime system must agree on the format of runtime data; many schemes have been used successfully [1,14,5].

When the word length of the machine is longer than the size of an address, then each pointer or integer can be tagged with a descriptor. A pointer to a two-word record (a cons cell, for example) would have a different tag than a pointer to a five-word record, etc. Then the garbage collector can know how much data to copy (or mark, in a mark-and-sweep collector) as it follows each pointer.

When the word length is not much longer than an address (as is increasingly the case), then a 1-bit tag can be used just to distinguish pointers from non-pointers. On modern 32-bit byte-addressible machines, where pointers tend to be multiples of 4 anyway, the low-order bit is typically used for this tag. Then it is necessary to put a descriptor at the beginning of each record explaining its length and format. A refinement of this method is to group records of a commonly-used format together in one range of addresses; then one descriptor suffices for a large group of records, as long as the garbage collector knows about the address-range convention. (See Chapter 1 for more on tagging schemes.)

In some implementations, it is undesirable to restrict the range of representable integers, so even a 1-bit tag is an intrusion. One solution is to encode in the record descriptor not just the number of fields, but an indication of which ones are pointers. This solution works well for Algol-like languages where the types of records are known at compile-time, but is awkward for languages like LISP and ML, where the descriptor would have to be constructed on-the-fly for each allocated record.

For statically-typed languages like Pascal or ML, the compiler can provide a map of the static typing to the collector [3]. Then, if the collector is told the types of the root pointers, it can follow the type-map with one hand while it follows the data with the other, and no tag bits at all are required! For polymorphic languages like ML it's not quite so easy, however, as some work is required to determine the types of the root pointers.

Finally, in some environments it is impossible to tell whether a word is a pointer or a non-pointer. This may be because of insufficiently strong compile-time type systems combined with a lack of run-time type information (e.g. in the C language), or in mixed-language systems. Mark-and-sweep collection can still be used here [9]; some objects may be spuriously marked because an integer was incorrectly seen as a pointer, but these objects just waste some storage and don't cause incorrect program behaviour. Obviously, copying and compacting collectors are more difficult to use here, since a "potential" pointer cannot be adjusted (when the object it points to is moved) in case it is really an integer. However, copying collection is still possible with sufficient care [8].

References

[1] J. Allen. *Anatomy of LISP*. McGraw-Hill, New York, 1978.

[2] A. W. Appel. Garbage collection can be faster than stack allocation. *Information Processing Letters*, 25(4):275–279, 1987.

[3] A. W. Appel. Runtime tags aren't necessary. *LISP and Symbolic Computation*, 2:153–162, 1989.

[4] A. W. Appel. Simple generational garbage collection and fast allocation. *Software – Practice/Experience*, 19(2):171–183, 1989.

[5] A. W. Appel. A runtime system. *LISP and Symbolic Computation*, 3(to appear), 1990.

[6] A. W. Appel, J. R. Ellis, and K. Li. Real-time concurrent collection on stock multiprocessors. *SIGPLAN Notices (Proc. SIGPLAN '88 Conf. on Prog. Lang. Design and Implementation)*, 23(7):11–20, 1988.

[7] H. G. Baker. List processing in real time on a serial computer. *Communications of the ACM*, 21(4):280–294, 1978.

[8] J. F. Bartlett. Compacting garbage collection with ambiguous roots. Technical Report 88/2, Digital Western Research Laboratory, Palo Alto, CA, 1988.

[9] H.-J. Boehm and M. Weiser. Garbage collection in an uncooperative environment. *Software – Practice/Experience*, 18(9):807–820, 1988.

[10] C. J. Cheney. A nonrecursive list compacting algorithm. *Communications of the ACM*, 13(11):677–678, 1970.

[11] J. Cohen. Garbage collection of linked data structures. *Computing Surveys*, 13(3):341–367, 1981.

[12] G. E. Collins. A method for overlapping and erasure of lists. *Communications of the ACM*, 3(12):655–657, 1960.

[13] R. R. Fenichel and J. C. Yochelson. A LISP garbage-collector for virtual-memory computer systems. *Communications of the ACM*, 12(11):611–612, 1969.

[14] R. E. Griswold and M. T. Griswold. *The Implementation of the Icon Programming Language*. Princeton University Press, Princeton, NJ, 1986.

[15] D. E. Knuth. *The Art of Computer Programming, vol. I: Fundamental Algorithms*. Addison Wesley, Reading, Mass., 1973.

[16] H. Lieberman and C. Hewitt. A real-time garbage collector based on the lifetimes of objects. *Communications of the ACM*, 23(6):419–429, 1983.

[17] J. McCarthy. Recursive functions of symbolic expressions and their computation by machine - I. *Communications of the ACM*, 3(1):184–195, 1960.

[18] R. A. Shaw. Improving garbage collector performance in virtual memory. Technical Report CSL-TR-87-323, Stanford University, 1987.

[19] D. M. Ungar. *The Design and Evaluation of a High Performance Smalltalk System*. MIT Press, Cambridge, Mass., 1986.

5   Concurrent Garbage Collection for C++

David L. Detlefs

5.1 Introduction

Automatic storage management, or garbage collection, is a feature usually associated with languages oriented toward "symbolic processing," such as Lisp or Prolog; it is seldom associated with "systems" languages, such as C and C++. The advantages of automatic storage management are obvious: since the system reliably determines when storage may be reclaimed, programs are simpler and less error-prone. Reasons typically cited for not providing garbage collection in a language are implementation difficulty and performance penalties. It is usually argued that garbage collection overhead is unacceptable for languages intended to support low-level systems work. This argument certainly has merit; however, its merit has declined for two reasons: 1) advances in garbage collection technology have made garbage collection overhead smaller, and 2) the boundary between "systems" and "applications" languages have become blurred. This paper will present measurements to support the first point. The second point is illustrated by the fact that Lisp is used as a "systems" language in the Lisp Machine operating system, while C extensions such as C++ [15] and Objective-C [7] are often used to build high-level applications. Other examples of languages intended to support a wide spectrum of applications include Cedar/Mesa, Modula-2+ and Modula-3, Clu, ML, and Eiffel; all provide garbage collection.

This chapter explores techniques for implementing garbage collection for C and C++. In particular, I present a concurrent, copying collection algorithm for C++: the program proper may proceed concurrently with the garbage collector. This concurrency results in performance improvements (of different kinds) on both unprocessors and multiprocessors. The rest of this paper is organized as follows: Section 5.2 poses two fundamental questions that any garbage collector must answer, and explains why these questions present difficulties for garbage collectors for C or C++. Section 5.3 describes how previous researchers have approached these problems. Section 5.5 discusses concurrent garbage collection, and how I merge concurrent collection with garbage collection techniques for C and C++. Section 5.6 presents some performance measurements. Section 5.7 describes some problems that my collector does not solve. Section 5.8 presents conclusions and suggestions for future work.

5.2   The Two Fundamental Garbage Collection Questions

Every garbage collection implementation must have a policy for answering two fundamental questions:

I. Given an object, what pointers does it contain?

II. Given a pointer, where is the start and end of the object it points to?

Question I is necessary to ensure that all accessible objects are found. Question II is
necessary to ensure that when a pointer is found, the (entire) object it actually points to
is retained.

The answers to these questions may be quite trivial. Lisp systems often settle Question
I by using *tagged data*; each data item contains a code indicating whether it is a pointer
or some "immediate" type, such as an integer. These tags are checked at run time to
determine how operations such as "+" should be executed. The garbage collectors may
use tags to decide which words in an object contain pointers. (See Chapter 1 for more
about tagging scheme.) Question II may be answered by requiring that all pointers refer
to the beginning of objects, and that all variable-sized objects contain an encoding of
their length. Fixed-size objects such as **cons** cells are often allocated in distinguished
areas of memory – the object size is known by the fact that it resides in the **cons** area.

Unfortunately, these simple answers are unsuitable for C and C++. The emphasis
these languages place on performance precludes the use of run-time type checking via
tags. Lisp compilers for stock hardware must generate instructions that mask off tag
bits from data values to recreate a "raw" data value suitable for the arithmetic or pointer
operations of the machine. Other instructions are needed to place tag bits in newly created
instructions. Measurements indicate that tag checking and manipulation can constitute as
much as 30% of the running time of a Lisp program [14]. The requirement that mutator
code behave differently in order to enable the garbage collector to function also limits
portability, since a special compiler must be used. Again, this is an example of mutator
cooperation. All these considerations indicate that for C and C++, tagged data is not an
adequate answer to Question I.

Question II also becomes more complicated, because C and C++ semantics allow
pointers into the interiors of objects. Consider the following C++ program:

```
char* str = new char[26];
strcpy(str, "This is a 25 char string.");
str += 10;
// GC occurs now;
str -= 10;
cout << str << "\n";
```

When the collection occurs, **str** is an *interior pointer*; it points into the interior of the object it references, rather than at the head of the object. A correct garbage collection must preserve the complete body of each accessible object, even objects that are only referenced by interior pointers. The code fragment above illustrates this: the programmer has every right to assume that the first ten characters of **str** will still be there after garbage collection. Thus, the collector must be able to locate the start of the string object referred to by the interior pointer **str**, as well as the end of the object.

5.3 Previous Work

This section describes approaches other researchers have taken to provide solutions to the questions of the previous section for C-like languages. The first two will be mark and sweep collectors, and the last a "mostly copying" collector.

5.3.1 *Conservative Mark and Sweep Collectors*

One possible answer to Question I results from observing that a collector need not collect *all* storage that the program is not using. Uncollected garbage will not affect the correctness of the program[1] as long as enough garbage is collected to allow allocation to continue. A collector that may leave some garbage uncollected is called a *conservative* collector. This strategy forms the basis for C garbage collection strategies proposed by Boehm and Weiser [5] and Caplinger [6].

The Boehm and Weiser collector and the Caplinger collector are both mark and sweep algorithms. Both answer Question I in the most conservative way: all properly aligned words are assumed to be "possible" pointers. If the value a word contains "points" into the heap when interpreted as a pointer, then the object "pointed" to is assumed to be accessible, and is marked. This conservative strategy could fail if many non-pointer data values are interpreted as pointers, causing many objects that are actually garbage to be retained in the collection. Neither Boehm and Weiser nor Caplinger observed this problem in the use of their collectors. The problem is probably avoided because even a large heap occupies only a small fraction of a full 32-bit address space, making the likelihood of an incorrect interpretation small. (Non-pointer data items are often integers, and integer variables tend to have quite small values.)

Each algorithm starts by considering the *roots* of the program; that is, the stack(s) and global variables. Each properly aligned word is considered as a pointer; if the word "points" to an unmarked object, that object is marked. When either collector finds that an object is referenced by a value that may be a pointer, it marks the object and

---

[1]In fact, one correct storage management policy would be never to attempt to reclaim unused storage at all. This may be a reasonable choice for short-lived programs with relatively small memory requirements.

considers the words in the object as pointers, recursively giving the same treatment to any umarked objects to which the words "point." (Caplinger explicitly presents this depth-first recursive marking procedure, which may consume large amounts of stack space in the collector. Boehm and Weiser do not specify a strategy. Note that constant-space marking algorithms exist [10].) When all the root objects have been considered, then all accessible objects are marked. Each algorithm then collects all unmarked storage.

Neither the Caplinger algorithm nor the Boehm and Weiser algorithm adequately answer Question II. Only pointers that point directly to the beginnings of objects will cause those objects to be retained. Thus, the garbage collector will malfunction if an object is referenced only by interior pointers. Interestingly, sufficient information is maintained by the Caplinger collector to deal with Question II, but it is not used. (See Section 5.4.3.) Boehm and Weiser note that they could have solved Question II at the cost of a more complicated marking algorithm, but did not implement this extension.

5.3.2 *"Mostly Copying" Collection*

The advantages of compaction make it desirable to design a copying garbage collector for C or C++. However, the problem of answering Question I without tagged data makes this a difficult undertaking. When a copying collector moves an object, it must update all pointers to that object. This means that the collector must be able to *reliably* locate all pointers in the system: it must exactly identify the set of words that contain pointers. It would be incorrect to simply assume that all data items that might be pointers are pointers, as is done in the conservative mark-and-sweep collectors discussed above. To see why, consider the following code fragment:

```
Foo* f = new foo;        // f happens to get 0x53f36
f = NULL;
int i = 0x53f36;         // Happens to be a relevant value
// Collection occurs now...
```

When the collection occurs, the stack contains a value for the integer variable i that looks like a pointer to the object allocated in the first line. However, if the collector treats i as a "real" pointer, it will copy the object and update the "pointer" i to refer to the new location. The program will observe this as a spontaneous change in the value of the integer variable i. Bartlett proposed a solution to this dilemma [3]. Essentially, his idea is to be conservative in the roots, but rely on "perfect knowledge" in the heap.

The first part of Bartlett's scheme is implemented by *promoting* pages containing objects that may be referenced from pointers in the stacks and globals instead of copying those objects. Unlike a traditional copying collector, Bartlett's heap does not contain two physically distinct semi-spaces. Instead, each page has an associated "space identifier"

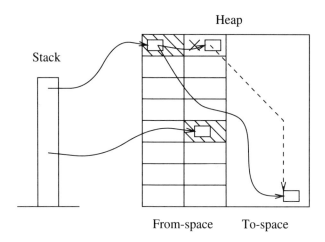

Figure 5.1: Bartlett's "mostly copying" collector.

indicating what space it is currently a member of. Thus, "from-space" and "to-space" may be distributed throughout the heap. When a stack value is found that (when interpreted as a pointer) would point to a heap object, the space identifier for that page is changed to that of "to-space." This conceptually "copies" all the objects on that page into to-space. However, since the objects do not actually change location, the data value that "pointed" to the object (which may not be a pointer at all) is not modified. Figure 5.1 illustrates this process. The shaded from-space pages have been promoted because they contain objects that are referenced by possible pointers in the roots. These are now part of to-space. After the roots have been scanned, a normal copying collection begins. The figure shows an object on a non-promoted page in from-space that was referenced by an objects on a promoted page. Following the normal copying collection algorithm, the object on the non-promoted page has been copied to a to-space page, a forwarding pointer (shown with a dashed line) left in the from-space copy, and the pointer in the object on the promoted page updated to refer to the new location. This technique is used to "copy" all objects that may be referenced from the stacks or globals into to-space; the objects that may be referenced are marked during this phase.

In order to do some copying and achieve some compaction, another technique must be used in the heap. Bartlett relies on a pair of conventions:

1. All **struct**'s must be coded so that all pointer fields occur contiguously at the beginning of the **struct**.

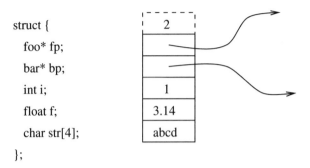

```
struct {
    foo* fp;
    bar* bp;
    int i;
    float f;
    char str[4];
};
```

Figure 5.2: Header structure in Bartlett's collector.

2. All calls to **malloc** are replaced by calls to Bartlett's **gc_alloc**, which takes the same *size* argument as **malloc**, but also an additional argument indicating the number of pointer fields in the type being allocated.

Gc_alloc inserts its second argument into a word preceding the block it allocates for the object, as shown in Figure 5.2. The collector can then use this field to determine how many fields in the beginning of an object to interpret as pointers. If the programmer correctly provides this information to **gc_alloc**, then the collector can safely copy the objects these pointers refer to, and update the pointers.

A final problem that Bartlett's collector must solve is the problem of "unsure references." For Bartlett, these arise when a program creates a continuation object, which essentially results in register values and part of a stack being stored in the heap. When scanning continuation objects, the collector has no more knowledge about which parts are pointers than it does for the stack: the references in the continuation are "unsure." In general-purpose C and C++ code, unsure references can arise because of **union** types, as shown below.

```
union Unsure {
  char* str;
  int i;
};
```

At collection time, the collector does not know whether this **union** contains a pointer or an integer.

Bartlett solves the problem of unsure references in the heap in same way as for the stack: the pages containing the objects the unsure references "point" to are promoted.

However, this raises a different problem. Assume that the collector scans object A, finding a sure reference to object X. It copies X and updates A's pointer. Later in the collection, object B is found to contain an unsure reference to X. If the collector promotes X's page, the sharing structure of the program is not preserved; after the collection A and B will no longer point to the same object. Bartlett solves this by making collection a two pass process. In the first pass, the detection of a pointer to a from-space object causes that object to be copied to to-space, and a forwarding pointer to the new-location to be inserted into the from-space copy. However, the pointer that caused the object to be copied is not changed. Similarly, pointers referring to from-space objects that have already been copied are not updated by following the forwarding pointer, as they would be in a normal copying collection. Unsure references found during this pass cause page promotions. Since all retained objects are scanned in this first pass, all unsure references will be found. Thus, all promoted pages are identified in this first pass. The second pass adjusts pointers. If a pointer is found to point to a from-space page, then it is updated by following the forwarding pointer left by the first pass. If it points to a to-space page, the page it points to must be a promoted page, so the pointer is not modified.

Bartlett's algorithm successfully integrates conservative and copying collection. One cost of this integration is the space wasted on promoted pages by objects that are not marked; that space is never utilized. However, his measurements show that this waste is small for the test cases he tried; only a few pages are promoted during each collection. Still, Bartlett's algorithm is incomplete in some respects; Section 5.4.1 examines these deficiencies and how my algorithm remedies them. (Note that this incompleteness is deliberate; Bartlett's system was intended for use by C code generated by his Scheme-to-C translator, not as a general purpose collector for C or C++.)

5.3.3 Mark and Sweep vs. Copying

I will complete this section by comparing the mark and sweep algorithms with the copying algorithm. A major advantage of the mark and sweep algorithms is that they allow the program to continue to use explicit **free** (**delete** in C++) commands in cases when the programmer has determined that storage is no longer in use. Both Boehm and Weiser's and Caplinger's collectors offer this facility.[2] Such collectors can also be used as "**malloc** debuggers" for programs not intended to use garbage collection. In this mode, an explicit **free** sets a flag in the header of the freed object. If the collector

---

[2]The Boehm & Weiser collector is intended for use with a C-producing compiler for Boehm's language Russell, much as Bartlett's collector is intended for use with his Scheme-to-C compiler. Compile-time analysis can sometimes determine with complete safety that an object is inaccessible, and the compiler can explicitly **free** the object in the C code it emits.

determines that an object with this flag set is probably accessible, it can emit an error message indicating that the object may have been deallocated prematurely. Support for explicit **free** could probably be grafted onto a copying collector, but it would make the allocation routine more complicated and slower, since it would have to check to see if an allocation request could be satisfied from a free list. Finally, mark and sweep collectors do not move objects, preserving the "normal" C property that an object's address does not change during its lifetime. Section 5.7.1 examines how violation of this property can invalidate some programs.

Copying collection has several advantages. The obvious advantage is that copying collection offers compaction. Another advantage is in algorithmic complexity: copying collection takes time proportional to the amount of retained storage, whereas mark and sweep algorithms, because of the sweep phase, must traverse the entire heap. In modern virtual memory systems, where very large heaps are practical, the ratio of retained memory to total heap size can approach zero [2]. Finally, copying collection is compatible with advanced techniques that can make garbage collection less intrusive: *generational* collection and *concurrent* collection. Each of these strives to minimize interruptions caused by garbage collection. Generational collection attempts to break collection into a number of small, fast collections. Bartlett has recently modified his "mostly copying" collector to use generational techniques [4]. Generational collection is also discussed in Chapter 3 of this book. Concurrent collection allows the mutator to proceed concurrently with the collector. I have taken this latter path; Section 5.5 details this work, as well as briefly discussing generational techniques.

5.4   My Copying Collector for C++

5.4.1   Incompleteness of Bartlett's System

Bartlett's collector was intended to support only the subset of C emitted by his Scheme-to-C compiler. As a result, there are several ways in which Bartlett's collector is not adequate for general purpose C or C++. The goal of my collector will be to eliminate those inadequacies to the greatest extent possible, producing a compiler/collector system that will work for most off-the-shelf C++ programs.

One problem with using Bartlett's collector is that programmers must manually modify code to use it. Structures must have pointers only at the beginnings of their extent, and all calls to **malloc** must be replaced with a call to **gc_alloc** that correctly gives the number of pointers in the structure being allocated. The latter point is an only an inconvenience, but still source of possible error. The requirement that all structures contain pointers only at the beginning is a more serious deficiency; some programs cannot be modified to meet this requirement, as the following example shows.

```
struct A {              struct B{
  int i;                  A aaa[3];
  char* str;              int j;
  Foo* f;               };
  float f;
};
```

Struct A can be reorganized so that all pointers are at the start, but **struct** B cannot. Thus, some more complicated encoding of pointer locations must be used.

Another problem with Bartlett's collector is that, like the other collectors for C and C++, it does not completely address Question II: it does not guarantee that an object will survive collection even if it is only referenced by one or more interior pointers. One of the variations of his algorithm that Bartlett presents ("**GC-2**," [3, p. 20]) handles interior pointers found in the roots, but not interior pointers found in heap objects. It may be that Bartlett's Scheme compiler guarantees that no interior pointers appear in heap objects. In any case, arbitrary C or C++ code can contain interior pointers in heap objects, so Bartlett's algorithm must be extended. Section 5.4.3 details how I use a technique similar to Bartlett's to handle all interior pointers.

5.4.2 Finding Pointers

As noted above, a mechanism more general than Bartlett's "number-of-pointers-at-the-front" scheme is needed to allow a collector to reliably find pointers in heap objects. In [4], Bartlett proposes and implements a *callback* mechanism. At allocation time, the user provides the address of a user-written "pointer-finding" procedure. This address is stored in the object header. When the collector needs to find the pointers in the object, it calls this procedure, which then calls a publicly-declared garbage collection function with the address of each pointer in the object. This scheme is completely general, since the user has complete control over the pointer-finding procedure. Moreover, this scheme can eliminate the unsure reference problem for **union**'s: such **union**'s are almost always used in conjunction with another structure field indicating which member of the union is currently in use. The user can write the pointer-finding procedure to incorporate this knowledge.[3]

A disadvantage of this callback scheme is that programmers, rather than a compiler, must generate the pointer-finding procedures for their classes. While this requirement allows Bartlett's collector to work with any compiler, it is an inconvenience to program-mers, and increases the likelihood of errors that will be particularly difficult to discover.

---

[3]This does not eliminate the unsure reference problem for continuations, since no such external knowledge is available for continuations.

For example, consider a user who adds a pointer field to a class, but neglects to update the pointer-finding procedure of the class. Bartlett's collector has a mode in which it uses conservative-style heuristics to attempt to detect such omissions, but users may neglect to use this mode.[4] Since the purpose of garbage collection is to make programs safer, I have chosen to use only automated methods that require as little user modification of programs as possible.

The mechanism used to locate pointers in my collector is a more sophisticated version of Bartlett's original scheme. The allocation routine inserts an *object header* preceding each object. One of the elements of an object header is an *object descriptor*, which takes one of the following forms:

- A *bitmap*: a word in which the "1" bits correspond to words containing pointers in the actual object. Bitmap descriptors are used only for objects that do not contain any unsure references and whose pointers only occupy the first 32 words (assuming a 32-bit architecture).

- An *indirect* descriptor. This is a pointer to an array of bytes that is interpreted by the collector. Different byte values encode sure references, unsure references, skips (non-pointer data), and repeated instances of smaller descriptions. Repeats are useful for encoding arrays, and nested repeats allow objects of any finite size to be represented.

- A *fast indirect* descriptor. Byte-interpretation of indirect descriptors turns out to be somewhat slow, so for all but the most complicated types the fast indirect representation is used. Here the object descriptor is a pointer to an array of integers. The first integer in the array is a repetition count, indicating how many times the rest of the the descriptor should be scanned. This convention allows fast indirect descriptors to describe large arrays. Each integer after the first indicates the number of words that must be skipped to find each successive pointer in the object. A negative integer indicates that the next reference is found by skipping the absolute value of the integer, but that the reference is unsure. Zero terminates the array.

To illustrate these object descriptors, consider the following types:

```
struct X {              struct Y {
  int i;                  X aaa[3];
  char* str;              union {
  float* fp;                int i;
  int j;                    char* s;
}                         }
                        }
```

---

[4]Consider the use of **lint** by C programmers...

Struct X can be described by a bitmap descriptor 0x6 – the second and the third bits
are on. **Struct Y** cannot be described by a bitmap descriptor, because it contains an
unsure reference. It must be described by an indirect descriptor pointing to a byte array
corresponding to

REPEAT(3), SKIP(1), SURE(2) SKIP(1), REPEAT_END, UNSURE(1), DESC_END.

Alternatively, **struct Y** can be described by a fast indirect descriptor, a pointer to the
integer array [1, 2, 1, 3, 1, 3, 1, -2, 0].

Much as Bartlett's allocation function requires an argument indicating the number of
pointers in the object or a pointer to a callback procedure, my allocator requires an
object descriptor for the type being allocated. It would obviously be time-consuming
and error prone to require users to create these fairly complicated encodings. Instead,
I have modified the AT&T C++ 1.2.1 compiler (**cfront**) to derive these encodings
automatically. Section 5.5.3 describes this implementation more fully.

5.4.3   Finding Objects

Previous collectors for C and C++ have not adequately addressed Question II, how
to reliably identify the whole object pointed to by a pointer. The Boehm and Weiser
collector was intended to work with machine-generated code that was known not to use
interior pointers. Caplinger argued that interior pointers were rare, and therefore not
worth handling.[5] Bartlett presents a variation on his basic algorithm that handles derived
pointers, but apparently only when they occur in the stack or registers [3, p. 20]. It
would be preferable to find a solution that correctly handles interior pointers wherever
they occur without imposing much cost in the normal case, where pointers point to object
heads.

The version of Bartlett's collector that recognizes some interior pointers does so using
an *allocation bitmap*, an array of bits separate from the heap. Each bit in the bitmap
corresponds to a word in the heap. The allocation routine of the garbage collector
maintains the invariant that a bit in the bitmap is set if and only if the corresponding
word in the heap is the start of an object. My collector maintains the same data structure,
but uses it to locate the start of the object referenced by each pointer, not just pointers
in the stacks or globals. Since most pointers actually point to the head of an object,
rather than to an object interior, the collector optimizes this case using a C++ inline
function. This function quickly checks the bit corresponding to the pointer, returning the
pointer if the bit is set. It is only if the the pointer is an interior pointer and the bit is

---

[5]Still, Caplinger found that his collector would not work with the Sun window system, and speculated that
interior pointers may have been caused the problem.

not set that a search procedure is called. This procedure locates the start of the object referenced by an interior pointer by scanning the bitmap for the first "1" bit preceding the bit corresponding to the pointer. The word corresponding to the "1" bit begins an object. An object header will immediately precede this object in the heap. For safety, the search procedure verifies that the original pointer lies within the extent of the object, as determined by the object start and the size field of the object header.

5.5   Concurrent Copying Collection for C++

5.5.1   Concurrent Garbage Collection

Even if a garbage collector entails little overhead when amortized over the lifetime of a program, its use may still be unacceptable in some applications if the mutator must halt for the duration of each collection. This is especially true of interactive applications. This section describes how concurrent collection can meet these real-time constraints, and presents an implementation that combines garbage collection for C and C++ with concurrent collection.

Concurrent collection allows the mutator to resume while garbage collection is still in progress. When run on a multiprocessor, concurrent collection can decrease total running time by allowing the collector and mutator to work at the same time. As always, the collector must ensure that all accessible objects are retained. Concurrency makes this more complicated, since the mutator may change references while collection is in progress. Consider an object X referenced by a pointer in object A at the start of a collection. If the mutator destroys this reference and moves it elsewhere before the collector scans A, X may never be copied (or marked.) Thus, the mutator and the collector must somehow be coordinated. Dijkstra, Lamport, Martin, Scholten and Steffens [8] and Kung and Song [11] present algorithms for doing concurrent mark-and-sweep collection. These require mutator cooperation: the mutator must "color" an object whenever it creates a reference to it during collection. Again, I will not consider algorithms requiring mutator cooperation.

Another way to coordinate the mutator and collector is to *serialize* a copying collection, so that the entire collection appears to the mutator to occur at one point in time. Before this point, the mutator observers only pointers into from-space; after this point, only pointers into to-space. North and Reppy achieve approximately this result for their language Pegasus by requiring the mutator and the collector to perform all object updates atomically, presumably using a lock in each object [12]. The mutator must not modify an object without holding the object lock, and the collector must obtain the object lock before scanning it. Their concurrent collection is not completely serialized; the mutator can observe from-space pointers during collection. They maintain correctness by requiring their compiler to insert extra code into each operation that modifies an object. This extra code checks whether a collection is in progress and the object has already been scanned; if so, it causes the collector to rescan the object. Without rescanning, the mutator could insert a pointer to an otherwise-unreferenced from-space object into a scanned object, and the collection would not copy the from-space object to to-space. I will not consider this scheme further because of the required mutator cooperation.

Ellis, Li, and Appel [9] present an algorithm that is somewhat similar to North and Reppy's, but achieves complete serialization without requiring mutator cooperation. When a collection begins, the mutator is suspended for a short time while the objects accessible from the roots are copied to to-space. These objects are "locked" by the collector, preventing mutator access. When the root scan is finished, the mutator is allowed to resume while the to-space objects are scanned. Whenever the mutator attempts to access a to-space object, it must wait until the collector has scanned it and "unlocked" it. This maintains the invariant that the mutator never observes from-space pointers during a collection. The main innovation of Ellis, Li, and Appel is the use of virtual memory primitives to simulate locking. To "lock" the objects on a page, the collector protects the page from the mutator. It also sets up an exception handler to field any protection faults caused by an attempted mutator access to the protected page. The exception handler causes the mutator to wait until the collector has scanned and unprotected the page, and then allows the mutator to resume.

5.5.2 Adaptation of Concurrent Collection to C++

It was fairly easy to incorporate the techniques of Ellis, Li, and Appel to my C++ collector. Since the mutator and the collector both perform allocation during a collection, I had to add mutual exclusion locks to create critical sections in appropriate places. Ellis, Li, and Appel [9] describe an implementation for the Taos [17] operating system used on the DEC Firefly multiprocessor workstation. In order to allow the collector to protect pages from the mutator, they needed to add special kernel calls to the operating system. I targeted my collector for the Mach [1] operating system. The Mach interface allowed me to implement their algorithm using only existing user-level calls.

The garbage collector takes the form of a separate Mach task. I will describe the interaction between the collector and mutator tasks here; details of the concurrent collection algorithm are later in this section. The collector task is created only when the first collection occurs; hence, a program that never needs a collection does not incur the overhead of task creation. The collector and mutator tasks share the heap and the data structures needed to manage the heap. At the start of the first collection, the mutator task creates the collector task and sends the new task its Mach *task port*. This gives the collector task the capability to perform kernel calls on behalf of the mutator task. The collector now enters a loop where it waits for a STARTGC message from the mutator. The mutator then sends one of these messages. To initiate subsequent collections, the mutator will simply send another STARTGC message, without creating another task. Following the algorithm of [9], the collector task now uses the Mach **task_suspend** call to temporarily halt the mutator task. The collector next calls Mach's **vm_read** primitive to map the pages containing the stack(s) of the mutator task into its address space. (Tasks that share stack pages are highly unlikely to work correctly, so shared memory cannot be used here.) The collector task uses these copied stacks as the roots of the collection. Any from-space page containing an object referenced from a mutator stack is promoted to to-space. When the root scan is complete, the collector allows the mutator to **task_resume**, but not before creating a new *exception port* for the mutator task. The collector creates a *handler dispatch* thread that waits for messages on this port. When the collector allocates a to-space page to hold objects it copies from from-space, it protects the page from the mutator task using the **vm_protect** call. The page is only unprotected after the collector has scanned it and transformed all its pointers into to-space pointers. When a mutator thread attempts to access a protected page, Mach translates this protection violation into a message to the exception port. The handler dispatch thread receives this message, and creates a new *handler* thread that waits until the desired page has been scanned and unprotected, and then sends a return code message that allows the appropriate mutator thread to resume. Before waiting, the handler thread also moves the desired page to the front of the list of pages to be scanned. This causes the collector to scan and unprotect it sooner, decreasing the time the mutator must be idle.

Another way in which Mach eased the implementation of my collector was in its handling of virtual memory. When virtual memory is allocated in Mach, no cost is incurred until the page is actually accessed. Thus, it is very easy to expand the heap. I initially allocate a very large heap of 128 Mbytes, of which I use only 1 Mbyte. (Of course, the programmer may adjust the initial heap size.) After each collection, the fraction of storage retained is evaluated; if this exceeds a threshold, then the portion of the heap currently used is doubled in size. This keeps collection costs down by always making retained storage a small fraction of the heap size. Some advantage might be gained by measuring system resource utilization to decide between collection and heap expansion. If physical memory and sufficient swap space are available, then it is probably preferable to do a cheap heap expansion instead of a relatively expensive collection.

Concurrent collection imposes a constraint on the C++ programs that use it: programs using concurrent collection cannot contain unsure references. Section 5.3.2 explained why unsure references necessitated a two-pass algorithm, where one pass scans and copies objects, and the other pass adjusts pointers. If a two-pass algorithm is used, however, most concurrency is lost. The collector cannot unprotect a to-space page until it contains no pointers into from-space. Since pointers are only adjusted during the second pass, no pages may be unprotected during the first pass. The mutator would essentially be halted completely for the first half of the collection.

To avoid this problem, my modified C++ compiler (described more fully in Section 5.5.3) forbids the existence of unsure references in the heap. Presently, an error message is generated whenever code is encountered that attempts to **new** a type containing an unsure reference. Note that the compiler could automatically eliminate unsure references in almost all cases by a simple transformation:

```
                                    struct A {
                                      union {
                                        int i;
     union A {                        float f;
       int i;                       };
       char* s;      becomes         union {
       float f;                        char* s;
       foo* fp;                        foo* fp;
     };                             };
                                    };
```

The **union** becomes a **struct** whose members are *anonymous unions*. In C++, a **struct** may contain unnamed **union**'s. The members of such a **union** share storage, but may be named as if they were independent members of the **struct**. All the pointer members in the **union** are moved to one **union** in the **struct**, and all non-pointer members are moved to another. The space requirements of the type increase by at most a factor of two. Though this would handle essentially all cases that occur in practice, pathological cases complicate the construction of a general algorithm.

Forbidding unsure references in the heap allows a one-pass instead of a two-pass algorithm. Pointers to from-space objects can be updated to point to to-space copies of those objects during the scanning pass.

5.5.3 Implementation

My garbage collector takes the form of an instance of a C++ class called **GcHeap**. **GcHeap** has a member function **alloc** that allocates storage from the heap, beginning garbage collections when there is not enough free space in the heap to satisfy allocation requests. The implementation of this class and its supporting types form a Unix library, **libGc.a**. Because my goal was the ability to make existing C++ programs use garbage collection automatically, I created a special version of a C++ compiler oriented towards my allocator. As previously mentioned, I modified AT&T **cfront** 1.2.1. (This is a compiler that uses C as an assembly language, for portability.) When this modified compiler compiles a C++ file, it first implicitly includes a header file that declares the **GcHeap** type, so that the **alloc** function can be used. The compiler computes and remembers an appropriate object descriptor for each type declared in a program. All calls to the C++ operator **new** are changed to calls to **GcHeap::alloc**. This function expects an extra **ObjHead** argument containing an object descriptor for the type being allocated; this object descriptor is provided by looking in the previously constructed table. If the object descriptor is one of the indirect descriptors, then the compiler defines the appropriate static array of characters or integers. An indirect object descriptor is only defined once per type per file, and only if an object of that type is allocated in the file. An object descriptor is also associated with each global variable containing pointers in the program, and a list of the addresses of all such variables is defined for later use by the collector. Calls to **delete** are ignored by translating them into null C statements, and destructors are similarly eliminated. (Section 5.7.2 discusses how this decision alters the semantics of the language.)

The collector works in much the same way as Bartlett's. As previously mentioned, the storage allocator inserts an object header before each object, containing the size of the object and an object descriptor. The complete definition of an object header adds space for a *marked* bit and a *scanned* bit. These are reset at allocation time. As in Bartlett's algorithm, my collector maintains a queue of new space pages, the *ns_queue*. A page is on the queue if and only if it contains objects that need to be scanned. My collector also uses a queue of object addresses called the *lmo_queue* (for *late marked object queue*) to handle intra-page references found while it scans a promoted page.

Figure 5.3 shows the top level of the collection algorithm. A collection starts by setting the *ns_queue* to the empty queue. It then scans the stacks of all mutator threads. Whenever the collector finds a word on a stack that references a heap object when interpreted as a pointer, it sets the marked bit of that object, promotes the page(s) on which the object resides, and appends the page to the *ns_queue*. The collector then scans every global data object, and every page on the *ns_queue*. All objects on non-promoted heap pages are scanned. When scanning a promoted page, however, the collector considers only marked objects. When the collector finishes scanning a marked object, it resets the *marked* bit, and sets the *scanned* bit. This prevents it from scanning the object again. Scanning objects on a promoted page may reveal further accessible objects on the page that must be scanned. The **scan_object** procedure (described below) enqueues the addresses of these objects on the *lmo_queue*. Therefore, the collector scans all objects on the *lmo_queue* before finishing with a promoted page.

```
void collect() {
   ns_queue = empty_queue();
   scan_stacks();
   scan_globals();
   scan_heap();
}

void scan_heap() {
   while (!ns_queue.empty()) {
      int page = ns_queue.deq();
      scan_page(page);
      unprotect(page);
   }
}

void scan_page(int page) {
   if (promoted(page)) {
      lmo_queue = empty_queue();
      for (each marked object O on page) {
         scan_object(O);
         set scanned bit and clear marked bit of O;
      }
      while (!lmo_queue.empty()) {
         O = lmo_queue.deq();
         scan_object(O);
      }

   } else {   // Not a promoted page: scan all objects.
      for (each object O on page)
         scan_object(O);
   }
}
```

Figure 5.3: Overall concurrent collection algorithm.

Figure 5.4 shows the algorithm used to scan individual objects. **Scan_object**
considers each object referenced by the object being scanned. Nothing needs to be done
if the referenced object has already been scanned or copied. If the referenced object has
not been scanned, the collector must ensure that it is scanned later. How it does this
depends on the state of the page the referenced object resides on. Consider first the case
in which the page is promoted. For such pages, the collector first considers whether the
page has been scanned or not. If the page has not been scanned, then merely marking
the object will ensure that it is considered when the page is eventually scanned. If the
page happens to be the page currently being scanned, the address of the referenced object
is enqueued on the *lmo_queue*. The scanned bit of the object is also set to prevent the
object from being inserted on the queue twice. Finally, if the page has already been
scanned, then the referenced object is marked, and the page is moved to the end of the
ns_queue to ensure that it is scanned again. Until the referenced object is scanned, it
may contain from-space pointers. To preserve the fundamental invariant of concurrent
collection, the mutator must be prevented from accessing this object until the object
is scanned. The collector therefore reprotects the page. Now consider the case where
the page of the referenced object is not promoted. The collector copies the referenced
object to a new-space page and leaves a forwarding pointer in the object header of the
from-space copy (overwriting the object descriptor). If the page the object is copied to
has already been scanned, then it must be reprotected and enqueued on the *ns_queue*.
This case arises only rarely.

5.6   Performance Measurements

5.6.1   Test Cases

I have measured garbage collection performance on three non-trivial programs. The first
is **cfront** itself. I used my modified **cfront** compiler (henceforth **gc_cfront**) to
compile a version of **cfront** that uses garbage collection. I then ran this on a C++
input file large enough to cause garbage collection. (Coincidentally, I use one of the
source files of **cfront** as this input file.) The second test case is a simulator for
communications traffic in a hypercube network, courtesy of Donald Lindsay at Carnegie
Mellon University. I will refer to this as **hyper**. The third test program, **grobner**,
is from computer algebra, courtesy of Jean-Philippe Vidal and Edmund Clarke, also at
CMU. It computes the *Grobner basis* of a set of polynomials. The Grobner basis allows
the efficient solution of the question of whether a new polynomial is a member of the
algebraic ideal formed by original set of polynomials. This program is distinguished
by the fact that it is a parallel program that exhibits approximately linear speedup on a
multiprocessor.

```
void scan_object(Object O) {
    for (each possible pointer P in O) {
        Object O2 = *P;
        if (O2 has a forwarding pointer F) {
            P = F;
            return;
        }
        if (O2 has scanned bit set)] return;
        // Otherwise...
        int page = obj2page(O2);
        if (promoted(page)) {
            if (unscanned(page)) {
                set marked bit of O2;
            } else if (being_scanned(page)) {
                set scanned bit of O2;
                lmo_queue.enq(O2);
            } else {
                // Page must have been scanned already.
                set marked bit of O2;
                protect(page);
                ns_queue.enq(page);
            }
        } else { // The page of O2 is promoted.
            // Note that unsure references are not allowed.
            Object O3 = GcHeap::alloc(sizeof(O2), ObjHead(O2));
            O3 = O2;
            set forwarding pointer in O2 to address of O3;
            set P to point to O3;
            int O3_page = obj2page(O3));
            if (scanned(O3_page)) {
                ns_queue.enq(O3_page);
                protect(O3_page);
            }
        }
    }
}
```

Figure 5.4: Concurrent **scan_object** algorithm.

5.6.2   Allocation Efficiency

The first set of measurements I present considers allocation only, ignoring collection. Allocation in a garbage collected heap can be quite efficient, since the allocator normally needs only to increment a pointer by the size of the object, and return that pointer's old value. In fact, Appel has shown how architecture-specific optimizations and virtual memory protection manipulation can be used to reduce heap allocation to as few as two machine instructions on some architectures (e.g., Vax) [2]. Allocation in my heap cannot be quite this efficient, unfortunately, since the allocator must insert an object header before the object and set the appropriate bit in the allocation bitmap to enable later garbage collection. Figure 5.5 compares the cost of the allocator used in my garbage-collected heap (call this `gc-alloc`) with the cost of two other storage allocators. `Malloc` is the allocator in the local C library at my site. This implementation of `malloc` is a "power-of-two" allocator: the size of every allocated block is a power of two, and all unused blocks of the same size are linked together in a free list. An allocation request is rounded to the next higher power of two, and satisfied by returning the head of the corresponding free list. `Falloc` represents a family of fixed-size allocators. Each object size in Figure 5.5 corresponds to an allocator built especially for that object size. Each `falloc` allocates a relatively large chunk of storage, and breaks it up into blocks of the given size, linked in a free list. Requests are satisfied from this free list until it is exhausted, and another chunk must be allocated. This test was performed on a Digital Equipment Corporation MicroVax III.[6]

Figure 5.5 shows that for a given object size, a fixed-size allocator is always better than either `malloc` or `gc-alloc`. A `falloc` should be better than `malloc` because it avoids the computation `malloc` performs to find the appropriate free list to allocate from. Also, it allocates only as much storage as is needed. `Malloc` and `gc-alloc` perform similarly for object sizes that are close to powers of two. `Gc-alloc` shows an advantage, though, for an object size that is between powers of two, such as 75. Here, `malloc` returns a 128 byte block for each request, wasting almost half of each block. `Gc-alloc` can allocate contiguous blocks of any size, wasting no storage. Thus, for "in-between" object sizes, malloc requires more virtual memory pages from the operating system than `gc-alloc` (or a `falloc` for that object size) requires, and therefore takes more time.

5.6.3   Garbage Collection Overhead

In this section, I will investigate the performance impact of garbage collection for the three test programs described above. I will first consider the cost of garbage collection

---

[6]MicroVax is a trademark of the Digital Equipment Corporation.

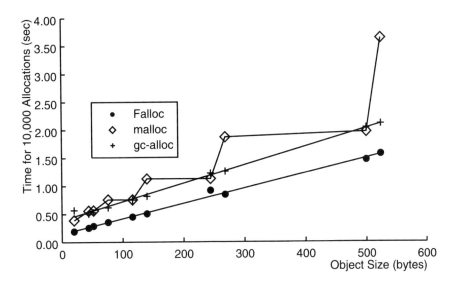

Figure 5.5: Comparing various storage allocators.

independent of concurrency concerns. Table 5.1 shows measurements of all three test programs, run on the same MicroVax III uniprocessor used in the previous test. Each program was run with a flag set causing the collector to inhibit concurrency; the mutator task was suspended for the duration of each collection, exactly as in a classical stop-and-copy collector. Each test used the default initial heap size of 1 Mbyte. I ran each test 4 times; the results shown are the averages of the best 3 of those runs.

Row 4 ("% Freed Storage") gives the average fraction of a semi-space that was freed by collection. Row 7 ("Total GC Time") sums the elapsed times of the garbage collections. The number in in parentheses is the percentage of total execution time used by garbage collection. Row 8 shows the percentage of total elapsed time during which collection was in progress. Row 9 ("Elapsed Time/GC") gives the length of an average collection. Row 10 ("Time/Mbyte collected") divides the garbage collection time by the amount of storage collected, i.e., the size of a semi-space. For comparison, Boehm and Weiser quote measurements of 2.4 seconds/Mbyte for their mark-and-sweep collector running on a Sun 3/260 [5]. Row 11 ("Time w/o GC") gives the performance of the "normal" program on the given input.[7] Row 12 ("GC Overhead") shows the fraction by which the

---

[7]For **cfront**, I interpreted "normal" to exclude AT&T allocation optimizations that essentially create a **falloc**-style fixed-size allocator for each important class. The version of **cfront** whose performance is shown in Row 10 uses the standard Unix **malloc/free** routines. I felt that this was a fairer comparison, given the amount of programming effort involved in these optimizations. For the other two programs, Row 10

Measurement	cfront	hyper	grobner
1. Objects allocated (1000's)	49.0	11.3	163.3
2. Mbytes allocated	1.48	0.58	4.07
3. Final Heap Size (Mbyte)	4.0	2.0	1.0
4. Freed Storage	45%	54%	88%
5. Total Elapsed Time (sec)	23.7	61.1	43.9
6. Number of Collections	2	1	11
7. Total GC Time (sec)	8.6	6.2	4.8
8. GC as percent of ET	36%	10%	11%
9. Elapsed Time/GC (sec)	4.3	6.2	0.4
10. Time/Mbyte collected (sec)	5.7	12.5	0.9
11. Time w/o GC (sec)	18.4	56.1	43.2
12. **GC Overhead**	**29%**	**9%**	**2%**

Table 5.1: Non-concurrent collection on a uniprocessor.

total running time of the garbage collecting version (Row 5) exceeds the running time of the "normal" program.

In the `cfront` test, garbage collection is in progress for approximately one-third (36%) of execution, making the running time 29% longer than non-GC'ing `cfront`. These are comparable with numbers reported in the literature for Lisp programs [18,13]. The `hyper` test requires only one collection, consuming 10% of the running time. **Hyper**'s single collection is dominated by the cost of scanning a single large static array that contains pointers. The `grobner` example shows excellent performance. Collection is in progress for about 11% of the total running time of the program. Though there are a relatively large number of collections, each is quite short. The running time of garbage-collecting `grobner` is only 2% greater than the running time of the original program shown in Row 10. Apparently, faster allocation almost balances collection overhead.

One lesson to draw from this data is that the performance of a garbage collector can depend heavily on properties of the program being collected, such as average object size, number of pointers per object, rate at which objects become garbage, etc. **Cfront** is in some ways a worst case for copying garbage collection, because compilers construct and retain large data structures (parse trees, symbol tables, etc.) during compilation. In

shows the result of running the program as I received it.

the runs above, an average of 55% of the allocated storage was retained in a collection, despite the fact that the heap size was doubled twice. Thus, collections free relatively little storage, and copy and scan a large amount of retained storage. A generational collector would probably perform better on compiler-like programs, because long-lived data would be moved to a seldom-collected generation. On the other hand, theorem provers such as the **grobner** example are well suited to copying collection, because they allocate much memory for short-term calculation, but retain little storage. For programs of this type, a full copying collection is similar in cost to a generational collection.

5.6.4   Concurrency

Even if the overall overhead due to garbage collection is acceptable, the use of garbage collection may still impose delays unacceptable in some applications. Interactive and real-time systems are the obvious examples. This section examines to what extent concurrent garbage collection can minimize these delays.

There are two ways in which a user of a program using concurrent garbage collection may notice the effects of collection. First, the collector may require the mutator to stop completely for some period of time. For example, in the current implementation of my collector, the mutator must stop completely while the collector scans stacks and global variables. Even if the individual delays are too short to be individually noticable, the user may notice the second effect: the aggregate effect of the delays may cause the perceived execution rate of the program to decrease. I will attempt to measure the magnitude of both forms of interruption. I will first consider uniprocessor measurements, then multiprocessor measurements.

Table 5.2 shows data on the duration of garbage collector interruptions in each of the test programs. Again, this test was run on a MicroVax III uniprocessor. Concurrent collection interrupts the mutator for two reasons: for *root scans*, that is, scanning stack(s) and global variables, and *mutator waits*, times when the mutator must wait for the collector to scan and unprotect a page the mutator needs to access. In the **cfront** and **grobner** tests, root scans took no more than 0.19 seconds in any collection. These are close to being acceptable interruptions even in interactive programs. For all three programs, mutator waits are quite small, averaging less than 50 msec. The maximum mutator wait is less than the average root scan time. The anomaly in this data is in the the **hyper** example, where the root scan takes more than four seconds (68% of total garbage collection time). Thus, the mutator is blocked for most of collection time in **hyper**. This root scan is lengthy because the roots include a large global data structure containing pointers into the heap. Ellis, Li, and Appel point out that this kind of interruption could be reduced by treating global objects in the same way as objects in

Measurement	cfront	hyper	grobner
Max Root Scan Time (sec)	0.19	4.27	0.14
Avg Root Scan Time (sec)	0.19	4.24	0.12
Max Mutator Wait (msec)	168	22	96
Avg. Mutator Wait (msec)	41	14	27

Table 5.2: GC interruptions of mutator on a uniprocessor.

the heap. Pages containing global objects could be protected from the mutator until all the objects on the page have been scanned. The same treatment could be given to stack pages. I believe that such optimizations are likely to produce significant improvements only if the collection is organized so that these pages, like heap pages, can be scanned in the order the mutator wants to access them.

If we agree that the magnitude of the individual interruptions are small enough to approach imperceptibility, then the next question to ask is what rate of execution an end-user of a program will perceive during collection. I will refer to this rate (expressed as a fraction of the between-allocation execution rate) as the *overlap*. Overlap can be expressed as

$$Overlap = \frac{Mutator\ work\ during\ GC}{Elapsed\ time\ of\ GC}$$

The elapsed time of garbage collection is easy to measure. The difficulty is in measuring the mutator work accomplished during collection. In principle, this is simple: I know the elapsed time of the total execution, and the elapsed time of garbage collection. The difference is the time the mutator spends between garbage collection.

Mutator work between GC = Elapsed time of program − Elapsed time of GC

If I know the total amount of mutator work done in the run, then

Mutator work during GC = Total mutator work − Mutator work between GC

After considering a number of alternatives, I chose to estimate *total mutator work* by running each program with an initial heap size large enough to eliminate the need for collection. Table 5.3 presents the calculation of overlap for each of the three test cases. Again, each test is the average of the best three of four runs on a MicroVax III. The *active time* of a collection is the time during which the mutator is not suspended; i.e., the elapsed time of the collection minus the time taken for the root scan. The *adjusted*

Measurement	cfront	hyper	grobner
Elapsed time of program *(sec)*	19.8	61.7	42.7
Elapsed time of GC *(sec)*	5.2	7.9	7.8
Mutator work between GC *(sec)*	14.5	53.8	34.9
Total mutator work *(sec)*	16.7	55.8	39.8
Mutator work during GC *(sec)*	2.2	2.0	4.9
Overlap	**42%**	**25%**	**63%**
Active time *(sec)*	5.0	3.6	7.0
Adjusted overlap	44%	54%	70%

Table 5.3: Overlap on a uniprocessor.

overlap divides *mutator work during GC* by the active time, to obtain the perceived execution rate after the root scan is completed. The *adjusted overlap* gives a truer picture of the perceived execution rate after the root scan for the **hyper** example, where the root scan time is larger than the active time.

These results are quite encouraging. Table 5.2 shows that the individual interruptions caused by garbage collection are quite short, except when the roots contain a large global variable. Table 5.3 shows that performance does not degrade to unacceptable levels during a collection. Even on a uniprocessor, where the mutator and collector tasks must share machine resources, perceived performance of the **cfront** and **grobner** programs during collection was 42% and 63%, respectively, of their between-collection rates. The **hyper** example does less well because of the long root scan, but once that is completed, overlap is 54% for the remainder of collection.

I should stress that using concurrent collection on a uniprocessor does not decrease the overall running time of the program.[8] Indeed, one might fear that the extra overhead of handling protection exceptions and moving pages around in the *ns_queue* might increase running time. Happily, this increase is quite small. When concurrent and non-concurrent runs of the three programs, adjusted to perform the same number of garbage collections, are compared the concurrent version takes less than 3% more time than the non-concurrent version in each case.

---

[8]There is the potential of "real" overlap between mutator I/O and collection, but I did not find any evidence of this.

Measurement	cfront	grobner
Max Root Scan Time (sec)	0.34	0.31
Avg Root Scan Time (sec)	0.30	0.21
Max Mutator Wait (msec)	146	48
Avg. Mutator Wait (msec)	38	18

Table 5.4: GC interruptions of mutator on a multiprocessor.

I next ported my collector and two of the test programs (**cfront** and **grobner**) to an 8-processor shared memory multiprocessor, a Digital Equipment Corporation VAX[9] 8800. The multiprocessor tests were intended to measure "real" concurrency between the mutator and collector. Since previous tests had determined that collections in the **hyper** example were dominated by scanning a global variable, very little concurrency would be possible. Therefore, I did not port the **hyper** program to the 8800.

Again, the first question to ask is whether the individual interruptions are noticable. Table 5.4 shows these numbers. The interruptions are generally short, though the root scan times are greater than they were on the MicroVax III for the same programs, despite the fact that the 8800 is the faster machine. I will speculate on the reason for this increase later.

Table 5.5 shows measurements of mutator/collector overlap for **cfront** and **grobner**. The measure of overlap calculated in Table 5.3 is calculated here as well, and called **Overlap-1**. In addition, a second calculation overlap (**Overlap-2**) is shown. This calculation uses a more direct measure of *Mutator_Work_During_GC*: subtract the elapsed time of the program with mutator/GC concurrency from the elapsed time with concurrency disabled. If the amount of garbage collection work is the same in both cases, the difference should be the mutator work accomplished in parallel with collection.

Overlap for **cfront** approaches 50%, while the overlap for the **grobner** example is less than 20%. Two questions arise from these measurements. First, why is not overlap greater on a multiprocessor than a uniprocessor? Second, why, in the case of **grobner**, is it actually worse?

The first question should actually be rephrased: how does collection on a uniprocessor do so well? The answer lies in the implementation of the collector. Whenever the main thread of the collector task scans and unprotects a page, it makes a system call to suspend itself if any other runnable threads are waiting. This has the effect of giving the mutator priority over the collector. This enhances overlap, but also stretches out collection.

---

[9]Vax is a trademark of the Digital Equipment Corporation.

Measurement	cfront	grobner
Elapsed_Time_of_Program *(sec)*	14.9	33.1
Elapsed_Time_of_GC *(sec)*	5.2	5.3
Mutator_Work_Between_GC *(sec)*	9.6	27.9
Total_Mutator_Work *(sec)*	11.9	28.7
Mutator_Work_During_GC *(sec)*	2.3	0.8
Overlap-1	**43%**	**16%**
Elapsed time, no concurrency *(sec)*	17.5	33.4
Decrease in elapsed time *(sec)*	2.6	0.3
Overlap-2	**50%**	**6%**

Table 5.5: Mutator/collector overlap on a multiprocessor.

Collection in **cfront** takes 10.5 seconds per Mbyte collected on the Microvax III, but only 3.5 seconds per Mbyte on the 8800. If we correct for the difference in raw speed of the machines,[10] collection still takes 2.1 times longer per Mbyte collected on the uniprocessor than it does on the multiprocessor. We should note also that non-zero overlap on a multiprocessor means that the actual running time of the program is reduced.

The second question still remains: why does **grobner** do poorly? Recall from Tables 5.4 and 5.2 that root scans on the 8800 take longer than on the MicroVax III, despite the greater speed of the 8800. Doing the root scan requires operating system calls to map the pages containing mutator stack(s) and globals into the collector's address space, and to retrieve the registers of the mutator's threads. These system calls require locking on a multiprocessor that is not required on a uniprocessor, which may account for the greater root scan time. This hypothesis should be investigated further. In any case, root scanning time consumes a much larger fraction (45%) of collection time on the 8800 than it does on the MicroVax III (10%). This immediately decreases the potential overlap. In defense of the collection algorithm, concurrency is not very important for programs like **grobner**, which retain little storage. The individual collections on the

---

[10]The ratio of machine speeds is estimated by comparing the elapsed times with a heap large enough to obviate collection; by this measure, the MicroVax III takes 1.4 times as long as the 8800 to execute the same code.

Program	norm-grobner	grobner	grobner	grobner
Initial heap size (Mbyte)	—	12	4	1
# of collections	—	0	2	11
1-worker time (sec)	31.0	29.0	29.7	33.2
Collection time (sec)	—	—	1.3	5.3
Overlap	—	—	*44%*	*20%*
2-worker time (sec)	17.3	17.8	18.9	23.4
Collection time (sec)	—	—	1.3	6.3
Overlap	—	—	*15%*	*12%*
4-worker time (sec)	10.6	12.9	14.1	18.8
Collection time (sec)	—	—	1.7	7.1
Overlap	—	—	*29%*	*17%*

Table 5.6: Collector performance for a multi-threaded program.

8800 are very short, averaging about 0.5 seconds. The performance of the collector for the **grobner** case is roughly equivalent to what a generational collector would achieve. It is only when collection lasts for significant time periods, as with **cfront**, that concurrency is really necessary.

The final test I performed measured the performance of **grobner** when it used multiple threads. Table 5.6 shows the results of this experiment. The numbers given are the elapsed times of the different experiments using different numbers of worker threads. **Norm-grobner** is the original **grobner** program, not using garbage collection. **Grobner** is the garbage-collecting version of **grobner** that we have been discussing. The *overlaps* shown arc determined using the same calculation used in Table 5.3. The first point to draw from this data is found by comparing the first and second columns. If no collections are performed, **grobner** using the garbage-collecting alloctor exhibits speedups similar, but not quite as good, as the original version of the program. The difference may be explained by the use of spin-locks in the default multi-threaded allocator versus a full mutual exclusion locks in the garbage-collecting allocator, but this must be investigated further. Section 5.8.2 suggests another possible method of avoiding allocation contention. The second point, unfortunately, is that speedup decreases when collections are performed. The low level of overlap in the **grobner** example means that collection costs remain essentially fixed while mutator parellism decreases overall mutator elapsed time. Thus, collection takes a larger fraction of total running time as more worker threads are added. A multi-threaded collector might be able to reverse this trend; Section 5.8.2 discusses this possibility.

One final optimistic note: one of the assumptions behind concurrent collection is that

Program	First Half	Second Half
cfront, uniprocessor	66%	34%
cfront, multiprocessor	76%	24%
grobner, uniprocessor	87%	13%
grobner, multiprocessor	68%	32%

Table 5.7: Distribution of mutator waits.

a program will tend to have a "working set" of pages that it will cause to be scanned first, and that once those pages are scanned, mutator waits will be rare. Table 5.7 shows that this assumption is borne out by my data. The percentages show the fraction of mutator waits that begin in the first and second halves, respectively, of the active time of the collection. At least two-thirds of mutator waits begin in the first half of active time. This would seem to imply that perceived performance would approach between-collection performance in long-running collections.

5.7   Remaining Problems

My compiler/collector system will preserve the semantics of the most C++ programs. However, there are some classes of programs that will fail. These fall into two basic categories.

5.7.1   Pointers as Values

If a program converts a pointer to a non-pointer value, my system may fail. If a program converts a object pointer into an integer value, destroys the original pointer, stores that integer value in an integer field in a heap object, and has no other references to the object pointed to, then that object may not be copied. The program may fail if it converts the integer value back to a pointer and attempts to dereference the pointer. This is perhaps not so serious: converting pointers to integers and vice-versa is non-portable at best, and most compilers will at least give a warning when this is done. This is not a problem for collectors that are conservative everywhere, such as Boehm and Weiser's collector or Caplinger's collector.

A more insidious class of error can occur in programs that are portable. Many C++ programs rely on an assumption that the address of an object will not change during the lifetime of the program. Consider a program containing a hash table, where the objects in the table are hashed on their address. A garbage collection will completely destroy the invariants of this hash table. To be used in a system using copying garbage collection, such a hash table would be rewritten to use some intrinsic address-independent property of the member objects as a hash key. Alternatively, objects such as this hash table could register a "reorganize" procedure with the garbage collector, and the collector could call this procedure at the end of collection for all registered objects that survived the collection. In either case, the program will have to be changed to work properly. The compiler can at least detect all such cases by issuing warnings whenever it encounters any pointer operation other than dereferencing. Again, this problem does not occur in mark-and-sweep collectors such as Boehm and Weiser's or Caplinger's, where objects are not moved.

A final class of pointer error occurs when if a programmer temporarily loses access to an object. This could occur, for example, if the only reference to an array is used to traverse the array in a loop, so that it points past the end of the array at the termination of the loop. The example below illustrates this case.

```
Foo* foo_arr_ptr = new Foo[10];
for (int i = 0; i < 10; i++) {
    do_something(foo++);
}
// If collection occurs now, no pointer to the array exists.
foo_arr_ptr -= 10;
```

This example is somewhat contrived but still legal. Note that this problem is shared with all C/C++ collectors we have considered.

5.7.2 Destructors with Side Effects

C++ allows users to specify *destructors* to be invoked whenever an object is deallocated via the **delete** operation. Destructors often simply take care of deallocating other objects, and have no other side effects. In this case, my system preserves semantics by simply eliminating **delete**'s and destructors. Garbage collection takes care of eventually performing "deallocation." Sometimes, however, destructors do have side effects. For example, a class might have a static (global) integer member that indicates the number of objects of that class currently present in the system. The constructor of the class would increment this integer, and the destructor would decrement it. By eliminating **delete**'s my system would change the semantics of the program.

One possible answer to this problem would be to reinstate **delete**'s, and perform all side effects of destructors except for deallocation. However, the logic behind this proposal is somewhat specious. The main reason for using garbage collection is to free the programmer of the burden and the danger of deciding when storage can be deallocated. The side effects of a destructor can be just as dangerous as deallocation if performed at the wrong time; a program still carries the same burden and danger if it invokes destructors with side effects. It is hard to see why one would use garbage collection if one still had to decide when deallocation could be performed safely.

A more reasonable proposal would be to reinterpret the semantics of C++ so that destructor invocation occurs at some unspecified time after the object becomes inaccessible. The compiler could analyze the program to determine which classes have destructors with side effects, and have the allocator function maintain a list of the addresses of all objects of these types that survived the last collection or have been allocated since. After a collection, the collector could go through this list, invoking destructors on all objects that did not survive the collection.[11] This proposal also has some difficulties. Note that destructors may potentially be executed concurrently with the mutator. If a destructor and another part of the program both access a data structure, their access might have to be synchronized. This would be difficult to even warn about at compile time, and would almost certainly require programmer intervention to correct. Another difficulty is that programs that rely on current C++ semantics may break under the reinterpreted semantics. In particular, the order of invocation of destructors is not necessarily preserved by the proposed mechanism. Programs written to rely on this order would not be guaranteed to work. It would be difficult to detect such programs at compile time.

Probably the most sensible solution to this problem would be to allow the user to specify on a per-class basis (perhaps using a **#pragma**) those classes that should and should not use garbage collection. Garbage-collected classes would be required to have no destructors.

5.8 Conclusions and Future Work

5.8.1 Summary

Though garbage collection is almost always associated with "high-level" languages such as Lisp, ML, Prolog, and Smalltalk, there is no conceptual reason why garbage collection cannot be used with languages such as C and C++. Indeed, collectors such as [5], [6], [3], [4], and the current work indicate that a full range of garbage collection algorithms are adaptable to these languages.

Automatic storage management always makes programming simpler; objections to its use are usually based on fears of performance degradation. Two kinds of overhead are relevant. For some programs (e.g., compilers), the overall running time is all that

---

[11] The collector could determine what destructor to invoke by having the compiler automatically make destructors with side effects *virtual*, requiring that a virtual destructor is always the first function in the virtual function table of a class.

matters. For these programs, the total excess time taken by garbage collection should be minimized. Other programs, particularly interactive programs, have real-time constraints. Users are likely to be annoyed if garbage collection interrupts the program for more than a fraction of a second.

The performance measurements in this paper indicate that total garbage collection overhead can be surprisingly small, even for C and C++ programs. When I compared programs using standard Unix explicit storage management (i.e., `malloc/free`)[12] with their garbage collecting counterparts, I found that total running time increased by less than 30% in all cases, and for one program was almost negligible.

One possible future trend in computer architecture is towards multiprocessor work-stations. If the cost of adding an extra processor to a machine approaches the cost of the processor chip, this will become an attractive method of increasing performance. If such machines become common, then concurrent garbage collection will become a very attractive technique. On a multiprocessor, concurrent collection reduces total collection overhead, by overlapping mutator and collector activity. Collection overhead was decreased by almost 50% in some cases. Concurrent collection also decreases the maximum interruption observed by the mutator to consistently less than a half a second on the architectures tested, on uniprocessors as well as multiprocessors.

A final argument in favor of the use of garbage collection is that easy software reuse may almost be impossible without it. Stroustrup is considering extending C++ by adding *parameterized classes* [16]. This extension will allow programmers to design, for example, container classes such as `Set`'s without explicitly specifying the member type of the set. Different `Set` types can be made by instantiating `Set<T>` with different type values for `T`. This kind of construct presents a problem for explicit storage management: what should be done in the destructor of `Set<T>`? If `T` is a pointer type, then the destructor will have to decide somehow whether or not to `delete` the objects pointed to. But the implementation of `Set` has no way of knowing whether other pointers to those objects exist or not. Garbage collection alleviates such worries, allowing such general-purpose classes to written more easily and cleanly.

5.8.2 Future Work

Generational collection (see Section 5.5) is the main alternative to concurrent collection for reducing collection overhead and interruption. As others have pointed out, it might be interesting to attempt to combine concurrent and generational techniques. Such a collector could guarantee interactive performance for collections of the larger old area

---

[12]Again, I explicitly eliminated hand-coded optimized allocators in the `cfront` program to perform this comparison.

as well as the small new area. Also, such a "combination" collector could use a larger new area than is usually used in generational collectors, because the mutator is allowed to resume before a new area collection completes. Finally, one of the difficulties in implementing a generational collector is the need to keep track of pointers from the old area into the new area. Some systems require mutator cooperation, adding every new old-area-to-new-area pointer to a list at the time of its creation. This can impose a substantial overhead on the mutator. Another alternative is to use a memory protection like the one used for concurrent collection to inspect every changed old area pointer. In a concurrent collector, old-area-to-new-area pointers might be found *lazily*. In this scheme, collection of the new area proceeds as in concurrent copying collection. After objects pointed to by the roots and globals have been copied to the new-space of the new area, all of the heap, including the old area, is protected from the mutator. The mutator is then allowed to resume, and the collector proceeds to scan and unprotect pages. All old area pages are added to the list of pages to be scanned; however, the collector only looks for pointers into the new area when it scans an old area page. Such pointers are likely to be rare, so scanning such pages should be fast. Attempted mutator access to protected old area pages could cause the collector to scan them sooner, just as with new-space pages in non-generational concurrent collection.

Another interesting avenue for future work is introducing parallelism into the collector. Currently, mutator allocation is a potential bottleneck, since each allocation occurs in a critical section. This also adds non-trivial locking overhead to allocation. A possible remedy would be to have multiple *allocation points*, so that each mutator thread is allocating new objects on a different point in the heap. Synchronization would only be required when an allocation required a new page. This would not be difficult to implement; the allocation point mechanism already exists to allow mutator and collector allocation to occur in parallel. A possible problem with this plan is that it could lead to a fragmented heap, in which it is difficult to allocate large multi-page objects.

A more interesting form of parallelism would be the introduction of multiple scanning threads into the collector. This might appear to be simple. The collector maintains a queue of pages to be scanned; except in the case of pages containing objects crossing page boundaries, the order in which the pages are scanned is largely irrelevant. Thus, each scanning thread could pick the next page off the head of this queue. The problem arises when these threads follow pointers into old-space. If two parallel scanning threads encounter pointers to the same uncopied old-space object at the same time, they could conceivably both copy that object to different new-space locations. Thus, these threads must somehow synchronize access to old-space objects. One method would be to associate a mutual exclusion lock with each page of old-space, and require that scanning threads obtain this lock before reading or modifying old-space forwarding pointers. A possibly faster method would be to use architecture-dependent atomic instructions, such as *test-and-set*, to insert forwarding pointers. This seems to me to be a very exciting area for future research.

References

[1] M. Accetta, R. Baron, W. Bolosky, D. Golub, R. Rashid, A. Tevanian, and M. Young. Mach: a new kernel foundation for unix development. In *Proceedings of Summer Usenix*, July 1986.

[2] A. W. Appel. Garbage collection can be faster than stack allocation. *Information Processing Letters*, 24(4):275–279, 1987.

[3] J. F. Bartlett. Compacting garbage collection with ambiguous roots. Technical Report 88/2, DEC Western Research Laboratory, February 1988.

[4] J. F. Bartlett. Mostly-copying collection picks up generations and C++. Technical Report TN-12, DEC Western Research Laboratory, October 1989.

[5] H.-J. Boehm and M. Weiser. Garbage collection in an uncooperative environment. *Software Practice and Experience*, 18(9):807–820, September 1988.

[6] M. Caplinger. A memory allocator with garbage collection for C. In *USENIX Winter Conference*, pages 323–3. USENIX, USENIX, 1988.

[7] B. J. Cox. *Object Oriented Programming: An Evolutionary Approach*. Addison-Wesley, Reading, MA, 1986.

[8] E. W. Dijkstra, L. Lamport, A. J. Martin, C. S. Scholten, and E. F. M. Steffens. On-the-fly garbage collection: An exercise in cooperation. E. W. Dijkstra Note EWD496, June 1975.

[9] J. R. Ellis, K. Li, and A. W. Appel. Real-time concurrent collection on stock multiprocessors. Technical Report 25, DEC Systems Research Center, February 1988.

[10] D. Knuth. *The Art of Computer Programming, vol. I: Fundamental Algorithms*. Addison Wesley, Reading, Mass., 1973.

[11] H. T. Kung and S. Song. An efficient parallel garbage collector and its correctness proof. Technical report, Carnegie-Mellon University, September 1977.

[12] S. C. North and J. H. Reppy. *Concurrent Garbage Collection on Stock Hardware*, volume 274 of *LNCS*, pages 113–133. Springer-Verlag, Berlin, Germany, 1987.

[13] G. L. Steele, Jr. Multiprocessing compactifying garbage collection. *CACM*, 18(9):495–508, September 1975.

[14] P. A. Steenkiste. The implementation of tags and run-time checking. In Peter Lee, editor, *Topics in Advanced Language Implementation*, chapter 1, pages 3–24. The MIT Press, Cambridge, MA, 1990.

[15] B. Stroustrup. *The C++ Programming Language*. Addison-Wesley, Reading, MA, 1986.

[16] B. Stroustrup. Parameterized types for C++. In *Proceedings of the 1988 USENIX C++ Conference*, pages 1–18, Berkeley, CA 94710, 1988. USENIX Association, USENIX Association.

[17] C. P. Thacker and L. C. Stewart. Firefly: A multiprocessor workstation. In *Proceedings of the Second International Conference on Architectural Support for Programming Languages and Operating Systems*, pages 164–172. ACM, 1987.

[18] D. Ungar. Generation scavenging: a non-disruptive high performance storage reclamation algorithm. *SIGPLAN Notices*, 19(5):157–167, May 1984.

Part II
Practice and Experience with Advanced Language Implementations

---

In contrast to conventional programming languages such as FORTRAN, Pascal and C, advanced languages generally allow one to write programs at higher levels of abstraction. This means that the implementation, as opposed to the programmer, is given more of the burden of providing the basic mechanisms of computation. For example, Lisp, Scheme, and ML all provide implicit allocation and deallocation of heap storage, in contrast to Pascal and C which force the programmer to manage the heap explicitly. As another obvious example, consider FORTRAN, which forces the programmer to use stacks (represented by arrays) along with a looping construct, instead of the higher-level mechanism of recursion. Many other examples of high-level features of advanced languages abound, such as first-class functions and continuations, generic functions, and pattern matching.

Clearly, then, there is a much work involved in implementing an advanced language. And because one generally wishes for the programmer not to be forced to pay a performance penalty for using an advanced language, one is often led to a system design in which aspects of the implementation are made highly interdependent. For example, the type system of Scheme has a direct bearing on the representation of data, but the design of the data representations must also take into account the hardware architecture, operating system, and run-time system requirements. Add on top of this the desire to generate optimized code, and you have an extremely challenging design problem indeed!

In this part, we consider the design considerations that went into three actual systems. Chapter 6 by Scott E. Fahlman (*Design Considerations for CMU Common Lisp*) describes the basic design of the current CMU Common Lisp system. This system, which is in worldwide use and forms the basis for some commercial implementations of Common Lisp, was originally designed at a time when less was known about advanced language implementation, and the Common Lisp standard was still a rapidly moving target. Fahlman's description of what went wrong and what went right in the whole experience makes for quite educational reading. Chapter 7 by Uwe F. Pleban (*Compilation Issues in the Screme Implementation for the 88000*) describes in great detail the design of a run-time system for a Scheme system targeted to the Motorola 88000 RISC processor. The design is very "up-to-date" and so should provide good information for other practitioners. What is more interesting, however, is how much the concerns of code generation, data representation, and hardware architecture must be considered in designing a run-time system for a production-quality implementation. Finally, Chapter 8 by Barak A. Pearlmutter and Kevin J. Lang (*The Implementation of Oaklisp*) describes the major elements of the implementation of the Oaklisp object-oriented programming language. The design is particularly interesting in the layout of objects, methods, and inheritance structure. In addition, the design of Oaklisp's byte-coded abstract machine makes the entire implementation highly portable, as demonstrated by its availability large variety of machines, with high-level support for continuations, objects, and so on.

As in Part I, there are many other systems that are worthwhile to study. These include (at the very least) Rabbit, Orbit, and Standard ML of New Jersey. The interested reader is once again encouraged to look these up.

References

[1] A. W. Appel. A runtime system. To appear in *Lisp and Symbolic Computation*, 1990.

[2] A. W. Appel and D. B. MacQueen. A Standard ML compiler. *Functional Programming Languages and Computer Architecture, Lecture Notes in Computer Science*, Vol. 274, September 1987, 301–324.

[3] D. A. Kranz. Orbit: an optimizing compiler for Scheme. Ph.D. Thesis, Yale University, New Haven, 1988.

[4] G. L. Steele. Rabbit: a compiler for Scheme. Technical Report AI-TR-474, MIT AI Lab, Cambridge, 1978.

6 Design Considerations for CMU Common Lisp

Scott E. Fahlman and David B. McDonald

CMU Common Lisp is a complete public-domain implementation of the Common Lisp programming language [9], plus an extensive set of software tools to aid the programmer in developing Common Lisp programs [4,3,2]. CMU Common Lisp was developed within the School of Computer Science at Carnegie Mellon University. It was initially developed on the Perq workstation and currently runs on the IBM RT workstation [10] under CMU's Mach operating system [8]. Ports of CMU Common Lisp to additional machines and CPU types are now under way. In addition to being heavily used within the university, CMU Common Lisp has been used by a number of computer manufacturers and software companies as the basis for their own commercial Common Lisp implementations.

Because it is optimized for evolutionary, experimental programming, Lisp presents some unusual challenges to the implementor. The Lisp function-call interface is very flexible and general, and it must allow for relinking of individual functions at run time. Storage is allocated dynamically, and a garbage collector is employed to reclaim the memory space occupied by abandoned data structures. The language includes a very large, user-extensible run-time library of built-in functions and data types. Despite all these advanced features, we want compiled Lisp programs to run as fast as possible.

In this chapter we will explore the tricks and tradeoffs used in the CMU Common Lisp implementation as it attempts to satisfy these conflicting demands. (Additional low-level details can be found in [5].) We will also look at the process by which this implementation was developed and bootstrapped; the process was complicated because the Common Lisp language was still being designed at the time.

6.1 Development of CMU Common Lisp

In 1980, the Computer Science Department of Carnegie Mellon University began the Spice Project, a five-year effort to develop an innovative computing environment for the high-powered workstations that we believed (correctly) would be available and affordable by the end of the five years. Since the Spice environment was meant to cover our day-to-day computing needs in all areas of computer research, including Artificial

Intelligence, the development of a first-rate Lisp system was an important part of the Spice effort. This "Spice Lisp" project was headed by Scott Fahlman. A substantial part of the programming was done by CMU undergraduates. The system was developed initially on the Perq workstations built by Perq Systems Corporation; it was always our intention to port the system to more popular, higher powered workstations as they became available.

At that time there was no widely accepted standard for Lisp systems. We decided that Spice Lisp should resemble Zetalisp [6], the dialect then running on the MIT Lisp Machine, but that Spice Lisp should be cleaner and simpler, omitting many Zetalisp features that were controversial or that were not portable to machines that lacked special hardware for Lisp.

In the spring of 1981, a meeting of Lisp implementors was called by DARPA, the government agency sponsoring most of the implementation efforts, to discuss the alarming and expensive proliferation of Lisp dialects. As a result of this meeting, a number of implementation groups, including the group at CMU, began to develop the specification for a single, "common" Lisp dialect that we could all agree upon. The design discussions, involving dozens of people at companies and universities worldwide, were conducted almost entirely by electronic mail. Guy L. Steele Jr., then part of the Spice Lisp effort at CMU, was chosen to write the manual for this new language; Steele and Fahlman moderated the design discussions. After five years and thousands of computer mail messages, the result was an informal but comprehensive specification for Common Lisp [9].

Spice Lisp was modified to conform to the new Common Lisp standard, changing from week to week as the definition of Common Lisp changed. Because the Spice Lisp code was in the public domain, it was used as a starting point for the development of many other Common Lisp systems, both in academia and in industry. It is fair to say that the free availability of the Spice Lisp code was one of the reasons why Common Lisp became common.

By 1985, our initial implementation effort was finished. Work continued in two major areas: increasing the speed and quality of our Common Lisp implementation and developing software tools that would run on top of Common Lisp. We decided to port our Common Lisp system from the Perq to one of the newer, more powerful workstations that were appearing on the market. We chose the IBM RT because of its clean RISC architecture and because many of these machines were available within our department. At the same time, CMU's Spice Project evolved into the Mach Project. Mach is an operating system combining many of the innovative ideas explored in Spice with a new emphasis on parallel processing and on external compatibility with the popular Unix programming environment. Since the Spice project had ended, our system was renamed

"CMU Common Lisp." The port of CMU Common Lisp to the IBM RT was done at CMU by David B. McDonald.

The CMU Common Lisp implementation comprises a large body of code (the Lisp interpreter and run-time system) written in Common Lisp, plus a compiler that converts this code into native instructions for the machine on which the system is to run. On the Perq we used a special Lisp-oriented instruction set, implemented in microcode [11]. On non-microcodable machines like the RT, the compiler generates a mixture of native machine instructions and calls to a number of small, hand-coded support routines.

Our compiler and most of our run-time system are written in Common Lisp itself. The use of this strategy would present little problem today: one would simply cross-compile our code from another machine running some existing Common Lisp implementation. However, because CMU Common Lisp was the first Common Lisp implementation to be generally available, cross-compilation from another Common Lisp was not an option. Fortunately, Common Lisp is fairly close to being a superset of Maclisp [7], which was available to us on the Decsystem 20. By writing our compiler in this common subset, and by using Lisp macros to simulate some Common Lisp features missing in Maclisp, we were able to cross-compile the initial versions of the system from Maclisp. Some parts of the run-time system were also written in this restricted subset of Common Lisp so that they could be run and debugged under Maclisp. Once we had a preliminary version of CMU Common Lisp running well on the Perq, we were able to move to that environment for subsequent compilation and testing, and the need to remain within the Maclisp-compatible subset was eliminated. By now, almost all traces of the early Maclisp compatibility have vanished from our code.

If Common Lisp and Maclisp had not been so similar, we would have been forced to write two distinct compilers: a cross-compiler for bootstrapping, followed by the production-quality compiler that runs within Common Lisp. An alternative approach, followed by many earlier Lisp systems, was to write the Lisp interpreter and run-time system in some existing language (typically assembler or C), to write the compiler in Lisp, and to bootstrap the compiler by running in the interpreter. We did not seriously consider this course. We very much wanted our run-time system to be in Common Lisp itself, so that we could more easily change and maintain it. In addition, we felt that a compiler running on top of a Common Lisp interpreter would be too slow even for bootstrapping purposes.

The task of building the first version of CMU Common Lisp was complicated by the fact that the Common Lisp design was not stable at the time the work was being done. Every time the Common Lisp design group would change a feature, we had to make corresponding changes in our implementation. A few of these changes, such as the decision to use lexical variable binding and to provide lexical closures, led to major rewrites of our compiler and interpreter. Despite this, we were able to track the evolving Common Lisp design through all of its many mutations. In some cases we were able to alert the design group of implementation problems that certain design decisions had caused while it was still possible to revise the language specification.

The revisions to to the Common Lisp specification continue to this day (early 1990). The revision process is now being driven by the efforts of the X3J13 committee to produce a solid, precise ANSI standard for Common Lisp and (if certain problems of international politics can be overcome) an ISO Lisp standard as well. However, there are now many commercial users of Common Lisp and a number of companies selling implementations. These commercial interests demand a certain degree of stability in the language. This means that the changes now being contemplated are rather limited in scope and can be added to our existing system without major upheavals.

Some major new language features can now be added by incorporating portable public-domain Common Lisp code (or copyrighted but freely distributed code) from other organizations: we currently use code from Gregor Kiczales and Daniel Borrow of Xerox to implement the Common Lisp Object System, code from Dick Waters of MIT to implement the pretty printer, code from Kent Pitman of Symbolics to implement the error and condition-signalling system, and code from LaMott Oren of Texas Instruments to implement the CLX interface between Common Lisp and the X window system. We have been careful not to incorporate into our code any external software that we are not allowed to pass on to others, as this would compromise our role as a resource for any group wanting to undertake a Common Lisp implementation.

In principle, CMU Common Lisp can be ported to a new machine simply by putting a new code-generation module in the compiler and recompiling the entire run-time system for the new instruction set. The resulting code must be linked together with a number of hand-coded routines to handle such low-level tasks as garbage collection, arithmetic, and interface to the new machine's operating system and I/O. Our code has now been ported via this process a number of times, both by members of our group and by other organizations. Of course, a port is never quite as simple as the description above might suggest. A new machine will always present a few new issues or will uncover a few bugs or unintentional machine-dependencies in our existing code.

At present, CMU Common Lisp represents over 30 person-years of effort; typically it requires from 1/2 to 2 person-years to port it to a new machine and to tune and polish the result. This assumes that the people doing the porting are good Lisp programmers and that they have excellent knowledge of the target machine and operating system. The port to the IBM RT was relatively quick because of the machine's simple RISC architecture and because McDonald had experience with earlier ports. Most of the problems he encountered were not with the Lisp system itself, but with unstable hardware and software on the pre-release prototypes of the RT workstation and Mach.

Our group at Carnegie Mellon is currently working on a completely new Common Lisp compiler, combining state-of-the-art Lisp compiler technology with some important ideas from compilers for conventional languages. Robert A. Maclachlan is the chief architect on this project. In addition to supporting much better code optimization than our current compiler, the new compiler will also be much easier to re-target to new machine architectures. The compiler's knowledge of the the target machine – the instruction set, classes of storage available, low-level data formats, and so on – is not woven into the code of the compiler; instead, this information is all kept in a series of easily-modifiable tables and declarative data structures. Once the new compiler is running well on the IBM RT, the CMU Common Lisp group intends to port our system to a number of other machines.

Since the new compiler is not yet completed, it would be premature to attempt a detailed description of it here. We will mention a few of its more interesting features at appropriate points in this paper, but unless otherwise specified, the system we describe here is the one built around the older compiler. This should serve equally well as an illustration of the the issues and trade-offs that must be considered in building a professional-quality Common Lisp system.

6.2 What's Different About Common Lisp?

People unfamiliar with Lisp tend to think of it as just another programming language, somewhat less efficient than most, but with certain list-processing features built in that are needed by Artificial Intelligence programs. Lisp users see the language in a different light: Lisp is first of all a language that is optimized for *evolutionary programming*. Conventional programming languages are based on the assumption that the user knows exactly what he wants before he begins programming. It is the job of such a language system to help the user create a program that will meet his (explicit or implicit) specification. These languages – Pascal and Ada are the best examples – emphasize safety and good programming discipline over power and flexibility for the individual programmer.

The evolutionary programming approach takes a different view: most of the time, most users have only a vague idea of what they want; they don't know what they *really* want a program to do, in full detail, until they have played around with a few prototypes and tried out some variations. This is obviously the situation for the sort of research-oriented programming that goes on in the field of AI. Software engineers don't like to admit this, but in fact most of the world's programming is evolutionary in nature. It is extremely rare to find a large software project in which the program's behavior has been fully specified in advance and in which the specification is not changed after the programming has begun. (See [1] for further elaboration of this point.)

Rather than attempting to stamp out the evolutionary style of programming or pretending that this style does not exist, Lisp attempts to provide tools to make evolutionary programming as easy and productive as possible. The goal is to make it as easy as possible to get a prototype program running quickly, to test various components and observe what they are doing, and to modify a program as needed, sometimes while it is running. Other programming languages – Smalltalk, ML, Forth, APL, and perhaps Prolog – share this orientation toward evolutionary programming to some degree, but Common Lisp is more heavily used than these other languages for writing very large, complex programs.

The same features that make Common Lisp a good language for evolutionary programming create some serious problems for the implementor. If these features are implemented in the obvious, straightforward way, they will exact a tremendous penalty in run-time performance of the program. Lisp's reputation as a very inefficient language was well deserved in Lisp's early days, when these features *were* implemented in a naive way. Over the years, Lisp implementors have developed a few tricks to speed up the language without sacrificing desirable features. In this section we will quickly survey some of the problems that must be addressed; in later sections we will look at some of the ways in which CMU Common Lisp attempts to solve the problems.

6.2.1   Storage Management

Common Lisp provides an extensive array of built-in data types: lists, symbols, arrays, strings, bit vectors, many types of numbers, and user-defined records, classes, and objects. These objects, which come in a variety of sizes, are allocated in heap storage as needed. A "garbage collector" (sometimes referred to as a "GC") is responsible for reclaiming the storage used by any objects that have been abandoned and are no longer accessible. As it eliminates dead data objects, the garbage collector also compresses the live objects into a contiguous block of storage, reducing the working set of the program and improving paging performance. The garbage collector may also linearize lists and other data structures in memory, minimizing the amount of paging that will occur when a program scans along a list in the usual order.

Lisp's use of dynamic storage allocation for everything, not just for selected parts of programs that cannot be written any other way, is a controversial feature. Lisp advocates claim that relieving the programmer of the burden of storage allocation is a good way to improve programmer productivity. When the programmer must handle allocation and de-allocation of objects explicitly, this process is a source of many subtle and hard-to-find bugs. It also leads to a rigid style of programming in which early decisions about the size and shape of various data structures cannot easily be changed later, and in which programs break when some data set grows larger than the programmer anticipated. On the other hand, there is a certain cost to be paid for automatic storage management. It is the job of the Lisp implementor to make this cost as small as possible.

6.2.2 Built-In Facilities

The code for a simple Lisp interpreter can be just a few kilobytes in length, but an industrial-strength Lisp dialect like Common Lisp augments this interpreter with an extensive built-in collection of run-time functions and facilities: formatted printing routines, sorting routines, debugging tools, arithmetic functions defined for a host of exotic number types, and so on. In many languages, such facilities (if available at all) would be relegated to an external library; in Common Lisp, they are built into the run-time Lisp system. This makes life easy for the programmer, who can make use of any of these facilities at any time, without having to explicitly locate, load, and link modules from the library. The typical Lisp programmer writes very little code at the lowest levels; most of his "programming" is just a matter of plugging together large, pre-existing functions to do whatever job he needs.

Because of this large built-in library, the run-time core-image of a Common Lisp system is very large – anywhere from two to ten megabytes – even if the user's own program is small. For program development on a machine with a large address space and a good virtual memory system, this presents no real problem: most of the core image is paged out to disk most of the time, where it costs no more than the equivalent code in an external program library. There is a problem, however, when development is over and the user wants to deliver a small Lisp-based application program on a machine with a small memory. Instead of providing the user with a small "delivery subset" of Common Lisp, most commercial implementations now provide some form of "tree-shaking" garbage collection: the user's completed program is retained, along with all of the built-in Lisp facilities that it calls, directly or indirectly; everything else is stripped out of the core image. This can result in a delivered Lisp program that is a small fraction of the size of the Common Lisp system itself.

6.2.3 Generic Operations

Another feature of Common Lisp that is valuable for evolutionary programming is the extensive use of *generic functions*: operators that will work on more than one type of object, and that adapt their behavior to fit the type of object actually received. For example, almost all of the Common Lisp arithmetic operations are defined to work on numbers of any type in any combination. Common Lisp operations that work on "sequences" will accept any of the one-dimensional data types: lists, character strings, or any type of vectors. CLOS, the Common Lisp Object System, provides facilities by which the user can define his own hierarchy of types and objects, and can define new *generic functions* that work on collections of these types, perhaps applying a different computational *method* depending on the type of argument actually received.

Common Lisp programmers are allowed to declare the exact type of a data object, or some constraint on the type of a data object, at any point in the program. A good compiler will make use of this information to generate more efficient code, eliminating some run-time dispatching on object-type. Such declarations, particularly at the interface between major modules or between the program and its user, may also play an important role in detecting errors and making the program more robust. Common Lisp differs from the "strongly typed" languages because in Lisp it is also possible *not* to declare the type of an object. While most programming languages require the programmer to declare everything, Lisp provides a continuum: the programmer can declare as much or as little as he likes.

This flexibility can be extremely useful during evolutionary program development – it means that the user can easily change the representation of certain data types as the program evolves and as new needs and constraints are discovered. A Common Lisp programmer will typically use generic operations during the program-development phase, declaring types only at major inter-module boundaries. After the design of the program has settled down, additional type declarations may be added for greater efficiency, especially in the inner loops where the program spends most of its time.

This flexibility in the type system also makes it easier to create libraries of reusable code in Lisp than in other languages. Library modules can be written in Lisp that accept a broad range of arguments types and that "do the right thing" for each type they encounter. Similar modules in other languages usually make much more specific assumptions about the type and range of their arguments and the surrounding environment, so these routines are less likely to be of use in a given situation.

It is the job of the Lisp system implementor to provide this added flexibility while minimizing the cost in terms of run-time performance and code size. Since some run-time type-checking and type-dispatching is going to occur, the data formats must be designed to make type checking as fast as possible. A common technique is to optimize the code to favor those types that occur most frequently in performance-critical code. For example, a generic 2-operand "+" operator may encode single-word integer addition inline, preceded by a test that will jump off to a subroutine if either of the operands is of some other, less common number format. Some CPU architectures allow the type check to take place concurrently with with the addition itself; if the type is not the one anticipated, the addition is aborted before any damage is done, and the program branches off to a subroutine that does a full type-dispatch.

A clever compiler (such as the new compiler being developed for CMU Common Lisp) can often move the type check out of a loop to a point in the program where the test can be performed just once. Such techniques can give the Lisp programmer the flexibility and safety of extensive run-time type checking while only increasing the time required by the program by a few percent.

In evolutionary programming, when you do declare the type of a data object, it desirable to declare it in only one place. Then, if you change your mind about the type of data structure you want to use, you can easily change the program. If the type of an object is specified in many different places, it can be very difficult to track down all the declarations and make the program consistent once again. In addition, we would like the compiler to figure out as much as possible about the object types in a program, without requiring the user to put in extra declarations. For example, if the types of the operands to an addition are known at compile time, the type of the result can also be determined. These goals can only be accomplished if the compiler does a good job of type-inference and type-propagation. (See Chater 3 for an in-depth discussion of this topic.)

Unfortunately, most existing Common Lisp compilers (including the old compiler for CMU Common Lisp) are very weak in this respect, requiring the user to put in redundant declarations in order to get the greatest possible efficiency. Our new compiler will have extensive facilities for type inference and propagation. This, in turn, enables many type-specific optimizations in the code.

6.2.4 Fine-Grained Modularity

Lisp programs use the function-calling mechanism as a sort of universal glue, holding together small modules written by the user, obtained from a library, or built into the Lisp system. A typical lisp program is not structured as a large block of code, but rather as a set of small functions, each one typically a screenful of code or less. Each function provides a single, simple procedure: it may call a few other functions in sequence, perform some tests, and perhaps provide one iteration loop or one level of recursion. Because Lisp programs are structured in this way, they do a lot of function calling compared to other languages. Therefore, the speed of a Lisp system depends critically on the efficiency of the implementation's function-calling machinery.

This modular structure makes it relatively easy to modify a Lisp program, often just by changing what a single function does and loading the modified version into an already running program. There is no separate linking phase – the loader must handle those issues that are handled by the linker in other languages. Since users value the ability to replace any function with a new definition at any time, most Lisp compilers treat each function as a separate compilation module: code is carefully optimized within each function, but there is no attempt to perform optimizations across function boundaries. A call from function A to function B cannot be optimized too tightly by the compiler; such calls must be handled in a way that allows for the definition of B to change at run time.

The situation is complicated by the generality of the function-calling interface in Common Lisp. Older Lisp dialects required each function to take a fixed number of arguments and to return exactly one value as the result. Over the years, responding to the requests of many Lisp programmers, Lisp dialects added more complex function-calling options. In Common Lisp, a function can be defined to take any number of *required arguments*, followed by any number of *optional arguments*. A default value is computed at the time of the call for each optional argument not supplied. A function may also be defined to take an unlimited number of *rest arguments*, which are turned into a list at the time of the call. Finally, a function may accept *keyword arguments*, in which the caller explicitly labels the arguments he passes in, rather than passing the arguments in some particular order. A Common Lisp function may return any number of values; if the caller is expecting only a single value, any others are discarded.

If handled in a naive way, Common Lisp's combination of frequent function calls, the ability to change function definitions at run time, and very flexible function-calling conventions could lead to very poor performance. Fortunately, most of the added cost can be eliminated through the use of caching and a few other tricks. CMU Common Lisp's approach to this problem will be described in Section 6.4.

6.3   Types and Storage Management

CMU Common Lisp uses a *stop-and-copy* garbage collector. Starting from certain root structures, all accessible objects are recursively copied from one area of virtual address space to another. When this copying process is complete, any object left behind must be inaccessible and therefore is garbage. Objects are allocated in the new space until the time arrives for the next GC; the process is then repeated, with accessible objects being copied back into the space that was emptied by the previous GC.

Some older garbage collection techniques, including the *mark and sweep* and *reference count* methods, leave the accessible objects in place; the dead objects are strung together onto a "free list." Such techniques lead to fragmentation of memory, especially in Common Lisp where many of the objects are vectors or strings of irregular size. A copying GC can pack the objects together as it moves them into new space. In addition, lists can be *linearized* in memory so that adjacent list cells are usually on the same page.

In fact, our users generally run the garbage collector long before the available space has been exhausted in order to compact their working sets.

Early versions of our Lisp system on the Perq used an *incremental copying* garbage collection scheme, in which the copying of live objects from oldspace to newspace goes on continuously while the Lisp is running. This technique is essential for real-time applications in which it is unacceptable for the Lisp to become catatonic, even for a few seconds. However, this incremental GC scheme slows down the normal operation of the Lisp system by a significant factor because the copying process initiates a lot of extra page faults. We found that our users preferred the stop and copy scheme, which gives maximum speed most of the time and an occasional pause. If real-time Lisp applications ever become important in our environment, it would be a straightforward task to build a CMU Common Lisp version that uses an incremental GC scheme. Our data formats and storage layout can support either style.

A number of *generation scavenging* GC schemes have now been developed, in which the system continuously tries to reclaim recently created objects, but in which older objects are considered for reclamation much less frequently. The idea is that most objects that have been around for a certain length of time will probably continue to be of use in the future. Unless a program exhibits an unusual pattern of memory usages, a generation scavenging GC can often give the user the best of both worlds: continuous collection of short-lived objects at relatively little cost in run-time performance. We may add a GC scheme of this sort to CMU Common Lisp in the future, but this is not a high priority at present.

Every Lisp object must have a type associated with it. When handed an unknown object, a Lisp program must be able to determine the type of the object at run time. It is important that type checking be efficient, since it is a frequently performed operation. A Lisp object is represented as a 32 bit word and can either be an *immediate object*, which contains the information in the word itself, or a *pointer object*, which points to a block of data of arbitrary size allocated in heap storage. The use of pointer objects means that any Lisp variable (a 32-bit slot) can hold any one object, whether that object is a single ASCII character or an array of a million pixels. In some cases, the slot holds the data itself, and in some cases it holds a pointer to the data, but this distinction is invisible to the Lisp user.

Figure 6.1 shows the structure of these two types of objects in CMU Common Lisp.

Examples of immediate objects are fixnums (small integers), ASCII characters, and short floating point numbers. It is especially important to use an immediate format for small integers, since these are created and abandoned very frequently by iteration counters and the like; if they were allocated in heap storage, garbage collection would have to occur much more frequently. Certain internal markers used by the Lisp system

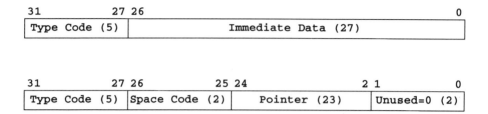

Figure 6.1: Immediate and pointer data types.

are also represented as immediate objects: an "illegal object trap" marker that is placed, for example, in the value slot of an unbound symbol, a marker that is used to signal that multiple values are being returned from a function, and so on.

Examples of pointer objects are symbols, list cells, arrays, vectors, and "structures" (the Common Lisp equivalent to a "record" in C or Pascal). The data for these objects is kept in heap storage and must be reclaimed by the GC when all pointers to the data area have been dropped. There is one distinguished pointer object, the gc-forward pointer, that is used only during GC; it is left behind in oldspace after an object has been copied, and points to the object's new location.

A problem for Lisp implementors is that Lisp needs room for a type code within every 32-bit immediate object, and most CPU's designed for more conventional languages do not allow for this need. The single-word integer formats used on most machines use the entire 32 bits for data. If some bits are used as a tag to indicate the object type, these type bits must be masked off before any arithmetic is done. Since single-word integer arithmetic is common, this can seriously degrade performance.

Our current "high tag" system deals with this problem by assigning the binary type code "00000" to positive short integers and "11111" to negative short integers. The data portion of the word contains the number itself in two's complement form. Since these codes coincide with the expected high-order bits for positive and negative integers in 32-bit format, arithmetic can be performed on these numbers with no masking or shifting. However, the system must check after the operation for any carry into the type-tag portion of the word. Integers whose signed representation does not fit into 28 bits must be converted to "bignums" – Common Lisp's infinite-precision numeric format. Bignums store the number in an array of arbitrary size, allocated on the heap.

An alternative scheme used by many Lisp systems is to employ two or three low-order bits to indicate the type of an object. For short integers, these bits are zero. Integers in this format can be added or subtracted without shifting or masking, and the machine's normal overflow machinery can be used to detect a carry out of the high end of the word. However, the data must be shifted to the right when such integers are multiplied or used for certain kinds of address arithmetic. In future versions of CMU Common Lisp, we may switch to a "low tag" scheme of this sort.

Efficiency is enhanced if a pointer object can be used directly as a memory address pointing to the object's data block, without any need for shifting and masking of the type field. In CMU Common Lisp on Mach, using the current high tag scheme, we are able to get away with this: the type bits are simply treated as high-order bits of a 32-bit address. In effect, this breaks the machine's address space into segments, since each type code points to some different part of the address space. All the objects with the "list" type code end up in one area; the objects of type "symbol" live in a different area, and so on, with multi-megabyte gaps between the areas actually being used. The Mach operating system supports this kind of sparse use of virtual memory with no additional overhead; other versions of Unix force the user to allocate memory in a single contiguous block, with no large gaps. In such systems, one must go to the extra expense of masking off the type fields before using the pointer.

The space code in a pointer object can take on one of four values:

1. Dynamic 0 space is used to allocate objects that may be freed later. For example, when a program allocates a cons cell as part of a list, it will be allocated in dynamic space.

2. Dynamic 1 space is similar to dynamic 0 space. Objects are initially allocated in Dynamic 0 space. The first garbage collection copies all live objects to dynamic 1 space. The pages of the old dynamic 0 space are then zeroed out or de-allocated. New Lisp objects are then allocated in dynamic 1 space until the next GC, at which time the live objects are copied back to dynamic 0 and the cycle repeats.

3. Static space contains objects that will exist over the lifetime of the Lisp session. For example, all the symbols defined by the Common Lisp specification are stored in static space, since they must always exist. These objects are scanned by the garbage collector, since they may contain pointers into dynamic space, but they are never moved.

4. Read-only space contains objects that will exist over the lifetime of the Lisp session and will never change. For example, compiled function objects for all the defined Common Lisp functions are placed in read-only space since they do not change and should only point at objects in static or read-only space. The garbage collector does not scan objects in read-only space.

With the type scheme and memory layout described above, the garbage collector is quite straightforward. (It is only a few pages of assembler code in the current implementation.) When a user-specifiable amount of dynamic memory has been allocated, a garbage collection occurs.

CMU Common Lisp's strategy for allocation and garbage collection is quite efficient on the RT: checking the type of an object for error detection can be done with three instructions (a shift, compare, and branch if error) and three cycles when no error is encountered. The use of separate spaces reduces the amount of work that the garbage collector needs to do since read-only objects are not scanned and static objects are not moved. This is especially important if the user's program is small compared to the Lisp system itself (most of which lives in static and read-only space).

One disadvantage of this scheme is that the address space available for any one type of object is only a small fraction of the machine's 32-bit address space. For example, only 32 megabytes of dynamic list cells can be in use at any one time. This limitation has not been a problem with any current applications – most users have less than 32M bytes of paging space on their local disks, at present – but some re-allocation of these spaces may be needed in the future, as programs and databases grow ever larger.

A second disadvantage of our current scheme is that free pointers must be maintained for all the spaces. These must be kept in main memory, since there are not enough registers available on the RT to hold them all. Using a single area for all heap storage would allow more efficient allocation routines, since the necessary pointers could be kept in registers, but type checking and garbage collection would become considerably more complex with many object types mixed together in a single heap.

6.4   Register Usage and Function Calling

Most early Lisp implementations used a stack for passing arguments to called functions, for the local variables allocated by the called function, and for passing back the return value. However, this scheme is not always well suited to the architecture of the target machine. The RT is a case in point. The RT has 16 general-purpose registers that can be accessed in a single instruction cycle; access to main memory is much slower – typically four instruction cycles or more. The original RT had no data cache to speed up references to the current stack frame in main memory. For efficiency, then, a Lisp implementation must make the best possible use of the registers.

While a Common Lisp function may accept any number of arguments and may return any number of values, an analysis of existing code showed that the overwhelming majority of function calls involve three or fewer arguments and return a single value. We therefore reserved three registers for argument passing; the single return value comes back in one of these. Any arguments after the first three and any return values after the first one are passed on the stack in main memory. The compiler must therefore generate somewhat different code for the first three arguments than for the others but this added complexity is justified by the greater speed of the resulting code. (In interpreted code, where speed is less important, all arguments and values are simply passed on the stack.)

Eight of the remaining registers are needed for internal use by the Lisp implementation: a program counter, various pointers into the Lisp stack and other important data areas, and two "non-lisp" scratch registers that can hold raw bit-patterns that do not have the tag bits that every legal Lisp object must have. The garbage collector must preserve the Lisp objects it finds in registers, and anything that these objects may point to, so we need a special place to put data that are *not* to be interpreted as Lisp objects, whatever their type bits may appear to be.

This leaves five registers that the compiler can allocate to the local variables of each function. Once again, any locals in excess of the first five are allocated in main memory, in the stack frame created when the function is called. It is not unusual for Lisp functions to require more than five locals. Our current compiler attempts to put the most heavily used local variables in the registers, based on the number of times each variable is referenced in the code. Our new compiler will base its allocation decisions on a flow analysis of the program, so it should make better decisions about which variables to favor.

The RT provides an instruction that writes a contiguous block of registers out to the stack in main memory at high speed, and another instruction that reads the block back in. This facility is used to preserve the local variables and some of the internal pointers across function calls. The argument-passing registers are not preserved, since they must be used in setting up the call. This means that if a function wants to preserve the arguments it received, it must copy them to local variables before that function calls another. The compiler handles this, making it invisible to the user.

As mentioned earlier, Common Lisp supports a very complex function-calling convention in which a function may accept a variable or unlimited number of arguments and return any number of values. Individual functions can be redefined at run time. If not handled carefully, this flexibility in function-calling can slow down Lisp programs considerably. In the most general case, the following steps must be performed when function A calls function B:

  1. Function A must arrange for its own local variables and control information to be preserved on the stack. A must then compute the arguments that it will pass to B, in left-to-right order, placing the first three values in registers and any additional values on the stack. (Of course, A may have to call other functions in the course of computing these arguments for B.)

2. Function A must check to ensure that function B is defined and must determine the proper entry point in the code for B. This normally cannot be done at compile or load time because the Lisp environment changes dynamically.

3. Function A then branches to the main entry point for function B.

4. Function B must determine how many arguments were actually passed. If it is not prepared to accept this number of arguments, it must signal an error. If it is prepared to accept this number, it must jump to the proper place in its own code to initialize any optional arguments that were not supplied by A, to turn any excess arguments into a list, and to parse any keyword arguments it may have received.

5. The body of function B now executes, perhaps calling other functions.

6. When B is ready to return, it puts the first return value in a register, and places any additional values on the stack. Then it restores the registers saved by function A and jumps to the proper return address.

7. Function A now harvests the return value(s). If function A wants only a single return value but receives more than one, it must remove the extra values from the stack.

This procedure includes a number of expensive steps that are not needed by more traditional (and less flexible) languages. Fortunately, most of the additional overhead can be eliminated most of the time through the clever use of caching and some other tricks.

It is possible in Lisp to put together an arbitrary function call at run time and then to execute it using APPLY, FUNCALL, or EVAL. In such cases, the very general function-call procedure described above must be used. However, in the overwhelming majority of function calls encountered in actual code, the call is explicitly present in the user's code at compiler time. The compiler can see the symbol that names the called function, the number of arguments that the caller intends to pass, and whether extra values will be discarded. Such cases can be optimized through the use of a *link table*. This table holds a collection of pointers that allow transfer of control from one function to another in a single indirect jump, even if the caller and and the called function were compiled at different times.

The procedure is as follows: Suppose function B is defined with two required arguments, one optional argument, and a "rest arg" that will collect into a list any arguments in excess of three. The compiler will create code for this function with three entry points for the two, three, and more-than-three argument cases. In addition to the code to be executed, a compiled function has a header that indicates, among other things, the maximum and minimum number of legal arguments and the entry points to be used for each case. The interpreter and the link-table machinery can examine this header whenever it is necessary to locate the proper entry point.

Now, suppose function A calls function B with three arguments. At the time A is being compiled, the only thing the compiler knows about function B is the symbol that names the function, so it cannot generate code to jump to B directly. Instead, it puts a special notation in the compiler output file indicating that A is calling a function named B with three arguments.

When the file containing the compiled code for A is loaded into the Lisp system, the loader will attempt to find a link table entry for function B called with three arguments; if this entry does not already exist, it will be created. (We will call this entry "B-3.") The code for function A is modified during the load, so that the call to B is replaced with an indirect jump through the address of the B-3 entry in the link table. By a similar mechanism, every function call from compiled code to a named function is turned into an indirect jump through a link table entry. All calls to a given function with a given number of arguments are mapped through the same entry in the table.

These link table entries are initialized to point to a special "first call" routine. The first time the B-3 entry is used, the first call routine locates the symbol B, verifies that it has a legal function definition at this point, looks in the function's header to determine that it is legal to call B with three arguments, and determines the proper entry point in the compiled code for B. This entry point is then placed in the B-3 link-table entry in place of the pointer to the first-call routine. Any subsequent calls to function B with three arguments, whether from A or from some other function, will simply be indirect jumps to the proper place.

One might imagine that the indirect jump through the link table could be eliminated. The first-call function could simply modify the code in the calling function to jump directly to the proper entry point. This is not done for two reasons. First, the user might choose at any time to load a new definition for B. When this is done, the system must locate all of the entries for B in the link table and turn them back into "first-call" pointers. This will ensure that the argument count checking is repeated for the new definition and that new entry points are used. Second, it is possible that a garbage collection will move the code for B; if this happens, the pointers to B in the link table must be updated properly. It would be very hard to perform either of these tasks if pointers into B were scattered through the code of many other functions.

The link table makes it possible for most function calls to be handled as a simple indirect jump most of the time. Of course, there is a price to be paid for this: extra work must be done during compilation and loading, at the time of the first call to a function, and whenever a function is redefined. Still, this is a good trade-off that, on the RT, results in an improvement of a factor of two in overall performance of typical Lisp programs, while still allowing the user to redefine any function at any time.

While the ability to redefine functions at run time is important during program development, there often comes a time when the program is "finished" and the user is willing to give up any remaining flexibility in exchange for more speed at run time. Our new compiler will provide an optional *block compilation* mode for this purpose. In block compilation, the compiler works on an entire set of functions at once, instead of compiling each function independently. Calls from one function to another within the block can be very highly optimized, perhaps requiring only a direct jump. Once it can examine both the caller and the callee, the compiler may be able to optimize the code in several ways: type-checking on arguments may be eliminated as unnecessary, register usage can be optimized across the call to eliminate some saving and restoring of registers, and argument passing can be streamlined. For example, caller and callee can agree that a "raw" number will be passed in a certain register, without the usual overhead of adding and removing type bits.

Function return is also optimized to favor the most common case: a function that returns a single value to a caller that is expecting only one value. When a function is interested in more than one value, it places a "multiple-values-requested" marker on the stack at the time of the call. If a called function wants to return more than one value, it must look for this marker: if it is present, the multiple values are returned on the stack; if not, only the first value is returned, and that is done in a register. This ensures that a function expecting only one returned value does not have to worry about cleaning excess values off the stack. Similarly, if a called function wants to return just one value, it simply does this in a register; if a caller was expecting multiple values, it must create the missing ones for itself. Thus, the possibility of multiple return values adds practically no overhead if neither the caller nor the called function use this facility.

We said earlier that our compiler generates a combination of inline code and calls to small, hand-coded assembler routines ("miscops") that perform various utility operations: allocating various kinds of object in storage, generic arithmetic, interface to the operating system, list and hash-table operations, and so on. There are over 200 of these small routines in the current system on the RT, most of them only a few instructions long. These internal subroutines are never seen or changed by the user, expect a fixed number of arguments passed in the argument registers, and return exactly one value in a register. It would be wasteful to use the full Common Lisp function call mechanism for these low-level internal calls; instead, we use the RT's simple subroutine jump and return instructions.

6.5 Summary

CMU Common Lisp for Mach and the IBM RT is efficient for a number of reasons. Care has been taken in the design of the data objects to eliminate wasted motion due to the type bits. In the general case, arguments, return values, and local variables must be kept on the stack in main memory, but in the most common cases we can keep all of these in registers. Common Lisp function calls are very complex and expensive in general, but again we have been able to optimize the most common cases through the use of caching and one level of indirection. These tricks, taken together, give performance that is competitive with traditional languages such as C, even with our present unsophisticated compiler. Our new compiler, with better optimization and block compilation, should give performance that is better still.

Acknowledgments

The mechanisms described in this paper were developed and implemented by members of the Spice Lisp and CMU Common Lisp project over a span of many years. It is very difficult to sort out individual contributions to this complex mixture, but particular credit must go to Bill Chiles, Robert A. Maclachlan, Guy L. Steele Jr., and Skef Wholey, all of whom contributed to the basic design of CMU Common Lisp.

References

[1] S. E. Fahlman. Common Lisp. In J. F. Traub et al., editor, *Annual Review of Computer Science, 1987*, pages 1–19. Annual Reviews, Inc., Palo Alto, CA, 1987.

[2] R. A. Maclachlan and B. Chiles. Hemlock command implementor's manual. Technical Report CMU-CS-89-134, Carnegie Mellon University, School of Computer Science, Pittsburgh, PA, 1989.

[3] R. A. Maclachlan and B. Chiles. Hemlock user's manual. Technical Report CMU-CS-89-133, Carnegie Mellon University, School of Computer Science, Pittsburgh, PA, 1989.

[4] D. B. McDonald (ed.). CMU Common Lisp user's manual, Mach/IBM RT PC edition. Technical Report CMU-CS-89-132, Carnegie Mellon University, School of Computer Science, Pittsburgh, PA, 1989.

[5] D. B. McDonald, S. E. Fahlman, and S. Wholey. Internal design of CMU Common Lisp. Technical Report CMU-CS-87-157, Carnegie Mellon University, School of Computer Science, Pittsburgh, PA, 1988.

[6] D. Moon, R. M. Stallman, and D. Weinreb. Lisp Machine manual, fifth edition. Technical report, MIT Artificial Intelligence Laboratory, Cambridge, MA, 1983.

[7] K. M. Pitman. The revised Maclisp manual. Technical Report MIT/LCS/TR 295, MIT Laboratory for Computer Science, Cambridge, MA, 1983.

[8] R. F. Rashid. Threads of a new system. *Unix Review*, 4(8):37–49, August 1986.

[9] G. L. Steele Jr. *Common Lisp: The Language*. Digital Press, 1984.

[10] F. Waters (ed.). *IBM RT Personal Computer Technology*. International Business Machines Corporation, 1986.

[11] S. Wholey and S. E. Fahlman. Design of an instruction set for Common Lisp. In *Proceedings, 1984 Conference on Lisp and Applicative Programming*. Association for Computing Machinery, 1984.

7 Compilation Issues in the Screme Implementation for the 88000

Uwe F. Pleban

This chapter discusses compilation issues which arose in the implementation of Screme, a high performance Scheme system for the Motorola 88000 RISC processor. It specifically focuses on the interaction between code generation and the overall design of the runtime system. We present the implementation of procedure calls as well as the inline coding of primitive operations in detail, in particular list processing and fixnum arithmetic. Our analysis of the Screme primops reveals that compile-time type and range analysis could be profitably applied in an optimizing Scheme compiler.

7.1 Introduction

The Screme system is a high performance implementation of the Lisp dialect Scheme on the Motorola 88000 RISC processor. One of its intended application areas are embedded systems applications. It was developed at Tektronix Laboratories over a period of almost three years. The components of the system include a *native-code optimizing compiler* with a "machine-independent" assembler, a *dynamic linker/loader*, *run-time support*, and a *run-time debugger*. With the exception of the garbage collector and the portion of the run-time library which deals with storage allocation, generic arithmetic, and the handling of continuations, the entire system is written in Scheme itself.

This chapter is a companion to the description of the Screme runtime environment in [25], and is structured as follows. The next section reviews Scheme, its fundamental implementation requirements, and the 88000 architecture. Section 7.3 summarizes important aspects of the Screme runtime environment. This is followed by a description of the Screme compiler, particularly the code generator. Section 7.5 examines in depth the implementation of critical Scheme operations on the 88000. The final section reviews the status of the project, and points to further research.

7.2 Review

7.2.1 Scheme, A Dialect of Lisp

The Lisp dialect Scheme [16] is based on the λ-calculus with assignment. It differs from low-level algorithmic languages like Pascal or C in several important aspects. First,

Scheme has *latent* as opposed to manifest *types*, which means that types are associated with values (objects) rather than variables. Non-numeric data types, including lists, symbols, and strings, are supported directly. In addition, *generic arithmetic* works on arbitrary precision integers, ratios, floating point and complex numbers. Second, all values have first class status, including *procedures and continuations*. Third, variables usually obtain values by *binding rather than assignment*. Fourth, objects created during a computation have *unlimited extent* and are automatically garbage collected when no longer needed. Finally, all implementations of Scheme are required to be *properly tail recursive*. This allows iteration to be expressed via recursive function application, while still retaining efficiency.

Like Common Lisp, Scheme is *lexically scoped*, and thus more amenable to efficient compilation than Lisp dialects with dynamic binding. In contrast to Common Lisp, Scheme is small[1], and was designed to have an exceptionally clear and simple semantics. Indeed, the core of the language can be expressed in terms of only seven fundamental constructs: *lambda abstraction, function application, sequencing*[2], *conditional, assignment, variable reference*, and *literal*. These are augmented with a rich set of predefined functions.

7.2.2 Approaches to Scheme Implementation

It is straightforward to construct an interpretive implementation for Scheme. The simplest approach trivially maps a source program to its syntax tree representation and interprets the resulting internal structure. A more complex method first compiles programs into byte code (a low-level abstract machine code), which is then interpreted. Alternatively, the byte code may be considered an intermediate code for a simple-minded instruction selector. The most difficult kind of implementation is a compiler which generates optimized native code.

It should be apparent that the efficient implementation of the following features is crucial to the overall success of a Scheme system:

- Procedure call and return.
- Primitive operations, such as list processing.
- Dynamic type-tag checks.
- The integer aspect of generic arithmetic.
- Environment access.
- Automatic storage management (garbage collection).

---

[1]... and small is beautiful, thus, by transitivity, Scheme is beautiful.

[2]Actually, sequencing can be expressed via application, but we consider it fundamental here.

- The handling of continuations.

This chapter addresses the first four items in detail. The reader may wish to consult other references for the handling of environments [20,11], garbage collection [24] (see also Chapters 4 and 5), and continuations [7].

7.2.3   The 88000 Architecture

The Motorola 88000 [14] is a Harvard-style load/store RISC architecture with pipelined instruction execution, thirty-two homogeneous[3] 32-bit registers, and instruction and data caches. The architecture uses a register scoreboard to stop the instruction pipeline whenever it is necessary to wait for a memory reference to complete; this allows multiple memory reads to occur simultaneously. All instructions occupy 4 bytes, and most of them execute in a single cycle.

The 88000 has five general classes of instructions: load/store, integer, bit manipulation, floating point, and transfer of control. The load/store, integer, and bit-manipulation instructions generally read either two registers or a register and an unsigned constant, and combine them to form a result. The branch instructions generally read a single register, from which a condition code or target address is determined.

The *load and store instructions* determine their address using either the sum of two registers, or the sum of a register and a 16-bit unsigned literal. Byte, halfword, fullword, and doubleword versions are available for each; byte and halfword loads can optionally be sign extended. Loading a register from memory incurs a 16-cycle latency, which is reduced to two cycles in case of a cache hit. Misaligned memory references either cause a trap, or produce undefined results; the choice between a trap or bizarre behavior depends on a user-settable status bit.

The usual complement of *arithmetic, relational, and logical instructions* is available. The result computed by the *compare* instruction is a bit-vector of condition code bits for all ten signed and unsigned comparisons. There is no hardware support for detecting arithmetic overflow without taking a trap. The floating-point instructions (together with integer multiplication and division) are directed to a separate function unit, which may execute in parallel with other instructions.

Bit-manipulation instructions include field extraction, masking, setting, clearing, and rotation. The extraction and masking instructions are generalizations of shift instructions. There is also a *find first bit* instruction which computes the position of the most significant zero/one within a word.

---

[3]Well, almost homogeneous: register **R0** always contains zero, and is not writable; and register **R1** is modified by the subroutine call instructions, which save the return address in it.

All *transfer of control instructions* come in two flavors. The ".n" version executes the instruction in the delay slot regardless of whether the branch is taken or not. The "standard" version suppresses the execution of the delay slot instruction if the branch is taken. The jump (**jmp**) and jump to subroutine (**jsr**) instructions use as a target address a value in a register. The branch to subroutine (**bsr**), branch on bit (**bb0**, **bb1**), and branch on condition (**bcnd**) instructions use a branch offset for specifying the target. The trap instructions are similar to the branch instructions. We will only make use of the conditional trap (**tcnd**) instruction in this chapter. Execution of the ".n" version of a transfer of control instruction always takes two cycles. The standard version takes two cycles if the branch is taken, and one cycle if not.

7.3   The Screme Run-time Environment

This section summarizes the salient characteristics of the Screme runtime environment. A more detailed discussion can be found in [25].

7.3.1   General Considerations

The design of the run-time environment for a language with run-time type checking is considerably more complex than for a language with manifest types [18,23,25]. First, none of the Scheme data types maps directly on a machine data type. Second, since type tags are inspected frequently [22], the overhead for tag testing by the most common *primops* (primitive operations), specifically fixnum arithmetic, basic list processing, and vector and string handling, must be minimized.

The ubiquity of procedure calls in Scheme programs makes an efficient call/return sequence absolutely essential. In addition, those primop applications which are expanded inline by the compiler should *minimize the number of instruction cycles* for the most commonly occurring cases, possibly at the expense of static code size.

The unlimited extent of every Scheme object mandates the presence of a garbage collector. This imposes fundamental invariants on the code and data structures, and allows for various time/space trade-offs.

The first class status of procedures and continuations warrants additional design considerations. Most importantly, programs which do not make use of these advanced features should not be unduly penalized by implementation overhead due to their potential presence. On the other hand, if such features are used, performance should not degrade drastically.

7.3.2 Partitioning of Operations

Based on experience gained during several years of using, implementing, and studying Scheme, the Screme team divided all run-time operations into three categories.

The first group of operations, whose execution-time efficiency had to be maximized "at all costs", includes procedure call/return, fixnum arithmetic, basic list processing, iteration, and garbage collection.

The second group of operations includes those which should be relatively fast: all storage allocation (for pairs, vectors, strings, and bytevectors), conditional branching on false, especially when the outcome of the test is determined by a primop call (in Scheme, both the boolean value #f and the empty list count as false), character, vector, string, and bytevector operations, uplevel variable references, and the use of continuations for loop exits.

The third group includes generic arithmetic, general uses of continuations, procedure calls with "rest" arguments, and operations with side-effects. Specifically, assignments may require that objects be "registered" with the garbage collector.

Some of the operations are implemented in *millicode* (termed "fastcall" operations in [4]). They are written in assembly language, have tailored calling sequences, and usually only reference the special millicode registers. All storage allocation as well as generic arithmetic is implemented via millicode.

Note that we are not interested in improving floating-point performance, due to the intended application areas of Screme. It remains to be seen whether floating-point operations can be compiled into efficient code in the absence of type declarations. See [3] for a Lisp compiler which uses declarations for generating clever numeric code.

7.3.3 Objects

Each object in the system is represented as a 32-bit quantity. The value of an *unboxed object* can be completely described in 32 bits. A *boxed object* is represented indirectly as a pointer to a heap-allocated structure.

The Screme implementation differentiates between three kinds of objects:

- *Exact fixnums* (unboxed), representing integers between -2^{28} and $2^{28} - 1$.

- *Immediates* (unboxed), which include booleans, characters, and the empty list.

- *Pointers* (boxed), which identify objects such as pairs, vectors, strings, procedures, etc..

The two least-significant bits in an object constitute an identifying *tag*, with **#b00** indicating a fixnum, **#b10** an immediate, and **#b11** a pointer. A tag value of **#b01** is illegal. The least significant bit is also known as the *pointer bit*; the one adjacent to it is called the *non-fixnum bit*, because an object is a fixnum if the non-fixnum bit is zero.

The choice of **#b00** as the fixnum tag allows many arithmetic operations such as addition to be performed *without any tag manipulation* [23]. Moreover, by disallowing a tag value of **#b01**, one obtains a one-instruction "branch on bit" test to determine if an object is a fixnum or a pointer. Furthermore, fixnums can be directly used as vector indices, since vector elements are aligned on word boundaries. Another benefit is that by using the low two bits as a tag, a number of runtime type violations can be caught "for free" using the *misaligned-access trap*.

A pointer refers to a structure in the heap, which contains *two header words* in addition to the object's data. The first header word usually encodes the object's class. However, for procedure objects, it points to the object's compiled code. The second header word contains a 23-bit length field, an internal object bit[4], and an 8-bit class tag field which (redundantly) encodes the object's class if the class is "known to the system". The latter allows many primitives to be implemented more efficiently; it is somewhat horizontally encoded to speed up the garbage collector.

7.3.4 Register Assignment

Each of the 32 general-purpose registers is dedicated to a particular use. At the highest level, the registers are divided into two categories, *rooted* and *unrooted*. The rooted registers are the only ones examined by the garbage collector. Therefore, the generated code must *ensure that during any period within which a garbage collection might occur, all rooted registers contain valid objects, and no live object is contained in an unrooted register*.

The set of 21 rooted registers is partitioned into various classes as follows.

- Twelve argument registers (**A0-A11**) are used for passing arguments to procedures. Although this seems like an excessively large number of argument registers, it should be remembered that syntactic forms such as **let** introduce local variables which are transformed into λ-applications by the macro preprocessing phase of the compiler. Local variables, therefore, are treated like arguments, and are typically stored in the argument registers. **A0** is special in that it contains the called object.

---

[4]If the *internal object bit* is set in the second header word, it is an indication that the structure is internal to some other structure. This effectively allows a pointer to refer to a location inside an object. In the Screme implementation this is used primarily for return addresses, entry points within code objects, and continuation frames within the frame cache.

This makes it possible for a procedure represented as a heap allocated closure to access its non-local variables.

- Six registers (**M0**-**M5**) are reserved for interfacing with millicode routines. Actually, the argument and millicode registers are contiguous, and their boundary can be negotiated by the code generator.

- The remaining four rooted registers contain system information. The **RETURN** register caches the current "return object", a relocatable encoding of the return address. The **CONT** register points to the current continuation frame, i.e., it is essentially a stack frame pointer. The stack limit is contained in the **LIMIT** register. Finally, the **RUNTIME** register points to a vector of "global" information, such as the values for all the global variables and the millicode routines.

Eleven of the 32 registers are unrooted: **R0** (**ZERO**) and **R1** (**CODE**), due to the hardware restrictions mentioned earlier; four scratch registers, **S0**-**S3**, which are available to the code generator for storing intermediate results of inline primop calls; the **INTPEND** register for interrupt polling; the **INARGS** register, used for passing the argument count on procedure calls; and registers **R29**-**R31**, which by convention are reserved by the operating system.

7.4 The Screme Compiler

The initial version of the Screme compiler is a *cross compiler* running on the Macintosh II under Lightship Scheme (formerly MacScheme). It interfaces with a machine independent assembler, which knows about instruction formats, takes care of ordering instruction blocks, generates descriptors for code objects, and inserts information for the linker.

7.4.1 Compiler Phases

The *reader* performs lexical and syntactic analysis, and converts a program into an S-expression. The *macro expander* then "explains away" the syntactic sweetener, yielding a program in the core language.

The *analysis phase* builds an abstract syntax tree, classifies variable references as global, local, and uplevel references, alpha-converts all non-global variable references, and identifies calls to primitive procedures (primops). It also performs *escape and assignment analysis*. During escape analysis, procedures are classified into those which need to be represented as heap-allocated closures, and those which may simply be compiled into machine code. Assignment analysis inspects all "**set!**" forms (many of which are usually generated by the macro expander), and introduces "cells" for variables which are multiply assigned. As a consequence, all other variables can safely be assumed to be bound to exactly one value, which may be freely substituted, provided that side effects are not duplicated. Note that, unlike other native code Scheme compilers, the analysis phase does not perform a conversion to CPS (continuation passing style) code [20,11].

The *code generator* first transforms the syntax tree into a lower-level representation suitable for instruction selection. It then performs a simple kind of *type inference* by propagating type information along execution paths. Another pass over the low level intermediate representation annotates variable references with *last use information*. Finally, storage is assigned and instructions are generated. Specifically, *variables are allocated in registers*, and spilled into stack frames when necessary. At the present time, no instruction scheduling for minimizing memory fetch latencies and branch delays is performed.

Since the analysis phase incorporates techniques which have been described elsewhere [20,11], we shall not dwell on it here. Instead, the next few subsections discuss aspects of the code generator in more detail.

7.4.2   *Core Language Transformations*

The syntax tree representation produced by the analysis phase could conceivably be used directly for code generation. However, a day of meditation quickly revealed that matching patterns in syntax trees would be overly complex and unwieldy. It was therefore decided to transform syntax trees into a lower-level intermediate representation (IR).

The transformation phase performs a number of simplifications by recognizing special cases of global definitions which can be handled directly by the assembler, transforming (`if` (`not` *cond*) *then else*) into (`if` *cond else then*), simplifying applications of the form ((`lambda` () *body*)) to *body*, etc. Most importantly, it specializes application nodes. Specifically, the IR operators distinguish between unknown calls, known calls, inline lambda applications, and primop calls, and whether the call is in tail position or not. The *recognition of local calls* allows the code generator to set up tailored calling sequences, suppress run-time argument-count checking, and use a shorter instruction sequence for the call.

Primop calls are specialized further by the *type tracking* phase. There may be several different implementations for an open coded primop, depending on whether the primop is used in a value producing or control flow context, and whether compile time knowledge of argument types and/or specific values allows specialized code sequences to be generated.

Usually, a primop is applied to arguments in order to produce a value. However, predicates such as **pair?** and **eq?** are almost always used in order to determine control flow within an **if** expression. Recognition of such uses in control flow context always leads to shorter code sequences.

For almost all primops, significantly better code (both in terms of space and execution time) can be generated if type and/or value information about arguments is known. For example, if one of the arguments to a numeric primop is a literal, its run-time tag test can usually be elided, as in the application (+ x 1). A literal with a particular value, such as a power of two, may even be more useful. For example, in Screme there exist three different implementations for the * primop, including one which uses a bitshift instead of a multiplication.

7.4.3 The Primop Database

All information concerning primops for which code is to be generated inline is contained in a set of tables called the primop database (PDB). The database was constructed in the following way. First, information concerning all inline primops was collected, including their syntax and semantics as prescribed by the R^3 Report [16], type checks performed, exceptions raised, assumptions concerning arguments and result, possible side effects on registers, scratch registers used, and the most general code sequence implementing each primop. The resulting file was then converted manually into a Scheme readable version, which was subsequently enriched with type tracking information. A utility program then produced suitable tables for the code generator.

Information for Type Tracking The PDB contains all the information necessary for driving the type tracking phase. Specifically, every primop definition contains type information for the result of the primop application (provided one is returned), and all constraints imposed on primop arguments after successful execution of the application. As an example, consider the call (car x), where x is a variable. The result value could be of any type, but if no exception is raised during the execution of the application, we may safely impose the constraint that along the execution path following (car x), x is bound to a pair. Therefore, if (car x) is subsequently followed along that path by (cdr x), the code sequence for cdr may elide the runtime tag check for x.

Another common case concerns type information available through explicit type tests by the programmer. For example, consider the form (if (pair? x) *then else*). The code generator can make use of the fact that within the *then* portion of the if form, x refers to a pair.

It should be clear that this kind of constraint propagation for variables crucially depends on the fact that the analysis phase has changed all mutable variables into cells. Also, if a CPS conversion had been applied to the syntax tree, type tracking could be performed on variables as well as all intermediate values exposed by the conversion. (See Chapter 3 for more on this subject.)

Information for Register Allocation   With few exceptions, every primop expects its arguments in registers, and delivers a result in a register. The database encodes the requirements on argument and result locations in two fields: **arg-regs** contains a list of location descriptors, one for each argument of the primop; and **result-reg** holds a location descriptor for the delivered result.

A location descriptor is in the set {**any-arg-reg, any-new-arg-reg, no-reg, literal, M0, M1, M2**}, with the following meanings:

- **any-arg-reg**: The argument/result may reside in any of the argument registers **A1-A11**; in particular, the result may be placed into a register holding one of the arguments, if the register targeting phase so chooses.

- **any-new-arg-reg**: This descriptor applies only to result locations. It indicates that the result must be in any argument register which differs from all registers holding arguments for the primop call. This is sometimes necessary in order to avoid overwriting the argument "too early". Typically, the type tests involving pointers to structures fall into this category.

- **no-reg**: This specifies that there is no result computed by the primop. It applies only to the result of setter primops, such as **set-car!** and **vector-set!**. Note that the control-flow version of a primop also does not deliver a result in a register. However, since the accompanying value producing version does compute a result, the **result-reg** field for the primop specifies something other than **no-reg**, and the control flow version simply ignores the specification.

- **literal**: This descriptor applies only to primop arguments. It means that the argument is not in a register, but is used as an immediate value in the code sequence for the primop application.

- **M0-M2**: These descriptors have the obvious meanings.

In addition, the **side-effect** field spells out which registers are destroyed by the primop application. Note that the fact that the specified result register is overwritten with a value is *not* considered a side effect here. With the aid of this information, register targeting for primop applications is vastly simplified.

A Sample PDB Entry   Figure 7.1 is a sample excerpt of the Scheme readable description of the **pair?** primop. Although it is relatively brief, it illustrates most of the remarks made in the preceding two subsections. The external database description mentions only fields with significant values. The others are automatically initialized by the table construction utility. In the example, the information contained in the **code** field is a

```
(pair?   ;(pair? obj)

 common

 (result-type       'boolean-type)
 (result-reg        'any-new-arg-reg)
 (type-effects
  '((along-true-branch  pair-type))     ;ignored in value context
 )
;;;----------------------------------------------------------------

(pair?   ;(pair? obj) in value context

 value

 (arg-types         '(any-type))
 (arg-regs          '(any-arg-reg))
 (side-effects      '(scratch S0))

 (code
  (lambda (tag Ak Ai)
   (let (($_FF (CG.new-false-label "pair?")))
    (_comment tag "pair? v")
    (_bb0.n   tag tagbit$pointer A1 $_FF)
                                ;if not pointer, to false exit
    (_or      tag Ak ZERO immediate$false)
                                ;...after returning #f
    (_ld.bu   tag S0 Ai object$$tag)
                                ;if so, get tag byte
    (_bcnd    tag 'ne0 S0 $_FF)    ;if not pair, to false exit
   ;$_TT:                          ;-> true exit
    (_or      tag Ak ZERO immediate$true)
                                ;return true
   ;$_FF:                          ;-> false exit
    (CG.connect-basic-blocks tag $_FF)
    $_FF)))                      ;false exit becomes new basic block
 )
;;;----------------------------------------------------------------
```

Figure 7.1: A sample excerpt of the Scheme readable description of the **pair?** primop.

```
(pair?    ;(pair? obj) in control-flow context

 control

 (arg-types        '(any-type))
 (arg-regs         '(any-arg-reg))
 (side-effects     '(scratch S0))

 (code
  (lambda (tag Ai $_FF)
   (_comment tag "pair? cf")
   (_bb0.n    tag tagbit$pointer Ai $_FF)
                                 ;if not pointer, to false exit
   (_ld.bu    tag S0 Ai object$$tag)
                                 ;get tag byte (only valid if
                                 ;pointer bit was set)
   (_bcnd     tag 'ne0 S0 $_FF)  ;if not pair, to false exit
   tag))
)
```

Figure 7.1: *cont.*

parameterized instruction selector for the particular primop application. Names such as **_bb0.n** refer to Scheme macros which expand into calls to the assembler.

As a result of the type tracking phase, every **call-primop** node in the IR points to the proper entry in the PDB. The code generator merely needs to call the routine stored in the **code** field of the entry in order to implement the primop. The interface to the code selection routine is dictated in part by the interface to the code block assembler. Since the assembler needs to be told to which basic block to append an instruction, the first argument to every code selection routine is an identification tag for the current block. This is followed by the result register, the argument registers (or literals) in order from left to right, and possibly branch targets for predicates used in control flow context. Each code selection routine returns a block tag as its result.

7.5 Implementation of Critical Operations

Previous research has demonstrated that certain compilation techniques such as closure and assignment analysis can significantly increase the performance of Scheme implementations [20,3,10]. Apart from compiler optimizations, however, the design of the run-time environment is just as important for good overall performance [18,25]. This section describes the interaction between code generation and the many low-level design issues in the Screme run-time system. Specifically, it discusses the implementation of procedure call and return, basic list processing, and the handling of fixnum arithmetic.

7.5.1 Procedure Call and Return

We have adopted a "caller saves" convention. The standard procedure calling sequence requires that the caller perform the following actions:

- Save any live registers in the current continuation frame. This frame is allocated upon entry to the caller. Also, variable values in live registers are spilled on the stack only once.

- Place the arguments in the argument registers **A1** through **A11**. If there are more than 10 arguments, the supernumerary arguments are placed in a vector, whose address is passed in **A11**.

- Load register **A0** with the procedure object. This allows the procedure to access its referencing environment, which is stored as part of each procedure object.

- *OR* together the argument count and the contents of the **INTPEND** register, and place the result in the **INARGS** register.

- Place the return object (which encodes the return address) in the **RETURN** register.

- Compute the procedure's "code object" and invoke it.

In Screme, every continuation frame is of fixed size. If the number of stack slots required by a procedure exceeds the number of slots in a frame, multiple frames must be allocated, which is slightly more expensive. The decision to have fixed-size frames is tied to considerations concerning the implementation of continuations [25]. Due to space limitations, this chapter will not discuss this issue any further.

An explicit check that the object in **A0** is a procedure is elided by using the following well-known technique: place a stub in the "code" slot of all boxed, non-procedure objects, such that its invocation causes a trap[5]. Thus an attempt to invoke any non-procedure object in the Screme system either raises an address alignment exception (if the object is unboxed), or traps to the debugger directly after issuing a suitable error message (if the object is boxed).

The called procedure checks the number of arguments and the interrupt bit. If it makes further procedure calls in non-tail position from within its body, it stores the return object in the continuation frame and allocates its own frame(s). However, if it

---

[5]The "code" slot doubles as the "class" slot for non-procedure objects.

only calls primops, or calls other procedures tail recursively, then the return address remains cached in the **RETURN** register, which saves both a store and a load instruction. This savings occurs for all procedures at the leaves of the execution tree, and is made possible because of the large number of registers in the 88000.

To simplify this discussion, we have ignored the complications introduced by "rest arguments". However, the additional expense is incurred only upon entry to procedures that expect such arguments.

Upon exit, the frame allocated on entry is deallocated, the return object is placed in the **RETURN** register, converted to a machine address, and a jump to that address is executed. At the call site, all live registers (possibly including **A0**) are restored, and execution proceeds.

Procedure Call   The following is the code skeleton for the most general kind of procedure call, a *non-tail call to an unknown procedure*. We assume that n arguments are passed. Note that names containing the string "$$" are integer offsets; the **addu** and **subu** instructions perform addition and subtraction, respectively, without trapping on overflow. Furthermore, instructions enclosed in square brackets are optional.

```
;;; at call site, in preparation for the call
;;;
   [st      A0,CONT,frame$$slot0    ;save A0, but only if live]
     <save all live registers in the frame>
     <load argument registers with n arguments>
     <load A0 with the procedure object>
     ld      CODE,A0,object$$class   ;1: load procedure's code object
     or      INARGS,INTPEND,n        ;2: pass # of args, include
                                     ;   interrupt bit
     addu    CODE,CODE,class$$instructions
                                     ;3: convert code object to entry
                                     ;   address
     jsr.n   CODE                    ;4: call procedure, after
                                     ;   converting ...
     subu    RETURN,CODE,1           ;5: ... return address to return
                                     ;   object
     <<three data words of return chunk info>>
;;;
;;;at call site, after call has completed
;;;
   [ld      A0,CONT,frame$$slot0    ;reload A0, if necessary]
     <restore all saved registers>
```

Thus, the most general call takes 5 core instructions, and executes in a minimum of 6 cycles, provided that the instruction loading the **CODE** register generates an address in the data cache.

Note that the garbage collector may have relocated the code object (commonly called "return chunk") following the fifth core instruction by the time execution returns from the called procedure. Because of this, the **RETURN** register contains a full fledged code object. Since it belongs to the set of rooted registers, its contents will be updated by the garbage collector to reflect any relocation of the return chunk.

For a *tail call to an unknown procedure*, the calling sequence can be shortened to the following:

```
<load argument registers with n arguments>
<deallocate frame, if necessary>
<load A0 with the procedure object>
ld      CODE,A0,object$$class   ;1: load procedure's code object
addu    CODE,CODE,class$$instructions
                                ;3: convert code object to entry
                                ;   address
jmp.n   CODE                    ;4: jump to procedure, after
                                ;   passing ...
or      INARGS,INTPEND,n        ;2: ... # of args, including
                                ;   interrupt bit
```

Thus a tail call does not save and restore live registers, reuses any allocated stack frames, elides the return chunk information, and the core sequence saves one instruction for the implementation of the call (which, however, executes in the same number of cycles as the non-tail call).

Calls to known procedures are considerably more efficient. Given a *non-tail call to a local procedure*, the five core instructions of the "unknown call" skeleton can be replaced by merely two instructions:

```
bsr.n   label(procedure)        ;4: call procedure, after
                                ;   converting ...
subu    RETURN,CODE,1           ;5: ... return address to return
                                ;   object
```

This elides the manipulation of the code object as well as setting up the argument count (since the procedure is known, its entry address and the number of arguments are known to the code generator). The core sequence now executes in two cycles.

Finally, a *tail call to a known procedure* has only a one instruction core:

```
<load argument registers with n arguments>
<deallocate frame, if necessary>
br      label(procedure)        ;4: call procedure
```

Moreover, if the code for the local procedure immediately follows the tail call, the branch instruction can be suppressed, and the call is made by simply "falling through". The assembler automatically takes care of this improvement.

Procedure Entry   Let us assume that the *"unknown" callee* expects m arguments, does not have "rest" arguments, calls other procedures, and needs to allocate one stack frame. Upon entry, the callee needs to check the argument count, poll the interrupt bit, save the cached return object, and allocate the stack frame. This is done as follows:

```
;;; argument and interrupt check
;;;
    cmp    S0,INARGS,m               ;check argument count and
                                     ; interrupt bit
    bb1    eq,S0,$noCheck            ;if ok, zoom on
    addu   CODE,RUNTIME,runtime$$poll
                                     ;otherwise investigate by ...
    jsr    CODE                      ;... calling millicode
    <<data word for polling routine>>
$noCheck:
    st     RETURN,CONT,frame$$return-chunk
                                     ;save return object in caller's
                                     ; frame
;;;
;;;frame allocation
;;;
    cmp    S0,CONT,LIMIT             ;check for frame cache overflow
    bb1.n  gt,S0,$ok                 ;if no overflow, to $ok,
    subu   CONT,CONT,frame-delta     ;after allocating one frame
    addu   CODE,RUNTIME,runtime$$cache-overflow
                                     ;otherwise, handle frame cache
    jsr    CODE                      ;overflow in millicode
    <<data word for overflow routine>>
$ok:
    <<code for procedure body>>
```

If all checks succeed, this entry sequence consumes 7 cycles. The entry sequence for a known procedure saves one instruction and one cycle because it only needs to test the interrupt bit in the **INTPEND** register. If a procedure needs to allocate more than one continuation frame, three additional instructions and cycles must be expended. Finally, the handling of rest arguments costs an additional four words and three cycles, as well as the time spent in setting up the list of rest arguments via millicode.

Procedure Exit   The code sequence for procedure exit is simple:

```
addu   CONT,CONT,frame-delta    ;deallocate frame
ld     RETURN,CONT,frame$$return-chunk
                               ;restore return object
addu   CODE,RETURN,chunk$$instructions
                               ;convert object to return
                               ; address
jmp    CODE                    ;return to caller
```

The load instruction incurs a memory delay, which may be avoided by an instruction scheduler. The one cycle delay due to the jump instruction may similarly be elided by proper scheduling. Under the assumption that the reloading of the return object hits the cache, and without code scheduling, this return sequence consumes 7 cycles.

Evaluation   In summary, a general procedure call costs 13 cycles, and the return costs another 7 cycles. Three of these cycles could potentially be eliminated through instruction reordering. For realistic programs, we would expect that one of them can always be avoided. For purposes of comparison, the Common Lisp implementation group for the IBM RT PC [13] reports that a simple function call of a symbol with no arguments takes 45 cycles, and that the returning of one value takes 35 cycles. This considerably larger cost is due to the more complex semantics of Common Lisp, and the fact that branch and call instructions on the RT take several cycles.

7.5.2   Basic List Processing

The list processing primops in Screme are the type tests **pair?** and **null?**, the selectors **car** and **cdr**, the constructor **cons**, and the setter operations **set-car!** and **set-cdr!**. We shall examine the selectors and the test for the empty list in more detail.

Selector Operations   Accessing the **car** or **cdr** field of a list cell (pair) involves the following steps:

1. Testing that the object is a pointer. This is done implicitly by relying on the address misalignment trap.

2. Testing that the structure pointed at is a pair. Since the pair tag is encoded as zero, a comparison instruction can be elided, though the conditional branch is still necessary.

3. Reading the data element from memory.

It is an error to take the **car** or **cdr** of the empty list or any other non-pair object.

The following code sequence implements the application **(car pair)**, where the value of **pair** is assumed to reside in register **Ai**, and the result is to be returned in register **Ak**.

```
ld.bu   S0,Ai,object$$tag        ;1:  get tag byte (may trap)
ld      S1,Ai,pair$$car          ;3a: get car (causes trap if not
                                  ;      pointer) (even if no trap,
                                  ;      may yield spurious value)
tcnd    ne0,S0,exception$not-a-pair
                                  ;2:  trap if not a pair
or      Ak,S1,ZERO               ;3b: copy car field to rooted
                                  ;      register
```

Note that the loading of the **car**-portion has been moved before the **tcnd** (trap on condition) instruction to reduce memory latency. Thus, **(car pair)** (and similarly, **(cdr pair)**) is compiled into 4 instructions, which execute in 5 cycles (including one cycle due to memory latency), assuming cache hits on both load instructions. The extra instruction which copies the result from a non-rooted to a rooted register is necessary to ensure that no rooted register contains an illegal value in the event of a trap caused by the second load instruction. By complicating the trap handler, it may be possible to eliminate the extra instruction.

Note that the obvious implementation

```
ld.bu   S0,Ai,object$$tag        ;1: get tag byte (may trap)
tcnd    ne0,S0,exception$not-a-pair
                                  ;2: trap if not a pair
ld      Ak,Ai,pair$$car          ;3: get car
```

occupies only three words, but executes in 7 cycles. Although four of these are due to memory latency, we did not expect an instruction scheduler to be able to eliminate more than one of them, and therefore opted for the slightly longer code sequence.

The instructions numbered 1 and 2 in the above code sequences are type checking overhead which can be eliminated if the code generator knows that the argument to **car** is indeed a pair. Furthermore, since no spurious value can be generated, the **car**-portion of the argument may be loaded directly in this case:

```
    ld      Ak,Ai,pair$$car          ;3: get car portion
```

Assuming a cache hit, the execution cost varies between one and three cycles, depending on whether the result register **Ak** is immediately referenced in the subsequent two instructions or not.

Testing for the Empty List   The application (**null? obj**) returns **#t** if **obj** is the empty list, otherwise it returns **#f**. In Screme, the empty list is not the same as the Boolean value **#f**, in anticipation of future revisions to Scheme which may no longer allow the representations of these two values to be identical. Thus, a suitable Scheme source code definition of **null?** would be (**define (null? x) (eq? x '())**).

The implementation of **null?** in value context consists of the following four instructions:

```
    cmp     S0,Ai,immediate$null     ;compare with '()
    bb0.n   eq,S0,$_FF               ;if not equal, to false exit...
    or      Ak,ZERO,immediate$false  ;... after returning #f
$_TT:                                ;-> true exit
    or      Ak,ZERO,immediate$true   ;if equal, return #t
$_FF:                                ;-> false exit
```

This assumes that the object to be tested is available in argument register **Ai**, and the result is returned in **Ak**, with **Ai=Ak** possible. Depending on whether the test succeeds or not, the above code sequence executes in four (three) cycles.

In control flow context, the cycle costs are the same, but only two instructions need to be generated:

```
    cmp     S0,Ai,immediate$null     ;compare with '()
    bb0     eq,S0,$_FF               ;if not equal, to false exit
$_TT:                                ;-> true exit
    ...
    br      $_Merge
$_FF:                                ;-> false exit
    ...
$_Merge:
```

Note that we have charged the "true exit" 2 cycles for the branch instruction which joins the computation paths together. Of course, the one cycle delay incurred by the **bb0** instruction could be eliminated by means of code scheduling.

Other Basic Operations   The implementation of the test **pair?** is quite similar to that for **null?**. It takes an additional instruction for loading the object header from memory, and three additional cycles, assuming cache hits.

The constructor **cons** is implemented in millicode. The interface to the millicode routine consists of two instructions and one data word.

The general implementation of the setter operations cost 10 instructions plus one data word. Three of the instructions check that the first argument to **set-car!** (**set-cdr!**) is indeed a pair, one instruction performs the field assignment, and the remaining six instructions register the assigned object with the generational garbage collector. This is necessary if the object is a pointer to a structure residing in a younger generation than the pair. Clearly, type tracking may eliminate the entire overhead, and reduce the implementation cost to one instruction and one cycle.

7.5.3   Fixnum Arithmetic

Most language implementations set a bound on the range of integers for which arithmetic operations are implemented; this bound generally coincides with the size of a machine word. A Scheme implementation, on the other hand, is expected to provide arbitrary-precision integer arithmetic. Arithmetic operations are additionally complicated by the fact that most operators must work on all available numeric types, which usually include floating point numbers, and possibly rational and complex numbers.

Clearly, such *generic arithmetic* must generally be implemented by calls to out-of-line procedures. However, since arithmetic on small integers is extremely common, always dispatching on the generic-arithmetic millicode would incur an unacceptable execution time penalty. Therefore, most implementations divide the space of integers into *unboxed fixnums*, which fit (along with tagging information) into a single machine word, and *boxed bignums*, which are represented via pointers to heap-allocated structures containing a multiword representation of the value [26].

The presence of differing type tags for fixnums and other numeric quantities means that arithmetic operators in the language cannot be directly mapped onto the standard machine instructions unless there is special hardware support. Without such support, arithmetic operations necessarily comprise arithmetic instructions as well as instructions for checking fixnum tags and detecting overflow.

In Screme, generic arithmetic is fully implemented in millicode. However, important fixnum operations such as the tests **zero?**, **positive?**, **negative?**, **odd?**, **even?**, the relational operators, addition, subtraction, multiplication, **quotient**, and **modulo** are open-coded for efficiency.

The following code sequence implements binary addition, with the operands in registers

Ai and **Ak**, and the result returned in a different register **Am**. Recall that a fixnum is indicated by the not-fixnum bit being zero.

```
    addu    Am,Ai,Ak                ;perform addition
    bb1     tagbit$not-fixnum,Ai,$_1
                                    ;test 1st operand for fixnum
    bb0.n   tagbit$not-fixnum,Ak,$_2
                                    ;test 2nd operand for fixnum
    clr     S0,Am,30<0>             ;prepare for overflow test
$_1:
    bsr     $_segment_generic       ;branch to generic millicode
    .word   <op=+,source1=Ai,source2=Ak,dest=Am,return=$_3>
$_2:
    bcnd    9,S0,$_1                ;check for overflow
$_3:
```

This code sequence occupies six instructions and one data word. In the case of both operands and the result being fixnums, it executes in 5 cycles. An overflow has occurred if the sign bit and the guard bit differ. We test this by masking off all but these two bits, and use the generality of the **bcnd** instruction to test if the masked value is either the most negative integer, or is positive.

If at least one of the arguments is not a fixnum, the generic millicode routine for addition is invoked in the following way:

- The inline code sequence branches to a code fragment at label **$_segment-_generic**, which actually calls the generic arithmetic millicode.

- The data word following the **bsr** instruction encodes the specific operation, the source locations, the destination register, and the return point.

- The out of line code sequence (one per code segment) loads the data word into millicode register **M1** and invokes the millicode. If one of the operands is a literal, the inline code sequence will have loaded it into register **M2**.

Note that even if the code generator knows that both arguments are fixnums, it can save only one cycle by replacing the two "branch on bit" instructions by a **br.n** instruction. However, if it is also known that the result of the addition cannot overflow, then the **addu** instruction alone suffices. Such constraints can be obtained from bounds analysis [8], and would constitute significant speed improvements for bounded loops.

7.5.4 *Analysis of Primop Implementation Costs*

Table 7.1 describes the implementation costs for all Screme primops. It considers both the static code size of the most general code sequence, as well as the cycle costs. The

primop	standard		value			control		
	w	c	w	c_{true}	c_{false}	w	c_{true}	c_{false}
(not obj)	—	—	5	5	4	3	5	4
(boolean? obj)	—	—	5	5	4	3	5	4
(eqv? obj1 obj2)	—	—	2	>3	>3	3	>5	>5
(eq? obj1 obj2)	—	—	4	4	3	2	4	3
(pair? obj)	—	—	5	$5+r$	$2;5+r$	3	$5+r$	$2;4+r$
(cons obj1 obj2)	2+1	>3	—	—	—	—	—	—
(car pair)	4	$4+max(r_1,r_2)-1$	—	—	—	—	—	—
(cdr pair)	4	$4+max(r_1,r_2)-1$	—	—	—	—	—	—
(set-car! pair obj)	10+1	$\geq 5+r$	—	—	—	—	—	—
(set-cdr! pair obj)	10+1	$\geq 5+r$	—	—	—	—	—	—
(null? obj)	—	—	4	4	3	2	4	3
(symbol? obj)	—	—	6	$6+r$	$2;6+r$	4	$6+r$	$2;5+r$
(zero? z)	—	—	8+1	2	4	4+1	4	3
(positive? x)	—	—	7+1	4	4	4+1	4	3
(negative? x)	—	—	7+1	4	4	4+1	4	3
(odd? n)	—	—	8+1	4	4	5+1	4	3
(even? n)	—	—	8+1	4	4	5+1	4	3
(relop? z1 z2)	—	—	8+1	6	5	5+1	6	5
(+ z1 z2)	6(7)+1	5	—	—	—	—	—	—
(* z1 z2)	18+1	15-17	—	—	—	—	—	—
(- z1 z2)	6(7)+1	5	—	—	—	—	—	—
(/ z1 z2)	1+1	many	—	—	—	—	—	—
(quotient n1 n2)	18+1	≥ 46	—	—	—	—	—	—

evaluation context

primop	standard w	standard c	value w	value c_{true}	value c_{false}	control w	control c_{true}	control c_{false}
(char? obj)	–	–	5	5	4	3	5	4
(char-relop? ch1 ch2)	–	–	10	10	9	8	10	9
(char->integer ch)	4	4	–	–	–	–	–	–
(integer->char n)	6	6	–	–	–	–	–	–
(string? obj)	–	–	6	$6+r$	$2;6+r$	4	$6+r$	$2;5+r$
(make-string k ch)	9+1	>9	–	–	–	–	–	–
(string-length str)	5	$5+r$	–	–	–	–	–	–
(string-ref str k)	13	$13+r_1-2+r_2$	–	–	–	–	–	–
(string-set! str k ch)	15	$15+max\{r-6,0\}$	–	–	–	–	–	–
(vector? obj)	–	–	6	$6+r$	$2;6+r$	4	$6+r$	$2;5+r$
(make-vector k fill)	4+1	>5	–	–	–	–	–	–
(vector-length vec)	5	$5+r$	–	–	–	–	–	–
(vector-ref vec k)	9	$9+r_1-1+r_2$	–	–	–	–	–	–
(vector-set! vec k obj)	15+1	$>10+r-1$	–	–	–	–	–	–
(procedure? obj)	–	–	7	$7+r$	$2;7+r$	–	$7+r$	$2;7+r$
(bytevector? obj)	–	–	6	$6+r$	$2;6+r$	4	$6+r$	$2;5+r$
(make-bytevector k)	11+1	$>11+r_1+r_2-2$	–	–	–	–	–	–
(bytevector-length bv)	5	$5+r$	–	–	–	–	–	–
(bytevector-ref bv k)	12	$12+r_1-2+r_2$	–	–	–	–	–	–
(bytevector-set! bv k by)	13	$13+max\{r-4,0\}$	–	–	–	–	–	–

Table 7.1: MC88000 code space and execution cycle costs for Screme primops.

relational operators for numbers are all captured by the entry named **relop?**; those for characters are captured by the entry named **char-relop?**.

The table distinguishes among three evaluation contexts. Predicates may be used in *value* or *control flow* context; all other primops appear only in the *standard* context. The cost in terms of instruction and data words is given in the columns headed by w; the cycle costs are in the c, c_{true}, and c_{false} columns. Since the cycle costs for predicates differ depending on whether they evaluate to *true* or *false*, both costs are indicated. The parameter r denotes the latency time for a memory read ($r = 2$ for a cache hit, $r = 16$ otherwise). If a code sequence issues two load instructions, the latency times are distinguished by subscripts.

Entries in the w column of the form $k + 1$ indicate that k instruction words and one dataword are used. The presence of a dataword always indicates that the code sequence interfaces with some millicode routine. *For the arithmetic primops, the cycle times assume that both operands pass the fixnum tag test*; all other cases are handled by the generic-arithmetic millicode and take considerably longer.

Some of the entries in the c_{false} column are of the form $c_1;c_2$. This indicates that the predicate returns *false* after either c_1 or c_2 cycles. This applies to all explicit type tests which inspect the pointer bit. If that bit is not set, the test fails; otherwise, additional testing must be performed.

All cycle costs in the c_{true} column of the control flow context include a 2 cycle charge for the branch which joins the two computation paths together. This makes the control flow cycle costs consistent with those in the value context column.

7.5.5 *Effects of Type Analysis*

It is instructive to classify the 88000 instruction sequences implementing Screme primops according to the purpose of each instruction. Table 7.2 breaks down the static code sequences into the following categories:

- *kernel*: Instructions which perform the "raw" work. Some of them also implicitly perform type checking by exploiting the misaligned address trap on the 88000.

- *type*: Instructions which check tag bits of an object and possibly the tag byte in the header prefixed to every structure.

- *bounds*: Instructions which check that values are not out of range (e.g., for vector and string bounds checks).

- *cvt*: Instructions which change the internal representation of a value (e.g., for indexing a string).

- *arith*: Instructions which interface with the generic-arithmetic millicode.

- *gc*: Instructions which interface with the garbage collector.

The last category is due to our use of a generation-scavenging garbage collector, and therefore specific to Screme. The other categories apply to any Scheme or Lisp implementation. Note that for predicates, only the code sequences in control flow context have been considered.

Clearly, the table shows that for most primops, the kernel instructions constitute merely a small fraction of the total number of instructions. All primops have significant type checking overhead (more so if the implicit type checking by means of 88000 traps were not available), and the primops dealing with characters, strings, vectors, and bytevectors often do a non-negligible amount of bounds checking. A sizeable fraction of the instructions for all the numeric primops deal with the interface to the generic-arithmetic millicode.

Ideally, the overhead introduced by run-time checks should be as small as possible. One possibility for reducing this overhead is by means of type declarations or type-specific operators to guide the compiler [3,10,4,21]. Unfortunately, this clutters up the code, and, at least for Scheme, would seriously compromise the elegance of the language. Another way to achieve efficiency is by simply ignoring certain checks. For example, the ORBIT compiler [10,11] generates efficient code for list manipulation and vector references by eliding type and/or bounds checks, thereby sacrificing security for efficiency. We have opted for a fully secure implementation of Scheme instead, and have tried to achieve performance by careful run-time system design, stressing execution-time efficiency over code size, and eliding run-time checks which the compiler could prove to be unnecessary due to type tracking.

Table 7.3 compares the cycle costs of the normal implementation of Screme primops with the smallest possible costs. To simplify the comparison, we have uniformly assumed that all values read from memory are in the data cache. For the smallest possible cycle cost we have assumed perfect type analysis, i.e, all arguments can be asserted to be of the required types at compile time. In addition, the following assumptions have been made:

- For **set-car!**, **set-cdr!**, and **vector-set!**, it is assumed that the **obj** to be assigned does not need to be registered with the garbage collector, either because it is an immediate literal, or because the compiler can prove that the pointer value is uninteresting to the collector.

- For + and -, it is assumed that the arguments as well as the result of the operation are fixnums.

- For *, **quotient**, and **modulo**, it is assumed that the second argument is a suitable power of 2.

primop	classification of instructions						
	total	kernel	type	bounds	cvt	arith	gc
(car pair)	4	1	3	-	-	-	-
(cdr pair)	4	1	3	-	-	-	-
(set-car! pair obj)	11	1	3	-	-	-	7
(set-cdr! pair obj)	11	1	3	-	-	-	7
(zero? z)	5	1	1	-	-	3	-
(positive? x)	5	1	1	-	-	3	-
(negative? x)	5	1	1	-	-	3	-
(odd? n)	6	1	1	-	-	4	-
(even? n)	6	1	1	-	-	4	-
(relop? z1 z2)	6	2	2	-	-	2	-
(+ z1 z2)	7	3	2	-	-	2	-
(* z1 z2)	19	14	2	-	-	3	-
(- z1 z2)	7	3	2	-	-	2	-
(quotient n1 n2)	19	12	2	-	-	5	-
(char-relop? ch1 ch2)	8	2	6	-	-	-	-
(char->integer ch)	4	3	1	-	-	-	-
(integer->char n)	6	2	2	2	-	-	-
(make-string k ch)	10	5	4	1	-	-	-
(string-length str)	5	1^a	3	-	1	-	-
(string-ref str k)	13	3^a	4	3	3	-	-
(string-set! str k ch)	15	3	7	3	2	-	-
(make-vector k fill)	5	3	1	1	-	-	-
(vector-length vec)	5	2^a	3	-	-	-	-
(vector-ref vec k)	9	3^b	3	3	-	-	-
(vector-set! vec k obj)	15	3^b	3	3	-	-	6
(make-bytevector k)	12	10	1	1	-	-	-
(bytevector-length bv)	5	2^a	3	-	-	-	-
(bytevector-ref bv k)	12	3^a	4	3	2	-	-
(bytevector-set! bv k by)	13	3^a	5	3	2	-	-

[a] one kernel instruction implicitly performs type checking
[b] two kernel instructions implicitly perform type checking

Table 7.2: Breakdown of MC88000 instruction sequences for Screme primops.

- For **vector-ref**, **vector-set!**, **string-ref**, **string-set!**, **byte-vector-ref**, and **bytevector-set!**, it is assumed that all bounds checks can be suppressed.

- For **string-ref**, **string-set!**, **bytevector-ref**, and **bytevector-set!**, none of the conversions between representations have been suppressed.

Although the ideal case will often not be achieved, we are still convinced that careful type analysis on Scheme programs can yield substantial improvements in both code space and execution time efficiency.

7.6 Current Status and Outlook

7.6.1 Status

As of the time of this writing, the Screme project has been put on indefinite hold for non-technical reasons, and most of the project members have left Tektronix Labs for greener pastures.

Unfortunately, the system was never completely operational. In particular, the last phase of the compiler (register targeting) was only designed, but never implemented. Moreover, neither floating point nor bignum arithmetic were ever written, although the generic arithmetic structure was in place. Finally, the debugging environment was not implemented.

7.6.2 Pseudo Benchmark

Since the compiler was never put together completely, we can only offer a "pseudo" benchmark at this point. Consider the definition of the **fib** procedure below.

```
(define (fib x)
   (letrec ((fibo (lambda (n)
      (if (< n 2)
          n
          (+ (fibo (- n 1)) (fibo (- n 2)))))))
   (fibo x)))
```

We have manually compiled the above fragment into 88000 code consisting of 53 instructions and 14 datawords (268 bytes total). A simple analysis reveals that this code will execute **(fib 20)** in roughly 470,600 cycles, or 23.5 milliseconds on a 20MHz 88000, provided that all referenced values are in the data cache. In comparison, the native code produced by Lightship Scheme on a Mac II for the same procedure takes 865 milliseconds to execute **(fib 20)**, which is about 37 times slower. In general,

primop	execution cycle costs		
	normal	*min*	*savings*
`(car pair)`	5	3	40%
`(cdr pair)`	5	3	40%
`(set-car! pair obj)`	11	1	91%
`(set-cdr! pair obj)`	11	1	91%
`(zero? z)`	4(3)	3(2)	25%(33%)
`(positive? x)`	4(3)	3(2)	25%(33%)
`(negative? x)`	4(3)	3(2)	25%(33%)
`(odd? n)`	4(3)	3(2)	25%(33%)
`(even? n)`	4(3)	3(2)	25%(33%)
`(relop? z1 z2)`	6(5)	4(3)	33%(40%)
`(+ z1 z2)`	5	1	80%
`(* z1 z2)`	15-17	6-7	60%
`(- z1 z2)`	5	1	80%
`(quotient n1 n2)`	46	5-7	$> 85\%$
`(modulo n1 n2)`	many	2	$> 90\%$
`(char-relop? ch1 ch2)`	10(9)	4(3)	60%
`(char->integer ch)`	4	1	75%
`(integer->char n)`	6	4	33%
`(make-string k ch)`	> 9	> 5	–
`(string-length str)`	7	4	43%
`(string-ref str k)`	15	10	33%
`(string-set! str k ch)`	15	5	66%
`(make-vector k fill)`	> 5	> 4	–
`(vector-length vec)`	7	4	43%
`(vector-ref vec k)`	12	4	66%
`(vector-set! vec k obj)`	> 11	2	$> 90\%$
`(make-bytevector k)`	> 13	> 11	–
`(bytevector-length bv)`	7	4	43%
`(bytevector-ref bv k)`	14	6	57%
`(bytevector-set! bv k by)`	13	4	69%

Table 7.3: Effect of type analysis on cycle costs for Screme primops under the assumption of cache hits.

well-informed sources have estimated that the 88000 runs about 15 times faster than the Mac II.

7.6.3 Improvements

In considering what might have been done differently in our implementation, three things come to mind. The first is that a significant execution penalty is paid to accommodate the possibility that code might be moved by the garbage collector. This leads to the representation of code addresses as full fledged objects, which requires a good deal of dynamic tag manipulation, as well as a considerable amount of space for code structure headers in the code itself. Because we expect the garbage collection of code to be a phenomenon that is (almost) exclusively utilized during program development, this amounts to a decision to slow down application programs in order to make it easier to implement an interactive programming environment. We would prefer either seeing this bookkeeping done in some other way, or having a compiler switch which would generate "application" code in which code addresses are represented in raw machine format.

Moreover, the storage needs for list cells (pairs) should be reexamined. In Screme, every list cell occupies 16 bytes, 8 of which are overhead. An alternate implementation technique would be to use a three-bit tag, with fixnums being `#b000`, immediates `#b100`, pairs `#b101`, and other pointers `#b110`; other tags would be illegal to allow one-instruction branches on fixnum, pointer, and pair. This would have advantages that include `car` and `cdr` being one-instruction operations (by exploiting the misaligned address trap), and pairs taking only 8 bytes of memory. These gains would seem to outweigh the disadvantages of requiring object allocation on 8-byte boundaries and the slowing down of vector operations by one or two cycles.

Finally, an instruction scheduler should be integrated into the code generator, as suggested in [2], and the type tracking phase should be supported by control and data flow analysis [19].

7.7 Future Research

A clever Scheme compiler should not only pay attention to language-specific features, such as procedure calls, primops, runtime type checks, environment access, and the handling of continuations, but also incorporate a variety of optimizations based on flow analysis. Shivers has demonstrated how to perform flow analysis in the presence of first class procedures and continuations [19] (see also Chapter 3). His techniques can be fruitfully applied to drive the following optimizations in a Scheme compiler:

- *Standard compiler optimizations*, such as elimination of common subexpressions, strength reduction, hoisting of loop invariant computations, elimination of induction variables, loop unrolling, etc. [1]. The Lisp compiler described in [3] includes some of these already.

- *Elimination of run-time type checks* based on compile-time type inference. These should be particularly effective in "counting" loops which process strings, vectors, and bytevectors, as well as in list processing.

- *Elimination of run-time bounds checks* based on compile-time analysis of the value ranges of variables [8]. Since the fixnum tag check is a special case of bounds checking, this could significantly improve the performance of fixnum arithmetic, particularly in bounded loops.

- *More efficient representation of index variables* based on representation analysis. This would allow the use of machine datatypes for index variables in string processing loops.

Recently, there has been renewed interest in optimizing storage management for late-bound languages [17,9]. However, based on our dissertation work in the area [15] we are convinced that suitable analyses are overly complicated and yield no practical benefits, except possibly in very specialized cases. It is interesting to note that none of the recent papers in this area has applied the advocated techniques to practical examples in a practical language (for example, one with recursive procedures). As was shown in [15] for Scheme, specific shapes of lists structures must be taken into account in order to obtain any useful data flow information at all. However, the required analysis appears to be rather expensive, and in the light of improved garbage collection techniques such as generation scavenging [24], not cost effective.

Instead, the aggressive compilation techniques developed by Ungar and his students [5,6] for SELF, an object-oriented language with very late binding times, should be explored in the context of Scheme. For example, the **fib** procedure could be compiled into two versions: a general version of the local **fibo** procedure, and a specialized one which assumes that **n** is a fixnum and the operations (**- n 1**) and (**- n 2**) also yield fixnums. Before calling **fibo**, the appropriate version is selected based on a runtime fixnum test of the value of **n**. It should not be too difficult to establish at compile time that the recursion "counts down" toward zero, which allows one to conclude that the subtraction operations cannot produce bignums when given a fixnum value for **n**. The fixnum version of **fibo** would execute in about 20.25 milliseconds, which is about 14% faster than the general version. Similarly, it may be possible to obtain good floating point code in Scheme with the help of the specialization techniques developed in the SELF compiler [5].

Finally, a good Scheme compiler should incorporate a good register allocator, which could be based on the TNBIND technique [3] or graph coloring [12]. Also, for RISC architectures, an instruction scheduler should be included to minimize delays due to memory latency and branching.

Acknowledgments

The Screme system was designed by Will Clinger, Norm Adams, Steve Vegdahl, and Ken Dickey. Uwe Pleban joined the group for about nine months to implement the backend of the compiler; he ended up learning and writing about what he considers a nifty system designed by Scheme experts. The entire team hopes that the work can be picked up by some other group interested in a high performance Scheme for the 88000.

References

[1] A. V. Aho, R. Sethi, and J. D. Ullman. *Compilers: Principles, Techniques, and Tools.* Addison-Wesley (1986).

[2] P. H. L. Bird. *Code generation and instruction scheduling for pipelined SISD machines.* Ph.D. thesis, University of Michigan (1987).

[3] R. A. Brooks, R. P. Gabriel, and G. L. Steele, Jr. "An optimizing compiler for lexically scoped LISP." *In Proceedings of the SIGPLAN '82 Symposium on Compiler Construction*, 261-275 (June 1982).

[4] R. A. Brooks, D. B. Posner, J. L. McDonald, J. L. White, E. Benson, and R. P. Gabriel. "Design of an optimizing, dynamically retargetable compiler for Common Lisp," *In Proceedings of the 1986 ACM Conference on Lisp and Functional Programming*, 67-85 (August 1986).

[5] C. Chambers and D. Ungar. "Customization: Optimizing compiler technology for SELF, a dynamically-typed, object-oriented programming language." *In Proceedings of the SIGPLAN '89 Conference on Programming Language Design and Implementation*, 146-160 (July 1989).

[6] C. Chambers, D. Ungar, and E. Lee. "An efficient implementation of SELF, a dynamically-typed object-oriented language based on prototypes." *Proc. OOPSLA '89*, 49-70 (October 1989).

[7] W. D. Clinger, A. H. Hartheimer, and E. M. Ost. "Implementation strategies for continuations." *Proc. 1988 ACM Conference on Lisp and Functional Programming*, 124-131 (July 1988).

[8] W. Harrison. "Compiler analysis of the value ranges for variables." IEEE Transactions on Software Engineering, Vol. SE-3, No. 3, 243-250 (May 1977).

[9] S. Horwitz, P. Pfeiffer, and T. Reps. "Dependence analysis for pointer variables." *Proc. SIGPLAN '89 Conference on Programming Language Design and Implementation*, 28-40 (June 1989).

[10] D. Kranz, R. Kelsey, J. Rees, P. Hudak, J. Philbin, and N. Adams. "ORBIT: An optimizing compiler for Scheme." *Proc. SIGPLAN '86 Symposium on Compiler Construction*, 219-233 (June 1986).

[11] D. A. Kranz. *ORBIT: An optimizing compiler for Scheme.* Ph.D. thesis, Yale University (1988).

[12] J. R. Larus and P. N. Hilfinger. "Register allocation in the SPUR Lisp compiler." *Proc. SIGPLAN '86 Symposium on Compiler Construction*, 255-263 (June 1986).

[13] D. B. McDonald, S. E. Fahlman, and A. Z. Spector. "An efficient Common Lisp for the IBM RT PC." Technical Report CMU-CS-87-134, Carnegie-Mellon University (July 1987).

[14] *MC88100 32-Bit third-generation microprocessor technical summary.* Document No. BR-588/D, Motorola, Inc. (1988).

[15] U. F. Pleban. *Preexecution analysis based on denotational semantics.* Ph.D. thesis, University of Kansas (1981).

[16] J. Rees and W. Clinger (Editors). "Revised revised revised report on the algorithmic language Scheme."
      ACM SIGPLAN Notices 21,12, 37-79 (December 1986).

[17] C. Ruggieri and T. P. Murtagh. "Lifetime analysis of dynamically allocated objects." *Proc. 15th POPL*,
      285-293 (January 1988).

[18] S. Shebs and R. Kessler. "Automatic design and implementation of language datatypes." *Proc. SIGPLAN
      '87 Symposium on Interpreters and Interpretive Techniques*, 26-37 (June 1987).

[19] O. Shivers. "Control flow analysis in Scheme." *Proc. SIGPLAN '88 Conference on Programming Lan-
      guage Design and Implementation*, 164-174, (June 1988).

[20] G. L. Steele, Jr. *Rabbit: A compiler for Scheme.* Technical Report 474, MIT Artificial Intelligence
      Laboratory (May 1978).

[21] G. L. Steele, Jr. *Common Lisp: The Language.* Digital Press (1984).

[22] P. Steenkiste and J. Hennessy. "LISP on a reduced-instruction-set-processor." *Proc. 1986 ACM Confer-
      ence on Lisp and Functional Programming*, 192-201 (August 1986).

[23] P. Steenkiste and J. Hennessy. "Tags and type-checking in LISP: Hardware and software approaches."
      Proc. ASPLOS-II, 50-59 (October 1987).

[24] D. Ungar. "Generation scavenging: A non-disruptive high performance storage reclamation algorithm."
      Proc. 1984 ACM Symposium on Practical Software Development Environments, 157-167, (April 1984).

[25] S. Vegdahl and U. F. Pleban. "The runtime environment for Screme, a Scheme implementation on the
      88000." *Proc. ASPLOS-III*, 172-182 (April 1989).

[26] J. L. White. "Reconfigurable, retargetable, bignums: A case study in efficient, portable Lisp system
      building." *Proc. 1986 ACM Conference on Lisp and Functional Programming*, 174-191 (August 1986).

8   The Implementation of Oaklisp

Barak A. Pearlmutter and Kevin J. Lang

8.1   Language Description

Oaklisp [4,5] is an object-oriented extension of Scheme; any program conforming to the R3RS Scheme standard [6] should run under Oaklisp with identical results. Thus, the most efficient way to describe Oaklisp is to mention the features that distinguish it from Scheme.

The fundamental computational model of Oaklisp is based on generic operations rather than functions. When an operation is applied to an object, the piece of code (or "method") that is actually invoked depends on the type of the object. For example, consider what happens when the expression (car mylist) is evaluated in Oaklisp. The variables car and mylist are dereferenced to yield two objects, the first of which is an operation – an anonymous token that denotes an abstract computation. This operation is then applied to the object to which the variable mylist was bound. If the object is an instance of the Oaklisp type cons-pair, [1] then a method is invoked which returns the contents of the first storage slot in the object. If the object is an instance of some type that doesn't have a car method, the run-time system checks to see whether a supertype of that type has a method for performing the operation. In case of conflict, the system invokes the method that would be found during a left-to-right, depth-first search of the multiple inheritance graph starting at the type of the object.

Syntactically, Oaklisp is similar to Scheme. Oaklisp has all the standard primitive special forms such as if and quote, but lambda is not primitive. In its place is the add-method special form, which associates a method with a type and an operation.

(add-method (*operation* (*type* . *ivarlist*) . *arglist*) *body*)   *Special Form*

Returns *operation* after adding a method for *operation* to the method table of *type*. The arguments to the method are specified by *arglist*, and instance variables that are referenced in the method's body are declared in *ivarlist*. Free variables in a method are evaluated in the lexical context in which they appear, with the bindings from the time the form was evaluated, just as with lambda in regular Scheme. The *operation* and *type* positions of the form are evaluated at run time.

---

[1] The phrase "the type cons-pair" means "the type to which the variable cons-pair is bound." We will use this convention throughout this chapter.

The Oaklisp run-time environment includes all of the standard Lisp types such as numbers, conses, and symbols. Unlike other dialects of Lisp, types in Oaklisp are explicitly represented by objects that can be manipulated at run time. Thus, Oaklisp types are first-class entities in the same sense as Scheme functions. Oaklisp types are instantiated by the **make** operation. For example, the call **(make hash-table)** causes a message containing the **make** operation to be sent to the **hash-table** type object, which then allocates, initializes, and returns a new hash table object. Similarly, one can create a new operation by applying **make** to the **operation** type, and one can create a new type by applying **make** to the **type** type.

To see how Oaklisp works in practice, let us define a new type of cons cell using **make**.

```
(set! mycons-cell
      (make type
            (list pair)                   ;supertypes
            (list 'slot1 'slot2)))        ;instance variable names
```

The **make** method for types takes two extra arguments: a list of the types from which the new type will inherit methods, and a list of names for the new type's instance variables. The type **mycons-cell** inherits from **pair**, which has methods for high-level list-processing operations such as **map** and **print**. These methods are written in terms of the accessor operations **car** and **cdr**, so we can cause instances of **mycons-cell** to be fully functional list components simply by supplying **car** and **cdr** methods for the type:

```
(add-method (car (mycons-cell slot1) self) slot1)

(add-method (cdr (mycons-cell slot2) self) slot2)
```

Now all we have to do is define the method for initializing instances of **mycons-cell**, and then we can instantiate the type using **make**:

```
(add-method (initialize (mycons-cell slot1 slot2) self x y)
  (set! slot1 x)
  (set! slot2 y))

(make mycons-cell 1 '(2 3))
```

The **make** operation really only needs to receive one argument (the object which denotes the type that is being instantiated) but our call contains the extra values 1 and '(2 3). Before returning our new object, the code for **make** sends the object an

initialize message which includes these two values. Our **initialize** method then uses these values to set up the object's internal state.

Because **mycons-cell** has **car** and **cdr** methods and inherits all of the system's list-processing methods from the supertype **pair**, our new object acts exactly like any other cons cell in the system. For example, when we apply the **print** operation to the object, it prints out as "(1 2 3)".

Although the type **mycons-cell** merely duplicates the functionality of the existing **cons-pair** type, we could just as easily define a radically different type of cons cell, such as a variety that contains thunks which aren't evaluated until their values are actually needed. Such a type would make it possible to build potentially infinite, lazily evaluated lists. In fact, in our implementation of Oaklisp, the variable **prime-list** is bound to a list of all prime numbers that was defined using this type of lazy cons cell.

Because Oaklisp types are represented by ordinary run-time objects, it is even possible to define new kinds of types at user level. For example, we have defined the **coercible-type** type, each instance of which is a type that responds to the **coercer** operation by returning the coercion operation for that type. For example, when the expression ((**coercer string**) '**foo**) is evaluated, the **coercer** operation is applied to the coercible type **string**, which returns the (anonymous) operation for coercing things to strings. This operation is then applied to the symbol 'foo, and because a method for the string-coercer operation has been defined for symbols, the result of this call is the string "**foo**".

This ability to add significant new features to Oaklisp at the user level is a result of the consistency of its semantics. Everything in the Oaklisp world is a full-fledged object with a type that fits into the inheritance hierarchy, and all computation occurs as the result of generic operation applications.

Due to the language's temporal consistency, **add-method** can be done at any time, and it is thus necessary for the method dispatch mechanisms to be dynamically modifiable. This is in contrast to statically compiled implementations of languages like C++, but is similar to interactive programming environments like Common Lisp's CLOS. Since these dynamic modification mechanisms must be present for processing incremental method addition, it seems capricious to deny the programmer run-time access to them.

8.2 Memory Format

Most objects, whether system- or user-defined, are stored in a standardized "boxed" format. The first word in this format is a reference to the object's type. The type of an object not only carries semantic weight, but also permits the run-time system to determine the answer to practical questions such as the number of storage cells that are included in a given object. The type is followed by storage for the object's instance variables.

The two objects shown here are instances of the pre-defined **cons-pair** type and a hypothetical, user-defined **lazy-cons-pair** type. Each of the objects contains a reference to the type of the object, followed by an appropriately sized block of storage for its instance variables.

Our implementation of Oaklisp currently runs only on machines with 32-bit words (although porting to a machine with slightly different word size, such as 36 or 24, should be very simple). These words are divided into two contiguous chunks: free words and allocated words. The *free pointer* points to the division between these two chunks, and it is incremented as memory is allocated. When allocating an object would push the free pointer beyond the limits of memory, a garbage collection is performed.

The allocated portion of memory is divided into *boxed objects* and *solitary cells*. Each aggregate object is a contiguous chunk of cells. The first cell of an object is a reference to its type; if the type is *variable length*, the second stores the length of the object, including the first two cells. The remainder of the cells hold the instance variables. Solitary cells are cells that are not part of any object, but are the targets of locatives, and are used heavily in the implementation of variables, discussed later.

8.2.1 Tags

The low two bits of each word contain a tag value which tells how the word should be interpreted. The most important question that the tag answers is whether a word should be interpreted as an "immediate" object or as a reference to a "boxed" object that lives elsewhere.

For example, if the tag has the value 00_2, the high 30 bits of the word are interpreted as an integer, but if the tag has the value 11_2, then the high 30 bits of the word are interpreted as a reference to the boxed object that resides at the address specified by those 30 bits.

While reserving 2 bits for a tag clearly costs us something in the case of an integer, the tag is free in the case of a reference to a boxed object because the 2 low bits of a word-aligned pointer always have the same value and hence carry no information.

Fixnums, locatives, and characters are stored as single-word, immediate objects whose types are specified by their tag bits.

31 30 29 28 27 26 ... 11 10 9 8	*7 6 5 4 3 2*	*1 0*	*type*
two's complement integer		0 0	fixnum
data	subtype	1 0	other immediate type
address		0 1	locative (pointer to cell)
address		1 1	reference to boxed object

To simplify garbage collection, we do not permit any exceptions to the tagging protocol. As a result, strings and code vectors are not as dense as they would be if raw binary data could be stored in memory.

8.2.2 *Efficient Access to Predefined Slots in Objects*

To justify this tagging scheme, consider what happens when the Oaklisp processor executes a **cdr** instruction, ignoring type checking for the moment. The processor first strips the tag value of 11_2 from the reference which is the instruction's argument to obtain a pointer to a memory location. The processor then fetches the contents of the second slot of the memory structure that begins at that location. An interesting optimization is possible: subtraction rather than bit-wise **and** can be used to strip the tag from the reference. Then the C expression to perform **cdr** on a reference r (an unsigned long) is

```
*((ref *)(r - 0x3) + 2)
```

which gets constant folded to

```
*(ref *)(r + 5)          /*    5 = 2*4 - 3    */
```

Most computers can use addressing modes to dereference a pointer with an offset, so the **cdr** operation can be performed by a single instruction of the form

```
ldl    5@r1 ,r2.
```

But even on computers that can't do this in one instruction, it is just as easy to add an offset of 5 as it would be to add an offset of 8 to access the cdr of a cons cell, so no efficiency is lost by using a tag value of 3 rather than a tag value of 0 for references.

The only time when a tag value of 0 would be better is when the machine must access the type field of an object. However, some machines ignore the low two bits when performing a long word fetch anyway, and on the remaining machines the advantage of avoiding tag manipulations on arithmetic seems to outweigh the overhead of slightly slower access to the type fields of boxed objects.

8.2.3 *Storage Reclamation*

Our garbage collector is of the popular stop-and-copy variety [1]; the spaces to be reclaimed are renamed *old*, all accessible objects in the old spaces are transported to a new space, and the old spaces are reclaimed. The data present in the initial world is considered static and is not part of old space in normal garbage collections, only in *full* garbage collections, which also move everything not reclaimed into static space. Before dumping the world to a save file, a modified full garbage collection is performed in which the stacks are left out of the root set.

Locatives can point to a single cell in the middle of a large object, and the garbage collector is able to deallocate all of an object except for those cells pointed to by locatives, which become solitary cells. Due to this complication, the collector makes an extra pass over the heap. A paper with more complete details on this technique is in press.

The weak pointer table is scanned at the end of garbage collection, and references to deallocated objects are discarded. Desired new space size is changed dynamically, being expanded after a garbage collection when the allocation system judges that it would have been better to have allocated more space. The entire garbage collector is written in C, and even in code that places heavy demands on the storage allocation subsystem, such as bignum arithmetic, the time spent in the garbage collector is a tiny fraction of the total time.

The user interface to the garbage collector is quite simple. Normally, the user need not be concerned with storage reclamation, as upon the exhaustion of storage the garbage collector is automatically invoked. A switch is provided to allow the user to turn off noise messages about garbage collection, and Oaklisp operations to force normal and full garbage collections are provided.

8.2.4 *Inheritance of Instance Variables*

reference to type *foo*
value of **foo-1**
value of **baz-1**
value of **baz-2**
value of **baz-3**
value of **bar-1**
value of **bar-2**

Pictured above is the memory format for an instance of a type *foo* which inherits from types *bar* and *baz*. The type *bar* has instance variables **bar-1** and **bar-2**, the type *baz* has instance variables **baz-1**, **baz-2** and **baz-3**, and *foo* has instance variable **foo-1**.

The sharp-eyed reader will note that the instance of *foo* is structured such that the instance variables associated with its constituent types *foo*, *bar*, and *baz* are stored in separate, contiguous memory blocks. Because Oaklisp methods are not allowed to contain direct references to the instance variables of supertypes, this memory format permits the compiler to implement all of the instance variable references in a method using a base-pointer-relative addressing mode. At run time, the processor's base-pointer is always set to the beginning of the instance variable block for the type which actually supplied the method which is currently being executed.

When a type inherits a type through two different routes, it only gets a single instance variable block for that type.[2] Because of our strict segregation of instance variables from the component types in a composite type, if the instance variables of two types inherited by a third have the same names, they are still distinct variables. This is in marked contrast to ZetaLisp Flavors or CLOS, in which references to instance variable must pass through mapping tables, resulting in considerable overhead. There are also important modularity considerations in favor of our scheme which are beyond the scope of this document, but are discussed in detail by Snyder [7]. Our semantics allow us to reference instance variables very quickly once the location of the relevant instance variable block for a given method has been determined. It also allows us to always use the same compiled code for a given method, regardless of whether it is being invoked upon an instance of the type for which it was originally defined or upon an instance of an inheriting type.

8.2.5 The Memory Format of Types and Operations

To show more of the character of the Oaklisp system, we will now look at the internal representation of instances of two important types. All objects, including these, have the same basic format as instances of user-defined types.

operation
`lambda?`
`cache-type`
`cache-method`
`cache-type-offset`

Operations are tokens whose only essential property is their identity. Thus, in our initial implementation, the memory format of an operation included only a single word: a reference to the **operation** type. Currently, operations contain some state that the

---

[2]This was a rather arbitrary implementation decision, and should not be relied upon by users. In fact, it will likely be changed in a future release.

run-time system uses to speed up message sending. For example, if an operation has only one method and that method is associated with the root of the type hierarchy, then it is possible to jump straight to this method whenever the operation must be performed. We indicate that an operation has this property by storing its sole method in its **lambda?** slot. (The instance variables associated with our method-caching scheme will be described later in this chapter.)

In order to allow the C code to refer to instance variables of important low-level system types as efficiently as possible, types whose instance variables are used directly by the C code are *top wired,* which forces the involved instance variables to appear first in memory. Except for the inability to inherit from more than one top-wired type at once, this top wiring is invisible to users. Most top-wired types have names like **%code-vector** or **%closed-environment**, and are not of interest to users anyway.

settable-operation
`lambda?`
`cache-type`
`cache-method`
`cache-type-offset`
`the-setter`

Settable operations [3] (a subtype of normal operations described below) contain two blocks of instance variables, one for the **settable-operation** type, and another for the **operation** type from which it inherits. Because **operation** is top wired, its instance variable block appears at the top of an instance of **settable-operation**.

Now we look at the memory format of a type. In particular, we will show the object which represents the **settable-operation** type. Thus, the reference in the header of the settable operation shown above points to this object:

type	
`instance-length`	6
`supertype-list`	`(#<Type OPERATION>)`
`ivar-list`	`(the-setter)`
`type-bp-alist`	`((#<Type SETTABLE-OPERATION> . 5)` `(#<Type OPERATION> . 1))`
`operation-method-alist`	`((#<Operation SETTER> . #<Method 3652>))`

As always, the first word in the object is a reference to its type, in this case, the **type** type. The second word in the object contains the value of its first instance variable, **instance-length**, which tells the system how many words of storage need to be allocated for each instance of the type. The garbage collector also uses this information when it copies instances of the type from old to new space.

The rest of the information in a type object governs the method lookup process which occurs when an operation is applied to an instance of the type. For example, the variable **operation-method-alist** stores the association between operations and methods for the type. However, this association list contains no information about the methods of the type's supertypes, so if a method can't be found locally for a given operation, a depth-first search of the inheritance graph is performed. The immediate supertypes of a type are recorded in the variable **supertype-list**.

Once a method has been found for an operation, the processor's base-pointer register is loaded with the address of the relevant instance variable block in the object that was the operation's first argument. The base pointer is set using to **type-bp-alist**, which describes the layout of the various instance variable blocks in instances of the object's type.

Finally, the field **ivar-list** specifies the layout of the variables in an instance variable block for the type. This map is used by the compiler to compute the offsets for the base-pointer-relative bytecodes that it emits for references to instance variables.

8.3   Processor Model

Our implementation of Oaklisp is based on a virtual processor that is emulated by a C program. The virtual processor contains three important registers: the program counter, the environment pointer, and the base pointer. When an operation is applied to an object by the **funcall-cxt** instruction, the processor pushes the values of these three registers on its context stack and then searches for a method for the operation, starting at the type of the object and continuing up the inheritance hierarchy if necessary. The **funcall-tail** instruction, which is identical to the **funcall-cxt** instruction except that it does not push anything onto the context stack, is used when the processor doesn't need to return to the current execution context and hence shouldn't save its state. The method which results from this search contains two parts: a reference to a vector of instructions, and a reference to a vector of storage cells which represents the method's lexical environment. These two references are used to set the processor's program counter and environment pointer. The base pointer is set to the top of the block of instance variables from the type the method was defined for.

8.3.1   Calling Conventions

The processor contains two stacks: one for values and one for saved processor state. This separation allows the value stack to smoothly accumulate values for function calls. Before a tail-recursive call, the parameters of the current call must be removed from the stack. Because return addresses do not have to be removed from the value stack during this process, stack motion is reduced. We feel that this dual stack system with an unframed value stack is primarily responsible for the efficiency of function calls in our implementation.

The calling protocol is illustrated by the following code vector, which the compiler generated for the expression (**lambda** (a b) (foo (bar b (baz b)) a)). The convention for verifying that the correct number of arguments is included in each function call can also be seen here; the processor has a **nargs** register whose value is set by callers and checked by callees.

Bytecode	Resulting value stack contents	English Description
(check-nargs 2)	... b a	The lambda's args are on the stack.
(load-stk 0 a)	... b a a	Preload second arg for **foo**.
(load-stk 2 b)	... b a a b	Load arg for **baz**.
(load-glo-con baz)	... b a a b baz	
(store-nargs 1)		
(funcall-cxt)	... b a a Z	Call **baz** and return, yielding second arg for **bar**.
(load-stk 3 b)	... b a a Z b	Load first arg for **bar**.
(load-glo-con bar)	... b a a Z b bar	
(store-nargs 2)		
(funcall-cxt)	... b a a R	Call **bar** and return, yielding first arg for **foo**.
(blt-stk 2 2)	... a R	blow away the lambda's args
(load-glo-con foo)	... a R foo	
(store-nargs 2)		
(funcall-tail)		call **foo**, but don't return.

8.3.2   C-Level Optimizations

In addition to optimizations discussed elsewhere in this chapter, a number of tricks at the C level were used to speed up the bytecode emulator.

Judicious use of register declarations and manual reuse of variables sped things up considerably, as did avoiding all procedure calls in common cases, and taking care that important system variables were able to live in registers. The latter was somewhat difficult because of interactions with the garbage collector. In our solution, storage allocation was done with a macro which incremented the free pointer and checked it against the upper limit of free space. Only if no storage was available was a procedure, namely the garbage collector, called. In order to allow register variables to hold members of the root set, such variables were pushed onto a special stack before calling the garbage collector, and popped off afterwards. Similarly, the value and context stack pointers were copied from local variables to global ones before calling the garbage collector. This allowed the context and value stack pointers, as well as emulator temporaries, to be kept in registers, which resulted in considerable speedup.

Tag checking was accomplished by macros, which were carefully tuned by benchmarking and examining the assembly level output of the compiler. Similarly, overflow checking for fixnum arithmetic was carefully tuned. In the case of overflow checking, we provided a number of different ways to detect overflows, selectable by compile time switches, because of extra constructs available on some machines. Much to our chagrin, although most machines raise an overflow flag, we were unable to find any way to access these flags, even by abandoning portable constructs. If this optimization were possible, we estimate that the tak benchmark could be sped up by about 10%.

Stack buffer overflow and underflow checking was another good target for optimization. Rather than doing bounds checking each time a value is pushed or popped, the code was modified to check only at strategic locations, where it was ensured that the stack buffer was in a state where it was appropriate to execute the entire next instruction. By making sure that there is always at least one element on the stack, unary instructions were able to dispense with buffer bounds checking entirely. Such instructions are quite common, including operators like `car` and `contents`, so this optimization alone was quite fruitful. All in all, efforts to economize on buffer bounds checking were well spent, resulting in about a 30% speed-up.

Since stack dumping or reloading procedures are called when the stack pointer exceeds the stack buffer bounds, and for speed reasons the stack pointers are kept in register variables, the stack buffer bounds checking macros load and unload the stack pointers from global structures across these procedure calls. Even more speed could be gained by using virtual memory facilities to trap at the edges of the stack buffer, obviating the need for explicit stack buffer bounds checking entirely, but at the loss of portablity.

8.4 Compilation

Our Oaklisp compiler implements the following primitive language constructs:

- variables
- combinations
- `quote`
- `if`
- `make-locative`
- `add-method`
- `labels`

All other special forms are macro-expanded in combinations of the primitive forms. For example, the familiar special forms **lambda** and **set!** are macro-expanded into combinations of function calls and **add-method** and **make-locative** forms.

8.4.1   Constant Folding and Frozen Variables

The compiler knows about the special properties of a number of operation subtypes, such as **open-coded-mixin** which informs the compiler that an operation can be open coded, **no-side-effects-mixin**, which permits constant folding, and **backward-args-mixin**, which causes the arguments to the operation to be pushed onto the stack in reverse order when the operation is open coded. These, in concert with a mechanism by which global variables can be declared *frozen,* which means that their values will never change, allow our simple compiler to perform a surprisingly wide range of optimizations.

For example, the **list** operation contains **backward-args-mixin** and **open-coded-mixin**, and is frozen. Thus, when compiling the expression (**list** 1 2 3), the compiler first generates code to push the arguments in reverse order:

    (load-imm 1) (load-imm 2) (load-imm 3)

and then calls **list**'s open-coder to obtain the following efficient bytecode sequence:

    (load-reg nil)(reverse-cons)(reverse-cons)(reverse-cons)

where the **reverse-cons** instruction is a version of the **cons** instruction that takes its arguments in reverse order.

Another example is the expression (**set!** (**car** **x**) **y**). This is macroexpanded to ((**setter** **car**) **x** **y**). Both **setter** and **car** are frozen, and the **setter** operation has **no-side-effects-mixin**, so the (**setter** **car**) expression is constant folded at compile time to an anonymous operation. This anonymous operation has **open-coded-mixin**, so it gets open coded as the instruction (**set-car**), and the whole code fragment thus compiles to

    (load-glo-con y) (load-glo-con x) (set-car).

8.4.2   Function Calls and Global Variables

The expansion of **lambda** makes use of the fact that all upward paths through the Oaklisp inheritance graph terminate at the distinguished type **object**, and so any method associated with this type functions as a "default" method that applies to objects of any type. Thus, (lambda (x y) (+ x y)) can be macro expanded to (add-method ((make operation) (object) x y) (+ x y)). When evaluated, this expansion generates a new anonymous operation and then associates it with a method at the top of the inheritance hierarchy.

The special form (set! foo 3) is macro-expanded into the combination ((setter contents) (make-locative foo) 3). This combination is compiled as follows. First, the compiler emits the instruction (LOAD-IMM 3) to load the immediate value 3 onto the stack.

Next, after determining that the variable foo is global, the compiler translates the special form (make-locative foo) into the pseudo-instruction load-glo, supplying the symbol foo as an argument. When this instruction is encountered by the Oaklisp loader, the relevant global namespace is consulted to find the memory location that is associated with the variable name foo. A locative to this memory cell is then created and plugged into the argument field of the instruction, which is then turned into an ordinary LOAD-IMM instruction.

Finally, the combination (setter contents) is constant folded to yield the anonymous operation for storing a value in the memory location referenced by a locative. The compiler then notices that the type of this operation includes the supertype **open-coded-mixin**, so a message is sent to the operation requesting a bytecode sequence for executing the operation directly (that is, without a function call). In this case, the operation returns the single instruction (set-contents).

So, the expression (set! foo 3) is macro expanded to ((setter contents) (make-locative foo) 3), which is compiled into the bytecode sequence (load-imm 3) (load-glo foo) (set-contents) and then converted by the loader into (load-imm 3) (load-imm <locative>) (set-contents).

Another specially marked version of load-imm called load-code is emitted when the compiler turns an **add-method** special form into a call to the **install-method** operation. The argument to this instruction is a symbolic representation of a code vector. The Oaklisp assembler turns this into a list of opcodes together with some symbolic variable-patching information, and then the Oaklisp loader resolves the variable references and constructs the actual code vector in memory. The load-code pseudo-instruction is then turned into an ordinary load-imm instruction whose argument is a reference to the code vector.

An example of the code that would be generated for an **add-method** special form is shown below. Note that the loader converts the pseudo-instruction load-glo-con into the instruction load-imm-con, which the processor treats as a load-imm instruction followed by the locative-dereferencing instruction contents.

```
(add-method (jump (frog x-pos color)
                  self distance)
  (set! x-pos (+ distance x-pos))
  (set! color 'greener))
```
$\Longrightarrow$
```
                     ;assumed ivar map
((load-code (code (x-pos color)
                  ((check-nargs 2)
                   (load-bp 0 x-pos)
                   (load-stk 2 distance)
                   (plus)
                   (store-bp 0)
                   (pop 3)
                   (load-imm greener)
                   (store-bp 1)
                   (return))))
  (load-glo-con jump)
  (load-glo-con frog)
  (load-glo-con install-method)
  (store-nargs 3)
  (funcall-tail))
```

8.4.3 Local Function Calls and Iteration

All looping is expressed vis tail recursion, as evident from the primitive forms the compiler recognizes listed above. Thus, in order for tight loops to be compiled efficiently it is necessary for the compiler to optimize heavily certain tail-recursive constructs. In particular, when the compiler encounters a **labels** form in which the labeled procedures are only called tail recursively and never referenced in any other way, it emits the code for the labeled procedures inline and compiles calls to them as simple branches, as in the following example.

This form describes how to append lists. Since **append** is so frequently used, it was written as a local tail-recursive loop.

```
(add-method (append (pair) oldcopy b)
  (let ((newcopy (cons (car oldcopy) b)))
    (let next ((oldpair (cdr oldcopy))
               (last-newpair newcopy))
      (if (not (null? oldpair))
          (next (cdr oldpair)
                (set! (cdr last-newpair)
                      (cons (car oldpair) b)))
          newcopy))))
```

This inner loop, which seems to involve procedure calls, nevertheless compiles into efficient code, as seen in the compiler's output.

```
        ((check-nargs 2)
         (load-stk 1 b)
         (load-stk 1 oldcopy)
         (car)
         (cons)
         (load-stk 0 newcopy)
         (load-stk 2 oldcopy)
         (cdr)
label0  (load-stk 0 oldpair)
         (branch-nil else1)
         (load-stk 4 b)
         (load-stk 1 oldpair)
         (car)
         (cons)
         (load-stk 2 last-newpair)
         (set-cdr)
         (blast 2)
         (cdr)
         (branch label0)
else1   (pop 2)
         (blt-stk 1 2)
         (return)))
```

8.5 List Optimizations

Because lists are so ubiquitous in lisp, it is desirable to expend some effort speeding up access to them. On the other hand, we designed Oaklisp so that cons cells would fit naturally into an extensible type hierarchy, as the example given in Section 8.1 shows. In initial versions of the system **car** and **cdr** were not specially handled, but were regular operations like any others. Because so much time was spent in these operations, we decided to make them into instructions. These instructions are very simple: they check if the object they are being applied to is a simple cons cell, of type **cons-pair**, which is held in a special C variable to make this check fast. If its argument is of the correct type, the instruction simply returns the appropriate value. Otherwise, the instruction traps and the normal method lookup takes place.

This optimization sped the system up by at least a factor of two. However, because it was made before method caching was inserted, it is not clear how much the system would slow down if it were to be disabled at this point.

Since the standard list processing operations, like **append!**, **map**, and **copy**, are called so frequently, the methods for these operations were carefully hand tuned.

8.6 Bignums

Bignums were implemented very late, and we didn't put much effort into them. They are represented in signed magnitude format, with the magnitude represented as a list of base 10,000 digits, for efficient printing and ease of carry manipulation during multiplication. Rather than the usual $O(nm)$ time multiplication algorithm, where n and m are the number of digits in the two numbers being multiplied, we use an $O(nm^{0.59})$ time algorithm, where $n > m$. In addition, because bignum division is so expensive, a division cache of the last two bignums divided is kept.

8.7 Locatives

Locatives are language-level pointer objects that permit the contents of memory cells to be retrieved and modified. Locatives are created with the special form **make-locative** and are derefenced with the operations **contents** and **(setter contents)**.

Locatives are employed throughout the Oaklisp system. For example, locales and closures contain locatives that point to the storage cells that actually contain the values associated with variable names.

Locatives are used to keep the value stack "clean," as required by the implementation of **call/cc** [3]. The code that is emitted to close over or side-effect a variable causes a locative to be made to that variable. When the compiler notices that a locative is being made to a stack variable, it generates a method preamble that allocates a cell for that variable in the heap, leaving a locative to this cell on the stack instead. For example, the code fragment

```
(let ((a (f1))
      (b (f2)))
  (foo a b)
  (set! b (f3))
  (bar a b))
```

keeps **a** on the stack but puts the cell for **b** in the heap:

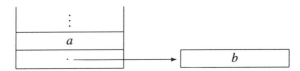

Locatives can be made to refer to any sort of variable, which after all are not distinguished at the language level. If one is made to an instance variable, the surrounding object can get garbage collected, leaving a solitary storage cell.

Locatives obey the following identities.

$$(\texttt{contents (make-locative } \textit{var})) \equiv \textit{var}$$
$$(\texttt{make-locative (contents } \textit{loc})) \equiv \textit{loc}$$

Although locatives complicate the garbage collector slightly, we found them so useful that we consider them well worth the price of a dedicated tag code and a somewhat slower garbage collector.

8.8 Methods

In describing how methods are created, represented, and looked up, we find ourselves concerned with references to instance variables, so we shall also describe how that works.

A method has two instance variables, one of which holds the code object that implements the method. The other contains the environment vector that holds references to lexical, or non-global, variables that were closed over. Global variable references are implemented as inline locatives to value cells.

8.8.1 Code Vectors

Code is represented by vectors of integers, which are interpreted as instructions by the bytecode emulator. This format allows code to be stored in the same space as all other objects, and allows the garbage collector to be ignorant of its existence, treating code vectors like any other vector. Bytecodes are 16 bits long, with the low 2 bits always 0. Here is an example taken from the middle of a code vector:

$\vdots$					
8 bit inline arg	6 bit opcode	0 0	8 bit inline arg	6 bit opcode	0 0
14 bit instruction		0 0	8 bit inline arg	6 bit opcode	0 0
14 bit relative address		0 0	8 bit inline arg	6 bit opcode	0 0
8 bit inline arg	6 bit opcode	0 0	8 bit inline arg	6 bit opcode	0 0
14 bit instruction		0 0	14 bit instruction		0 0
arbitrary reference used by last instruction of previous word					
14 bit instruction		0 0	8 bit inline arg	6 bit opcode	0 0
$\vdots$					

Note the reference to an arbitrary object in the middle of the code. To allow the garbage collector to properly handle code vectors, as well as to allow the processor to fetch the cell efficiently, this reference must be cell aligned. When the processor encounters an instruction that requires such an inline argument, if the program counter is not currently pointing to an aligned location then it is suitably incremented. This means that the assembler must sometimes emit a padding instuction, which will be ignored, between instructions that require inline arguments and their arguments.

8.8.2   Environment Vectors

An environment vector is a block of cells, each of which contains a locative to a cell. When the running code needs to reference a closed-over variable, it finds the location of the cell by indexing into the environment vector. This index is calculated at compile time, and such references consume only one instruction.

Just as it is possible for a number of methods to share the same code, differing only in the associated environment, it is also possible for a number of methods to share the same environment, differing only in the associated code, a possibility proposed by Sussman and Steele [8] and partially implemented by the Orbit compiler's *closure-hoisting* [3]. Currently the Oaklisp compiler does not generate such sophisticated constructs.

8.8.3   Invoking Methods

Methods are looked up by by doing a depth-first search of the inheritance tree. Some Oaklisp code to find a method would look like this,

```
(define (%find-method op typ)
  (let ((here (assq op (type-operation-method-alist typ))))
    (if (null? here)
        (any? (lambda (typ) (%find-method op typ))
              (type-supertype-list typ))
        (list typ (cdr here)))))
```

Once this information is found, we need to find the offset of the appropriate block of instance variables, put a pointer to the instance-variable frame in the **bp** register, set the other registers correctly, and branch.

```
(define (%send-operation op obj)
  (let ((typ (get-type obj)))
    (destructure (found-typ method) (%find-method op typ)
      (set! ((%register 'current-method)) method)
      (set! ((%register 'bp))
            (%increment-locative
```

```
            (%crunch (%data obj) %loc-tag)
            (cdr (assq found-typ (type-bp-offset-alist typ)))))))
    (set! ((%register 'env)) (method-env method))
    (set! ((%register 'pc))
          (code-body-instr (method-code (%method)))))))))
```

Of course, the actual code to find a method is written in C and has a number of tricks to improve efficiency.

- Simple lambdas (operations which have only one method defined at the type **object**) are ubiquitous, so the overhead of method lookup is avoided for them by having a **lambda?** slot in each operation. This slot holds a zero if no methods are defined for the given operation. If the only method defined for the operation is for the type **object** then the **lambda?** slot holds that method, and the method is not incorporated in the **operation-method-alist** of type **object**. If neither of these conditions holds, the **lambda?** slot holds **#f**.

- To reduce the frequency of full-blown method lookup, each operation has three slots devoted to a method cache. When *op* is sent to *obj*, we check if the **cache-type** slot of *op* is equal to the type of *obj*. If so, instead of doing a method search and finding the instance-variable frame offset, we can use the cached values from **cache-method** and **cache-offset**. In addition, after each full-blown method search, the results of the search are inserted into the cache.

  The method cache can be completely disabled by defining **NO_METH_CACHE** when compiling the emulator. We note in passing that we have one method cache for each operation. In contrast, the Smalltalk-80 [2] system has an analogous cache at each call point. We know of no head-to-head comparison of the two techniques, but suspect that if we were to switch to the Smalltalk-80 technique we would achieve a higher hit rate at considerable cost in storage.

- In order to speed up full-blown method searches, a move-to-front heuristic reorders the association lists inside the types. In addition, the C code for method lookup was tuned for speed, is coded inline, and uses an internal stack to avoid recursion.

8.8.4 Adding Methods

A serious complication results from the fact that the type field in an **add-method** form is not evaluated until the method is installed at run time. Since the target type for the method is unknown at compile time, the appropriate instance-variable map is also unknown, and hence the correct instance-variable offsets cannot be determined. Our solution is to have the compiler guess the order (by attempting to evaluate the type expression at compile time) or simply invent one, compile the offsets accordingly, and incorporate this map in the header of the emitted code block. When the **add-method** form is actually executed at run time, the assumed instance-variable map is compared to the actual map for the type that is the recipient of the method, and the code is copied and patched if necessary. The code only needs to be copied in the rare case when a single **add-method** is performed on multiple types that require different offsets.

After instance-variable references in the code block have been resolved (which usually involves no work at all since the compiler almost always guesses correctly) the method can actually be created and installed. Creating the method involves pairing the code block with an appropriate environment vector containing references to variables that are in the lexical environment. Because this environment vector is frequently empty, a special empty environment vector is kept in the global variable **%empty-environment** so a new one doesn't have to be created on such occasions. All other environment vectors are created by pushing the elements of the environment onto the stack and executing the **make-closed-environment** opcode. With the exception of the empty environment, environment vectors are not shared.

After the method is created it must be installed. The method cache for the involved operation is invalidated, and the method is either put in the **lambda?** slot of the operation or the **operation-method-alist** of the type it is being installed in. If there is already a value in the **lambda?** slot and the new method is not being installed for type **object**, the **lambda?** slot is cleared and the method that used to reside there is added to the **operation-method-alist** of type **object**.

(**%install-method-with-env** *type operation code-body environment*)   *Operation*
This flushes the method cache of *operation*, ensures that the instance-variable maps of *code-body* and *type* agree (possibly by copying *code-body* and remapping the instance variable references), creates a method out of *code-body* and *environment*, and adds this method to the **operation-method-alist** of *type*, modulo the simple lambda optimization if *type* is **object**.

Some simplified variants of this are provided, both to optimize these specialized calls because of the extra assumptions about the arguments, and to save code volume in the callers.

(**%install-method** *type operation code-body*)
≡ (**%install-method-with-env** *type operation code-body*
    %empty-environment)
(**%install-lambda-with-env** *code-body environment*)
≡ (**%install-method-with-env** **object** (**make operation**) *code-body*
    environment)

(**%install-lambda** *code-body*)
≡ (**%install-method-with-env** **object** (**make operation**) *code-body*
    %empty-environment)

8.9 Stacks and Continuations

8.9.1 Stack Implementation

Although the value and context stacks are logically contiguous, they are sometimes physically noncontiguous. The instructions all assume that stacks are stored in a designated chunk of memory called the stack buffer. They check if they are about to overflow or underflow the stack buffer, and if so they take appropriate actions to fill or flush it, as appropriate, before proceeding.

If the stack buffer is about to overflow, most of it is copied to a *stack segment* that is allocated on the heap. These segments form a linked list, so upon stack underflow the top segment is removed from this list and copied back to the stack buffer.

There is one more circumstance in which the stack buffer is flushed. The `call/cc` construct of Scheme [6] is implemented in terms of *stack photos,* which are snapshots of the current state of the two stacks. A **FILL-CONTINUATION** instruction forces the stack buffers to be flushed and copies references to the linked lists of overflow segments into a continuation object.

Actually, in the above treatment we have simplified what happens when a stack buffer is flushed. The emulator constant **MAX_SEGMENT_SIZE** determines the maximum size of any flushed stack segment. When flushing the stack, if the buffer has more than that number of references then it is flushed into a number of segments. This provides some hysteresis, speeding up `call/cc` by taking advantage of coherence in its usage patterns. A possibility opened by our stack buffer scheme, which we do not currently exploit, is to use virtual memory faults to detect stack-buffer overflows, thus eliminating the overhead of explicitly checking for stack overflow and underflow.

As a historical note, an early version of Oaklisp did not use a stack buffer but instead implemented stacks as linked lists of segments which were always loacted in the heap. When exceeding the top of a segment, a couple of references were copied from the top of that segment onto a newly allocated segment, providing sufficient hysteresis to prevent inordinate overhead from repeated pushing and popping along a segment boundary. Regrettably, substantial storage is wasted by the hysteresis and the overflow and underflow limits vary dynamically whereas in the new system these limits are C link-time constants. Presumably due to these factors, timing experiments between the old system and the new system were definitively in favor of the new system.

8.9.2 Catch and Throw

We provide two different escape facilities: `call/cc` and `catch`. The `call/cc` construct is that described in the Scheme standard [6], and its implementation is described above. The **catch** facility provides the user with a second class *catch tag*, which is valid only within the dynamic extent of the **catch**.

The implementation of catch tags is very simple: they contain heights for the value and context stacks. When a catch tag is thrown to, the value and context stacks are truncated to the appropriate heights. The slot **saved-wind-count** is used for unwind protection and **saved-fluid-binding-list** is used for fluid variables.

type: escape-object
value stack height: 25
context stack height: 19
saved wind count: 3
saved fluid binding list: (**(print-length** . **#f)** ...)

Actually, there are two variants of **catch**. In the regular variant, which is compatible with T [3], the escape object is invoked by calling it like a procedure, as in (**catch a (+ (a 'done) 12)**). In the other variant, the escape object is not called but rather thrown to by using the **throw** operation, as in (**native-catch a (+ (throw a 'done) 12)**). Although the latter construct is slightly faster, the real motivation for its inclusion is to remind the user that the the escape object being thrown to is not first class. In order to ensure that an escape object is not used outside of the extent of its dynamic validity, references to them should not be retained beyond the appropriate dynamic context.

8.9.3 Fluid Variables and Unwind Protection

Fluid (or *dynamic* or *special,* depending on your background) variables are provided using the special forms (**fluid x**) to reference them and **bind** to bind them. Fluid variables are implemented with an association list, and constructs which break the normal flow of execution, such as **throw** or **call/cc**, restore the appropriate fluid-binding list when control is transfered nonlocally.

Another facility, unwind protection, is also provided. This allows chunks of code to be executed upon entry or exit from a particular dynamic context (**call/cc** allows a dynamic context to be reentered even after it has been exited.) The fluid-binding list could be maintained with the unwind protection facility, but for efficiency reasons we implemented it separately. The unwind protection actions form a tree, and each time a nonlocal transfer of control is made, either by **throw** or by invoking a continuation, the unwind protection entries along the path from the source to the destination are executed. Care is taken to restore the appropriate fluid-variable binding list for each unwind-protection action.

All of this is done at nearly user level, so the underlying primitive mechanisms for nonlocal transfer of control need not be concerned with either fluid variables or with unwind protection. In a multprocessor version of the implementation, a fluid binding list would have to be stored for each process. We considered adding a cache for fluid variables to avoid the overhead of looking them up, but such a tiny fraction of the system's time is spent looking up fluid variables on the fluid binding list that we decided it was not worth it.

8.10 Traps

Some operations, like **car** and **contents**, are open coded as calls to bytecodes. If the operand passed to the operation is not of the precise type expected by the system, it is necessary for a full-blown operation dispatch to be performed. In cases like this, a table containing a trap operation for each instruction is indexed, and the appropriate operation is called, after setting things up so that the instruction following the trapping instruction will be the next one executed when the trap code returns. This allows users to define freely methods for system operations for their own types, even when the system operation is open coded.

One issue that arises in this context is tail recursion. If **car** were not open coded, when it occured in a tail recursive position it would be coded as **(... (load-imm car) (funcall-tail))**. With **car** open coded, the code is **(... (car)(return))**. But if the **car** instruction traps, pushing the context of the trap point onto the context stack would make the call non-tail-recursive. To avoid this, when an instruction traps if the next instruction is a return then no context is pushed onto the context stack. Similar special cases are needed when a **funcall-tail** instruction traps.

In the above treatment we have discussed synchronous traps. Another class of traps are user interrupts, used to terminate infinite loops and the like. User interrupts set a flag, which is polled by certain instructions, such as branches, carefully chosen to interrupt any loop. By using polling, we avoid the overhead of determining where in the C code the program was when the signal was fielded, and then having to clean up memory to restore the heap and stack invariants. The polling solution has also proven quite portable.

8.11 Anonymity and Printed Representations

Oaklisp objects are anonymous, but when an object is stored in a global variable, it can be accessed through that variable.

When printing an object, the default print method tries to provide an expression that will evaluate to that object, such as **car** or **(setter contents)**. These expressions are generated relative to the current locale, and they are cached and rechecked for validity every time they are used.

When this fails, a *weak* (or non-garbage-collector-proof) pointer to the object is generated. These weak pointers are represented by small integers. To determine the value of **#<Object 427>**, evaluate the expression **(object-unhash 427)**. Weak pointers are also used in hash tables, so that an object which appears only as a key in a hash table can be deallocated by the garbage collector. For convenience, the **describe** operation, which describes arbitrary objects, and dereferences any weak pointers it is passed.)

This strategy of moving responsibility for finding names for objects into the printer avoids a trick used in most dialects of Scheme, in which many objects are created with a "name" slot which contains a symbol corresponding to the global variable in which the object in question is stored. This name slot is typically used by the printer, thus giving descriptive names to objects; but such a strategy requires storage for keeping redundant information, is susceptable to inconsistency as the system evolves, and subverts the anonymous spirit of Scheme.

8.12   Bootstrap and Portability Issues

8.12.1   Building the world

The Oaklisp world is built from files that define all of the types, operations, and other data structures that a user expects to have predefined. The most primitive of these, those which are necessary in order to load compiled files, are linked by an offline program into a cold world file that contains one huge method which builds the world from ground zero when invoked.

The cold-world linker also has to lay out a few skeletal data structures for quoted lists and symbols that appear as program constants, along with information about these structures are located so that they can be back-patched (with correct type descriptors, for example) after the world comes up. Also, a locale is built to provide access to the global environment that was implicitly in effect while the world was booting up.

The files that define the root of the type hierarchy, such as **type**, **object**, and **operation**, are carefully written using only operations that are compiled straight into bytecodes, because no function calls or **add-method**'s can occur until the machinery has been built to support them.

8.12.2   Endianity

The logical order of the instructions in a code vector depends on the byte order of the CPU running the emulator. If the machine is big-endian, i.e. addresses start at the most significant end of a word and go down (e.g. 68000 or IBM 370 series) then instructions are executed left to right. Conversely, on a little-endian machine (e.g. a VAX) instructions are executed right to left. Of course, the Oaklisp loader has to be able to pack instructions into words in the appropriate order. The format of cold world loads is insensitive to endianity, but binary world loads are sensitive to it, so binary worlds are distributed in both big endian (with extensions beginning with `.ol`) and little endian (with extensions beginning with `.lo`) versions. When a running Oaklisp loads a compiled file, a special instruction, `%big-endian?`, tells the running Oaklisp how to pack the instructions.

8.12.3 Strings

Characters are packed into strings more densely than one character per reference, so strings are not just vectors with odd print methods; they also have accessor methods which unpack characters from their internals. Unfortunately, it is not possible to pack four eight bit characters into a single reference without violating the memory format conventions by putting something other than `0 0` in the tag field. We could pack four seven bit characters into each reference, but some computers use eight bit fonts, and the characters within the string would not be aligned compatibly with C strings anyway. We therefore use a somewhat wasteful format, which is little endian regardless of the endianity of the host. Here we document it by example, showing how the string `"Oaklisp Rules!"` is represented:

31 ... 26	25 ... 18	17 ... 10	9 ... 2	1 0
string				
object length: 8				0 0
string length: 14				0 0
0 0 0 0 0 0	#\k	#\a	#\O	0 0
0 0 0 0 0 0	#\s	#\i	#\l	0 0
0 0 0 0 0 0	#\R	#\space	#\p	0 0
0 0 0 0 0 0	#\e	#\l	#\u	0 0
0 0 0 0 0 0	#\null	#\!	#\s	0 0

The unused high bits of each word are set to zero to simplify equality testing and hash key computation. No trailing null character is required, although one is present two thirds of the time due to padding. When interfacing to C routines that require string arguments, such as when opening files, a special translation routine written in C is used to convert Oaklisp strings to C strings.

The representation of strings is probably the first thing that would be changed if facilities were added to permit raw binary data to exist in memory. Since the bulk of

I/O time is spent doing string manipulation, they could be a fruitful source of useful optimizations, especially considering that they have not been optimized at all yet. The easiest thing to do would be to move manipulation of simple strings into C in the same way that manipulation of simple cons cells was moved into C, but if strings were being optimized it would probably be worth modifying the garbage collector to handle raw binary data first so that they could be stored in a C-compatible fashion. Time constraints prevented us from experimenting with such measures.

8.13   Getting a Copy

Copies of the Oaklisp language and implementation manuals can be obtained by sending a request to

Catherine Copetas
School of Computer Science
Carnegie Mellon University
Pittsburgh, PA 15213

or **Catherine.Copetas@CS.CMU.EDU** by computer mail. The most recent released version of Oaklisp is available for FTP from the host **DOGHEN.BOLTZ.CS.CMU.EDU** (**128.2.222.37**), user **anonymous**, with no particular password. The proper file to retrieve is **oaklisp/release.tar.Z**, which is a compressed tar file. This file is binary so you must put FTP into binary mode before transferring it. For those without access to FTP, a tape can be obtained by making suitable arrangements with Catherine Copetas. There is a distribution fee.

8.14   Conclusions

The Oaklisp implementation effort was a success. In less than one year of full-time work, a team of two experienced programmers implemented not just new language features, with new techniques for their efficient implementation, but also the remainder of a full featured Scheme, from rationals to bignums to hash tables. Through judicious design decisions, with feedback from repeated profiling of the evolving implementation, speed rivaling (and sometimes even surpassing!) that of contemporary native-code implementations was obtained in a portable implementation.

As a result of our experience, we have come to the strong conclusion that most Lisp implementation efforts spend a great deal of time optimizing portions of the implementation that are rarely used, and spend insufficient time worrying about the tradeoff between access to processor resources within procedures and speed of procedure calls. Our watchwords were *profile* and *experiment*. We implemented dozens of "optimizations" which we were sure would speed the system up, only to remove them after profiling revealed the inadequacy of our intuition.

Another trick we used constantly was that of amortized optimization: techniques which save time on the average. Caching is such an optimization, as it slows down the worst case in order to speed up the average case. Our stack fragmentation technique is another example. In the worst case, `call/cc` needs to copy the entire stack onto the heap, which can take unbounded time. But if `call/cc` is used frequently, most of the stack has already been copied to the heap, so making the new continuation is cheap. The bring-to-front heuristic for method lookup is yet another. Almost every time we added an optimization in this class, we observed a speedup.

Because of our choice of memory formats, it would be a straightforward task to add a native code compiler if extreme speed was desired on a particular platform. If this implementation is to fill more than its current niche as a reasonably fast Scheme system that can be ported quickly to a new machine, to be used until native code implementation are retargetted, it will be necessary to add such native-code back ends.

References

[1] R. R. Fenichel and J. C. Yochelson. A Lisp garbage collector for virtual memory computer systems. *Communications of the ACM*, 12(11), November 1969.

[2] A. J. Goldberg and D. Robson. *Smalltalk-80: The Language and its Implementation*. Addison-Wesley, 1983.

[3] D. Kranz. *Orbit: An optimizing compiler for Scheme*. PhD thesis, Yale University, 1988.

[4] K. J. Lang and B. A. Pearlmutter. Oaklisp: an object-oriented Scheme with first class types. In *ACM Conference on Object-Oriented Systems, Programming, Languages and Applications*, pages 30–37, September 1986.

[5] K. J. Lang and B. A. Pearlmutter. Oaklisp: an object-oriented dialect of Scheme. *Lisp and Symbolic Computation*, 1(1):39–51, May 1988.

[6] J. A. Rees, W. Clinger, et al. The revised[3] report on the algorithmic language scheme. *SIGPLAN Notices*, 21(12):37–79, December 1986.

[7] A. Snyder. Encapsulation and inheritance in object-oriented programming languages. In *ACM Conference on Object-Oriented Systems, Programming, Languages and Applications*, pages 38–45, September 1986.

[8] G. L. Steele Jr. Lambda: the ultimate declarative. Technical Report AI Memo 379, MIT AI Lab, 1976.

Part III
Languages for Parallel and Distributed Systems

Parallel and distributed computer systems have been around for many years. Yet, relatively little is known about how to exploit them fully. For programs using mainly simple control structures (such as FORTRAN DO loops) and flat data structures (such as arrays), there are now well-established methods for achieving good speedups on vector and multiprocessor machines. Programs for scientific computing often fall into this class. On the other hand, advanced programming languages are often used for symbolic computations which, in contrast to scientific computation, usually exhibit much less regularity in both the control and data structures used. This makes it difficult both to control the amount of parallelism and to predict the grain size of the parallel tasks. In addition, certain features in advanced languages, such as first-class functions and dynamic typing, often seem to preclude the possibility of good parallel performance.

Given these difficulties, it is no surprise that current implementations tend to be experimental and hence fail in many instances to live up to expected, or even acceptable, performance standards. But the progress in recent years has been very good, with a number of advanced languages for parallel and distributed computing coming quite close to achieving a measure of practicality.

In this part of the book we consider some of the issues involved in compiling for parallel and distributed systems. In all three chapters, the languages considered are explicitly parallel. Hence, the emphasis is on the management of concurrent and distributed activities on multiple processing units, rather than on program analysis to identify opportunities for parallelism. Chapter 9 by Alessandro Forin (*Futures*) describes some of the hard issues in the implementation of the "future" construct, which is found in Multilisp and Mul-T. Futures represent an example of so-called "control parallelism," in which good scheduling and synchronization are the key concerns of the compiler. It is interesting to see how important hardware and operating system interactions become here.

Chapter 10 by Skef Wholey (*An Experimental Implementation of Connection Machine Lisp*) describes an experience in implementing Connection Machine Lisp, which features the "xapping" data type. In contrast to Multilisp futures, xappings are an example of a "data parallel" construct. In data parallelism, the idea is to exploit regularities in the problem to achieve massive parallelism. Of particular interest are the problems posed by the Common Lisp base language, which supports dynamic typing and garbage collection. Such dynamic features make it extremely challenging to compile for the Connection Machine.

Finally, Chapter 11 by David L. Detlefs, Maurice P. Herlihy, and Jeannette M. Wing (*Inheritance of Synchronization and Recovery Properties in Avalon/C++*, which originally appeared in *IEEE Computer*, December 1988, pp. 57–69), describes how the implementation of synchronization properties for distributed computing can be standardized in a useful way. The approach provides such standardization as part of the Avalon/C++ language, as opposed to the more conventional approach of providing such features in a library.

These chapters tend to focus on implementation issues. For more information about the languages themselves, the following readings are recommended.

References

[1] G. Blelloch. *Vector Models for Data-Parallel Computing*. MIT Press, 1990.

[2] R. Goldman and R. Gabriel. Preliminary results with the initial implementation of Qlisp. *Proceedings of the 1988 Conference on Lisp and Functional Programming*, Snow Bird, Utah, August 1988, 143–152.

[3] R. Halstead. Multilisp: A language for concurrent symbolic computation. *ACM Transactions on Programming Languages and Systems*, Vol. 7, No. 4, October 1985, 501–538.

[4] D. Kranz, R. Halstead, and E. Mohr. Mul-T: A high performance parallel Lisp. *Proceedings of the 1989 Conference on Programming Language Design and Implementation*, Portland, Oregon, June 1989, 81–90.

[5] B. Liskov and R. Scheifler. Guardians and actions: Linguistic support for robust, distributed programs. *ACM Transactions on Programming Languages and Systems*, Vol. 5, No. 3, July 1983, 381–404.

[6] G. Steele, Jr. and D. Hillis. Connection Machine Lisp: Fine-Grained Parallel Symbolic Processing. *Proceedings of the 1986 ACM Conference on Lisp and Functional Programming*, Cambridge, Massachusetts, August 1986, 279–297.

9   Futures

Alessandro Forin

Parallel Lisp languages have moved in recent times from the realm of design to the realm of implementation and practical use. Notable examples are Multilisp [7], MultiScheme [11], Qlisp [6], and more recently Mul-T [10] and the Gambit compiler [5]. The idea that is central to all of these languages is the one of a *future* – a Lisp object that is usable even if its value might not have been computed by some other parallel activity. In this chapter we illustrate the techniques used to implement this construct on stock hardware, as well as the various implementation and performance problems that go with it. The notion of queue-based parallel processing which is provided in Qlisp is also discussed to some extent. Particular attention is paid to issues such as locking, scheduling and garbage collection which appear to be crucial to a good-performing parallel Lisp system. We are only concerned here with implementation issues. The design of the languages or the programming styles that are most appropriate for their use are not discussed.

Sequential Lisp systems have benefited in the past from special operating system support, for example a virtual memory system that supports large and sparse address spaces such as in the Mach operating system [12]. With this in mind, we describe which other features of Mach have proved useful in the implementation of Multilisp and Mul-T, and which ones have not and why.

9.1   Introduction

Parallel Lisp languages are targeted at *symbolic* computations, which have some particular properties that make them different from other common parallel applications. Programs that are commonly referred to as *scientific parallel programs* have much more predictable data access patterns and sometimes the program spends all of its time in a single iteration, for instance computing some function of large matrices. *Real-time* programs might well do some symbolic computation, but their stringent property is that they must execute within predefined, limited time bounds.

Of the many designs for parallel Lisps, there are two that currently receive the widest attention, Multilisp and Qlisp. They both are based on the idea of extending an existing Lisp with some simple constructs that turn it into a parallel language. Multilisp and its successor Mul-T are based on Scheme [9], while Qlisp is based on Common Lisp

Figure 9.1: Reusing existing sequential Lisp code.

[8]. They all reflect the spirit of the original language, for instance Multilisp emphasizes simplicity and minimality while Qlisp provides a much richer set of constructs for parallel programming.

One of the many reasons a parallel Lisp is attractive is the prospect of leveraging on the large existing body of Lisp code and applications, as depicted in Figure 9.1. Even the standard Lisp environment has the potential for a great deal of parallelism. Actually, the problem faced by the designers and implementors of both Multilisp and Qlisp is rather the excess of parallelism! Generating too many parallel activities without enough processors/memory to devote to them leads to slower execution times. The solutions provided by the two languages are very different. Qlisp exposes this issue to the programmer, permitting program control over the creation of new parallel activities, for example based on the number of available processors on the machine. Multilisp relies on the run-time system to employ the best scheduling strategies, perhaps making use of other run-time information, such as the length of the run queues, to decide when to stop creating new computations.

Both languages provide a new construct, the *future*. Any Lisp expression can be evaluated within a future wrapper, producing an object of the **future** type, and (potentially) creating a new parallel activity to actually evaluate the expression. Eventually the expression will be evaluated, and the future object will take on the result value of the evaluation. The future object can however be used immediately in non-strict operations. For instance consing it at the beginning of a list has no side-effect whatsoever. Using the object in a strict operation, for instance in an arithmetic operation, will instead produce a different behavior. If the parallel activity that is supposed to evaluate the future expression has not yet completed the evaluation, the future has no value and the arithmetic operation cannot be performed. Therefore its evaluator will be suspended until the parallel activity has determined a value for the future. At that point the future object changes into a *determined future*, which is henceforth indistinguishable from its value. Indeed, the garbage collector will replace it with its value at the first opportunity. A simple analogy for futures is lazy-evaluation, since the value is computed when needed. But if there are enough cycles available the evaluation could actually be eager-evaluation, which will provide faster execution time if the value is actually used later on. On the other hand, this style of parallelism is named *optimistic*, because the eager-evaluation might actually prove to be a waste of cycles if the value is then never actually used.

As a quick example, let us consider the Fibonacci function. A sequential version might look like:

```
(define (fib x)
  (cond ((> 2 x) x)
        (1 (+ (fib (sub1 x))
              (fib (- x 2))))))
```

The most useful place to use futures is in the recursive calls, as in this parallelized version:

```
(define (pfib x)
  (cond ((> 2 x) x)
        (1 (+ (future (pfib (sub1 x)))
              (future (pfib (- x 2)))))))
```

To imagine how execution will proceed in the parallel version one can think of the call graph for the sequential version and place future creations at each node: the parent will in fact stop immediately in the strict operator +, waiting for the two branches to complete. For best performance this wait is unnecessary: the best parallelized version of the Fibonacci function only actually uses one future – readers might wish to discover where as a simple exercise. Note that if in this function template we substitute the strict operator + with some non-strict one such as *cons*, evaluation would be very different. The parent would immediately return from the function with a future value, without waiting for the children to complete. It is from this second type of function that we would expect the greatest gains in the use of futures.

9.2 Multilisp

Since it originates from Scheme, Multilisp aims for simplicity and minimality. The only two basic constructs that a programmer should really need to use are:

1. *futures* – to create new parallel computations, and

2. *semaphores* – to exercise control over side-effects.

With futures, any Lisp form can be evaluated in parallel and the result used immediately. For example, the following expressions are all equivalent (provided they are side-effect free), and they differ only in the way they are evaluated:

```
(cons A B)
(future (cons A B))
(cons (future A)(future B))
```

as they respectively produce zero, one, and two parallel computations. Parallel computations are called *tasks* in Multilisp, and it is not uncommon to generate thousands of them during a computation. Clearly, futures are meant to be used even for extremely fine-grained parallel programs, but it is likely that this will become a reality only with special hardware support, not on stock hardware. We will get back to performance issues in Section 9.9.

Semaphores are the only high-level synchronization primitive, and the operations defined on semaphores are

- **make-sema** – Create and initialize a semaphore.

- **wait-sema** – Suspend this task if semaphore is *busy*.

- **signal-sema** – Make semaphore *free* and restart the first suspended task.

The Multilisp implementation actually defines various other lower-level functions for atomicity in side-effects (**scar scdr rplaca-eq rplacd-eq rplaca rplacd**) and task suspension/reactivation (**suspend activate**) but they are only supposed to be used to implement higher-level primitives, such as the above mentioned semaphore abstraction. Making up an analogy between memory locations in C and lists in Lisp, it is easy to figure what these low-level operations do. Spin-locks, for instance, would be implemented as in:

```
(define spin-init (cons '*unlocked* nil))

(define (spin-lock lock)
  (if (not (rplaca-eq lock '*locked* '*unlocked*))
      (spin-lock lock)))

(define (spin-unlock lock)
  (rplaca lock '*unlocked*))
```

Other uses of the low-level primitives will be illustrated later in Section 9.5.

The **pcall** (parallel call) form, which has formed the basis for various past parallel Lisp designs, is implemented by the Multilisp compiler in terms of *pcons*, with various optimizations for simple cases like cons, list, and so on.

```
(define-syntax (pcons first rest)
  '(rplacd (future (cons ,first nil))
           ,rest))
```

The idea in `pcall` is to simply evaluate the arguments of a function call in parallel. This turns out to be a relatively unflexible primitive, because many function invocations have relatively simple arguments. On the other hand many of these function evaluations can profitably happen in parallel. Futures provide control over both the evaluation of function arguments and the evaluation of the function itself, as well as the evaluation of any other Lisp expression.

9.3 Mul-T

Mul-T is a parallel version of the T3 Scheme system from Yale University [13]. Besides dynamic binding and other modifications to the T3 run-time system, Mul-T offers the same parallel constructs as Multilisp, with the added notion of *task groups* to allow explicit process control from the top-level. The most important difference in Mul-T is the use of an optimizing compiler to boost performance. A syntax package is available to compile largely unmodified Multilisp programs in Mul-T.

A task group is the collection of tasks created to evaluate a single top-level form. It can be started, stopped, resumed, killed and debugged independently of other task groups. The Mul-T user interface is based on this mechanism. A new task group is created to evaluate any form typed by the user at the top-level; all tasks created during evaluation of this form are also part of the task group. Should an exception occur within any of the member tasks the whole group is stopped. Groups are identified by simple numeric identifiers, and there is a notion of a current group and last group. Indeed, task group control was designed after the job control capabilities provided by the Unix C-shell, so that users will find it familiar. Working with the current task group is much like working in sequential T.

Within a task group individual tasks are also assigned numeric identifiers which only have a local meaning. It is only possible to refer to tasks in the current group, and there is a notion of the current task equivalent to the notion of the current group. A task group will be in one of the following states:

1. `normal` – Normal or completion state.
2. `error` – Non-fatal error in some task.
3. `nc-error` – Fatal error in some task.
4. `interrupted` – Stopped by keyboard interrupt.
5. `killed` – Abnormal completion state.
6. `blocked-on-io` – Some task within is waiting for I/O completion.

Within a stopped task group it is possible to enquire about the state of individual tasks to monitor execution. A task will be in one of the following states:

1. **new** – Not yet scheduled for execution.

2. **error** – Non-fatal error.

3. **nc-error** – Fatal error.

4. **interrupted** – Suspended.

5. **blocked-on-io** – Waiting on I/O completion.

9.4 Qlisp

The programming paradigm for Qlisp is "Queue-based multiprocessing": the programmer explicitly controls the amount of parallelism that is generated. The Fibonacci function can be written in Qlisp using the *qlet* construct:

```
(defun qfib (n depth)
  (if (<= n 1) 1
      (qlet (> depth 0) ;; no parallel if false
            ((n1 (qfib (- n 1) (- depth 1)))
             (n2 (qfib (- n 2) (- depth 1))))
            (+ n1 n2)))))
```

which is just like **let*** in Common Lisp, only in this case evaluation really happens in parallel. In this example, the control predicate for **qlet** is based on the **depth** argument and will prevent the recursive calls from being evaluated in parallel when the depth of the evaluation tree is too low. Note that the relation between the number of parallel activities and the controlling parameters might become much more involved than in this simple example. Another problem with explicit programmer control is how to correlate the control parameters of different, possibly nested parallel modules.

The visible and controllable entities that perform computations are called processes in Qlisp. They are generated with the *qlambda* construct, as in the following example:

```
(let ((worker-process
        (qlambda t (parameters)
          (....))))
    ...
    (funcall worker-process arguments))
```

The elements of the Qlisp "queues" are therefore function invocations, and they are posted with the funcall device. Clearly, this supports well a programming paradigm based on the notion of cooperating processes and perhaps on remote procedure calling. Qlisp also supports finer-grain parallelism with futures, although this was a late addition to the language. In the following, we will mainly refer to Qlisp as a basis for comparison, as our implementation experience has been limited to the former languages.

9.5   Implementation Issues

Programming in Multilisp is quite similar to programming in Mul-T, but the implementations of the two languages are different enough to cover a large part of the design space available to the implementor. In this section we will consider in detail the most important issues for the users, namely how a programmer can control the creation of futures and their scheduling. Sections 9.6 and 9.7 will concentrate on Multilisp and Mul-T, respectively.

9.5.1   Types of futures

Multilisp provides four types of *futures*:

1. `future` – Create a new task for "parent," enqueue it in LIFO order,

2. `sfuture` – Create a new task for "parent," enqueue it in FIFO order,

3. `dfuture` – Create a new task for "child," enqueue it in LIFO order,

4. `delay` – Create a new task for "child," do not enqueue it.

but only two, namely future and delay, have been actually defined as proper parts of the language. The difference between them is only in the immediate effects on scheduling, and therefore on the creation of other futures. For regular **future**s, the child is the one that is scheduled first while the parent will have to wait for the first rescheduling before resuming execution. Similarly for **sfuture**s, but in this case the parent will presumably be stopped for a longer time, as all tasks that are currently sitting in the run queue will execute before it. This type of scheduling behaviour is advantageous, for instance, in stream-like processing of data, hence the name. For **dfuture**s the parent is rescheduled first, and the child will wait for it to be descheduled before actually starting to execute. This type of future could be used in parallel applications where a main task spawns a number of other tasks and then waits for their completion.

Readers familiar with the Unix OS might have noticed that there is some similarity (at least from the scheduler's point of view) between what happens when a new future is created and what happens when a new process is created in Unix via the *fork()* system call. More precisely, most Unix schedulers will follow the same scheduling as for Multilisp's *futures*. If Unix supports the *vfork* system call this scheduling is actually the only permissible one.

A **delay** future is perhaps the closest thing to lazy-evaluation, as no activity whatsoever is scheduled for execution, and the parent just proceeds its sequential flow. Only if-and-when the value of the delay future is needed will the evaluation take place, perhaps by the very same task that needs its value. Consider for instance the following function:

```
(define (make-counter initial-value)
  (lambda ()
    (let ((value initial-value))
    (set! initial-value (delay (+ value 1)))
    value )))
```

On every invocation of the counter a new, monotonically increasing value is returned. The value is, however, a future and only if touched will it reveal its real value. Until that point no computation at all is performed. When the ith value of the counter is touched all values preceding it are also touched, but not the values following it. The identity operator **touch** can be used to force evaluation of a future.

Mul-T provides only two types of futures, equivalent to the **dfuture** and **delay** of Multilisp. However, it is possible to *inline* futures that should only be evaluated in parallel when the machine is lightly loaded. At run-time a quick check is made on the length of the run-queues on the local processor, and only when the length is greater than a threshold limit is a new task actually created, much in the spirit of Qlisp. Beyond the threshold evaluation is sequential. This optimization is equivalent to removing the future altogether, hence the name.

9.5.2   Scheduling

The real synchronization primitives provided by the Multilisp interpreter, on which the ones exported to the user are based are:

- (**suspend** *closure*) – Suspend the invoking task, evaluate *closure* in a new task, return (after suspension) whatever the activator indicates.

- (**activate** *task value*) – Push *value* on *task*'s stack, reschedule *task* in LIFO order, return *value*

- (**quit**) – Terminate the invoking task.

While in Mul-T semaphore primitives are really primitives and part of the run-time system, in Multilisp they are implemented using the lower-level atomic list manipulation functions and the synchronization primitives, as the following code illustrates:

```
(define make-sema (list '*semaphore* '*free*))

(define (wait-sema S)
  (let ((identifier 1))
    (suspend (lambda (tsk)
               (nconc S (set! identifier (list tsk)))
               (activate-next-sema S)
```

```
                    (quit))))
        identifier))

(define (signal-sema S)
  (rplaca (cdr S) '*free*)
  (activate-next-sema S))

(define (activate-next-sema S)
  (if (cddr S)
      (if (rplaca-eq (cdr S) '*busy* '*free*)
          (if (cddr S)
              (block (rplacd S (cddr S))
                     (activate (cadr S) nil))
              (block (rplaca (cdr S) '*free*)
                     (activate-next-sema S))))))
```

In **wait-sema**, **suspend** will put the invoking task in a suspended state, and before actually blocking it will execute its first argument lambda expression, with argument the task itself. In this case, the task enqueues itself (atomically) in the semaphore's queue, possibly activates the first task in the queue, and finally suspends itself. Note that logically it is a new task that executes the lambda expression, hence the invocation to the task termination primitive **quit**.

Signalling a semaphore means atomically setting its value to ***free***, and invoking the activating function. This in turn does what is essentially a "test and test-and-set" operation on the semaphore, only in terms of list values rather than integer values. Note that the semaphore is kept busy during evaluation of the inner form, and recursion is used to activate tasks that might have been enqueued in the meantime.

Mul-T completely hides the scheduling of tasks from the programmer. A translation of suspend/activate for Mul-T might be:

```
(define-syntax (suspend proc)
  '(call/cc ,proc))

(define (activate task value)
  (task value))
```

Note however that these simple macros cannot guarantee the scheduling effects as in Multilisp, and therefore they are not fully equivalent. The second one, for instance, activates the given task but only in a coroutine manner and not in parallel as it is supposed to in Multilisp. It is necessary to use a more elaborate translation and a combination of futures and **call/cc** to provide a more faithful translation, as in the following example:

```
(define-syntax (suspend proc)
  '(call/cc (lambda (c)
                    (future (let ((v (proc (cons '*suspended* c))))
                                (c v)
                                (quit)))
             (quit)))))

(define (activate task value)
  (if (eq? (car task) '*suspended)
      (error "arg not a suspended task")
      (block
            (future
                    (block
                          ((cdr task) value)
                          (quit)))
            value)))

(define (quit)
  (let ((x nil))
       (set! x (delay (touch x)))
       (touch x)))
```

Low-level functions exist in Mul-T such as test-and-set and task queue manipulations, but since they require deep knowledge of the core system, users are not likely to make use of them.

It is interesting to show how **call/cc** can be implemented in Multilisp in terms of suspend/activate combinations:

```
(define (call/cc function)
  (suspend (lambda (tsk)
                   (function
                    (lambda (return-val)
                      (activate tsk return-val)
                      (quit))))))
```

The current continuation is invoked by a new task after the current one is suspended. It receives as its continuation a form that will terminate the task after resuming the original one. The value returned by **function** is passed along to the original task.

9.6   Multilisp Implementation

Multilisp was originally implemented at MIT on the Concert multiprocessor, a multibus-based machine where each processor is a Motorola 68000 with local memory. Each

lock	value	oldspace	mark	type	unused
1	**22**	**1**	**1**	**6**	**1**

Figure 9.2: Encoding of Lisp Objects in Multilisp

processor can also access the memory on other processors, but with a longer access time (about twice). Each processor executes a (local) copy of the Multilisp interpreter code, which is a byte-code interpreter written in C. There is no operating system on the Concert, only some ROM functions to download applications and interact with them. Two sequential interpreters for Multilisp were also developed at MIT: one for the Vax under Unix, and one for the Lisp machine.

To port Multilisp to a general purpose multiprocessor under the Mach operating system, we decided to use Mach's features to simulate the bare-bones Concert machine. The most interesting byproduct of this decision is that we could then easily transport the resulting Mach-Multilisp system to a variety of machines running Mach, even uniprocessors like the Sun3 and the IBM RT. The interesting machines are, of course, the real multiprocessors and so we ported both to the Encore Multimax and to various Vax multiprocessors such as the 62xx series. Since Multilisp is interpreted, the port was completed in a very short period of time.

9.6.1   Multilisp Objects

Multilisp uses a tagged data representation. A generic Lisp object is represented as in Figure 9.2. The *lock* bit is set while the value is being updated, or to call attention to exceptional circumstances (e.g., forwarding pointers). Also, on the Concert, it is set when fetching a value to insure atomicity. The value field is either a pointer or integer value. For pointers, a 24-bit machine pointer is formed by appending two 0 bits to the 22-bit **value**, which is permissible because all objects are aligned on word boundaries. This limitation in the addressing capability caused some complication on the IBM RT, where the 24-bit value had to be considered rather an offset from the beginning of the data segment. The *Oldspace* flag is set in pointers to old space when relocation is occurring, and in pointers located in the old space to indicate that they have already been moved. The *mark* bit is only used as a sanity check during garbage collection. The *type* field indicates the type (tag) of the Lisp value.

Tag types include cons, fixnum, string, symbol, task, environment, closure, future and various others. The details of the Multilisp virtual machine (the M-code) are not important, but various considerations are generally applicable.

The lock bit must be checked *on each data fetch*, using hardware interlocked instructions. On the 68000 this means using the test-and-set machine instruction, which is why the bit was located in the highest position. Some architectures like the Vax or the NS32000 define flexible interlocked bit instructions which allowed us to use the same object representations. But in the case of the IBM RT we had a real problem. The only interlocked instruction in this case only works on a 16bit word, which gets clobbered entirely by the "tsh" machine instruction. Since this was really only a uniprocessor we quickly solved the problem with a set of internal locks: depending on the object's address we hashed into one of the real locks and then attempted to lock it. Protected by this real lock, the object's lock bit could then be set safely. We used a test/test-and-set scheme to avoid useless collisions on the real locks. Note also that since memory in Multilisp is divided in per-processor slices the idea of hashing on the object's address is in general very effective to reduce contention on the internal locks.

We tried the same code on the Encore multiprocessor, and it worked without noticeable performance degradation, perhaps because the overhead is unnoticeable in the relatively slow Multilisp interpreter. Note that a solution like this is needed on machines where strange hardware primitives are provided, or when there is no hardware support at all for atomic operations. For instance, some existing multiprocessors only give users a limited number of locks which are specially supported by the hardware.

The *Oldspace* flag is dependent on the particular generational GC algorithm used in Multilisp (see section 9.6.3), and might not be needed for different algorithms. Mul-T does not use it, for instance. If it is used, the idea of keeping the lock bit set for objects that still require moving into new space might be useful, for instance to implement a truly parallel garbage collector.

A **FUTURE** object contains a pointer to a future value which contains the following fields:

1. **queue** – list of tasks waiting for values to be calculated.

2. **value** – the value when calculated.

3. **thunk** – possible task to calculate a value for this future.

4. **exc-handler** – exception handler for this task.

5. **doc** – some kind of documentation for this future.

6. **id** – unique identifier, used for monitoring

If the **thunk** of a future is **DETERMINED** then its value has been calculated; otherwise it has not. This saves some extra memory operations and locking, since if the future is not determined it is necessary to wake up the task that is supposed to compute it, or to create one if no such task exists.

When creating a new future, the various fields are initialized and the exception handler is set either to the default or to the user-supplied one. The stack cache is flushed to memory,[1] and a new task is created and enqueued on this processor's queue, unless this is a *delay* future. For *delay* futures the thunk is set to the new task, and execution simply proceeds. Otherwise a new stack is allocated, and execution proceeds either on the new stack for *futures* and *sfutures* or on the old stack for *dfutures*. In all cases the same environment is used.

9.6.2 The Multilisp scheduler

A *task* in Multilisp is the schedulable entity that evaluates futures. A task has both some machine state associated with it and an evaluation stack. Tasks ready for execution are placed in a number of runnable queues, one queue per physical processor. Each processor runs one task at a time. When short of tasks to run, the scheduler looks into the queues of

1. processors on the same *memory slice* (defined as the set of memory boards that provide equal access to the participant processors)

2. all other processors.

The design of the Concert multiprocessor accounts for a non-uniform memory system. More than one processor could potentially be attached to the same memory slice and have slower access to other memory slices. Various dynamic configurations might be possible, and therefore it is important that the scheduler attempts to maintain as much locality as possible, avoiding redundant and potentially expensive migrations of tasks from slice to slice. For instance, tasks are always inserted in the local processor's queue and not on some other queue. An idle processor will take it off that queue later, according to the above selection algorithm.

Scheduling is normally round-robin among tasks on the same processor. A task will release the processor after executing at most 2000 instructions, and put itself at the tail of the processor's run queue. There is one exception to this scheme: the I/O processor. On the Concert there is only one processor board that has a communication line attached to it, and therefore when a task starts an I/O operation it reschedules itself onto the I/O processor's queue. Since many I/O devices might be attached to the I/O processor, scheduling here is done specially for better performance. The I/O processor will also run normal tasks when idle.]

This I/O scheme also works very well on the Mach "Virtual Concert" (see Figure 9.3), with the added advantage that OS-level state such as file descriptors is nicely kept in

---

[1]Multilisp uses a small cache to improve locality, as the stack might be on a remote node.

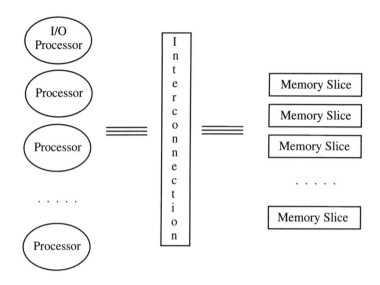

Figure 9.3: The virtual concert.

the same process. Interactions with the user's terminal also happen in an orderly fashion despite possible program synchronization mistakes, because only one process is ever attempting to read characters from the user's terminal. Note that in this scheme an I/O intensive program might continuously bounce between the I/O processor and some other processor. But since symbolic programs are rarely I/O intensive this is rarely a problem for Multilisp.

Halstead [7] notes that scheduling in Multilisp is not fair, and for very good reasons. A fair scheduler would give to all tasks an equal chance of running to completion, which in absence of I/O or synchronizations means an equal amount of instructions to each one. The act of creating a future, for instance, would have no bearing whatsoever on the scheduling of a task. It is easy to understand that in these conditions the programmer has no way to limit the number of futures that are created, and in many programs this would simply clog the machine with futures waiting for execution, not to mention the bad impact on memory usage. If an opportunistic scheduler is therefore needed, what better place to make its decisions than at future creation time? It becomes possible, for instance, to disable entirely the creation of futures and fall back to regular sequential execution, perhaps because memory utilization has become too high or some upper limit on the number of futures has been reached, or just as a special case optimization like in Mul-T's inlining.

9.6.3 Garbage Collection

The garbage collector used in Multilisp is an incremental copying one derived from Baker's [2], modified to be run in parallel on multiple processors. The heap is modeled after the physical memory on the Concert multiprocessor, with multiple separate segments (*parcels*). The memory on each memory board is divided up into parcels at initialization, and all parcels are linked in a per-processor list of free parcels. A processor allocates memory out of the current parcel, which it takes off its free list. When this becomes exhausted the processor is entitled to steal a parcel from some other processor's free list, but the system can also be instructed not to do so, and just trigger a general garbage collection. A user therefore has the option to trade higher memory utilization at the possible expense of slower execution. Under Mach, memory is uniform and better memory utilization is the default choice, things might be different on other non-uniform memory systems. There is probably another trade-off in the size of the parcels, since smaller parcels lead to higher memory utilization but also to more work in the GC flip, but we have not investigated this issue at all. Note also that the largest possible Lisp object must fit in a parcel, which gives a lower bound on their size.

Each parcel is subdivided into *Newspace* and *Oldspace*, allocation of new objects happens in Newspace, which is further divided as in Figure 9.4. Garbage collection is done incrementally by all processors when allocating memory, and most importantly *when idle* or waiting for file operations. An internal function in the interpreter can be called almost at any time to move up to a given number of objects from Oldspace to Newspace. Pointers into Oldspace are recognized because they are specially tagged. At garbage collection time all processors synchronize twice to flip Oldspaces and Newspaces, and although flip itself is not a zero-cost operation the result is much better than in any stop-and-copy algorithm. Processors are stuck only at GC flip time and not during the entire garbage collection procedure.

9.7 Mul-T Implementation

Mul-T was initially developed under the UMAX operating system for the Encore Multimax multiprocessor, and subsequently ported to Mach on the same machine by D. Kranz at MIT. Not many modifications at all were applied to the original version, as Mach is largely compatible with UMAX in providing a Unix 4.3 BSD interface. The only modifications necessary were in the initial allocation of shared memory. Interestingly, a synchronization bug was discovered in the initial startup under Mach which was never apparent under UMAX.

The structure of the Mul-T system is very much like the one of Multilisp under

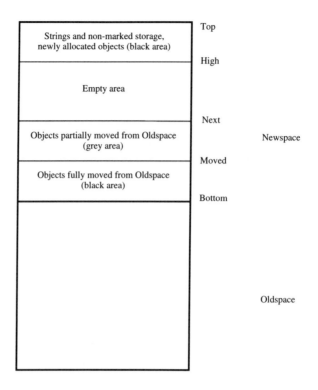

Figure 9.4: A Multilisp memory parcel.

Mach, with multiple processes sharing memory and a single process devoted to the I/O operations. One difference is that I/O operations are requested of the I/O process via requests posted in shared memory rather than rescheduling the task on the I/O process itself. The motivation for this was to eliminate the consequent task migration and the possible bad performance effects on the caches. Much work was necessary to transform the T3 run-time system into a parallel language kernel, including a special variable binding mechanism to provide per-processor global variables. Amazingly enough, not much work at all was needed on the compiler to support the future construct itself. The relevant transformation is:

```
(define-local-syntax (future exp)
  '(if (inline? 1)
       ,exp
       (*future (lambda () ,exp)))))
```

where ***future** is a run-time function which enqueues a new task on the run queue to evaluate the closure. Note that due to the lexical scoping of the language the compiler already must copy all free variables in **exp** into the heap.

A future object is tagged appropriately, and tags are kept in the lower bits. A future value contains the following fields:

- **future-header** – contains
    - **tag** – includes the *determined?* bit
    - **status** – whether evaluation has been started or not
    - **lock** – for queueing operations
- **future-value** – the value of the future, if any
- **future-queue** – the queue of tasks waiting for this future
- **future-stack** – the evaluation stack
- **future-dynamic-state** – dynamic binding information
- **future-fluid-state** – fluid binding information
- **future-processor** – which processor is evaluating this future
- **future-group** – task group this future belongs to

The garbage collection algorithm used in Mul-T is largely the same used for T3 [3], which is a stop-and-copy one. It is executed in parallel by all processors by locking each object before moving it, so that the elapsed time for garbage collection can be decreased. Some details on the algorithm can be found in [10].

Work on Mul-T has identified at least two problems that impede performance of a compiled parallel Lisp: the cost of stack checks and the cost of tag checking. A sequential Lisp either uses only one stack, or uses some memory protection techniques to isolate the binding stack and evaluation stacks. In a parallel Lisp the number of stacks grows with the number of processors and the problem becomes acute. Mach supports sparse address spaces, so all stacks can be allocated in separate regions of memory. Trap handlers can perform the appropriate actions when a stack overflows and causes an addressing exception. Unix has a much more primitive virtual memory support, and therefore explicit checks must be carefully added to the compiled code. This was the case, for instance, for the UMAX OS.

More devastating is the cost of tag checking. Any object could be a future, and checks against this eventuality must be inserted potentially in each and every object access. Even the use of declarations is largely defeated: knowing that a given future can only evaluate to a fixnum is of no use. Only preliminary work was done on this issue in Mul-T. New compiler techniques must be devised to minimize the number of tag checks.

Perhaps flow-analysis techniques [14] might help here. Alternatives might include, again, memory management techniques: if undetermined future values are "allocated" in non-readable memory, all accesses to them will generate traps. There are two problems with this solution: it might not apply to important cases such as fixnums because the value is presumably contained in the object itself and not pointed to, and unless the machine/OS provides a very fast exception recovery mechanism the price paid on undetermined future accesses might be too high, e.g. under Unix on a Vax.

9.8 Operating System Support

Concert is a bare-bones machine, dedicated to Multilisp. It is also a single-user machine. To use Multilisp on a general-purpose multiprocessor, new issues arise:

1. how is memory allocated, deallocated, shared?

2. which are the right synchronization primitives?

3. how do computations (threads) get created, synchronized, scheduled?

4. how are processors allocated, deallocated?

The Concert is a shared-memory multiprocessor; therefore the most obvious memory system for Multilisp and Mul-T under Mach was a shared-memory based one. Other parallel languages such as Ada have benefited from Mach's message-passing primitives, but the shared heap of Lisp makes this an unattractive alternative. Also, it is straight forward to use the shared-memory model of Mach since it can transparently extend over a communication network. The Concert implementation did not have virtual memory; therefore it was an easy decision to allocate all the heap memory in advance, without further extending it. If this were not the case we could still solve the problem in Mach, but not in other operating systems that provide a Unix System-V-like shared memory, because this comes only in fixed size segments. Having shared virtual memory also gives users the freedom of experimenting with different configurations and memory topologies, which is not available on a bare-bones machine.

The advanced virtual memory functionality that Mach offers has been used in the past to implement Lisp tagging: the high bits of the object serve both as address and tag of the data. Mach supports large, sparse address spaces efficiently, so this approach works well in practice in the CMU Common Lisp system for the IBM RT [4] (see also Chapter 6). This system also uses memory de-allocation as a way to clean up old space efficiently. None of these features was used for Mach Multilisp, with the only exception that memory slices are allocated sparsely to mimic a non-uniform memory system. An attractive idea would be to use Mach's ability to control protection of individual memory pages to implement a garbage collector that uses an algorithm along the lines of the one described in [1]. The basic trick is to simply remove all access rights to pages in old space that have not been moved yet, so that a thread chasing a pointer into old space would take a fault and the page be cleaned as part of the fault handling by the external memory manager.

The external synchronization primitives that Multilisp offers to users (semaphores) could be implemented both in terms of spin locks and in terms of message exchanges: a future blocked on a semaphore could correspond to a thread waiting for an IPC message. This is not really the case, though. As illustrated above, the implementation of both semaphores and scheduling primitives clearly requires atomic operations on lists, and in a well behaved parallel program they will typically *not* generate contention. Indeed, a functional language such as Multilisp will hopefully encourage users to write largely-functional programs where side-effects on shared variables are kept to a minimum. Therefore simple spin locks are the most appropriate support for the Multilisp run-time system. The argument is even stronger for Mul-T where the compiler generates inline code as much as possible, which should waste the minimum time synchronizing the access to data. One case where Mach IPC would help is in the case of I/O, which clearly models well as an RPC to the I/O process. Another one is internal synchronizations, say to trigger garbage collection: the solution used in Mul-T (Unix signals) is quite inefficient and distasteful, and only justified by portability reasons.

There are two ways in which processors could be simulated in Mach: with multiple threads within the same process, or with multiple threads in different processes sharing a segment of their address space. Only the latter approach would be viable on most other operating systems, with the further limitation of one thread per process. Multilisp futures are much finer-grained than Mach threads: creation and destruction operations cannot map one to one because the times to create a kernel thread are, say, in the order of a thousand machine instructions. Therefore threads should at the very least be reused. A pool of available threads can be allocated initially, and a Multilisp thread creation would therefore only entail a much cheaper thread synchronization operation – most likely the exchange of a single Mach IPC message. After looking at the interpreter's code we realized that the amount of per-processor global state was relevant, and various variables needed very efficient access. Since per-thread memory can only be obtained via indirection with Mach C-Threads, we chose the simpler solution of using multiple processes, each providing transparent local state. Despite being simpler, this solution is more expensive in terms of OS level resources, e.g. page tables on a Vax.

Scheduling is also finer-grained in Multilisp than OS scheduling. For example, when running on a uniprocessor, or with more virtual processors than physically available on the machine, it is the language's run-time system that knows which virtual processor (Mach thread) should be scheduled next, e.g. the one with the longer task queue. Also, the language might boost the priority of some virtual processor because the value of a future or chain of futures is known to be needed "right now." The OS scheduler should therefore only be used as a firewall to share the machine among multiple users.

One more Mach feature which has only been available recently, with which we could not experiment, is the capability of controlling processor allocation at the user level. A user can create a *processor-set* of a given size and assign threads to it. Mach guarantees that only those threads, at any given time, will run on the given set of processors. For instance, it is possible to allocate all the machine's processors to a processor-set and then bind threads to it, obtaining guaranteed exclusive use of the machine in the time slices where the application runs. In this way our "Virtual Concert" becomes a real physical Concert, as there is no operating system or other user interference during its execution. A processor-set can also vary its size dynamically, and processors can be added/removed from it at the user's leisure. In this way the use of processing resources could be automatically controlled by the language, releasing processors during long-lasting idle states. This is quite apparent when we consider Mul-T's task groups. One simple mapping strategy could be to allocate a processor set per task group and release the entire processor group when the task group becomes suspended.

Another reason for using a dynamic number of processors is fault-tolerance: when a processor fails it is just removed from the pool of available processors and the application proceeds undisturbed. We have only experimented with adding processors dynamically to the system to see the effects on performance, but adding a controlled shutdown should not be a major problem, provided there is a way to recognize and isolate the faulty processor.

9.9   Performance Indicators

What exactly are the performance indicators that we should be looking for in a parallel Lisp system? Which tests should we run to compare two different systems? Since there is no such thing as a portable parallel program, which simple tests should we try? Some simple performance indicators that can be used are

- Overhead of wrapping code into a future

- Overhead of tag checking

- Speedups of trivial programs, such as the Fibonacci function

- Speedups/slowdowns on recognized benchmarks, such as the Gabriel ones.

The various performance figures for Multilisp are what one would expect from a bytecode interpreter. An empty function call, for instance, costs 1.6 milliseconds on a Concert which is about 3 times less than a future-wrapping of the same code. This makes futures relatively inexpensive to use and the system well balanced, but does not really show the fundamental limitations and overheads in the future construct. Every data access, for instance, has to lock the object in memory which adds two or more instructions. In an interpreter this might involve a limited overhead when compared with the average number of instructions needed to interpret one bytecoded instruction. In compiled code the overhead is substantial. Kranz [10] measured a maximum overhead ratio of 25:1 for the same empty function, or about 200 instructions versus 8.

In Mul-T, a comparison between two objects requires two future tag checks, turning a one instruction sequence into a 7 instruction sequence. When the same object is used multiple times, however, the first successful test for a non-future value makes the others unnecessary. Applying this optimization can reduce the overhead by as much as 40%. The effect of future tags is therefore basically equivalent to removing all the optimizations that a compiler might apply, in the same way that not using declarations introduces extra tag checks.

For Multilisp, it really only makes sense to compare the speedups of a parallel version of a program with the (best) sequential versions of it for Multilisp. Very good results were obtained both at MIT and CMU, quite often with linear speedups up to the number of physical processors. But Mul-T is aimed at production-quality environments, and therefore the comparisons must be against the best sequential Lisp on the same hardware. Which incidentally happens to be, again, T3. This time the results are less enthusiastic: it takes at least two processors to get better execution times on a number of programs, and the average is about a factor of two slowdown for a one-processor execution of the Mul-T version of the program. With 8 processors the speedup over the best sequential Boyer program is 3.6. Other application programs show wide variations, ranging from a 1.3 low to a 6.4 high when using 8 processors.

The Qlisp implementation was done on on an Alliant FX machine, with 4+2 processors which are equivalent to the 68000. It uses the Lucid compiler, which is a well-reputed commercial compiler, and adds to it support for `Qlet, Qlambda, Futures` and locks. Garbage collection is done simply with a stop-and-copy algorithm. Besides various poor interactions with the operating system, such as the inability to make system calls in parallel (which highly impedes I/O), Gabriel [6] reports limited speedups for application benchmarks, for instance less than a factor of 2 with four processors for the Boyer program. Gabriel also challenges the assumption that using multiple scheduler queues is a good idea, which is contrary to what most other researchers in the field have observed. Perhaps this might be due to the preliminary nature of the system on which the measurements were done.

9.10   Conclusions

Parallel Lisp languages have now just reached the production-quality level of other Lisps with Mul-T. Their use in various research projects has shown that they are indeed a simple vehicle to introduce parallelism in symbolic programs. Tools have been developped to ease the transition into parallel Lisp programming, but their applicability in industrial settings is still to be assessed.

The effect of the future construct on the implementation of Lisp, both in compilers and in interpreters, has been studied in some detail, but much work remains to be done to eliminate overhead and interference with other optimization techniques. The most important problem that must be solved is how to reduce the extra tag checks in compiled code that the potential presence of futures requires.

Despite this problem, a number of parallel Lisp programs exist that show substantial speedups versus their sequential counterparts, even on multiprocessors with a limited number of processors. The new incoming wave of non-uniform memory multiprocessors should also do well with parallel Lisps, as indicated by the experiences with Multilisp.

Acknowledgments

Peter Lee helped me in getting this paper in proper shape, Randy Osborne pointed out a number of mistakes and omissions in earlier versions and fixed the translation of the suspend/resume macros. Their help was greatly appreciated.

References

[1]   A. Appel, J. Ellis, and K. Li. Real-time concurrent collection on stock multiprocessors. In *Proceedings of the 1988 Conference on Programming Language Design and Implementation, Atlanta, GA*, pages 11–20. ACM, June 1988.

[2]   H. G. Baker. List processing in real time on a serial computer. *Communications of the ACM*, 21(4):280–294, 1978.

[3]   D. W. Clark. An efficient list-moving algorithm using constant workspace. *Communications of the ACM*, 19(6):352–354, June 1976.

[4]   D. McDonald editor. CMU Common Lisp user's manual. Mach/IBM RT PC edition. Technical Report CMU-CS-87-156, Carnegie-Mellon University, September 1987.

[5]   M. Feeley and J. S. Miller. A parallel virtual machine for efficient Scheme compilation. In *Proceedings of the 1990 Conference on List and Functional Programming, , Nice France*. ACM, June 1990.

[6]   R. Goldman and R. Gabriel. Preliminary results with the initial implementation of qlisp. In *Proceedings of the 1988 Conference on Lisp and Functional Programming, Snow Bird UT*, pages 143–152, Lucid, Inc., August 1988. ACM.

[7]   R. Halstead. Multilisp: A language for concurrent symbolic computation. *ACM TOPLAS*, 7(4):501–538, October 1985.

[8]   G. L. Steele Jr. *Common LISP: The Language*. Digital Press, 1984.

[9] G. L. Steele Jr. and G. J. Sussman. The revised report on scheme: A dialect of lisp. AI Memo 452, MIT Artificial Intelligence Lab., Cambridge, MA, January 1978.

[10] D. Kranz, R. Halstead, and E. Mohr. Mul-T: A high performance parallel Lisp. In *Proceedings of the 1989 Conference on Language Design and Implementation, Portland OR*, pages 81–90. ACM, June 1989.

[11] J. S. Miller. *MultiScheme: A Parallel Procesing System Based on MIT Scheme*. PhD thesis, MIT, 1987.

[12] R. Rashid, R. Baron, A. Forin, D. Golub, M. Jones, D. Julin, D. Orr, and R. Sanzi. Mach: A foundation for open systems. In *Proceedings of the Second Workshop on Workstation Operating Systems*, pages 109–113. IEEE Computer Society, September 1989.

[13] J. Rees, N. Adams, and J. Meehan. *The T Manual*, 4th edition, January 1984.

[14] O. Shivers. Control flow analysis in Scheme. In *Proceedings of the 1988 Conference on Programming Language Design and Implementation, Atlanta, GA*, pages 64–74. ACM, June 1988.

10 An Experimental Implementation of Connection Machine Lisp

Skef Wholey

The massively parallel architecture of the Connection Machine has inspired several new programming languages built around the notion of data-oriented parallelism. Of these, Connection Machine Lisp is one of the more abstract, higher-level languages, and poses challenging implementation problems. We present here a description of and our experiences in building an experimental, "quick and dirty" implementation of Connection Machine Lisp. In addition to helping us identify key issues in the implementation of such higher-level languages, this exercise gave us some insight into how different language features can interact with massive parallelism in ways that can hinder performance of programs.

10.1 Introduction

The Connection Machine [4,8] is a high-performance computer consisting of tens of thousands of simple, low-performance processors. The sheer number of processors gives the machine its power – but the processors must work in concert if this power is to be realized in actual programs.

The central problem in programming parallel computers is making effective use of processing resources. One strives to maximize the time each processor spends doing "useful work" while minimizing both the work duplicated among processors and the time spent coordinating the activities of different processors. These complex goals give rise to abstractions and paradigms that in turn lead to new programming languages. The wide variety of parallel architectures, each with its own set of performance tradeoffs and idiosyncrasies, has led to an even wider variety of parallel programming languages. In this respect, the Connection Machine is no exception.

Connection Machine Lisp [7,11] is a dialect of Common Lisp [6] extended to be suitable for massively parallel computers like the Connection Machine. Its data structures and control constructs are more abstract than those of other languages developed for the same hardware (e.g., *Lisp [9], C* [5,10]) and pose unique problems to the language implementor. We present here the details of an experimental implementation of Connection Machine Lisp and the lessons we learned while working on it.

The rest of this chapter is organized as follows. Section 10.2 provides a brief description of the Connection Machine hardware, which motivated the design of the language and is, of course, relevant in its implementation. Section 10.3 describes the principal ways in which Connection Machine Lisp extends Common Lisp, and includes a short programming example. Section 10.4 describes our "quick and dirty" implementation of Connection Machine Lisp, the goal of which was to increase our understanding of both the language and its implementation. Finally, Section 10.5 discusses what we learned.

10.2   The Connection Machine

There are several important features of the Connection Machine architecture that influence both programming paradigms and language implementation:

- It has many processors – where "many" is between 1000 and 100000 (65536 processors on a "full" CM-2). The set of physical processors may be time-multiplexed to simulate an even larger set of *virtual processors*. Henceforth, when we say "processor" without qualification, we will mean "virtual processor."

- Each physical processor has a small local memory (8192 bytes on a CM-2). The larger the ratio of virtual processors to physical processors, of course, the smaller the memory associated with each virtual processor.

- Single instruction, multiple data (SIMD) execution. A *front-end* computer (a general purpose machine, such as a DEC VAX) issues instructions to the Connection Machine over a dedicated bus. Every processor executes from the same instruction stream, although any set of processors can "ignore" instructions via their *context flags*. Processors in which the context flag is **true** are called *active* and execute all instructions; processors in which the context flag is **false** are called *inactive* and execute only unconditional instructions.

  Note that SIMD execution means control decisions are made by the front-end (possibly based on data read from the Connection Machine) and thus there are no control-flow instructions in the Connection Machine instruction set. Programs reside on the front end, whereas data reside on the Connection Machine.

- A general-purpose router connects all processors. In a single instruction, every processor can send a message to any other processor. The details of how such messages are routed and the complexity of this operation are hidden by the instruction set.

A less important feature from a high-level programming standpoint is that the CM-2's processors operate *bit-serially*, working on objects one bit at a time. Most instructions take field lengths as arguments, allowing, for example, multiplication of two 3-bit numbers to form a 6-bit result.

Apart from the omission of control flow instructions and the addition of communication instructions, the Connection Machine instruction set is not unlike that of other computers. Some common instructions are:

Set-Context

Sets the context flag to **true** in all processors, unconditionally.

Logand-Context *src*

Sets the context flag in all processors to the logical AND of the current context flag and the one-bit field *src*, thus (possibly) narrowing the set of active processors.

S-Add-3-1L *dest*, *src1*, *src2*, *len*

In every active processor, the signed *len*-bit number stored starting at *src1* is added to the number stored at *src2*, and the result is written to *dest*.

S-Add-2-1L *dest*/*src1*, *src2*, *len*

In every active processor, the signed *len*-bit number stored starting at *dest*/*src1* is added to the number stored at *src2*, and the result is written to *dest*/*src1*.

Logand-3-1L *dest*, *src1*, *src2*, *len*

In every active processor, the *len*-bit number stored starting at *src1* is logically AND'ed with the number stored at *src2*, and the result is written to *dest*.

Global-Logand-1L *src*, *len*

Returns (to the front-end) the logical AND of the *len*-bit numbers starting at address *src* in all active processors.

Send-1L *dest*, *addr*, *src*, *len*

Sends a *len*-bit message from every active processor to the processors whose numbers are stored at *addr*. Messages are read from *src* in the sending processors and written to *dest* in the destination processors. If the same processor receives more than one message, the result in that processor is undefined.

Send-With-S-Add-1L *dest*, *addr*, *src*, *len*

Like **Send-1L**, but if the same processor receives multiple messages, the messages, interpreted as *len*-bit signed integers, are summed.

10.3 The Language

Connection Machine Lisp extends Common Lisp in three basic ways, by adding:

- A new primitive data type: the *xapping*.

- *Parallel function call* via α syntax.

- *Reduction* and *combination* via β syntax.

In addition, a small number of library functions are added, and others are extended to operate on the new data type.

10.3.1 Xappings

Connection Machine Lisp is based on fine-grained, data-oriented parallelism, as opposed to the relatively coarse-grained, control-oriented parallelism of other parallel Lisps such as QLAMBDA [2] or Multilisp [3]. The parallelism in the language is built around a data structure called the *xapping*. Xappings are similar in function to arrays or hash tables, but differ in one essential way: operations on the entries of a xapping may be performed in parallel, as if each element of the xapping were contained in its own processor. Xappings, like other Lisp objects, are dynamically allocated and automatically garbage collected.

A xapping is an unordered collection of ordered pairs. The first item of each pair is called its *index*, and the second its *value*. Pairs are written as *index→value*, and all the pairs in a xapping are written surrounded by braces. For example

{rent→625 food→300 electricity→15}

is a xapping which maps **rent** to **625**, **food** to **300**, and **electricity** to **15**. All the indices in a given xapping must be distinct, but their values need not be. (The Common Lisp function **eql** determines sameness.) One may think of the indices as abstract names for Connection Machine processors and the values as the data stored within those processors.

Special "infinite" xappings are provided which map all indices to a given value. For example

{→5}

maps all indices to **5**. Infinite xappings may have a finite number of index/value exceptions. For example

{boy→blue girl→pink →green}

maps **boy** to **blue**, **girl** to **pink**, and all other Lisp objects to **green**.

A xector is a xapping whose indices run from 0 to some positive integer n. Xectors may be written in an abbreviated form – just the values in order surrounded by brackets:

{0→a 1→b 2→c} ≡ [a b c]

10.3.2 *Parallel Function Call and* α *Syntax*

Connection Machine Lisp extends the function call mechanism of Common Lisp to allow xappings of functions to be called *as* functions, provided that all arguments to a xapping of functions are themselves xappings. The result of such a call is a xapping of results, one element for each index that appears in all argument xappings and the function xapping. The value associated with each such index in the result xapping is computed by applying the value of the function xapping at that index to the values of the argument xappings at that index. For example

```
(funcall '{→+} '[10 20 30] '{→3}) ⇒ [13 23 33]
```

Connection Machine Lisp defines $\alpha X \equiv \{\to X\}$. This allows us to express the above more concisely:

```
(α+ '[10 20 30] α3) ⇒ [13 23 33]
```

Furthermore, α distributes over function call, and • is the inverse of alpha. Thus:

```
α(+ •'[10 20 30] 3) ⇒ [13 23 33]
```

The idea that xappings of functions can be called as functions is extended to xappings of xappings, xappings of xappings of xappings, and so forth. The arguments in such function calls must be similarly nested xappings. For example:

```
(αα+ '[[1 2 3] [3 2 1] [2 3 1]]
     '[[5 5 5] [3 2 0] {→10}])
⇒ [[6 7 8] [6 4 1] [12 13 11]]
```

In general, α of special forms and macros is an error, but Connection Machine Lisp defines the behavior for certain useful and intuitive cases:

α**let**

Establishes "parallel" variable bindings.

```
α(let ((a •'[1 2 3 4]))
   (* a a a))
⇒ [1 8 27 64]
```

α**function**

Creates a parallel function, which closes over any parallel variable bindings currently in effect.

αif

This provides the high-level equivalent of the hardware context flag. The "then" clause is executed for indices in which the test is non-nil; the "else" clause is executed for indices in which the test is nil. Both clauses are always executed, but at distinct sets of indices. The result is a xapping which maps each index in the condition to the result of the appropriate clause.

```
(αif '[t nil t] '[all good men] '{→groovy})
⇒ [all groovy men]
```

αsetf

Modifies elements of its "left hand side" xapping based on its "right hand side" xapping. Indices not mentioned in the RHS remain untouched.

αlet*, αcond, $\alpha$and, αor, ...

These are the natural extensions of their serial equivalents based on the above.

10.3.3 Communication and β Syntax

One way to think about α is that it broadcasts data and programs to any number of indices (i.e., processors). To gather data from many indices or route it between indices, we use β.

The simplest use of β is *reduction*. (βf x) reduces the values in the xapping **x** using the two-argument *combining function* **f**. So:

```
(β+ '[3 5 10 4]) ⇒ 22
```

When the combining function is +, the result is the sum of all the values; when it is *, the result is the product, and so on. In general, the order in which the values are accumulated is unpredictable, so the combining function should be both associative and commutative.

The more general use of β is *combination*. (βf d x) yields a xapping whose indices are specified by the values in d and whose values come from combining the values in x at corresponding indices. For every distinct value q in d there will be a pair q→s in the result. If q appears in more than one pair of d, then s is the result of reducing all the corresponding values from x. For example:

```
(β+ '{giants→nfc redskins→nfc steelers→afc dolphins→afc}
     '{giants→12  redskins→42  steelers→3   dolphins→93})
⇒ {nfc→54 afc→96}
```

The Giants and Redskins are in the NFC; the Steelers and Dolphins are in the AFC. The scores for the teams in each conference are combined using **+**. The hardware analog of this operation is **Send-With-S-Add-1L**: each processor sends its score to the appropriate destination (NFC or AFC), and scores are summed if more than one arrives at any processor.

10.3.4 Library Functions

Common Lisp provides a large library of functions; Connection Machine Lisp extends this library in two ways:

- by adding a small number of new functions, and
- by extending the behavior of existing functions.

Many of the extensions of the first sort provide xapping analogs to array functions, for example:

(**xref** *x i*)

> Returns the element of the xapping *x* at index *i*. This is similar to **aref** or **gethash**. Elements can be set using **setf** of **xref**.
>
> (xref '[martha and the muffins] 3) ⇒ muffins
> (xref '{→boring} 'job) ⇒ boring

(**make-xector** *length*)

> Returns a xector of the specified *length*. Keyword options may be used to specify initial contents, as with **make-array**.
>
> (make-xector 5 :initial-element 'yow)
> ⇒ [yow yow yow yow yow]

A few functions provide completely new features to facilitate the data-oriented programming style. For example:

(**iota** n)

> Returns a xector of the integers from 0 to $n - 1$. This is inspired by the ι operator of APL.
>
> (iota 5) ⇒ [0 1 2 3 4]

Most of the extensions of the second sort are modifications of Common Lisp's "generic sequence functions." In Connection Machine Lisp, the type **sequence** includes xappings as well as arrays and lists. Thus, we have:

(subseq '[a b c d e] 1 3) ⇒ [b c]
(position 'c '[a b c d e]) ⇒ 2
(reverse '[a b c d e]) ⇒ [e d c b a]

10.3.5   A Short Example

The sieve method of finding prime numbers can be coded very naturally in Connection Machine Lisp. We use two xectors: **possible** is **t** for indices that might be prime, and **prime** is **t** at each prime index we've found so far. On each iteration we find the next prime (the lowest **possible** prime), record it in **primes**, and eliminate its multiples from **possible**.

```
(defun primes (n)
  (let ((possible (make-xector n :initial-element t))
        (primes (make-xector n :initial-element nil)))
    (αsetf possible '[nil nil])
    (do ((next-prime 2 (position t possible)))
        ((null next-prime)
         primes)
      (setf (xref primes next-prime) t)
      α(setf •possible
             (and •possible
                  (not (zerop (mod •(iota n) next-prime)))))))))
```

Thus:

```
(primes 10)  ⇒  [nil nil t t nil t nil t nil nil]
```

10.4   An Experimental Implementation

We undertook the initial implementation effort with two goals:

- To quickly bring up a useful subset of the language, so that we could have some experience programming in it.

- To identify the hard problems involved in implementing the full language.

The first goal led directly to our "piggyback" strategy: building a Connection Machine Lisp on top of an existing serial Common Lisp. This saved much work, because we didn't have to duplicate the serial functionality of Common Lisp – still a large part of the parallel dialect – and also because we had the power of a Common Lisp programming environment in which to work. This approach, however, was not without its problems, as we shall discuss in Section 10.5.

The subset we chose to implement is restricted in the following ways:

- Only simple Lisp objects reside on the Connection Machine. These include integers, floating-point numbers, and characters. Other objects (such as symbols or lists) reside on the front-end. They can be pointed to by the Connection Machine, but parallel operations can manipulate only the simple objects actually stored in Connection Machine memory.

- While one is permitted to nest α's to any depth, only the innermost nesting of α'ed function calls are actually carried out in parallel.

In the remainder of this section we describe the runtime system and the compiler of our experimental implementation.

10.4.1   The Runtime System

Primitive Data Structures   Xappings are represented by Lisp structures in the front-end that "point to" areas of data in the Connection Machine.

```
(defstruct xapping
  domain            ; xec of indices
  range             ; xec of values
  default           ; for infinite xappings
  xector-p)         ; t if it's a xector
```

The domain and range each refer to data stored in Connection Machine processors described by **xec** structures (see below). Xectors are an important class of xappings, and are treated specially. A xector's domain can be quickly inferred from the length of its range, so it need not be stored explicitly. If **xector-p** is **t**, the **domain** slot of a xapping is **nil**.

A **xec** is used as a "pointer" into an area of the Connection Machine. Each **xec** refers to a number of Lisp objects stored across a set of processors:

```
(defstruct xec
  first-processor   ; first processor of xec
  length            ; number of processors
  address)          ; address in all processors
```

The objects in Connection Machine processors consist of a 2-bit type tag and a 32-bit data portion, yielding a 34-bit object size (which is of course no problem on a bit-addressed machine). The four type codes, in binary, are:

00 Integer.

> The data part is interpreted as a 32-bit signed integer.

01 Float.

> The data part is interpreted as an IEEE single precision floating-point number.

10 Pointer.

> The data part identifies object residing on front-end. Several pointer numbers are reserved for important Lisp objects such as **nil** and **t** and for character objects.

11 Free block header.
    Described in Storage Allocation section, below.

Storing pointers on the Connection Machine to front-end Lisp objects poses several problems. First, a front-end garbage collection may move objects, changing their addresses. This means that raw front-end addresses cannot be used as the data part of pointer objects. Another problem is that objects on the front-end referred to only by the Connection Machine must be known to be referenced, so front-end garbage collection doesn't reclaim them. Both of these problems are solved by entering every object that passes from the front-end to the Connection Machine in a special table on the front-end, the *front-end pointer table*. The data part of a pointer object is the index into this table at which the object resides.

Rendezvous Mechanism   The storage representation is in fact somewhat more complicated than outlined above. During parallel function call, values from the argument xappings must be brought together according to their indices: values with a given index must find their way into the same processor before the actual computation can take place. We call this process *rendezvous*.

Rendezvous is facilitated by representing domain xecs specially. The object stored in each element of a domain xec is not the index, but rather the number of the processor which serves as the rendezvous point for that index. Rendezvous points are assigned to objects that appear as indices as those objects pass from the front-end to the Connection Machine.

Storage Allocation and Garbage Collection   Connection Machine objects with tag **11** are free block headers. The data part of these objects encodes the number of free processors following the header (inclusive) at the free block header's address.

To allocate storage for a xec of length n, we choose an address and broadcast to all processors a request for all free block headers at the given address that head blocks of at least n elements to identify themselves. We then choose one of these free blocks and use the first n elements of it as storage for our xec, creating a new free block header for the remaining portion (if any). If no free block of the required size is found at one address, we try the next highest address (incrementing by the object size – 34 bits), wrapping around at the top of the heap. If we run out of addresses, we initiate garbage collection.

For garbage collection, we maintain a *weak set* of xec structures on the front-end. A weak set retains objects that are pointed to by structures other than the weak set itself; when all references but the weak set's reference are dropped, the object is effectively removed from the weak set. Weak sets are not a standard part of Common Lisp; however, the Symbolics Common Lisp we used provides enough storage management hooks for us to construct our own.

To collect garbage xecs, we simply mark all the live xecs (i.e., all xecs in the weak set), and construct free blocks out of the unmarked cells. This basic scheme is complicated in a number of ways by objects which point from the front-end to the Connection Machine and vice versa.

First, the system needs to drop objects from the front-end pointer table that are no longer referenced by the Connection Machine, so that these objects can be garbage collected. This requires at least time proportional to the number of objects to be dropped from the front-end pointer table, since this must happen serially on the front-end.

Then, if xappings are referenced by the Connection Machine through the front-end pointer table, cleaning that table may free additional xecs, which may in turn lead to more objects being dropped from the table, and so on. Circular xappings will never be collected using this scheme.

10.4.2   The Compiler

The compiler translates Connection Machine Lisp programs into Common Lisp programs containing calls to run-time system functions and Connection Machine operations. The resulting Common Lisp programs are then compiled by the front-end Lisp compiler. The translation process occurs in three phases: annotation, optimization, and code generation. These phases are not distinct passes over the whole program, but are rather collections of analysis and transformation functions that mutually recurse on one another as the forms and subforms of each function are processed.

Annotation   The annotator walks the code tree adding information it infers about the program. After translating α of macros and special forms, it examines each function call to determine types, storage classes, and side-effects.

Straightforward translation of Connection Machine Lisp into lower-level operations yields code that does a great amount of heap allocation of xappings, and therefore causes frequent garbage collection. While intermediate results of parallel function calls are conceptually xappings, by specially treating such quantities we reduce the amount of heap allocation. The storage class information deduced by the annotator is used in allocating intermediate results and local variables – if a xapping is proven to be confined to a particular scope, it can be allocated on the stack.

The annotator receives a form to be compiled and passes an annotated form onto the optimizer. The annotator works much like a Lisp evaluator or compiler, repeatedly macroexpanding a form until the expansion results in a function call or special form. Function calls are processed accordingly, using stored information about argument and result types and side-effects. The various special forms are handled separately by specialized annotation functions, one for each Common Lisp special form.

Optimization The annotator works on special forms and macros, treating all function calls similarly. The optimizer uses the type, storage class, and side-effect information provided by the annotator to convert calls of Connection Machine Lisp functions into calls of more efficient internal functions. The function name is used to dispatch to a function-specific optimizer. Often these optimizers will provide additional type information that can be of use to the code generator. For example, the optimizer for `iota` has the knowledge that the result of a call to `iota` is a xector of integers. If the length argument is known at compile time, then the `iota` optimizer knows the length of the xector result as well.

Code Generation The code generator uses type information provided by the previous phases to efficiently translate parallel function calls into Connection Machine instructions. A database mapping Common Lisp functions to Connection Machine instructions facilitates this translation. The database is constructed using calls to the macro `defcmop` (for "DEFine CM OPeration"). As an example of the sort of information used during code generation, consider the `defcmop` for `+`:

```
(defcmop (+ :alu)
  :identity 0
  :unary cm:s-move-11
  :binary (:fixnum cm:s-add-3-11
           :flonum cm:f-add-3-11)
  :n-ary t
  :reducer (:fixnum cm:global-s-add-11
            :flonum cm:global-f-add-11)
  :combiner (:fixnum cm:send-with-s-add-11
             :flonum cm:send-with-f-add-11))
```

The first parameter gives the name and general class of the Lisp function whose translation is being defined; in this case, the function is `+`, a simple ALU operation. Keyword arguments provide detailed information:

`:identity`
> indicates that the result of a zero-argument call to `+` is 0.

`:unary`
> specifies that a one-argument call to `+` is simply a move from the argument's range xec to the result's range xec.

`:binary`

specifies which operations are to be used for two-argument calls to `+`. Integers (fixnums) are to be added using the `S-Add-3-1L` instruction; floating-point numbers (flonums) are to be added using the `F-Add-3-1L` instruction. Mixed-mode operations follow the Common Lisp rules of floating-point contagion: first integers are converted to floating-point, and then a floating-point addition is performed.

`:n-ary`

indicates that calls to `+` with more than two arguments are legal, and that such calls accumulate into the result using the two-argument form.

`:reducer`

specifies that reduction with $\beta+$ is carried out using the `Global-S-Add-1L` instruction for integers, and the `Global-F-Add-1L` instruction for floating-point numbers.

`:combiner`

specifies that combination with $\beta+$ is carried out using the `Send-With-S-Add-1L` instruction for integers, and the `Send-With-F-Add-1L` instruction for floating-point numbers.

10.5 Conclusions

The difficulties we encountered during our experimental implementation and the shortcomings of the resulting system arose from two sources: our particular approach to implementation (the piggyback strategy), and certain features of the Connection Machine Lisp language.

By building our implementation on top of an existing Common Lisp we eased some problems while exacerbating others. Connection Machine Lisp is a language that changes behavior of Common Lisp in deep, sometimes subtle ways.

The treatment of xappings of functions as functions fundamentally changes the function call mechanism. For the most part we were able to produce the right behavior through source-level code transformations, but there are some rough edges. For example, one can not store a xapping of functions in the function cell of a symbol and invoke that symbol as a function; xappings of functions are therefore not quite functions.

Another problem is the dichotomy between objects stored on the front-end and those stored on the Connection Machine. This complicates the garbage collector and, at least for our "quick and dirty" version, can cripple it when circularities cross from the Connection Machine to the front-end.

The language itself poses a number of obstacles to efficient execution of programs. Connection Machine Lisp of course inherits all the complications of Common Lisp:

dynamic data typing, first-class functions, and so on. While these problems had been studied and, for the most part, solved for serial systems, they interact badly with massive parallelism, creating new problems.

Parallel computation on elements of nested xector-like objects is an important high-level programming abstraction. For some languages, nested parallel computations can be mapped onto a "flat" massively parallel machine, as done in [1]. The loose typing and mutability of xapping indices and values makes it difficult to apply the same kinds of techniques to Connection Machine Lisp.

Another feature of Lisp that can cause problems for a massively parallel language is the pervasiveness of implicit pointers. Consider an array of structures. To manipulate a particular element of this array we must dereference the pointer stored in the array. Manipulating a xapping of such structures would entail, in general, a parallel pointer dereferencing operation which is, relatively speaking, many times more expensive than its serial counterpart (on current machines like the CM-2). Furthermore, there is no guarantee that the elements are unique or are pointed to by only one other data structure, so they can't simply be allocated in the same processors that point to them.

We believe that some features of Lisp-like languages are currently of questionable utility in the massively parallel arena. However, as compiler and hardware technology evolve, the tradeoffs inherent in using such higher-level abstractions will undoubtedly change.

Acknowledgments

Connection Machine Lisp was originally devised by Danny Hillis, and was later refined by Guy Steele, Skef Wholey, Norman Rubin, and Michael Berry. The system described here was implemented at Thinking Machines Corporation.

References

[1] G. E. Blelloch and G. W. Sabot. Compiling Collection-Oriented Languages onto Massively Parallel Computers. In *Proceedings Frontiers of Massively Parallel Computation*. (October 1988).

[2] R. P. Gabriel and J. McCarthy. Queue-based Multiprocessing Lisp. In *Proc. 1984 ACM Symposium on Lisp and Functional Programming*. ACM SIGPLAN/SIGACT/SIGART (Austin, Texas, August 1984), 25–44.

[3] R. H. Halstead. Multilisp: A Language for Concurrent Symbolic Computation. *ACM Transactions on Programming Languages and Systems 7*, 4 (October 1985), 501–538

[4] W. D. Hillis. *The Connection Machine*. MIT Press (Cambridge, Massachusetts, 1985).

[5] J. R. Rose, and G. L. Steele Jr. C*: An Extended C Language for Data Parallel Computing. In *Proc. Second International Conference on Supercomputing*. (Santa Clara, California, May 1987).

[6] G. L. Steele Jr., S. E. Fahlman, R. P. Gabriel, D. A. Moon, and D. L. Weinreb. *Common Lisp: The Language*. Digital Press (Burlington, Massachusetts, 1984).

[7] G. L. Steele Jr. and W. D. Hillis. Connection Machine Lisp: Fine-Grained Parallel Symbolic Processing. In *Proc. 1986 ACM Conference on Lisp and Functional Programming*. ACM SIG-PLAN/SIGACT/SIGART (Cambridge, Massachusetts, August 1986), 279–297.

[8] Thinking Machines Corporation. *Connection Machine Model CM-2 Technical Summary*. Thinking Machines Technical Report HA87-4. (April 1987).

[9] Thinking Machines Corporation. *The Essential *Lisp Manual*. (July 1986).

[10] Thinking Machines Corporation. *C* Reference Manual*. (August 1987).

[11] S. Wholey and G. L. Steele Jr. Connection Machine Lisp: A Dialect of Common Lisp for Data Parallel Programming. In *Proc. Second International Conference on Supercomputing*. (Santa Clara, California, May 1987).

11 Inheritance of Synchronization and Recovery Properties in Avalon/C++

David L. Detlefs, Maurice P. Herlihy, and Jeannette M. Wing

Many "object-oriented" programming languages provide inheritance mechanisms that allow new data types to be defined as extensions of previously existing types. By supporting incremental modification, inheritance mechanisms are generally thought to enhance modularity and reusability. In this chapter, we describe our experience adapting inheritance mechanisms to a new application domain: reliable distributed systems. We give an overview of Avalon/C++, a programming language currently under development at Carnegie Mellon. Avalon/C++ allows programmers to "customize" the synchronization and fault-tolerance properties of new data types by inheriting from a library of basic types providing properties such as serializability and crash recovery. We believe that inheritance can facilitate implementing and reasoning about programs that must cope with the complex behavior associated with concurrency and failures.

Reliable distributed systems are inherently more complex than their conventional sequential counterparts. In addition to the usual concerns about functional correctness, the programmer must address issues arising from concurrency and fault-tolerance. In the presence of concurrency and failures, the data these systems manage must satisfy application-dependent *consistency constraints*, which may encompass objects stored at multiple nodes in a distributed system. The data must be highly *available*, that is, highly likely to be accessible when needed. Data must be *reliable*, that is, unlikely to be lost or corrupted by system failures. Examples of applications that require such properties include databases, airline reservations, and electronic banking systems, where incorrect or unavailable data may be extremely expensive.

This chapter is organized as follows: Section 11.1 describes the transaction model used to organize distributed computations, some relevant features of C++, and an overview of the Avalon/C++ base hierarchy; Sections 11.2, 11.3, and 11.4 describe each of the hierarchy's classes in more detail; Section 11.5 describes some restrictions on the use of these classes that must be obeyed to preserve their semantic intent. Section 11.6 describes an extended example of an implementation of a directory type that makes use of all three of the base classes. Finally, Section 11.7 presents related work and a discussion.

11.1 Background

11.1.1 Transaction Model of Computation

A *distributed system* consists of multiple computers (called *nodes*) that communicate through a network. Distributed systems are typically subject to several kinds of failures: nodes may crash, perhaps destroying local disk storage, and communications may fail, via lost messages or network partitions. A widely-accepted technique for preserving consistency in the presence of failures and concurrency is to organize computations as sequential processes called *transactions*. Transactions are *atomic*, that is, serializable, transaction-consistent, and persistent. *Serializability* means that transactions appear to execute in a serial order. *Transaction-consistency* ("all-or-nothing") means that a transaction either succeeds completely and *commits*, or *aborts* and has no effect. *Persistence* means that the effects of a committed transaction survive failures.

A program in Avalon consists of a set of *servers*, each of which encapsulates a set of objects and exports a set of *operations* and a set of *constructors*. A server resides at a single physical node, but each node may be home to multiple servers. An application program may explicitly create a server at a specified node by calling one of its constructors. Rather than sharing data directly, servers communicate by calling one another's operations. An operation call is a remote procedure call with call-by-value transmission of arguments and results. Objects within a server may be *stable* or *volatile*; stable objects survive crashes, while volatile objects do not. Avalon/C++ includes a variety of primitives (not discussed here) for creating transactions in sequence or in parallel, and for aborting and committing transactions. Each transaction is the execution of a sequence of operations; each is identified with a single process.

Transactions in Avalon/C++ may be nested. A subtransaction's commit is dependent on that of its parent; aborting a parent will cause a committed child's effects to be rolled back. A transaction's effects become permanent only when it commits at the top level. We use standard tree terminology when discussing nested transactions: a transaction T has a unique parent, a (possibly empty) set of siblings, and sets of ancestors and descendants. A transaction is considered its own ancestor or descendant.

Avalon/C++ provides transaction semantics via *atomic objects*. Atomic objects ensure the serializability, transaction-consistency, and persistence of the transactions that use their operations. All objects shared by transactions must be atomic. Avalon/C++ provides a collection of built-in atomic types, and users may define their own atomic types by inheriting from the built-in types.

Sometimes it may be too expensive to guarantee atomicity at all levels of a system. Instead it is often useful to implement atomic objects from non-atomic components. In

Avalon, such components are called *recoverable* objects; they guarantee persistence in the presence of crashes.

Avalon relies on the Camelot system [13] to handle operating-system level details of transaction management, inter-node communication, commit protocols, and automatic crash recovery.

11.1.2   Overview of C++

Readers familiar with C++ can skip this section. C++ [15,16] is an object-oriented extension of C [6], designed to combine advantages of C, such as concise syntax, efficient object code, and portability, with important features of object-oriented programming, such as abstract data types, inheritance, and generic functions.

Abstract data types are defined in C++ using the *class* construct.[1] A class is declared to contain *members*, which are objects, including functions, of any C++ type. For example, one might enforce bounds checking on array accesses by the following **vector** class:

```
class vector {
  int* elts;                      // Array of elements.
  int count;                      // Size of array.
 public:
  vector(int sz)                  // Create vector.
  ~vector();                      // Destroy vector.
  int size();                     // Number of elements.
  virtual void store(int e, int i); // Store element at index.
  virtual int fetch(int i);       // Fetch element from index.
};

int vector::fetch(int i) {
  if (i < 0 || i >= count) error("vector index out of range");
  return elts[i];
}

// Implementations of other vector operations omitted ...
```

The **elts** and **count** members are *private*; they are accessible to the operations of the **vector** class, but not to external *clients* of the class. The other members are *public*; they provide the only means for clients to manipulate the object. Here, bounds checking is ensured by allowing clients to access the vector elements only through the **store** and **fetch** operations. Declaring **store** to be **void** indicates that it is an operation that returns no results.

---

[1]We use the terms "class" and "data type" interchangeably.

New classes in C++ can also be defined by *inheritance* from an existing class. The old class is said to be the *superclass*, and the new class the *derived* class. Each derived class has a single, explicit superclass.[2] The public members of the superclass become public members of the derived class. The derived class does *not* have access to the superclass's private members; thus, even in the derived class implementation, the inherited superclass object must be manipulated using its public members. For example, let us define a **vector2** class that extends the **vector** class by allowing a lower index bound other than zero.

```
class vector2: public vector {
  int lbound;                    // Low bound.
 public:
  vector2(int sz, int lb);       // Create vector.
  ~vector2();                    // Destroy vector.
  int low();                     // Return low bound.
  void store(int e, int i);      // Store element at index.
  int fetch(int i);     // Fetch from index.
};

int vector2::fetch(int i) {
  return vector::fetch(i - lbound);
}

// Implementations of other vector2 operations omitted ...
```

Vector2 keeps track of the index lower bound in the private member **lbound**. It directly inherits the **size** operation, but it *overloads* the **fetch** and **store** operations with slightly modified operations that explicitly call the corresponding operations of the superclass. C++ provides the facility to declare operations of a class to be *virtual*. A virtual operation of one class can be overloaded by any of its derived classes, but a derived class that does not need a special version of a virtual operation need not provide one; instead the operation of the superclass (or its superclass, etc.) is used. C++ guarantees that the most specific operation is invoked at run-time. Many other languages would call virtual operations *generic* functions.

Class **vector** is a *public* base class of class **vector2**. This means that a public member of class **vector** is a public member of **vector2**. Omitting the keyword **public** means that a public member of the superclass would become a private member of the derived class.

The more recent versions of C++ also recognize that finer control over the visibility of inherited members is sometimes necessary, and adds a new member classification

---

[2]A newer version of C++ supports multiple inheritance.

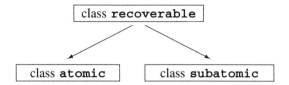

Figure 11.1: Inheritance hierarchy of the three Avalon/C++ base classes.

called *protected*. Protected members are something of a compromise between public and private members: when a class with protected members is inherited, its protected members become private members of the derived class.

11.1.3 Overview of Avalon/C++ Base Hierarchy

In conventional sequential languages, inheritance is typically used to implement an object's "functional" properties, properties whose meaning can be given by simple pre- and postconditions. In Avalon/C++, however, we use inheritance to implement more complex "non-functional" properties such as serializability, transaction-consistency, and persistence.

The Avalon/C++ base hierarchy consists of three classes, as shown in Figure 11.1, and as explained in detail in the next three sections. Each base class provides primitives for implementors of derived classes to ensure the "non-functional" properties of objects of the derived classes. The **recoverable** class provides primitives for ensuring persistence, and thus a means of defining recoverable types. Both **atomic** and **subatomic** provide primitives for ensuring atomicity, and thus two different means of defining atomic types. Putting class **recoverable** at the root of the hierarchy makes sense since atomicity encompasses persistence. Moreover, factoring out **recoverable**'s operations from those of the other two classes lets programmers define non-atomic (but recoverable) objects, such as objects for which synchronization is not a concern (usually because correct synchronization is provided by objects that contain them at a higher-level). The difference between class **atomic** and class **subatomic** is that class **subatomic** gives programmers a finer-grained control over synchronization and crash recovery.

Programmers define their own recoverable or atomic types by deriving from the appropriate class. It must be emphasized that persistence and atomicity, like more conventional "functional" properties, cannot be inherited automatically. Instead, the Avalon base classes provide the *means* by which the implementor of the derived class can ensure these properties. Users of the derived class can then rely on the guarantee provided by the implementor. For example, an implementor of **atomic_set** type would derive from class **atomic**, making explicit use of the inherited locking primitives to implement operations of **atomic_set**. Users of class **atomic_set** are then free to treat objects of that type as atomic, without need for additional explicit synchronization. Although inheritance of persistence and atomicity is not automatic, we will give simple guidelines that guarantee persistence of classes derived from **recoverable**, and atomicity of classes derived from **atomic**.

11.2 The Recoverable Class

The most basic class in our hierarchy is **recoverable**, which provides the means for its derived classes to ensure *persistence*: the restored state of a recoverable object is guaranteed to reflect all operations performed by transactions that committed before the crash, and possibly some operations of transactions uncommitted at the time of the crash. Before presenting the class definition for **recoverable**, we first describe our underlying model of storage.

11.2.1   Three-Level Model of Storage

Conceptually, there are three kinds of storage for objects: volatile, non-volatile, and stable. We assume that local storage of nodes of a distributed system is structured as a virtual memory system, where *volatile* semiconductor memory serves as a cache for memory pages from *non-volatile* backing store, such as magnetic disk. Recoverable objects reside in this local storage of nodes. Since nodes are subject to crashes that destroy all their local storage, if recoverable objects are to survive such crashes, they must be written to *stable storage*, a storage medium that survives crashes with high probability. (Stable storage may be implemented by replicating data.) If every recoverable object is *logged* to stable storage after modifying operations are performed on it, then a consistent state may be recovered after a crash by "replaying" the log.

Replaying the log is sufficient to restore a system's state (indeed, it is used by the Argus system [7]). Nevertheless, recovering the system state entirely from the log is time-consuming. Camelot hastens crash recovery by exploiting the observation that crashes can be divided into two classes: node failures and media failures. In a *media failure*, both volatile and non-volatile storage are destroyed, while in a *node failure*, only volatile storage is lost. In practice, node failures are far more common than media failures. To optimize recovery from node failures, a protocol known as *write-ahead logging* [4] is used. An object is modified in the following steps:

1. The page(s) containing the object are *pinned* in volatile storage; they cannot be returned to non-volatile storage until they are *unpinned*.

2. Modifications are made to the object in volatile memory.

```
class recoverable {
 public:
  virtual void pin(int size);    // Pins object in physical memory.
  virtual void unpin(int size);  // Unpins & logs object to stable
                                 // storage.
}
```

Figure 11.2: The **recoverable** class.

3. The modifications are logged on stable storage.

4. The page(s) are unpinned.

This protocol ensures that a recoverable object can be restored to a consistent state quickly and efficiently (for details, see [13]). Of course, modifications must still be logged to stable storage to protect against media failure.

11.2.2 Class Definition

Figure 11.2 shows the class header for **recoverable**. Classes derived from **recoverable** inherit **pin** and **unpin** operations, which can be used to ensure persistence for the derived class. The **pin** operation causes the pages containing the object to be pinned, as required by the write-ahead logging protocol, while **unpin** logs the modifications to the object and unpins its pages. A recoverable object must be pinned before it is modified, and unpinned afterwards. After a crash, a recoverable object will be restored to a previous state in which it was not pinned. Further, if a transaction makes nested **pin** calls, then the changes made within inner **pin**/**unpin** pairs do not become persistent until the outermost **unpin** is executed. This allows implementors of classes derived from **recoverable** to guarantee persistence by enclosing all modifications between calls to **pin** and **unpin**.

The **pin** and **unpin** operations are usually not called explicitly by programmers; instead, Avalon/C++ provides a special control structure, the **pinning** block, both for syntactic convenience and as a safety measure. The statement:

```
pinning (object) <stmnt>;
```

is equivalent to

```
object->pin(sizeof(*object));
<stmnt>;
object->unpin(sizeof(*object));
```

with the additional guarantee that the **unpin** will be executed even if **<stmnt>** causes control to pass outside the block prematurely, e.g., by executing a **break** or **return**. If the object name is omitted in a **pinning** statement within a class definition, then it defaults to the value **this**, which refers to the object whose member is being defined.

11.2.3   Using Class Recoverable

Consider a class **rec_X** derived from **recoverable**, containing a member **X**, and an operation **modify** that modifies **X**. The class definition would look like this:

```
class rec_X: public recoverable {
  X_type X;
 public:
  void modify();
};

void rec_X::modify() {
  pinning() {
    // ...modify X...
  }
}
```

Without the **pinning** block, the modification to **X** would never be written to stable storage. Persistence could then be violated if a transaction that executes the **rec_X** operation commits. If a crash then occurs, that transaction's effects would not survive.

The **pin** and **unpin** operations are public members of **recoverable**, and are therefore public members of classes derived from **recoverable**. To see why it is useful for **pin** and **unpin** to be public, consider a recoverable array of integers, **rec_int_array**. An object of this type should provide normal array operations such as **store** and **fetch**, but should do so to ensure persistence. We could implement **rec_int_array** as a derived class of **recoverable** as follows:

```
class rec_int_array: public recoverable {
  int elts[100];
 public:
  rec_int_array(int initial = 0);
  int fetch(int index);
  void store(int index, int value);
  void operator=(rec_int_array& source);     // Array copy.
};
```

```
rec_int_array::rec_int_array(int initial) {
  pinning ()
    for (int i = 0; i < 100; i++) elts[i] = initial;
}

void rec_int_array::store(int index, int value) {
  pinning () elts[index] = value;
}

int rec_int_array::fetch(int index) {
  return elts[index];
}

void rec_int_array::operator=(rec_int_array& source) {
  pinning()
    for (int i = 0; i < 100; i++) elts[i] = source.fetch(i);
}
```

Now, suppose we have a **rec_int_array** of 100 integers, and we want to add 1 to each element. We can use a loop where each element is fetched, incremented, and stored back into the array. Given the above implementation of **store**, we would make 100 calls to each of **pin** and **unpin**. Unfortunately, the log write done by **unpin** is expensive, both in terms of space taken on stable storage, which is a scarce resource, and in terms of time. Clients can avoid this expense by explicitly enclosing the loop in a **pinning** block:

```
// Pin and log only once instead of 100 times.
pinning(&a)
  for (int i = 0; i < 100; i++) a.store(i, a.fetch(i) + 1);
```

Here, the **pin** and **unpin** calls made by **store** are much less expensive, because the implementations of **pin** and **unpin** recognize when an object is already pinned, and return immediately.

The **pin** and **unpin** operations can be overloaded. To see why such overloading might be useful, consider how one might implement a recoverable array whose size can be adjusted dynamically. The dynamic array is implemented as a list, where each list element includes a 100-element integer array, a size indicating how much of that array is used, and a pointer to the next list element, possibly *null*.

```
class rec_dyn_array : public recoverable {
  int elts[100]; // 100 element array
  int size; // How much of elts is used
  rec_dyn_array* next; // Null => end of list
 public:
  ...
};
```

This implementation, however, has the disadvantage that the **pin** operation exported by **rec_dyn_array** pins only the first list element. If the array is repeatedly updated in a loop, as discussed above, then each access to a subsequent list element will generate a new log record. A simple remedy is to overload the **pin** and **unpin** operations to dereference and pin the next list element.

```
void rec_dyn_array::pin(int size) {
  recoverable::pin(size);
  if (next) next->pin(sizeof(*next));   // Pin next element
}

void rec_dyn_array::unpin(int size) {
  recoverable::unpin(size);
  if (next) next->unpin(sizeof(*next)); // Unpin next element
}
```

The redefined **pin** pins the first list element by an explicit call to the **pin** operation provided by **recoverable**, and then recursively pins its successor. This example illustrates how the combination of inheritance and overloading can be used to customize properties such as failure recovery.

In summary, recoverable types can be defined as subclasses of **recoverable**. If an operation that modifies a recoverable object calls the inherited **pin** and **unpin** operations properly, the object will be persistent. If a client calls an object's operations many times, as in a loop, performance can be enhanced by enclosing those operations in a **pinning** block.

11.3 The Atomic Class

The second base class in our hierarchy is **atomic**. **Atomic** is a subclass of **recoverable**, specialized to provide two-phase read/write locking and automatic recovery. Locking is used to ensure serializability, and an automatic recovery mechanism for **atomic** objects is used to ensure transaction-consistency.

```
class atomic: public recoverable {
 public:
   // "Pin" and "unpin" are inherited from "recoverable."
   // Atomically obtains a long-term write lock.
   virtual void write_lock();
   // Atomically obtains a long-term read lock.
   virtual void read_lock();
}
```

Figure 11.3: The **atomic** class.

11.3.1   Class Definition

Figure 11.3 gives the class header for **atomic**.

We now discuss in more detail how serializability, transaction-consistency, and persistence can be ensured of objects derived from **atomic**. Atomic objects should be thought of as containing *long-term locks*. **Read_lock** gains a *read lock* for its caller. Many transactions may simultaneously hold read locks on an object. **Write_lock** gains a *write lock* for its caller; if one transaction holds a write lock on an object, no other transaction may hold either kind of lock. Transactions hold locks until they commit or abort. **Read_lock** and **write_lock** suspend the calling transaction until the requested lock can be granted, which may involve waiting for other transactions to complete and release their locks. If **read_lock** or **write_lock** is called while the calling transaction already holds the appropriate lock on an object, it returns immediately.

Classes derived from **atomic** should divide their operations into *writers* and *readers*, that is, operations that do and do not modify the objects of the class. To ensure serializability, reader operations should call **read_lock** on entry, and writer operations should call **write_lock**. Note that no short-term mutual exclusion lock on the object is necessary: if any transaction holds a read lock on an object, then no transaction holds a write lock, so all are free to read the object without fear of its being modified as they read it; conversely, if one transaction holds a write lock on an object, no other transaction may hold either type of lock, so it need not fear interference.

Atomic objects must also be transaction-consistent, that is, the effects of aborted transactions, including those aborted by crashes, must be undone. The Avalon runtime system guarantees transaction-consistency by performing special abort processing that "undoes" the effects of aborted transactions. Thus, implementors of atomic types derived from **atomic** need not provide explicit commit or abort operations.

Finally, persistence is "inherited" from **recoverable**. Since **atomic** is a subclass of **recoverable**, the **pin** and **unpin** operations of **recoverable** are public operations of **atomic**, and may be used in the same way to ensure persistence.

11.3.2   Using Class Atomic

Below is an implementation of an **at_int_array** class that inherits from **atomic**.

```
class at_int_array: public atomic {
  rec_int_array elems;

 public:
  at_int_array(int initial = 0) : elems(initial) {};

  void store(int index, int value) {
    write_lock();
    elems.store(index, value);
  }

  int fetch(int index) {
    read_lock();
    return elems.fetch(index);
  }
};
```

write_lock and **read_lock** are public operations of **atomic**, and thus may be called by clients of classes derived from **atomic**. Clients might want to call these locking operations explicitly to decrease the likelihood of *deadlock*. Two transactions T1 and T2 might each want to obtain write locks on objects A and B; if T1 gets A and T2 gets B, there will be a deadlock – neither will be able to make any progress. Deadlock can be avoided if all transactions obtain locks on the objects they require in some system-wide canonical order. Therefore, clients might want to structure their code so that each transaction obtains all the locks it requires before executing any operations. They would do this with explicit calls to **read_lock** and **write_lock**.

Atomic uses specially optimized facilities provided by the Camelot system, and is therefore quite efficient. It is probably appropriate for deriving most atomic types.

11.4   The Subatomic Class

The third, and perhaps most interesting, base class in our hierarchy is **subatomic**. Like **atomic**, **subatomic** provides the means for objects of its derived classes to ensure atomicity. While **atomic** provides a quick and convenient way to define new atomic objects, **subatomic** provides more complex primitives to give programmers

```
class trans_id: public recoverable {
    ...                                  // Hidden representation.
public:
    trans_id();                          // Constructor.
    bool operator==(trans_id& t);        // Equality.
    bool operator<(trans_id& t);         // Serialized before?
    bool operator>(trans_id& t);         // Serialized after?
    // Is 1st a child of 2nd?
    friend bool descendant(trans_id& t1, trans_id& t2);
};
```

Figure 11.4: The **trans_id** class.

more detailed control over their objects' synchronization and recovery mechanisms. This control can be used to exploit type-specific properties of objects to permit higher levels of concurrency and more efficient recovery. Before presenting the class definition for **subatomic**, we first describe the Avalon **trans_id** class, used to create and test transaction identifiers.

11.4.1 Transaction Identifiers

Figure 11.4 shows the class header for the **trans_id** class. Note that Avalon/C++ defines **bool** to be an enumeration type with **TRUE** set to 1 and **FALSE** set to 0.

A new **trans_id** is created by a call to the constructor:

```
trans_id tid = trans_id();
```

Rather than simply returning the calling transaction's identifier, the **trans_id** constructor creates and commits a (dummy) subtransaction, returning the subtransaction's **trans_id** to the parent. This alternative semantics was chosen because it is often convenient for a transaction to generate multiple **trans_id**'s (for example, one for each of its operations) ordered in the serialization order of their creation events.

The system's current knowledge about the transaction serialization ordering can be tested by the overloaded operators < and >. For example, if the expression:

```
t1 < t2
```

evaluates to true, then if **t2** commits, **t1** will also commit and be serialized before **t2**. Note that < induces a *partial* order on **trans_id**'s; if **t1** and **t2** are active concurrently, both **t1** < **t2** and **t2** < **t1** will evaluate to false.

```
class subatomic: public recoverable {
 protected:
  void seize();          // Gains short-term lock.
  void release();        // Releases short-term lock.
  void pause();          // Temporarily releases short-term lock
 public:
  // "Pin" and "unpin" are public, by inheritance
  // from "recoverable."

  // Called after transaction commit.
  virtual void commit(trans_id& t);

  // Called after transaction abort.
  virtual void abort(trans_id& t);
}
```

Figure 11.5: The **subatomic** class.

It is sometimes convenient to test whether one transaction is a descendant of another in the transaction tree. If the following expression evaluates to true,

```
descendant(t1, t2)
```

then **t1** is a descendant of **t2**. (A **friend** in C++ is a nonmember operation that is allowed access to the private part of a class.)

11.4.2 Class Definition

Figure 11.5 gives the class header for **subatomic**. We now discuss how the primitives provided by **subatomic** may be combined to satisfy the three aspects of atomicity: serializability, transaction-consistency, and persistence.

A subatomic object must synchronize concurrent accesses at two levels: *short-term* synchronization ensures that concurrently invoked operations are executed in mutual exclusion, and *long-term* synchronization ensures that the effects of transactions are serializable. Short-term synchronization is used to guarantee *operation-consistency* of objects derived from **subatomic**. Operation-consistency means that an operation completes entirely or not at all. Since a transaction is a sequence of operations, operation-consistency is a weaker property than transaction-consistency; it permits the effects of aborted transactions to be observed, while transaction-consistency does not.

Subatomic provides the **seize**, **release**, and **pause** operations for operation-level synchronization. Each subatomic object contains a *short-term lock*, similar to a monitor lock or semaphore. Only one transaction may hold the short-term lock at a time. The **seize** operation obtains the short-term lock, and **release** relinquishes it. **Pause** releases the short-term lock, waits for some duration, and reacquires it before returning. Thus, these operations allow transactions mutually exclusive access to subatomic objects. Note that these operations are protected members of the **subatomic** class. They are not provided to clients of derived classes, since it would not be useful for clients to call them.

Like **pin** and **unpin**, Avalon/C++ programmers are typically not expected to call these operations directly. Instead, Avalon/C++ provides a special control construct, the **when** statement, to enhance safety and syntactic convenience:

```
when ( <TEST> ) {
   <...BODY...>
}
```

The **when** statement is a kind of conditional critical region. The calling process calls **seize** to acquire the object's short-term lock, repeatedly calls **pause** until the condition becomes true, and then executes the body. It calls **release** when control leaves the body, either normally or by statements such as **break** or **return**. In addition, the **when** statement can be used to ensure operation-consistency: Avalon guarantees that if a failure occurs in the middle of the execution of a **when** no partial effects are observed.

To implement transaction-consistency, **subatomic** provides **commit** and **abort** operations. Whenever a top-level transaction commits (aborts), the Avalon run-time system calls the **commit** (**abort**) operation of all objects derived from **subatomic** accessed by that transaction or its descendants. **Abort** operations are also called when nested transactions "voluntarily" abort. **Abort** operations usually undo the effects of aborted transactions, while **commit** operations discard recovery information that is no longer needed. Since **commit** and **abort** are C++ virtual operations, classes derived from **subatomic** are allowed (and in this case, expected) to reimplement these operations. When **commit** or **abort** is called by the system, the most specific implementation for the object will be called. Thus, **subatomic** allows type-specific commit and abort processing, which is useful and often necessary in implementing user-defined atomic types efficiently, as exemplified in the next section and Section 11.6. Notice that users need not invoke **commit** and **abort** explicitly; the system automatically invokes them when appropriate.

Finally, as for **atomic**, persistence is "inherited" from **recoverable** since **subatomic** is a subclass of **recoverable**.

11.4.3 Using Class Subatomic

Consider how one would implement an atomic first-in-first-out (FIFO) queue. The easiest way to define such a queue is to inherit from **atomic**. A limitation of this approach is that **enq** and **deq** operations would both be classified as writers, permitting little concurrency. Instead, we show how a highly concurrent atomic FIFO queue can be implemented by inheriting from **subatomic**. Our implementation is interesting for two reasons. First, it supports more concurrency than commutativity-based concurrency control schemes such as two-phase locking. For example, it permits concurrent **enq** operations, even though **enq**'s do not commute. Second, it supports more concurrency than any locking-based protocol, because it takes advantage of state information. For example, it permits concurrent **enq** and **deq** operations while the queue is non-empty.

The Representation Information about **enq** invocations is recorded in the following **struct**:

```
struct enq_rec {
  int item;               // Item enqueued.
  trans_id enqr;          // Who enqueued it.
  enq_rec(int i, trans_id& en) { item = i; enqr = en; }
};
```

The **item** component is the enqueued item. The **enqr** component is a **trans_id** generated by the enqueuing transaction, and the last component defines a constructor operation for initializing the struct.

Information about **deq** invocations is recorded similarly:

```
struct deq_rec {
  int item;               // Item dequeued.
  trans_id enqr;          // Who enqueued it.
  trans_id deqr;          // Who dequeued it.
  deq_rec(int i, trans_id& en, trans_id& de);
   { item = i; enqr = en; deqr = de; }
};
```

The queue is represented as follows:

```
class atomic_queue : public subatomic {
  deq_stack deqd;         // Stack of deq records.
  enq_heap enqd;          // Heap of enq records.
 public:
  atomic_queue() {};      // Create empty queue.
  void enq(int item);     // Enqueue an item.
```

```
int deq();                  // Dequeue an item.
void commit(trans_id& t);
void abort(trans_id& t);
~atomic_queue();            // Destroy queue.
};
```

The **deqd** component is a stack of **deq_rec**'s used to undo aborted **deq** operations. The **enqd** component is a *partially ordered heap* of **enq_rec**'s, ordered by their **enqr** fields. A partially ordered heap provides operations to enqueue an **enq_rec**, to test whether there exists a unique oldest **enq_rec**, to dequeue it if it exists, and to discard all **enq_rec**'s committed with respect to a particular transaction identifier.

Our implementation satisfies the following representation invariant: First, assuming all items enqueued are distinct, an item is either "enqueued' or "dequeued," but not both: if an **enq_rec** containing **[x, enq_tid]** is in the **enqd** component, then there is no **deq_rec** containing **[x, enq_tid, deq_tid]** in the **deqd** component, and vice-versa. Second, the stack order of two items mirrors both their enqueuing order and their dequeuing order: if **d1** is below **d2** in the **deqd** stack, then **d1.enqr < d2.enqr** and **d1.deqr < d2.deqr**. Finally, any dequeued item must previously have been enqueued: for all **deq_rec**'s **d**, **d.enqr < d.deqr**.

The Operations   **Enq** and **deq** operations may proceed under the following conditions. A transaction P may dequeue an item if (1) the most recent dequeuing transaction is committed with respect to P, and (2) there exists a unique oldest element in the queue whose enqueuing transaction is committed with respect to P. The first condition ensures that P will not have dequeued the wrong item if the earlier dequeuer aborts, and the second condition ensures that there is something for P to dequeue. Similarly, P may enqueue an item if the last item dequeued was enqueued by a transaction Q committed with respect to P. This condition ensures that P will not be serialized before Q, violating the FIFO ordering. Given these conditions, **enq** and **deq** are implemented as follows:

```
void atomic_queue::enq(int item) {
  trans_id tid = trans_id();
  when (deqd.is_empty() || (deqd.top()->enqr < tid))
    enqd.insert(item, tid);
}

int atomic_queue::deq() {
  trans_id tid = trans_id();
  when ((deqd.is_empty() || deqd.top()->deqr < tid)
        && enqd.min_exists() && (enqd.get_min()->enqr < tid)) {
    enq_rec* min_er = enqd.delete_min();
```

```
    deq_rec dr(*min_er, tid);
    deqd.push(dr);
    return min_er->item;
  }
}
```

Enq checks whether the item most recently dequeued was enqueued by a transaction committed with respect to the caller. If so, the current **trans_id** and the new item are inserted in **enqd**. Otherwise, the transaction releases the short-term lock and tries again later. **Deq** tests whether the most recent dequeuing transaction has committed with respect to the caller, and whether **enqd** has a unique oldest item. If the transaction that enqueued this item has committed with respect to the caller, it removes the item from **enqd** and records it in **deqd**. Otherwise, the caller releases the short-term lock, suspends execution, and tries again later.

Commit and **Abort** are implemented as follows:

```
void atomic_queue::commit(trans_id& committer) {
  when (TRUE)
    if (!deqd.is_empty() &&
        descendant(deqd.top()->deqr, committer)) {
      deqd.clear();
    }
}
```

```
void atomic_queue::abort(trans_id& aborter) {
  when (TRUE) {
    while (!deqd.is_empty() &&
           descendant(deqd.top()->deqr, aborter)) {
      deq_rec* d = deqd.pop();
      enqd.insert(d->item, d->enqr);
    }
    enqd.discard(aborter);
  }
}
```

When a top-level transaction commits, it discards **deq_rec**'s no longer needed for recovery. (The representation invariant ensures that all **deq_rec**'s below the top are also superfluous, and can be discarded.) **Abort** has more work to do. It undoes every operation executed by a transaction that is a descendant of the aborting transaction. It interprets **deqd** as an undo log, popping records for aborted operations, and inserting the items back in **enqd**. Abort then flushes all items enqueued by the aborted transaction and its descendants.

11.5   Restrictions on Containers

Some types are (conceptually) parameterized over the types of objects that they can contain. In order to preserve the intended meaning of the type, some restrictions are necessary on the types that can be used to instantiate these parameterized container types.

11.5.1   Restrictions for Recoverable

Let us consider the class **rec_array**, a generalization of the **rec_int_array** class that is parameterized over the element type of the array. It is necessary to ask what kinds of objects we can put in **rec_array**'s, and still maintain recoverability of the array object considered as a whole. First, any type that is stored *in-line* is permissible. An in-line type is any type that contains no pointers. The fundamental types of C++ (**char**, **int**, or **float**) are in-line. A **struct** whose members are all in-line is in-line. Similarly, a (C++) **array** whose elements are all in-line is in-line. Note that if a **rec_array** has an in-line element type, then logging the array to stable storage will log all the elements as well.

Problems arise when we start to consider pointer types. If we declare **A** to be a **rec_array** of pointers to **int**'s, is **A** a recoverable object? The answer is no, since **A[1]** points to an **int**, which is not a recoverable object. We could change the value of this **int** during a transaction, thus conceptually modifying the state of the array, but no record of this modification would ever reach stable storage, allowing persistence to be violated.

Here, then, is a rule for ensuring that a type is recoverable: if objects of a type may contain other objects, and the containing type is intended to be recoverable, then the type of the contained objects must either be an in-line type, or it must be a pointer to a recoverable object. This rule ensures that the latest version of a recoverable object will be written to stable storage every time an operation that modifies it completes.

The inverse problem occurs when we have a object that is not meant to be recoverable, but conceptually contains some recoverable object. The Camelot system requires that recoverable and non-recoverable data be allocated in different sections of memory. If we allow a non-recoverable object to contain an in-line recoverable object, then we must allocate space for the aggregate object in one of these sections of memory. We cannot put it in the non-recoverable section of memory since then the recoverable object would not be recoverable. We also cannot put the object in the recoverable section of memory, for a more subtle reason. If we were to allocate memory there, and there were a node crash, the non-recoverable part of the object would become meaningless after recovery: the storage allocator would think it had been allocated, although no variables reference it. This type of garbage would build up over time. Therefore, as a rule we forbid non-recoverable objects to contain recoverable objects "in-line;" they can only point to recoverable objects.

11.5.2   Restrictions for Serializability

Similar restrictions apply to serializability. If a container type is intended to ensure serializability of the transactions accessing it, then it should be instantiated either with an in-line type or with a pointer to another type that ensures serializability. Care must be taken that nested atomic objects do not lead to deadlock.

11.6   An Extended Example

We now demonstrate how all three base classes can be combined to implement an atomic directory type. A *directory* stores pairs of values, where one value (the *key*) is used to retrieve the other (the *item*). The *insert* operation,

```
bool directory::insert(key k, item i)
```

inserts a new binding in the directory, returning **FALSE** if the key was already present, and **TRUE** otherwise. The *remove* operation,

```
bool directory::remove(key k)
```

removes the item bound to the given key, returning **TRUE** if the key is in the directory, and **FALSE** otherwise. The *alter* operation,

```
bool directory::alter(key k, item i)
```

alters the item bound to the given key, returning **FALSE** if the key is absent. Finally, the *lookup* operation,

```
item directory::lookup(key k)
```

returns the item bound to the given key. For brevity, we assume the key is bound.

   The directory example provides a further illustration of how the Avalon/C++ synchronization primitives can be used for type-specific synchronization. Here, all synchronization is done on a per-key basis, so transactions that operate on disjoint sets of keys never interfere. Internally, concurrent operations synchronize by strict two-phase locks. The lock conflict table appears in Figure 11.6. An interesting aspect of this scheme is that lock conflicts take into account not only the names and arguments to operations, but also the operations' results. For example, because an unsuccessful **insert** (denoted

	insert/T, remove/T	*insert/F, remove/F*	*alter/T*	*alter/F*	*lookup*
insert/T, remove/T	Conflict	Conflict	Conflict	Conflict	Conflict
insert/F, remove/F	Conflict		Conflict		
alter/T	Conflict	Conflict	Conflict	Conflict	Conflict
alter/F	Conflict		Conflict		
lookup	Conflict		Conflict		

Figure 11.6: Lock conflicts for directory.

by *insert/F*) does not modify the key's binding, it need not conflict with a concurrent **lookup** operation on the same key. On the other hand, a successful **insert** (*insert/T*) does modify the key's binding, hence it must conflict with **lookup**.

The directory example also illustrates the utility of user-defined commit and abort processing. For objects inheriting from **atomic**, transaction recovery is straightforward. When a transaction is aborted, the object's earlier value is restored by a bit-wise copy, while if it commits, the recovery data is discarded. This "bit-wise recovery" is done directly by Camelot, and it is used in the directory example for operations such as **alter** that "overwrite" existing bindings. Bit-wise recovery, however, is inadequate for more complex operations such as **insert** and **remove** that create or destroy bindings. Instead, commit and abort processing for these operations relies on the **commit** and **abort** operations inherited from **subatomic** and overloaded by the directory implementation.

11.6.1 Class Definition

As shown in Figure 11.7, lock modes for each operation are defined by the enumeration type **mode**. The **insert**, **remove**, and **alter** operations have different lock modes depending on whether they return successfully or not. For example, an **insert** that returns **TRUE** must acquire a lock of mode **INSERT_T_LOCK**, while one that returns **FALSE** must acquire **INSERT_F_LOCK**. A *lock manager* is a recoverable object that keeps track of locks. It provides operations to acquire a lock, to release a lock, and to test whether another transaction holds a conflicting lock.

Each key in the directory is associated with a *binding*, which is a recoverable struct with two fields. The **target** field is a pointer to an atomic struct (that is, a *cell*) that holds the item itself. The **present** field serves as a count of the number of committed inserts minus the number of committed removes. Thus, **present** is 1 if the key is bound in the directory's committed state; otherwise, **present** is 0 and the key appears unbound. **Present** is initially 1 because new bindings are created only when insertions are performed. A binding can be discarded when it is unlocked (true if and only if there are no active insertions or removals) and **present** is 0.

The association between keys and bindings is maintained by a recoverable *map* object, also shown in Figure 11.7. A map provides operations to insert new bindings, to remove existing bindings, to find the binding associated with a given key, and to test whether a particular key is bound.

Finally, the **directory** itself (Figure 11.8) inherits from **subatomic**. As private members, it has a lock manager **locks**, a map **data**, and a collection of auxiliary procedures used to test synchronization conditions.

The simplest operation is **lookup**. It generates a new transaction identifier, and enters its critical section when the lock manager reports that no other transaction holds a conflicting lock for that key. Inside the critical section, the transaction locks the key in lookup mode, finds the key's binding, and returns the associated item.

```
item directory::lookup(key k) {
  trans_id tid = trans_id();
  when (!locks.conflict(k, LOOKUP_LOCK, tid)) {
    locks.acquire(k, LOOKUP_LOCK, tid);
    binding* b = data.lookup(k);
    return *(b->target);
  }
}
```

The **insert** operation is more complex. Since the operation's lock depends on whether the insert is successful, it must first check to see whether the key has a binding. This test is performed by the auxiliary **insert_check** procedure, which tests the status of the binding and the state of the lock manager, returning a value of an enumeration type. A value of **PRESENT** indicates that the key is bound and the caller may acquire an **INSERT_F_LOCK** on that key, a value of **ABSENT** indicates that the key is unbound and the caller may acquire an **INSERT_T_LOCK** on that key, and a value of **BUSY** indicates that lock conflicts prevent the binding's status from being determined. The **insert** operation itself uses the result of **insert_check** to determine how to proceed in its critical region. The **whenswitch** statement is a generalization of the **when** statement that replaces the boolean expression with an expression of an enumeration type. If the key is absent, the caller acquires the appropriate lock, then creates (and initializes) a new binding for the key. If the key is present it simply acquires a lock and returns.

```
// Lock modes depend on whether a key is bound.

status directory::insert_check(trans_id& tid, key k) {
  binding* b = data.lookup(k);
  if ((b && b->present==1) &&
      !locks.conflict(k, INSERT_F_LOCK, tid))
    return PRESENT;
  if ((!b || b->present==0) &&
      !locks.conflict(k, INSERT_T_LOCK, tid))
    return ABSENT;
  return BUSY;
}


bool directory::insert(key k, item i) {
  trans_id tid = trans_id();
  whenswitch (insert_check(tid, k)) {
    case ABSENT:
      locks.acquire(k, INSERT_T_LOCK, tid);
      binding* b = new binding(i);
      data.insert(k, b);
      return TRUE;
    case PRESENT:
      locks.acquire(k, INSERT_F_LOCK, tid);
      return FALSE;
  }
}
```

The implementations of **remove**, **remove_check**, **alter**, and **alter_check** are similar, and are omitted for brevity.

The **commit** operation enters its critical section, iterates through the locks held by the committing transaction, and discards any unlocked binding where **present** is zero.

```
void directory::commit(trans_id& tid) {
  lock_info* info;
  when (TRUE)      // Always ok to commit.
    while (info = locks.release(tid)) {
      key k = info->k;
      binding* b = data.lookup(k);
      if ((b->present==0) && !locks.is_locked(k))
        data.remove(k);
    }
}
```

Handling aborts, in particular for **insert** and **remove** operations, is a little more complex. For each successful **remove** lock, the **abort** operation locates the associated binding and increments the **present** field; for each successful **insert** lock, it decrements **present**; finally, it discards superfluous bindings. Note that because a key's item is stored in a cell that inherits from **atomic**, the effects of aborted **alter** operations are automatically undone when the **atomic** cell is recovered.

```
void directory::abort(trans_id& tid) {
  lock_info* info;
  when (TRUE)
    while (info = locks.release(tid)) {
      key k = info->k;
      binding* b = data.lookup(k);
      switch (info->m) {
case REMOVE_T_LOCK:
  pinning(b) b->present++;
  break;
case INSERT_T_LOCK:
  pinning(b) b->present--;
      }
      if ((b->present==0) && !locks.is_locked(k))
        data.remove(k);
    }
}
```

11.7   Related Work and Discussion

The use of inheritance to provide recoverability and atomicity in Avalon/C++ is not closely tied to the details of the C++ inheritance mechanism. It could be adapted to inheritance mechanisms in languages such as Smalltalk [3], Flavors [8], CommonLoops [2], CommonObjects [12], and Owl [10]. Our extensions would undoubtedly take a slightly different form in a language allowing *multiple* inheritance [16], where a class may inherit from more than one superclass.

Avalon/C++ is based on a transaction model of computation. It should be possible to exploit **subatomic**'s provision of user-defined commit and abort operations to support non-transaction based approaches to crash recovery, which typically use optimistic recovery schemes [5,14] based on rollbacks and replays.

Other projects investigating an "object-oriented" transaction-based approach to managing persistent data include Exodus [9] and Arjuna [11]. Avalon/C++ is in many ways similar to Argus [7], a language designed to provide support for fault-tolerant distributed computing. Although Avalon/C++ and Argus provide much of the same functionality,

```
// Lock modes
enum mode {
  INSERT_T_LOCK, // Successful insert.
  INSERT_F_LOCK, // Unsuccessful insert.
  REMOVE_T_LOCK, // Successful remove.
  REMOVE_F_LOCK, // Unsuccessful remove.
  ALTER_T_LOCK, // Successful alter.
  ALTER_F_LOCK, // Unsuccessful alter.
  LOOKUP_LOCK // Lookup.
};

// All synchronization is done through the lock manager.
struct lock_info {mode m; key k;};

class lock_mgr: public recoverable {
  // Private representation not shown ...
 public:
  lock_mgr();
  bool conflict(key k, mode m, trans_id& t); // Any conflicts?
  void acquire(key k, mode m, trans_id& t);  // Grant lock.
  bool is_locked(key k);                      // Is key locked?
  lock_info* release(trans_id& t);   // Release and return lock.
};

// Cells are atomic in order to get automatic commit
// and abort processing.
struct cell: public atomic {
  item value;
  cell(item i) { pinning() value = i; }
  item operator=(item rhs);       // Assign an item to the cell.
  operator item();                // Coercion from cell to item.
};

// Discard binding when unlocked and present = 0.
struct binding: public recoverable{
  int present; // inserts - removes.
  cell* target; // Current item.
  binding(item i) {
    pinning() { present = 1; target = new cell(i); }
  }
  ~binding() { delete target; }
};
```

Figure 11.7: Auxiliary definitions for directory example.

```
// Maps keys to bindings.
class map: public recoverable {
  // Private representation not shown ...
 public:
  map();
  void insert(key k, binding* b);
  void remove(key k);
  binding* lookup(key k);
};
```

Figure 11.7: *cont.*

```
enum status { PRESENT, ABSENT, BUSY };

class directory: public subatomic {
  lock_mgr locks;
  map data;
  status insert_check(trans_id& t, key k); // Internal proc.
  status remove_check(trans_id& t, key k); // Internal proc.
  status alter_check trans_id& t, key k); // Internal proc.
 public:
  directory();
  bool insert(key k, item i);
  bool alter(key k, item i);
  bool remove(key k);
  item lookup(key k);
  void commit(trans_id& t);
  void abort(trans_id& t);
};
```

Figure 11.8: Atomic directory definition.

such as support for transactions and atomic data types, programs in the two languages have a different flavor. In Avalon/C++, user-defined atomic objects are implemented by inheriting from the special built-in classes, while in Argus such objects are typically implemented by including atomic objects in the new object's representation. Avalon/C++ and Argus use different models of serializability. In Argus, concurrency control is based on a generalization of strict two-phase locking. In Avalon/C++, the ability to query the transaction serialization ordering at run-time (via the **trans_id** type) permits strictly more concurrency than two-phase locking, while remaining compatible with two-phase locking. Finally, Avalon/C++ and Argus use different recovery techniques. Avalon relies on the Camelot system for basic transaction management, using the write-ahead log protocol for efficient recovery from node failures. Argus recovers directly from the log.

We are currently implementing Avalon/C++ on IBM RT's, DEC MicroVaxes, and Sun 3's using Version 1.1 of C++. The implementation takes the form of a preprocessor that transforms Avalon code to C++ code. We make extensive use of the Camelot system for low-level transaction support; Camelot, in turn, relies on the Mach operating system [1] for memory management, inter-node communication, and lightweight processes. As of this writing, we are able to compile and run all the code presented in this chapter.

In conclusion, we believe that inheritance provides an effective way to customize and extend the kind of complex "non-functional" properties, such as serializability, transaction-consistency, and persistence, needed to support programs for reliable distributed applications. For each of these properties, there is a core of functionality, such as the basic mechanics of locking, pinning, and logging, that is best provided by the underlying language implementation. Nevertheless, support for user-defined data types sometimes requires extending or modifying that functionality, as illustrated by the example in which a recoverable object needs to pin a component object indirectly referenced through a pointer. The combination of inheritance and overloading provides a simple and flexible way to achieve incremental modification of these complex properties that lie outside the domain of conventional programming languages.

References

[1] M. Accetta, R. Baron, W. Bolosky, D. Golub, R. Rashid, A. Tevanian, and M. Young. Mach: A new kernel foundation for Unix development. In *Proceedings of Summer Usenix*, July 1986.

[2] D. G. Bobrow, K. Kahn, G. Kiczales, L. Masinter, M. Stefik, and F. Zdybel. CommonLoops: Merging Lisp and object-oriented programming. In *Proc. ACM Conference on Object-Oriented Systems, Languages, and Applications*, pages 17–29, New York, New York, 1986. Association for Computing Machinery.

[3] A. Goldberg and D. Robson. *SmallTalk-80: The Language and its Implementation*. Addison-Wesley, Reading, MA, 1983.

[4] J. Gray. Notes on database operationg systems. In *Operating Systems: an Advanced Course*, volume 60 of *Lecture Notes in Computer Science*. Springer-Verlag, Berlin, 1978.

[5] D. R. Jefferson. Virtual time. *ACM TOPLAS*, 7(3):404–425, July 1985.

[6] B. W. Kernighan and D. M. Ritchie. *The C Programming Language*. Prentice-Hall, Englewook Cliffs, NJ, 1978.

[7] B. Liskov and R. Scheifler. Guardians and actions: Linguistic support for robust, distributed programs. *ACM Transactions on Programming Language and Systems*, 5(3):382–404, July 1983.

[8] D. A. Moon. Object-oriented programming with flavors. In *Proc. ACM Conference on Object-Oriented Systems, Languages, and Applications*, pages 1–8, New York, New York, 1986. Association for Computing Machinery.

[9] J. E. Richardson and M. J. Carey. Programming constructs for database implementation in exodus. In *Proceedings of SIGMOD 87*, pages 208–219, May 1987.

[10] C. Schaffert, T. Cooper, B. Bullis, M. Kilian, and C. Wilpolt. An introduction to Trellis/Owl. In *Proc. ACM Conference on Object-Oriented Systems, Languages, and Applications*, pages 9–16, New York, New York, 1986. Association for Computing Machinery.

[11] S. K. Shrivastava, G. N. Dixon, F. Hedayati, G. D. Parrington, and S. M. Wheater. A technical overview of Arjuna: A system for reliable distributed computing. Technical report, Computing Laboratory, University of Newcastle upon Tyne, 1988.

[12] A. Snyder. Object-oriented programming for Common Lisp. Technical Report ATC-85-1, Software Technology Laboraty, Hewlett-Packard Laboratories, 1985.

[13] Alfred Z. Spector, Randy Pausch, and Gregory Bruell. Camelot: A flexible, distributed transaction processing system. In *Proceedings of Compcon 88*, February 1988.

[14] R. E. Strom and S. Yemini. Optimistic recovery in database systems. *ACM TOCS*, 3(3):204–226, August 1985.

[15] B. Stroustrup. *The C++ Programming Language*. Addison-Wesley, Reading, Massachusetts, 1986.

[16] B. Stroustrup. What is object-oriented programming? *IEEE Software*, pages 10–20, May 1988.

Part IV
New and Unconventional Languages and Techniques

The first three parts of this book have focused, for the most part, on the implementation of languages such as Lisp, Scheme, and ML. In recent years, however, there have been many new developments in programming language design, and also in software development methodology. Not surprisingly, these have presented challenging new problems, oftentimes requiring the implementor to adopt totally new approaches and techniques. The four chapters in this final part represent just a tiny fraction of such work on "unconventional" languages and techniques.

Chapter 12 by Conal Elliott and Frank Pfenning (*A Semi-functional Implementation of Higher-order Logic Programming*) gives a remarkably clear description of the interpretation of logic programs. The chapter presents interpreters, written in Standard ML, for a series of logic-programming languages. Beginning with a simple "propositional" language, this is extended to a Prolog-like language, and finally to a "higher-order" language in the spirit of λProlog. Such languages are really quite fascinating, and so the reader is encouraged to read more about the λProlog language itself. It should be noted that many Prolog systems compile for an abstract machine, called the Warren abstract machine, or WAM. A reference for a good description of the WAM is given below.

An important trend in programming methodology is the computer-assisted development of programs from formal specifications. Chapters 13 and 14 discuss some of the issues involved in implementing such computer assistance. One of the most basic issues is how to support the development and maintenance of mathematical "knowledge" in a programming environment. Chapter 13 by Joseph Bates (*The Architecture of the PRL Mathematics Environment*) recounts the experience gained from the various PRL mathematics-development systems. The insights and conclusions gained from this experience are sometimes quite surprising. The reader may find it useful to read more about PRL's approach to formal software development in the paper by Bates and Constable listed below.

Another critical requirement for such systems is persistence. The term "persistent object base" has become quite a buzzword of late, meaning very different things to different people. In Chapter 14 by Eugene J. Rollins (*A Simple Object Storage System for Common Lisp*), some of the "bare essentials" for persistence in sequential Common Lisp are described, along with an example implementation.

Finally, Chapter 15 by Philip J. Koopman, Jr. and Peter Lee (*Architectural Considerations for Combinator Graph Reduction*) describes an approach to compiling and executing lazy functional languages. The compilation technique is based on a standard approach called graph reduction, but the method for executing programs involves self-modifying code. To see whether such an approach is reasonable on modern hardware, the results of a cache simulation study are presented. Some of the results are quite surprising, and may have implications for other implementation techniques, such as garbage collection algorithms.

References

[1] H. Aït-Kaci. *The WAM: A (Real) Tutorial*. Research Report 5, DEC Systems Research Center, January 1990.

[2] J. Bates and R. Constable. Proofs as programs. *ACM Transactions on Programming Languages and Systems*, Vol. 7, No. 1, January 1985, 113–136.

[3] G. Nadathur and D. Miller. An overview of Prolog. *Logic Programming: Proceedings of the Fifth International Conference and Symposium, Volume 1*, R. Kowalski and K. Bowen (eds.), Cambridge, Massachusetts, August 1988, 810–827.

[4] S. L. Peyton Jones. *The Implementation of Functional Programming Languages*, Prentice-Hall, London, 1987.

12   A Semi-Functional Implementation of a Higher-Order Logic Programming Language

Conal Elliott and Frank Pfenning

12.1   Introduction

In this chapter we develop an interpreter of a higher-order constraint logic programming language in Standard ML (SML). The logic programming language is closely related to λProlog [25], though the type system supported by our implementation is more general, for example by allowing explicit abstraction over types. The implementation is closely modeled after eLP, an implementation of λProlog in the Ergo Support System [8,20] and may be considered as a rational reconstruction and explanation of the eLP implementation.

This is not a tutorial on λProlog (we present no λProlog programs at all), but for someone familiar with ML this should serve as a high-level operational semantics of a variant of the λProlog language. Prior knowledge of ML is assumed, but not at a very deep or sophisticated level (see [15] for an SML tutorial). We try to emphasize programming techniques as well as the gradual development of the interpreter in its full generality from a very simple starting point. For someone considering experimentation with variations on logic programming languages, this chapter should provide enough detail and techniques for the rapid implementation of a modified interpreter of related languages. Our approach is to write a true interpreter, and not to embed Prolog in ML the way Prolog is embedded in Scheme in [9] and [17]. The primary difference is that we separate carefully the name space of predicates of the logic programming language from the name space of functions in ML.

We do not address the use of the SML module system, nor do we discuss a number of features of λProlog such as its module system, input/output, and other built-in special predicates. Also omitted are the front end of the interpreter (parsing, unparsing, type inference) and, due to space constraints, we limit ourselves to a sketch of higher-order unification. We hope to write a companion paper which concentrates primarily on a development of higher-order unification and type reconstruction within the framework laid out in this chapter.

One might also miss a discussion of compilation, which is not very well understood in this context and is the subject of current research [24].

We begin with an interpreter for propositional Horn logic, which introduces the central technique of the success continuation, due to Carlsson [2]. We then move on to first-order Horn logic, which is very much in the tradition of Prolog. In Section 12.4 we generalize this to include embedded implication and universal quantification (see [1,11,21] for the motivation for these constructs) which complicates primarily unification. In Section 12.5 we introduce side-effects and assignment in the implementation in a controlled way to increase the efficiency of unification. This is refined in the next section where we address non-logical control constructs such as if-then-else and cut and introduce the concept of the trail. Section 12.7 sketches a more efficient clausal representation of programs which hitherto were simply formulas and hints at indexing. In Section 12.8 we generalize the underlying language of terms from first-order terms to typed λ-terms, at which point unification no longer generates most general unifiers and constraints enter the interpreter. Finally we discuss how to make the transition from terms to goals to allow true higher-order logic programming. Throughout this chapter we remark on the differences between the interpreter developed here and our Common Lisp implementation.

12.2   Propositional Horn Logic

We begin the development with a very simple propositional logic amenable to an interpretation as a programming language: propositional Horn logic. Our presentation is non-standard in that we do not require the formulas to be in *clausal form*: throughout our development we view this as a normal form, which must be justified by an appropriate metatheorem. A more efficient clausal representation for formulas will be introduced in Section 12.7.

12.2.1   The Language of Goals and Programs

The definition of propositional Horn logic is by induction in the form of a BNF grammar. G denotes the legal *goal* formulas (which are also the legal queries) and D the legal *program* formulas.[1] We sometimes refer to these classes as D-formulas and G-formulas, respectively, and collectively as *formulas*.

$$G ::= A \mid \top \mid G_1 \wedge G_2 \mid G_1 \vee G_2$$
$$D ::= A \mid \top \mid D_1 \wedge D_2 \mid G \rightarrow D$$

The letter A generally stands for atomic formulas; here this means propositional constants, $\top$ stands for truth, $\wedge$ stands for conjunction, $\vee$ for disjunction, and $\rightarrow$ for implication. In logic programming it is often more conspicuous to use $\leftarrow$, where $D \leftarrow G$ can be read as "D if G" and is a purely notational variant of $G \rightarrow D$.

---

[1] D is derived from *definite* as in *definite clauses*, though our definition is broader.

The following figure shows how this would be translated into a **datatype** definition in SML (comments are enclosed in **(* *)**).

```
datatype gform  =                       (* Goal formula *)
     Gtrue                              (* Truth *)
   | Gand of gform * gform              (* Conjunction *)
   | Gor of gform * gform               (* Disjunction *)
   | Gatom of string                   (* Atomic G formula *)

and dform =                             (* Program formula *)
     Dtrue                              (* Truth *)
   | Dand of dform * dform              (* Conjunction *)
   | Dimplies of gform * dform          (* Implication *)
   | Datom of string                   (* Atomic D formula *)
```

This defines *constructors* such as **Dand**, which, when applied to two D-formulas, yields a D-formula. For example, the program $p \land (p \rightarrow q)$ would be represented as

```
Dand(Datom("p"),Dimplies(Gatom("p"),Datom("q")))
```

A query, such as whether q is true, would be represented as

```
Gatom("q")
```

12.2.2 A First Interpreter

The next step is to give goals and programs an operational interpretation. For this simple logic this is straightforward, though the precise definition of "upon backtracking" is deferred to the actual interpreter in ML. First comes the reduction of a goal to its subgoals, then the analysis of whether an atomic goal follows from the program.

1. Given goal $\top$, succeed.

2. Given goal $G_1 \land G_2$, attempt to solve G_1 and, if it succeeds, attempt to solve G_2.

3. Given goal $G_1 \lor G_2$, attempt to solve G_1. If this succeeds, succeed. If this fails, attempt to solve G_2.

4. Given an atomic goal A, look through the program for ways to establish A following the control structure below.

If we assumed the program to be in clausal form, we would enumerate the clauses of the form $A \leftarrow G$ and attempt to solve G for each such clause. It is easy to see that the following program analysis will behave this way on the special case of clausal form programs. We assume we are given a program D, and atomic goal A. We also have an "accumulated subgoal" which is initialized to $\top$.

1. $D = D_1 \wedge D_2$. Attempt to infer A from D_1. If this fails, attempt to infer A from D_2.

2. $D = G \rightarrow D_1$. Attempt to infer A from D_1, but conjoin G to the subgoal that remains to be solved.

3. $D = A$. Attempt to solve the accumulated subgoal.

4. $D = B$ for atomic B distinct from A. In this case D is not helpful in the attempt to derive A and we backtrack.

Thus our program consists of two mutually recursive functions. **solve** analyzes a composite goal, and **match_atom** analyzes the program with respect to an atomic goal. The fundamental idea of the formulation as a functional program is that of a *success continuation* due to Carlsson [2]. The obvious arguments to **solve** are the current goal and program. The non-obvious argument is the success continuation **sc**. **sc** is a function (of no arguments) that is to be called when the current goal succeeds. Backtracking is achieved simply by returning from the current function with an uninteresting value (we have chosen () : **unit**). The function **match_atom** calls a local recursive function **rec_match**, which accumulates subgoals as outlined above.

```
fun solve (Gtrue) prog sc = sc ()
  | solve (Gand(g1,g2)) prog sc =
      solve g1 prog (fn () => solve g2 prog sc)
  | solve (Gor(g1,g2)) prog sc =
    ( solve g1 prog sc ; solve g2 prog sc )
  | solve (Gatom(goal_const)) prog sc =
    match_atom goal_const prog sc

and match_atom goal_const prog sc =
    let fun rec_match (Dtrue) subgoal = ()
          | rec_match (Dand(d1,d2)) subgoal =
              ( rec_match d1 subgoal ; rec_match d2 subgoal )
          | rec_match (Dimplies(g,d)) subgoal =
              rec_match d (Gand(subgoal,g))
          | rec_match (Datom(prog_const)) subgoal =
              if prog_const = goal_const
                then solve subgoal prog sc
                else ()
    in rec_match prog (Gtrue) end
```

Let us inspect this compact program line-by-line.

1. If the current goal is $\top$, we succeed by invoking the success continuation.

2. If the current goal is $G_1 \wedge G_2$, we attempt to solve G_1, but we also build a success continuation that will eventually solve G_2, which is necessary in order for the conjunction to succeed. `(fn () => ...)` is the SML way of constructing a function of no arguments.

3. If the current goal is $G_1 \vee G_2$, we attempt to solve G_1 with the same success continuation. If this should fail and thus return, we attempt to solve G_2. Semicolon is the SML sequencing operator. Note that in a purely functional setting without any side-effects, it would make no sense to try the left and right subgoals in succession: if solving the left subgoal succeeds, it must produce some record of this. In the framework of success continuations, this is achieved through the *initial success continuation*, which could be a function such as `(fn () => print "Goal succeeded!")` (see Section 12.2.3).

4. If the current goal is atomic we look through the program to find D-formulas that might help us prove the goal.

Next we consider the program analysis. We call **rec_match** with a current subgoal **Gtrue**, which will always succeed and the whole program **prog** as the current D-formula. Here are the cases for **rec_match**.

1. If the program is $\top$, any atomic goal (which excludes $\top$) will fail. We return to indicate failure.

2. If the program is a conjunction we attempt to use the left conjunct and then the right conjunct to derive the atomic goal. This is dual to the case of a disjunctive goal.

3. If the program is an implication $G \rightarrow D$, we conjoin G onto the subgoal that would have to be solved if D matched the atomic goal, and continue by attempting to use D to derive the atomic goal.

4. If the program is atomic and equal to the atomic goal, we attempt to solve the accumulated subgoal; otherwise we backtrack by returning.

There are some obvious inefficiencies in this control structure. Some of these will be addressed in later sections.

12.2.3 The Initial Success Continuation

From the exposition above we can see that

```
val solve : gform -> dform -> (unit -> unit) -> unit}
```

and **solve goal prog sc** may be read as "solve **goal** in program **prog** and call **sc** if successful, otherwise return." This is not quite accurate, since if **sc** *returns*, it will be called again for every way of proving **goal** the interpreter can find.

For example, let **val psc = (fn() => print "Success! ")**. Then **solve** p $(p \wedge p)$ **psc** will print **Success!** twice. On the other hand, due to the incompleteness of depth-first search, **solve** p $((p \rightarrow p) \wedge p)$ **psc** will get into an infinite loop, while **solve** p $(p \wedge (p \rightarrow p))$ **psc** will print an infinite stream of **Success!**'s.

At first this might seem like a serious limitation of this implementation technique. However, using exceptions we can prevent the initial success continuation from returning. For example, the following top-level interface would stop after the first solution is found.

```
fun one_solve goal prog =
   let exception Success
   in ( solve goal prog (fn () => raise Success) ;
        print "no " )
      handle Success => print "yes "
   end
```

It is also easy to add a query of the user that checks if more solutions are desired or not. The eLP implementation [8] plays even more tricks with the initial success continuation: it presents the first solution, but then works ahead without waiting for instructions as to whether additional solutions are required. If an externally visible side-effect is just about to be executed, it suspends. This has the advantage that we can often return to the top-level without user input if the query has only one solution.

12.3 First-Order Horn Logic

The interpreter from the previous section can be generalized and improved in several different directions. Before we introduce some improvements, we continue with a few generalizations. The most important and obvious step is that from a propositional to a first-order logic. This requires the introduction of *unification* and *substitution*. Interestingly, the basic structure of the interpreter stays intact: success continuations can be generalized to deal with unification and substitutions. This first version of an interpreter for first-order Horn logic requires no side-effects except for the presentation of solutions.

The definition of first-order Horn logic is again somewhat non-standard in that we do not require a clausal form.

$$
\begin{aligned}
G &\ ::=\ A \mid \top \mid G_1 \wedge G_2 \mid G_1 \vee G_2 \mid \exists x\, G \\
D &\ ::=\ A \mid \top \mid D_1 \wedge D_2 \mid G \rightarrow D \mid \forall x\, D
\end{aligned}
$$

We add two new cases for the quantifiers to the datatypes **gform** and **dform**, but we also have to change the definition of atomic formulas, since they now may consist of a predicate constant applied to a number of terms built from constants, function constants, and variables. Partly for reasons of simplicity and partly in preparation for a higher-order language, we do not distinguish between constants, function constants, and predicate constants. Thus atomic formulas are considered to be terms, which also means that not every **gform** or **dform** represents a well-formed formula of first-order Horn logic. However, this property can be checked statically and we thus consider it a problem for an appropriate front end for our interpreter that is beyond the scope of this chapter. Before we go into detail in the representation of terms, here is the changed definition of formulas.

```
datatype gform  =                 (* Goal formula *)
     Gtrue                        (* Truth *)
   | Gand of gform * gform        (* Conjunction *)
   | Gor of gform * gform         (* Disjunction *)
   | Gatom of term                (* Atomic G formula *)
   | Gexists of varbind * gform   (* Existential *)

and dform =                       (* Program formula *)
     Dtrue                        (* Truth *)
   | Dand of dform * dform        (* Conjunction *)
   | Dimplies of gform * dform    (* Implication *)
   | Datom of term                (* Atomic D formula *)
   | Dall of varbind * dform      (* Universal *)
```

12.3.1 Terms and Substitution

Our inductive definition of terms has three base cases: **Bvar** for *bound variables*, **Evar** for *logic variables*,[2] and **Const** for constants, including predicate and function constants. These variables and constants can be combined via *application* using the **Appl** constructor, giving the representation the flavor of a *curried form*, which will aid us in the transition to the higher-order language later on, but also leads to more compact code here.

```
datatype term =
     Bvar of string           (* Bound Variables *)
   | Evar of string * int     (* Logic Variables , Stamped *)
   | Const of string          (* Constants *)
   | Appl of term * term      (* Applications *)
and varbind = Varbind of string (* Variable binders *)
```

---

[2]The name is derived from *existential variables*, since logic variables may be viewed as variables that are existentially quantified in the meta-theory.

Varbind's are used to bind variables at quantifiers, but seem to belong to the term language rather than the formula language are thus implemented as a separate type rather than merely by strings. Later, in Section 12.8 a **Varbind** will also contain the bound variable's type.

Under this representation the Prolog clause *append*(nil, K, K) has an explicit quantifier on K and is represented as[3]

```
Dall(Varbind("K"),
  Datom(Appl(Appl(Appl(Const("append"),Const("nil")),Bvar("K")),
           Bvar("K")))))
```

Logic variables must be generated many times in such a way as not to conflict with previous logic variables of the same name. For example, every time a clause in Prolog is used, its free variables must be instantiated with fresh logic variables. In our setting, the quantification on the variables is explicit, since this approach lends itself more easily to later generalizations. Nonetheless, we must be able to generate new unique logic variables when instantiating universally quantified D-formulas (programs). We do this by attaching to each logic variable an integer stamp which makes it unique. We use the function **new_evar** to generate new logic variables from given variable names. In order to properly explain substitution and later unification, we will need to introduce some terminology. We say an occurrence of a **Bvar** is *loose* in a term or formula if it is not in the scope of a binding operator binding the same name. We say a term or formula is *tight* if it contains no loose **Bvar**'s, and it is *closed* if it is tight and also contains no **Evar**'s. Here are the types of some of the lower-level functions implemented below.

```
val new_evar : varbind -> term
val shadow : varbind -> varbind -> bool
val subst : term -> varbind -> term -> term
```

shadow determines if one variable binding shadows another and is used to correctly substitute in formulas such as $\forall x\,(P(x) \wedge \forall x\,Q(x))$. **subst** s x t substitutes the tight term s for all loose occurrences of x in t. The implementations are straightforward as renaming can be avoided, since t is required to contain no loose **Bvar**'s.

```
(* Externally invisible counter to create unique variables *)
local val varcount = ref 0
 in fun new_evar (Varbind(vname)) =
    ( varcount := !varcount + 1;
      Evar(vname,!varcount)  )
```

---

[3]Note that we use the conventional Prolog uncurried notation in the concrete syntax of examples for this first-order term language.

```
end   (* local val varcount *)

fun shadow (Varbind(vname1)) (Varbind(vname2)) = (vname1 = vname2)

fun subst s (Varbind(vname)) t =
  let fun sb (t as Bvar(bvname)) = if vname = bvname then s else t
        | sb (Appl(t1,t2)) = Appl(sb t1,sb t2)
        | sb t = t                   (* Evar , Const *)
    in sb t end
```

There are also functions that substitute in G-formulas and D-formulas. These are mutually recursive,[4] but each function changes only a subset of the arguments in the recursion. The following illustrates a general implementation technique for such a recursion structure.

```
local fun formsubst t x =
  let fun gsb (Gtrue) = Gtrue
        | gsb (Gand(g1,g2)) = Gand(gsb g1, gsb g2)
        | gsb (Gor(g1,g2)) = Gor(gsb g1, gsb g2)
        | gsb (Gexists(y,g)) =
            Gexists(y, if shadow x y then g else gsb g)
        | gsb (Gatom(s)) = Gatom(subst t vbd s)
      and dsb (Dtrue) = Dtrue
        | dsb (Dand(d1,d2)) = Dand(dsb d1, dsb d2)
        | dsb (Dimplies(g,d)) = Dimplies(gsb g, dsb d)
        | dsb (Datom(s)) = Datom(subst t vbd s)
        | dsb (Dall(y,d)) =
            Dall(y, if shadow x y then d else dsb d)
    in (gsb , dsb) end
in
  fun gsubst t x g =
        let val (gsb ,  _ ) = formsubst t x in gsb g end
  and dsubst t x d =
        let val ( _ , dsb) = formsubst t x in dsb d end
end
```

12.3.2   Unification

The basic new data structure we need is that of a *substitution*, which maps logic variables to terms. First, a section of the signature.

```
type substitution = (term * term) list
```

---

[4]Actually, in this version D-formulas may not occur in G-formulas, but this will change later on.

```
val unify : term -> term -> (substitution -> unit) ->
            substitution -> unit
```

The structure of **unify** is again based on the idea of a success continuation, except that we now need to communicate some information to the success continuation, namely the substitution that arises from unifying two terms. Thus **unify** s t sc $subst$ unifies s and t under the substitution $subst$ and applies sc to the resulting new substitution. This means that substitutions arising from unification are never explicitly applied, but when an **Evar** is encountered we need to see if it has been instantiated to a term by previous unifications. If unification fails, **unify** simply returns. **unify** requires the auxiliary function **lookup**, which returns the substitution term for a logical variable in a substitution, or the token **NONE** if no such term exists.[5]

First, we show a version that implements unsound unification as used in Prolog. Omitting the occurs-check as done here may be justified by efficiency arguments, but has the undesirable side-effect that X and $f(X)$ are unifiable (where X is the variable).

```
(* val lookup : term -> substitution -> term option *)
fun lookup (Evar(_,stamp)) subst =
  let fun lk nil = NONE
        | lk ((Evar(_,tstamp),t)::tail) =
              if stamp = tstamp then SOME(t) else lk tail
    in lk subst end

fun unify (s as Evar _) t sc subst = unify_evar s t sc subst
  | unify s (t as Evar _) sc subst = unify_evar t s sc subst
  | unify (Const(cname1)) (Const(cname2)) sc subst =
      if cname1 = cname2 then (sc subst) else ()
  | unify (Appl(s1,s2)) (Appl(t1,t2)) sc subst =
      unify s1 t1 (fn newsubst => unify s2 t2 sc newsubst) subst
  | unify _ _ sc subst = ()
and unify_evar e t sc subst =
      case (lookup e subst)
         of NONE => sc ((e,t)::subst)
                                 (* Instantiate e to t, succeed *)
          | SOME(s0) => unify s0 t sc subst
                                 (* e is instantiated to s0 *)
```

Adding the occurs-check requires a few auxiliary functions and a modification of the definition of **unify_evar**. The definitions of **occurs_in** and **same_evar** are straightforward and omitted here. The occurs-check is only called once we know that we

---

[5]The frequently used type **'a option** is not part of the definition of SML but defined as **datatype 'a option = NONE | SOME of 'a**.

are not trying to unify a variable with itself. The definition of **unify** remains unchanged
and the new definition of **unify_evar** is

```
unify_evar e t sc subst =
     case (lookup e subst)
        of NONE => if same_evar e t subst
                        then sc subst                    (* e = e *)
                        else if occurs_in e t subst
                                then ()   (* Occurs check fails *)
                                else sc ((e,t)::subst)
                                               (* Bind e to t *)
         | SOME(s0) => unify s0 t sc subst
```

   The obvious inefficiency in the structure of this function is that substitutions must be
built up, and that it may be very costly to continue to look up possible substitutions terms
for **Evar**'s. This can be corrected using destructive substitutions (see Section 12.5).

12.3.3   The Interpreter

The generalized version of the function **solve** now takes one additional argument (the
current substitution for **Evar**'s), and the success continuation also expects to be passed
a substitution.

```
fun solve (Gtrue) prog sc subst = sc subst
  | solve (Gand(g1,g2)) prog sc subst =
     solve g1 prog (fn newsubst => solve g2 prog sc newsubst)
          subst
  | solve (Gor(g1,g2)) prog sc subst =
     ( solve g1 prog sc subst ; solve g2 prog sc subst )
  | solve (Gatom(t)) prog sc subst =
     match_atom t prog sc subst
  | solve (Gexists(x,g)) prog sc subst =
     solve (gsubst (new_evar x) x g) prog sc subst

and match_atom t prog sc subst =
     let fun rec_match (Dtrue) subgoal = ()
            | rec_match (Dand(d1,d2)) subgoal =
               ( rec_match d1 subgoal ; rec_match d2 subgoal )
            | rec_match (Dimplies(g,d)) subgoal =
               rec_match d (Gand(subgoal,g))
            | rec_match (Datom(s)) subgoal =
               unify s t (fn newsubst => solve subgoal prog sc
                                            newsubst) subst
            | rec_match (Dall(x,d)) subgoal =
```

```
        rec_match (dsubst (new_evar x) d) subgoal
   in rec_match prog (Gtrue) end
```

Again, the question arises how we call this interpreter at the top-level. The initial success continuation will have to be slightly more complicated than before since we would like to present a substitution for the logic variables in the query. To this end we have functions

```
val project_substitution : term list -> substitution ->
                                        substitution
val print_substitution : substitution -> unit
```

project_substitution *evars* *subst* takes a list of **Evar**'s and determines their substitution terms in *subst*. This includes looking up all of the logic variables in the substitution terms that were instantiated during the unification. **print_substitution** *subst* just presents the substitution in a human readable format. For the sake of brevity we will not show the implementation of these straightforward functions. It will also be the responsibility of the front end to ensure that all free uppercase identifiers in the original query are converted into new logic variables, and that the final substitution is projected onto these variables and then printed.

12.4   Hereditary Harrop Logic

We now further generalize from the first-order Horn logic to allow hereditary Harrop formulas as goals. This means that a goal can be an implication (called *embedded implication*) or a universally quantified formula (*embedded universal quantification*). For some general motivation for these constructs refer to [1,12,11,21,25]. The mutually recursive definitions of the classes of goals and programs now become

$$G ::= A \mid \top \mid G_1 \wedge G_2 \mid G_1 \vee G_2 \mid \exists x\, G \mid D \to G \mid \forall x\, G$$
$$D ::= A \mid \top \mid D_1 \wedge D_2 \mid G \to D \mid \forall x\, D$$

The definition of **gform** is changed by adding two new cases.

```
 |  Gimplies of dform * gform        (* Embedded Implication *)
 |  Gall of varbind * gform          (* Embedded Universal *)
```

The operational interpretation of these new constructs follows the intuitionistic reading of implication and universal quantification.

- Given goal $D \to G$, assume D into the program and then attempt to solve G. The additional assumption is in effect only while solving G. D is added "to the beginning" of the program, which means that the most recently assumed formula is considered first when we are trying to solve an atomic goal.

- Given goal $\forall x\; G$, create a new parameter a and attempt to solve $[a/x]G$. "New" means that a is not allowed to occur in the current program or G.

As examples, consider the goals $p \to p$ (which clearly succeeds) and $\exists x\; (P(x) \to (P(1) \land P(2)))$, which fails (due to the intuitionistic reading of $\exists$) where the classically equivalent $(\forall x\; P(x)) \to (P(1) \land P(2))$ succeeds. Quantifier dependence now also becomes an issue, as one can see from the goals $\exists x\; \forall y\; (P(x) \to P(y))$ (which fails) and $\forall y\; \exists x\; (P(x) \to P(y))$ (which succeeds).

12.4.1 Embedded Implication

Embedded implication can be added trivially to the interpreter as we have developed it so far, since the program is an explicit parameter to the **solve** function. We just add a new case to the definition of **solve**:

```
| solve (Gimplies(d,g)) prog sc subst =
    solve g (Dand(d,prog)) sc subst
```

12.4.2 Embedded Universal Quantification

Embedded universal quantifiers require much more pervasive changes to the interpreter, since the dependence of existential and universal quantifiers on each other now must be taken into account. In theorem provers this is typically addressed by a one-time Skolemization pass during the preprocessing stage. Here this does not seem possible (since the logic is essentially intuitionistic). Moreover, we can take advantage of special properties of hereditary Harrop formulas to obtain a more efficient implementation.

First of all, we need to update the definition of the datatype of **term** to include the case that the term is a *parameter*. In our implementation we call these parameters **Uvar**'s, thinking of them as universally quantified at the meta-level. Note that in unification they act essentially like constants, except for certain quantifier dependence considerations. The way we implement quantifier dependence is for every **Evar** to explicitly contain a list of parameters on which it may depend.

```
datatype term =
    Bvar of string              (* Bound Variables *)
  | Evar of string * int * term list
                                (* Logic Variables , Stamped , *)
                                (* Depends on *)
  | Uvar of string * int        (* Parameters , Stamped *)
  | Const of string             (* Constants *)
  | Appl of term * term         (* Applications *)
and varbind = Varbind of string (* Variable binders *)
```

Consider, for example, the goal $\forall x \; \exists y \; G$. First we introduce a new parameter a for x and solve $\exists y \; [a/x]G$. Then we introduce a new logic variable Y and solve $G'' = [Y/y][a/x]G$. We are free to instantiate Y with terms which contain a, that is, Y may depend on a. If, on the other hand, our goal is $\exists y \; \forall x \; G$, we first introduce a logic variable Y for y and then a parameter a for x. Note that here Y may *not* contain occurrences of a!

In the interpreter this is implemented by adding a new argument to **solve**, namely the list of parameters (**Uvar**'s) which have been introduced so far and thus may occur in the substitution term for any logic variable (**Evar**) which is introduced subsequently. There are some additional minor interface changes. For example, the function **new_evar** must now be passed the list of **Uvar**'s on which the new **Evar** is allowed to depend on. Since the new parameter is passed along unchanged in all cases except the embedded universal quantifier, we only show this case in **solve**.

```
| solve (Gall(x,g)) prog uvars sc subst =
    let val a = new_uvar x
    in solve (gsubst a x g) prog (a::uvars) sc subst end
```

There are some further bookkeeping changes (for example, in substitution), but the crucial change now is in the unifier. More specifically, we have to extend the occurs-check to account for dependency. When the prospective substitution term **t** contains a **Uvar** on which the **Evar s** is not allowed to depend, we have to fail. However, this is not quite sufficient. Consider the problem of unifying X with $f(Y)$, where X and Y are logic variables, and X is allowed to depend only on parameter a, but Y is allowed to depend on parameters a and b. If we merely bind X to $f(Y)$, Y might later be instantiated to a term containing b, thus unwittingly violating the condition that the substitution term for X not depend on b. Thus we also need to restrict further instantiations of Y not to depend on b.

In general, all **Evar**'s Y embedded in a substitution term for an **Evar** X can depend only on the intersection of the parameters legal for X and Y. This is implemented by instantiating Y with a new **Evar** Y' whose **Uvar** list is thus restricted. We don't need to implement this in full generality due to a metatheorem: when we have to consider the lists of **Uvar**'s from two **Evar**'s during the execution of a logic program one of the lists will be an initial segment of the other.[6]

Rather than using two passes, we combine the occurs-check with the restriction of **Evar**'s. Since restriction of **Evar**'s is an instantiation process, the extended occurs-

---

[6]This also gives rise to the even more efficient implementation used in eLP, where whole lists of parameters are represented by their upper bound (a single integer).

check may need to change the substitution and thus is programmed using success continuations, just as **unify** itself.

```
fun init_seg uvars1 uvars2 = length uvars1 <= length uvars2

fun extended_occurs_check (Evar(_,stamp1,uvars1)) t sc subst =
  let fun eoc (e as Evar(x,stamp2,uvars2)) sc subst =
          (case (lookup e subst)
              of NONE => if (stamp1 = stamp2)
                         then ()    (* fail *)
                         else if init_seg uvars2 uvars1
                              then sc subst
                              else sc ((e,new_evar
                                          (Varbind(x)) uvars1)
                                        ::subst)
               | SOME t0 => eoc t0 sc subst)
       | eoc (Appl(t1,t2)) sc subst =
          eoc t1 (fn newsubst => eoc t2 sc newsubst) subst
       | eoc (Uvar(_,stamp2)) sc subst =
          if exists (fn (Uvar(_,stamp1)) => stamp1 = stamp2
                      | s => raise
                              subtype("eoc",s,"is not a Uvar"))
                    uvars1
          then sc subst
          else ()
       | eoc _ sc subst = sc subst
    in eoc t sc subst end
  | extended_occurs_check s _ _ _ =
      raise subtype("extended_occurs_check",s,"is not an Evar")
```

One more detail here is the use of a function **subtype** which generates an exception from a function name, term, and error message. The intent is that these exceptions signal an internal error, called **subtype**, because being a term, but not an **Evar** or **Uvar** constitutes a form of subtype violation (although subtypes are not supported in SML).

The extended occurs-check is called from **unify_evar**. The only subtlety here is perhaps that we have to postpone the substitution until the extended occurs-check has succeeded. Note also that we have to previously check if we are unifying an **Evar** with itself and succeed without changing the substitution – otherwise the occurs-check would fail for this case.

```
and unify_evar e t sc subst =
        case (lookup e subst)
```

```
       of NONE => if same_evar e t subst
                  then sc subst
                  else extended_occurs_check e t
                       (fn newsubst =>
                           sc ((e,t)::newsubst))
                       subst
       | SOME s0 => unify s0 t sc subst
```

12.5 Destructive Substitution

Of the code presented so far, the two most important optimizations will be (a) introduction of destructive substitution in order to avoid repeated lookup of the substitution terms for logic variables, and (b) the conversion of the program into clausal form in order to have ready access to the part of the program relevant to a particular predicate symbol. In this section we will deal with the first issue.

Up to now we were using almost exclusively purely functional code. Destructive substitutions will violate this principle, but in a relatively disciplined way. This means that whenever the unification algorithm instantiates a logic variable to a term it has to make provisions to undo this instantiation upon backtracking. Since backtracking is indicated simply by returning rather than calling the success continuation, this is easy to implement.[7]

Before plunging into the code, a brief word about assignment in SML. Traditionally in imperative languages we assign to variables. In SML, we assign to *references*. References are distinguished by their type (which will be `'a ref` for some type `'a`) and are created by applications of the function `ref` to a value. `ref` is also a constructor so that we can access the value stored in a location using match expressions as for usual function definitions. Thus the dereferencing operation `!` can be defined explicitly as `fun !` `(ref v) = v`.

In order to implement the idea of destructive substitutions, we give `Evar`'s an additional slot that could either hold the term to which the `Evar` was instantiated, or a token indicating that the `Evar` is not instantiated. We must be able to assign to this slot, and it will thus be a reference to an optional term. Here is the updated definition of the datatype of terms.

```
datatype term =
    Bvar of string          (* Bound Variables *)
  | Evar of string * int * term list * (term option) ref
                            (* Logic Variables , Stamped , *)
```

---

[7]In Section 12.6 we will be forced to abandon this assumption, and will thus require a more sophisticated implementation of instantiation and uninstantiation of variables.

```
                              (* Depends on , Inst'd to *)
  |  Uvar of string * int     (* Parameters , Stamped *)
  |  Const of string          (* Constants *)
  |  Appl of term * term      (* Applications *)
```

When a new **Evar** is created, it is uninstantiated and thus contains a reference to **NONE**. Now most operations will have to *dereference* **Evar**'s if they are instantiated to a term. This is illustrated, for example, in the second clause in the definition of **unify_evar** below.[8]

The most profound changes in **unify** are that (a) it no longer requires a substitution as an argument since it instantiates variables destructively, and (b) it needs to take action to uninstantiate variables upon failure of the success continuation. Instantiation is accomplished by an assignment to the reference in the value slot of an **Evar** uninstantiation assigns **NONE**. The instantiation is performed when the extended occurs-check succeeds and thus is passed in the success continuation to **extended_occurs_check**. The function for the extended occurs-check must also be changed in an analogous fashion.

```
fun unify (s as Evar _) t sc = unify_evar s t sc
  | unify s (t as Evar _) sc = unify_evar t s sc
  | unify (Const(cname1)) (Const(cname2)) sc =
        if cname1 = cname2 then sc () else ()
  | unify (Uvar(_,stamp1)) (Uvar(_,stamp2)) sc subst =
        if stamp1 = stamp2 then (sc subst) else ()
  | unify (Appl(s1,s2)) (Appl(t1,t2)) sc =
        unify s1 t1 (fn () => unify s2 t2 sc)
  | unify _ _ sc = ()
and unify_evar (e as Evar(_,_,_,(vslot as (ref NONE)))) t sc =
        if same_evar e t
            then sc ()
            else extended_occurs_check e t
                    (fn () => ( vslot := SOME t ; sc () ;
                                vslot := NONE ; () ))
  | unify_evar (Evar(_,_,_,ref (SOME s0))) t sc = unify s0 t sc
  | unify_evar s _ _ = raise
                        subtype("unify_evar",s,"is not an Evar")
```

The definition of G-formulas and D-formulas and the functions for substituting into formulas does not change from the previous section. The interpreter undergoes only a very minor change: since explicit substitutions are no longer required, **solve** and the success continuation both require one argument less than before.

---

[8]An important optimization arises from the invariant that an **Evar** is never instantiated to a term with a loose **Bvar**: In the operation of substituting for a **Bvar** in a term, if the term is an instantiated **Evar**, we can simply return it without dereferencing and further traversal.

12.6   Control Primitives and Trailing

So far, the only mechanism available for search control in our logic programming language has been clause ordering. There are many programs where this is insufficient and there are a number of ways one can address this deficiency. The most common construct is *cut* (!, in concrete Prolog syntax), though we will discuss this only briefly in Section 12.6.2. Our focus will be on what is commonly called *if-then-else* and written as **G1 -> G2 | G3** . In our abstract syntax we have a corresponding **guard** constructor. **guard** is general enough to allow a direct definition of the constructs **once** and **not** in a higher-order language (see Section 12.9), and most programs using cut can easily be transformed into programs using **guard**. We show that the **guard** control primitive can be implemented using SML exceptions without disturbing the general structure and organization of the interpreter. However, the use of exceptions relies on a non-local exit from a success continuation, which requires a different implementation of the uninstantiation of variables on backtracking. This alternative implementation technique for backtracking is referred to as *trailing*.

12.6.1   The guard Control Construct

The operational reading of $G_1 \to G_2 \mid G_3$ (not to be confused with implication) is

- Solve the guard G_1. If this succeeds, solve G_2 (with the new substitution). On backtracking, *do not* reconsider the choices made while solving G_1, but simply fail the overall goal $G_1 \to G_2 \mid G_3$.

- If solving G_1 fails, solve G_3 and fail the overall goal $G_1 \to G_2 \mid G_3$ on backtracking.

In the interpreter, we first augment the definition of the **gform** data type and modify the substitution function to include the obvious additional case. A first, as it turns out, incorrect attempt at the additional case for the interpreter (from Section 12.5) would be

```
| solve (Guard(g1,g2,g3)) prog sc =
    let exception Guard_success in
        ( solve g1 prog (fn () => raise Guard_success) ;
          solve g3 prog sc )
        handle Guard_success => solve g2 prog sc
    end
```

If we succeed in solving the guard **g1**, raising the exception **Guard_success** will transfer control back to the handler for the exception, bypassing all the choice points, and then solve **g2**. Choice points are established, for example, when solving a disjunction, or when descending through a conjunction when analyzing the program in

match_atom. One can now see what is wrong with this attempt: the code in the unifier which uninstantiates variables on backtracking (the assignment of **NONE** below)

```
extended_occurs_check e t
    (fn () => ( vslot := SOME t ; sc () ; vslot := NONE ; () ))
```

will not be executed when solving **g2** eventually backtracks, because the call **sc ()** exited with an exception, bypassing the second assignment.

The solution to this problem is move the responsibility for uninstantiating variables from the unifier to the choice points. Thus, in the case of a goal $G_1 \vee G_2$, for example, we have to keep track of all the variables which may have been instantiated during an attempt to solve G_1 and uninstantiate them before attempting to solve G_2. Keeping track of these variables is the purpose of the *trail*.

A SML variable **global_trail** contains a reference to a trail. When a variable is instantiated, it is added to the trail (which is accessed as a stack). At a choice point, when the first alternative backtracks, we uninstantiate all variables which have been pushed onto the trail and simultaneously unwind the trail (that is, pop the stack). This is bundled up into a few functions and the datatype **trail**. The function **trail**[9] is used by the interpreter at choice points: it remembers the global stack, evaluates its argument (by applying it to the unit element), and then uninstantiates all the "new" variables it finds on the stack. The function **instantiate_evar** is used by the unifier in order to instantiate logic variables and simultaneously push them onto the trail. The variable **global_trail** is local to a context with these functions, which guarantees that no other functions can obtain access to it and change the value of the location it refers to. In order to be able to properly unwind the trail, we must have a reference (= pointer) to a trail that we can compare with the result of unwinding it. Since the only way to compare for pointer equality is by comparing references, the tail of a trail must be implemented as a reference to a trail even though is never modified.

```
datatype trail =
    consTrail of term * (trail ref)
  | nilTrail

local val global_trail = ref (ref nilTrail)
in

fun unwind_trail shorter_trail longer_trail =
    if longer_trail = shorter_trail
       then (global_trail := shorter_trail; ())
```

---

[9]In Standard ML, functions and types occupy the same name space.

```
            else (case !longer_trail of
                     (consTrail (Evar(_,_,_,vslot),rest_trail)) =>
                         (vslot := NONE; unwind_trail shorter_trail
                                          rest_trail)
                   | _ => raise
                          Subtype("unwind_trail: Ill-formed trail."))

fun trail func =
    let val old_trail = !global_trail in
        (func () ; unwind_trail old_trail (!global_trail) ; ())
    end

fun instantiate_evar (s as Evar(_,_,_,vslot)) t =
    ( vslot := SOME t;
        global_trail := ref (consTrail(s,!global_trail)) )
  | instantiate_evar s _ =
        raise subtype("instantiate_evar",s,"is not an Evar")

end  (* local val global_trail *)
```

The main function of the unifier does not change, but **unify_evar** changes, since it no longer has the responsibility of uninstantiating variables upon backtracking. Thus the call to the extended occurs-check now looks like

```
extended_occurs_check e t (fn () =>
                                ( instantiate_evar e t ; sc () ))
```

The interpreter makes use of the functional **trail** where it establishes choice points. This happens in exactly three cases: **Gor**, **Guard**, and **Dand**. The argument to **trail** is protected by a vacuous abstraction in order to prohibit premature evaluation – just as in success continuations.

```
fun solve (Gtrue) prog uvars sc = sc ()
  | solve (Gand(g1,g2)) prog uvars sc =
        solve g1 prog uvars (fn () => solve g2 prog uvars sc)
  | solve (Gor(g1,g2)) prog uvars sc =
        ( trail (fn () => solve g1 prog uvars sc) ;
          solve g2 prog uvars sc )
  | solve (Gatom(t)) prog uvars sc =
        match_atom t prog uvars sc
  | solve (Gexists(x,g)) prog uvars sc =
        solve (gsubst (new_evar x uvars) x g) prog uvars sc
  | solve (Gimplies(d,g)) prog uvars sc =
        solve g (Dand(d,prog)) uvars sc
```

```
  | solve (Gall(x,g)) prog uvars sc =
     let val a = new_uvar x
      in solve (gsubst a x g) prog (a::uvars) sc end
  | solve (Guard(g1,g2,g3)) prog uvars sc =
     let exception Guard_success
      in ( trail (fn () => solve g1 prog uvars
               (fn () => raise Guard_success)) ;
            solve g3 prog uvars sc )
         handle Guard_success => solve g2 prog uvars sc
     end

and match_atom t prog uvars sc =
    let fun rec_match (Dtrue) subgoal = ()
          | rec_match (Dand(d1,d2)) subgoal =
               ( trail (fn () => rec_match d1 subgoal) ;
                 rec_match d2 subgoal )
          | rec_match (Dimplies(g,d)) subgoal =
               rec_match d (Gand(subgoal,g))
          | rec_match (Datom(s)) subgoal =
               unify s t (fn () => solve subgoal prog uvars sc)
          | rec_match (Dall(x,d)) subgoal =
               rec_match (dsubst (new_evar x uvars) x d) subgoal
      in rec_match prog (Gtrue) end
```

12.6.2   Cut

Instead of the **guard** construct, we can use cut (written as **!**) as a non-logical control primitive. The operational reading of cut is

- When encountering cut as a goal, succeed. When the interpreter backtracks to this point, do not simply backtrack further, but jump past all the choice points which have been created since the immediate atomic supergoal of the cut.

The reference to the "immediate atomic supergoal" requires the addition of another argument to **solve** and **match_atom**. This additional argument is an exception which, when raised, will transfer control back to the immediate atomic supergoal. This additional argument **ctag** is merely passed along in most cases in the interpreter, so we show only the critical changes to the previous incarnation of **solve**.

```
fun solve (Gatom(t)) prog uvars ctag sc =
    let exception new_ctag
     in (match_atom t prog uvars new_ctag sc)
        handle new_ctag => ()
    end
```

```
  | solve (Gcut) prog uvars ctag sc =
      ( sc () ; raise ctag )
   ...
and match_atom t prog uvars ctag sc =
    let fun rec_match (Datom(s)) subgoal =
            unify s t (fn () => solve subgoal prog uvars ctag sc)
        ...
    in rec_match prog (Gtrue) end
```

In addition to the initial success continuation (see Section 12.2.3) we now also need to create an initial exception to pass to **solve**. This is easily accomplished by

```
fun top_solve goal free_vars prog =
  let exception top_ctag
   in (trail (fn () => solve goal prog nil top_ctag
                            (fn () => print_substitution
                                        free_vars)))
       handle top_ctag => ()
  end
```

where **free_vars** is the list of variables (**Evar**'s) free in **goal**. Trailing is necessary so that **top_solve** does not have a side-effect on the variables among **free_vars** which are instantiated during the call to **solve**. Now we can also see how a Prolog-like top-level can be implemented: the initial success continuation could present the substitution and then require user input. If the user types a semi-colon "**;**" it returns, and otherwise is raises the exception **top_ctag**.

12.7 Clausal Form

One of the problems with the interpreter so far is the inefficiency of the program analysis. We would like to restrict the search for potentially applicable assumptions as much as possible. Here, the clausal form theorem for Horn logic (and hereditary Harrop logic) is helpful: any legal D-formula is equivalent to one in *clausal form*. The clausal form is defined by

$$
\begin{aligned}
D &::= \top \mid C \mid C \wedge D \\
C &::= G \rightarrow A \mid \forall x\, C
\end{aligned}
$$

where C is a clause, A (referred to as the *clause head*) stands for an atomic formula, and G (referred to as the *clause body*) stands for a G-formula as before. Atomic formulas have the form $P(t_1, \ldots, t_n)$ for a predicate symbol P and terms $t_1, \ldots, t_n$. We call P the *head* of A and, more generally, f the *head* of a term of the form $f(t_1, \ldots, t_n)$, including the cases where $n = 0$. We refer to the head of the clause head of a clause C

as the *head predicate* of C. Given an atomic goal A with head P, the interpreter, that is, **match_atom**, can only succeed in applying a clause if its head predicate is also P.

Thus we can represent an arbitrary program as a list of clauses, and store with each clause its head predicate, for direct comparison with the head of an atomic goal. In a first step, the program is searched clause by clause for one with a matching head predicate. A straightforward optimization, which we do not discuss here further, stores a list of clauses relevant to each head predicate in a hash table indexed by the head predicate. This can be carried even further by "indexing" on the head function symbol of one or more of the predicate arguments.

Recall that in our implementation atomic formulas are represented by terms, since this simplifies the code. We now add the definition of the datatype of **clause**:

```
datatype clause = Clause of head * varbind list * term * gform
```

head is a new type exported in the implementation of terms: it is the type of legal heads. Up to and including this section, a head can be only a constant and can be implemented simply as its name. The **varbind list** is the list of the universally quantified variables in the clause; **term** is the clause head; and **gform** is the clause body. Together with this we have a function that converts an arbitrary formula into clausal form. **clausify** carries three accumulator arguments: the body, the universally quantified variables, and a list of clauses. Thus **clausify** D **(Gtrue) nil nil** will convert a D-formula D into clausal form.

```
fun gand_opt (Gtrue,g) = g
  | gand_opt (g,Gtrue) = g
  | gand_opt (g1,g2) = Gand (g1,g2)

fun clausify Dtrue _ _ rest = rest
  | clausify (Dand(d1,d2)) body vars rest =
      clausify d1 body vars (clausify d2 body vars rest)
  | clausify (Dall(x,d)) body vars rest =
    if exists (fn y => shadow x y) vars
      then let val (new_x,sb) = rename_sb x
              in clausify (dapply_sb sb d) body (new_x::vars) rest
                 end
      else clausify d body (x::vars) rest
  | clausify (Dimplies(g,d)) body vars rest =
      clausify d (gand_opt (body,g)) vars rest
  | clausify (Datom(t)) body vars rest =
      Clause(head t,vars,t,body) :: rest
```

The function **gand_opt** eliminates some **Gtrue** subgoals. Bound variables may have to be renamed during the conversion to clausal form (consider, for example, the clausal form of $\forall x \ (P x \ \rightarrow \ \forall x \ (Q x \ \rightarrow \ R x)))$. **rename_sb** returns the new variable name and also a renaming substitution. This notion of substitution is different from the one discussed in Section 12.3: here we substitute for **Bvar**'s rather than for **Evar**'s. The new version of **match_atom** below takes a list of clauses, instead of a D-formula. It uses a function **new_evar_sb**, which takes a list of bound variables and returns a substitution that, when applied, substitutes new **Evar**'s for all the **Bvar**'s. Note that the body of a clause is not copied (that is, substituted into) until the unification of the atomic goal with the clause head has succeeded.

```
match_atom t clauses uvars sc =
    let val t_head = head t
        fun rec_match nil = ()
          | rec_match ((clause as
                        Clause(s_head,vars,s,gbody))::rest) =
                if head_equal s_head t_head
                    then let val nesb = new_evar_sb vars uvars in
                         ( trail (fn () =>
                             unify (apply_sb nesb s) t (fn () =>
                             solve (gapply_sb nesb gbody)
                               clauses uvars sc)) ;
                           rec_match rest )
                         end
                    else rec_match rest
    in rec_match clauses end
```

We could store the head of atoms in the atomic formula, to avoid the call to **head**. Along similar lines, we could statically convert D-formulas which appear on the left-hand sides of embedded implications into clauses rather than convert them at assumption time. This is an important optimization, but it requires substitution functions into the clausal representation, which we would like to avoid in the presentation. Thus the case for embedded implication in **solve** looks as follows:

```
  | solve (Gimplies(d,g)) prog uvars sc =
    solve g (clausify d (Gtrue) nil prog) uvars sc
```

Before, functions such as **gsubst** substituted for a single (bound) variable in order to achieve clause copying. Calls to this are now replaced with calls to **gapply_sb**, which achieves the more efficient simultaneous substitution. Checking of variable name conflicts is still avoided, except in a rare case during conversion of programs to clausal form. Changes to the corresponding substitution functions on formulas are straightforward, though with an interesting twist. When descending through a quantified formula, we augment the substitution by adding a pair substituting the bound variable for itself. Noting that this still cannot introduce "capturing," we rewrite the substitution as follows.

```
type sb = (varbind * term) list

exception Loose_Bvar of term

(* val lookup_vbind : string -> sb -> term *)
fun lookup_vbind vname sb =
    let fun lk ((Varbind(xname),t)::rest) =
                if vname = xname then t else lk rest
           | lk nil = raise Loose_Bvar(Bvar(vname))
    in lk sb end

(* val apply_sb : sb -> term -> term *)
fun apply_sb sb s =
    let fun asb (Bvar(vname)) = lookup_vbind vname sb
           | asb (Appl(s1,s2)) = Appl((asb s1),(asb s2))
           | asb t = t             (* Evar , Uvar , Const *)
    in asb s end
```

Remember that substitution due to unification is done destructively and not by the function above.

12.8 Higher-order Terms

So far we have been working with a first-order, untyped term language. We will now make the transition to a higher-order, typed term language. This necessitates handling constraints in the interpreter (a simple change) and a major change in unification, which may now branch and is no longer guaranteed to terminate.

12.8.1 The Interpreter

The modules defining propositions and the interpreter need to change very little. The primary change is that we have to introduce *constraints*, since the higher-order unification algorithm generates constraints, that is, sets of equations which are known to be satisfiable. Though somewhat more general through our use of types, implication, and explicit quantification, our language now becomes a constraint logic programming language in the sense of Jaffar and Lassez [19]. The way constraints are handled in the interpreter is reminiscent of the way we handled substitutions in Section 12.3.3 before the introduction of destructive instantiation of variables: where the success continuation previously expected a substitution **subst**, it now expects a constraint **con** as an argument.

```
fun solve (Gtrue) clauses uvars con sc = sc con
  | solve (Gand(g1,g2)) clauses uvars con sc =
      solve g1 clauses uvars con
          (fn newcon => solve g2 clauses uvars newcon sc)
  | solve (Gor(g1,g2)) clauses uvars con sc =
      ( trail (fn () => solve g1 clauses uvars con sc) ;
        solve g2 clauses uvars con sc )
  | solve (Gatom(M)) clauses uvars con sc =
      match_atom M clauses uvars con sc
  | solve (Gexists(x,g)) clauses uvars con sc =
      solve (gapply_sb (term_sb x (new_evar x uvars)) g)
          clauses uvars con sc
  | solve (Gimplies(d,g)) prog uvars con sc =
      solve g (clausify d (Gtrue) nil prog) uvars con sc
  | solve (Gall(x,g)) prog uvars con sc =
      let val a = new_uvar x
       in solve (gapply_sb (term_sb x a) g) prog (a::uvars)
          con sc end
  | solve (Guard(g1,g2,g3)) clauses uvars con sc =
      let exception Guard_success of constraint
       in ( trail (fn () =>
                  solve g1 clauses uvars con (fn newcon =>
                      raise Guard_success(newcon))) ;
              solve g3 clauses uvars con sc )
            handle Guard_success(newcon) =>
                solve g2 clauses uvars newcon sc
      end

and match_atom M clauses uvars con sc =
      let val M_head = head M
          fun rec_match nil = ()
            | rec_match ((clause as
                           Clause(N_head,vars,N,gbody))::rest) =
              if head_equal N_head M_head
              then let val nesb = new_evar_sb vars uvars
                    in ( trail (fn () =>
                                unify (apply_sb nesb N) M con
                                    (fn newcon => solve
                                        (gapply_sb nesb gbody)
                                        clauses uvars newcon
                                        sc)) ;
                            rec_match rest )
                   end
              else rec_match rest
       in rec_match clauses end
```

12.8.2   Representing Higher-Order Terms

For convenience, we use a single representation type **term** for both terms and types in
our calculus. If we were only interested in implementing a logic programming language
over the simply typed λ-calculus without polymorphism this would be unnecessarily
complicated, but we are interested in including dependent types (in the form of LF [14])
and polymorphism, at which point it is convenient to have to write only one function
each for substitution and unification, rather than two (one for unifying terms and one
for unifying types, for example). The algorithm we outline below will be complete only
for certain fragments of the full calculus, but we can now implement various subcalculi
merely by changing the type checking phase and the set of predeclared constants in
the front end. This basic approach, though different in various details, is taken in the
Calculus of Constructions [4]. The representation of terms is perhaps more direct, but
less efficient than deBruijn indices [5] which are used in eLP and almost all other modern
implementations of λ-calculi which require access to the internal structure of λ-terms.
Nonetheless, we were quite surprised how little of the code depends on the choice of the
representation of bound variables.

```
datatype term =
      Bvar of string              (* Bound Variables *)
    | Evar of varbind * int * term list * (term option) ref
                                  (* Logic Variables , Stamped , *)
                                  (* Depends on , Inst'd to *)
    | Uvar of varbind * int       (* Parameters , Stamped *)
    | Const of string             (* Constants *)
    | Appl of term * term         (* Applications *)
    | Abst of varbind * term      (* Abstractions *)
and varbind = Varbind of string * term
                                  (* Variable binders , Type *)
```

In the implementation of the term language and the type checker, we have two constants
type and **pi**. And, yes, **type** is a type, though this could be avoided by introducing
universes (see [16]) without any changes to the code of the unifier. As is customary, we
use $A \rightarrow B$ as an abbreviation for $\Pi x : A.\, B$ if x does not occur free in B. Also, however,
$\Pi x : A.\, B$ is an abbreviation for the application **pi** $A\,(\lambda x : A.\, B)$. In our formulation,
then, the constant **pi** has type $\Pi A : \texttt{type}.\,((A \rightarrow \texttt{type}) \rightarrow \texttt{type})$.

As an example consider a predicate constant **eq** of type $\Pi A : \texttt{type}.\, A \rightarrow A \rightarrow$
o (where o is the type of formulas as indicated in Section 12.9). The single clause
eq $A\,M\,M$. correctly models equality, that is, a goal of the form **eq** $A\,M\,N$ will succeed
if M and N are unifiable. The fact that unification now has to branch can be seen by

considering the goal **eq int** $(F\,1\,1)\,1$ which has three solutions for the functional logic variable F, namely $\lambda x\!:\!\mathtt{int}.\,\lambda y\!:\!\mathtt{int}.\,x$, $\lambda x\!:\!\mathtt{int}.\,\lambda y\!:\!\mathtt{int}.\,y$, and $\lambda x\!:\!\mathtt{int}.\,\lambda y\!:\!\mathtt{int}.\,1$.

The functions supporting substitution are extended in the obvious way. In particular, we now have to substitute inside **Varbind**'s, since they contain terms which may contain free variables. The type of a constant is accessible in a *signature* which maps names of constants to their types, implemented, for example, as a list of pairs of strings and types.

The unification procedure we use is based on the one in [6,7] for higher-order unification with dependent types, which itself is an extension of Huet's procedure for (higher-order) unification in the simply typed λ-calculus [18]. This procedure is most easily understood in terms of a collection of "transformations," some on terms, some on pairs of terms being unified, and some on sets of such pairs.

With the right control structure (such as iterative deepening) the unifier would be complete for the LF fragment of our calculus, but logic variables ranging over types destroy this completeness. The unifier detects if there is a possibility for incompleteness on a particular execution and can give a warning in such a case, if desired.

12.8.3   Rewriting

Because we are using transformations as a fundamental structuring device in the implementation of unification, we adopted a very elegant technique from Paulson's higher-order implementation of rewriting [27], which itself was patterned after the tactics and tacticals in LCF [13]. Because we are not worried about having our implementation *prove* the correctness of applications of its transformations, we can use a somewhat simpler implementation than in [27]. The basic kind of object we deal with we call a *rewriter*, which is simply a *partial* function from some type to itself – "partial" because it may fail to apply (which is communicated by a raised exception) as well as fail to terminate. Thus we have simply

```
type 'a rewriter = 'a -> 'a
```

The exception **Fail** may be raised in case a rewriter fails to apply and takes string as an argument, which is intended but not required to give some indication of reason for the failure of the rewriter to apply. Here are the general rewriting primitives we found useful.

```
exception Fail of string

fun rew_and rew1 rew2 = rew2 o rew1

fun rew_or rew1 rew2 x = (rew1 x) handle Fail _ => (rew2 x)
```

```
fun rew_id x = x

fun rew_try rew = rew_or rew rew_id

fun rew_repeat rew x = rew_try (rew_and rew (rew_repeat rew)) x

(* rew_first: 'a rewriter -> 'a list rewriter *)
fun rew_first rew nil = raise Fail("rew_first")
  | rew_first rew (x :: l) = (rew x) :: l

(* rew_rest: 'a list rewriter -> 'a list rewriter *)
fun rew_rest list_rew nil = nil
  | rew_rest list_rew (x :: l) = x :: (list_rew l)
```

12.8.4 Unification

The basic structure of the unifier involves maintaining a collection of pairs of terms to be unified simultaneously. Traditionally such pairs are called *disagreement pairs* and such a collection is called a *disagreement set* (though represented and used as a list).

```
datatype dpair = Dpair of term * term
type dset = dpair list
```

During unification, we transform terms, disagreement pairs, and disagreement sets, as described below. However, because some unification problems have more than just a single most general unifier, we will also have one branching step. This will be implemented using success continuations, thus meshing nicely with the interpreter.[10]

Normalization   One kind of rewriting we will need to do during unification is "weak head normalization" of terms. This just means normalizing enough to determine the top-level structure of the β-normal form of the term.[11] In mathematical notation, a weak head reduction step reduces a term of the form $(\lambda x : A. M) N_1 \dots N_n$ to the term $([N_1/x]M) N_2 \dots N_n$.[12] Thus the rewriter below fails if the given term does not have the form of the left-hand side of this rewriting rule (modulo dereferencing of instantiated **Evar**'s).

```
fun head_reduce_term (Appl(M,N)) =
```

---

[10]Success continuations can be used for rewriting as well, but they do not seem as appropriate in this context with only a very simple form of nondeterminism (succeed with the rewritten term or fail).

[11]More specifically, "weak" here refers to not doing any normalization inside of abstractions.

[12]Application associates to the left, so with parentheses the redex would be $(\dots ((\lambda x : A. M) N_1) \dots N_n)$.

```
    (let fun hrt (Abst(xofA,M0)) = apply_sb (term_sb xofA N) M0
           | hrt (Evar(_,_,_,ref(SOME M0))) = hrt M0
           | hrt _ = Appl(head_reduce_term M,N)
      in hrt M end)
  | head_reduce_term (Evar(_,_,_,ref(SOME M0))) =
                     head_reduce_term M0
  | head_reduce_term _ = raise Fail("head_reduce_term")
```

The conventions for naming ML variables in the code for the unifier are as follows: we use **M** and **N** for terms and **A**, **B**, and **C** for types.[13] Furthermore, we use **xofA** and **yofB** for **Varbind**'s (a pair consisting of a variable name and its type) and **Gamma** for contexts (lists of **Varbind**'s).

Next, we raise this from a term rewriter to a disagreement pair rewriter that tries to head reduce the left member of the pair and, if this fails, tries to reduce the right member. The functional **rew_dpair** does this kind of raising:

```
fun rew_dpair rew =
    rew_or (fn (Dpair(M,N)) => Dpair(rew M, N))
           (fn (Dpair(M,N)) => Dpair(M, rew N))

val head_reduce_dpair = rew_dpair head_reduce_term
```

Extensionality   The next transformation involves a disagreement pair made up of one or two abstraction terms. This can be justified by an extensionality principle or the η-rule. For example, consider unifying $\lambda x : A. M$ and $\lambda y : B. N$. In this case we introduce a new parameter a and reduce the problem to unifying $[a/x]M$ and $[a/y]N$. There are two similar cases in which only one of terms being unified is an abstraction where we simply form an application.

```
fun abst_reduce_dpair (Dpair(Evar(_,_,_,ref(SOME M0)),N)) =
    abst_reduce_dpair (Dpair(M0,N))
  | abst_reduce_dpair (Dpair(M,Evar(_,_,_,ref(SOME N0)))) =
    abst_reduce_dpair (Dpair(M,N0))
  | abst_reduce_dpair (Dpair(Abst(xofA,M0), Abst(yofA,N0))) =
    let val a = new_uvar xofA
      in Dpair(apply_sb (term_sb xofA a) M0,
               apply_sb (term_sb yofA a) N0)
    end
  | abst_reduce_dpair (Dpair(Abst(xofA,M0), N)) =
    let val a = new_uvar xofA
      in Dpair(apply_sb (term_sb xofA a) M0, Appl(N,a))
```

---

[13]"Types" are simply terms used in the capacity of types.

```
       end
  | abst_reduce_dpair (Dpair(M,Abst(yofA,N0))) =
      let val a = new_uvar yofA
       in Dpair(Appl(M,a),apply_sb (term_sb yofA a) N0)
      end
  | abst_reduce_dpair _ = raise Fail("abst_reduce_dpair")
```

Rigid pairs   We now focus on the case of unifying two terms, neither of which is subject to weak head reduction and neither of which is an abstraction. Of these, the simplest case is when each of the two terms is "rigid", i.e., its top-level structure does not change under substitution. This is the case when the head of a term is either a constant or a **Uvar**. The treatment in this case is to compare heads. If they are the same, we replace the disagreement pair with the corresponding pairs of arguments. Otherwise, we conclude that the two terms are non-unifiable, and hence the disagreement set containing them is non-unifiable as well.

To distinguish non-unifiability from non-applicability of a rewriter, we introduce a new exception with **exception Nonunifiable**. Rather than extracting the heads and lists of arguments first, in the implementation below, we accumulate disagreement pairs matching up the corresponding arguments while descending to the heads. When we get to a head, we either succeed or fail.

```
(* rigid_rigid : dpair -> dset -> dset,
   Adds result of rigid-rigid decomposition to the given dset.
   Fails if the dpair is not rigid-rigid.
   Can raise the exception Nonunifiable. *)

fun rigid_rigid (Dpair(Evar(_,_,_,ref (SOME M0)), N)) dset =
      rigid_rigid (Dpair(M0,N)) dset
  | rigid_rigid (Dpair(M, Evar(_,_,_,ref (SOME N0)))) dset =
      rigid_rigid (Dpair(M,N0)) dset
  | rigid_rigid (Dpair(Appl(M1,N1),Appl(M2,N2))) dset =
      (* Note the "head-recursion" *)
      rigid_rigid (Dpair(M1,M2)) (Dpair(N1,N2)::dset)
  | rigid_rigid (Dpair(Const(name1),Const(name2))) dset =
      if name1 = name2 then dset else raise Nonunifiable
  | rigid_rigid (Dpair(Uvar(_,stamp1),Uvar(_,stamp2))) dset =
      if stamp1 = stamp2 then dset else raise Nonunifiable
    (* Otherwise, either not rigid-rigid or unification fails. *)
  | rigid_rigid (Dpair(M,N)) _ =
      if (is_rigid M) andalso (is_rigid N)
         then raise Nonunifiable
         else raise Fail("rigid_rigid")
```

It is a simple matter to make this function into a disagreement set rewriter that attempts to apply **rigid_rigid** to the first disagreement pair in a disagreement set:

```
(* rigid_rigid_rew : dset rewriter *)
fun rigid_rigid_rew nil = raise Fail("rigid_rigid_rew")
  | rigid_rigid_rew (dp :: rest) = rigid_rigid dp rest
```

SIMPL   We can now assemble the previous rewriters into a main component of the unification algorithm, corresponding to Huet's "SIMPL" phase. One step of the SIMPL phase is accomplished by the following disagreement set rewriter, which tries first head reduction, then (if that fails to apply) extensionality, and finally rigid-rigid decomposition.

```
val SIMPL_rew =
    rew_or (rew_or (rew_first head_reduce_dpair)
                   (rew_first abst_reduce_dpair))
           rigid_rigid_rew
```

The complete SIMPL phase repeats **SIMPL_rew** as long as it applies, transforming the first disagreement pair, and then recursively works on the remaining disagreement pairs.

```
fun SIMPL ds =
    rew_and (rew_repeat SIMPL_rew)
            (* if SIMPL_rew fails, (rew_repeat SIMPL_rew)
               succeeds and either we have run out of
               disagreement pairs and are done, or the first
               is no longer rigid-rigid and we need to go on. *)
            (rew_rest SIMPL)
            ds
```

MATCH   The SIMPL phase leads either to non-unifiability or to a disagreement set made up completely of disagreement pairs relating two flexible (non-rigid) terms or one rigid and one flexible term. As in Huet's algorithm, we defer treating flexible-flexible disagreement pairs, as their treatment leads to an intractable explosion of the search space, or, if a particular solution is chosen, to an overcommitment which must be avoided in this setting of constraint logic programming. At least in the LF sub-calculus, these disagreement sets are always unifiable when they arise [6].

The "MATCH" phase examines a flexible-rigid disagreement pair, instantiates the logic variable at the head of the flexible term, and calls the success continuation on an augmented disagreement set. Upon backtracking, further instantiations may be tried. Once all possibilities are exhausted MATCH returns. The interested reader can consult [6] for an explanation and justification of these instantiations, as well as completeness proofs. Actually, completeness can in general only be guaranteed for a subcalculus where logic variables do not occur at the head of types. As logic variables ranging over types are extremely useful in practice (they provide for polymorphism), and the algorithm will often be complete even in this case, enforcing this restriction statically is counter-productive. Instead, we give a run-time warning if the unification procedure might be incomplete.

A full discussion of MATCH is beyond the scope of this chapter; we merely show some fragments of the code illustrating its control structure.

```
(* MATCH : dpair -> dset -> (dset -> unit) *)

fun MATCH (Dpair(flex,rigid)) ds sc =

 let val F as Evar(Varbind(Fname,Ftype),_,ok_uvars,_) =
             flex_term_head flex
    ...
    (* Try a substitution given a term and its type *)
    (* Given M and A such that  |- M : A
       instantiate F to M and constrain  Ftype == A
       (not necessary in the simply typed lambda-calculus) *)
    fun try_subst_term M A =
            ( instantiate_evar F M ;
              sc (Dpair(Ftype, A) :: ds) )

    ...
  in
    (* project_from and imitate enumerate the possible
       substitution terms for F, calling try_subst_term on each;
       expecting it to return upon backtracking. *)
    ( trail (fn () => imitate ()) ; project_from Gamma_w )
 end
```

There is no distinction in λProlog or our hypothetical language between choice points established during unification and choice points established during clause selection. Thus trailing must be done at choice points during unification, as in the interpreter.

Putting it together   Now we combine the various pieces into the function **unify_dset**. It expects a disagreement set and a success continuation, which is to be called on a possibly remaining constraint if the disagreement set is unifiable. If not, we simply return to signify failure and initiate backtracking. Constraints are nothing but disagreement sets with only flexible-flexible pairs.

```
type constraint = dset

(* unify_dset : dset -> (constraint -> unit) -> unit *)
fun unify_dset ds sc =
    (* First SIMPL.  This may raise exception Nonunifiable *)
    (* handled below. *)
    let val ds' = SIMPL ds
     in (* ds' will have only flex-rigid, rigid-flex, or
           flex-flex pairs.  Select a flex-rigid or rigid-flex
           and call MATCH. If there is none, we succeed with
           the remaining constraints. MATCH returns upon
           backtracking. *)
       case (find_flex_rigid ds')
         of SOME(dp) => MATCH dp ds' (fn match_ds =>
                                          unify_dset match_ds sc)
          | NONE => sc ds'  (* Success: only flex-flex left *)
    end
    handle Nonunifiable => ()  (* Failure in SIMPL *)

(* unify : term -> term -> constraint -> (constraint -> unit) ->
           unit *)
fun unify M N dset sc = unify_dset (Dpair(M,N) :: dset) sc
```

12.9 Higher-Order Logic

The language of higher-order terms introduced so far has not changed the underlying
logic of our logic programming language: it is still a first-order logic, though over a
very rich domain. This is sufficient for many application programs (see, for example, [10]), but there are instances where it is very elegant and natural to allow true
higher-order programming. By *higher-order programming* we mean the ability of programs to construct other programs (to be assumed) and other goals (to be invoked). In
Prolog some semblance of such a facility is provided through the **call** primitive. Here
we have a higher-order term language, and, following Church [3], we introduce a distinguished type of propositions (o) and constants representing the logical quantifiers and
connectives. For example, logical conjunction is represented by a constant **and** of type
$o \to o \to o$, and the existential quantifier is represented by a constant **exists** of type
$\Pi A : \textbf{type}. ((A \to o) \to o)$.

Two simple examples of higher-order programs in the sense given above are clauses
defining **once** and **not** (negation-as-failure), given the more general **guard** construct
we adopted in Section 12.6. $\bot$ is simply a goal which always fails.

$\quad$ **once**$(G) \leftarrow (G \to \top \mid \bot)$.
$\quad$ **not**$(G) \leftarrow (G \to \bot \mid \top)$.

Here G is a variable of type o and **once** and **not** are constants of type o $\rightarrow$ o. Note that the argument G will be passed as a term, but has to be converted to a goal before it can be invoked.

If we implemented strictly higher-order hereditary Harrop formulas (see [22]), some of the work below would not be necessary, but in practice it is important not to restrict *statically* to D-formulas and G-formulas whose predicate symbol is fixed and known at the time where terms are translated into propositions. Instead we introduce a new case in the definitions of the datatypes **gform** and **dform**, namely **Gflex of term** and **Dflex of term**, respectively. They convey that we do not yet know whether this term will be atomic, a conjunction, *etc.*, since it begins with a predicate variable which might be instantiated by unification *before* the current G-formula or D-formula is needed by the interpreter.

The functions **term_to_gform** and **term_to_dform** (not shown here) translate a term to a formula. They proceed by converting the term to head normal form and then deciding from the constant at the head of the term if it is a conjunction, disjunction, *etc.* If it matches none of the logical constants, it is either atomic (if the head is rigid) or "flex" if the head is an **Evar** or a **Bvar**. The quantifiers are represented as constants applied to abstractions.

All that is required to complete the interpreter is to modify the clausification function to allow **Dflex** formulas and the interpreter to allow **Gflex** formulas. In either case, the argument is again converted to a proposition. If the formula remains flexible, an error results. Recall that flexible formulas may become rigid through instantiation during unification. Consider, for example, $\exists x(x = \top \wedge x)$. At translation time, x is flexible, but by the time the goal x is encountered, it has been instantiated to $\top$, which should simply succeed. We thus add the following case to solve:

```
| solve (Gflex(M)) clauses uvars con sc =
    (case term_to_gform M
        of Gflex(M') =>
            raise error("solve: Goal " ^ term_makestring(M')
                        ^ " with variable head predicate.")
        | g => solve g clauses uvars con sc)
```

and a corresponding case to clausify

```
| clausify (Dflex(M)) body vars rest =
    (case term_to_dform M
        of Dflex(M') =>
            raise error("clausify: Program " ^ term_makestring(M')
                        ^ " with variable head predicate.")
        | d => clausify d body vars rest)
```

12.10   Conclusion

The interpreter we have developed is relatively close to eLP, our Common Lisp implementation of λProlog in the Ergo Support System [8,20]. Most of the differences have already been mentioned: eLP clauses are indexed and stored in a global hashtable; bound variables are represented by deBruijn indices; and parameters and logic variables are time-stamped for comparison and unification of terms that have not been Skolemized. There are also the front-end, that is, parsing, unparsing, and type reconstruction, the implementation of λProlog's module system, and "special" (non-logical) predicates which we ignored in this presentation, some of which are by no means trivial. Unification also differs: the algorithm given here supports a much richer λ-calculus, but it does not implement a number of important optimizations (see [23]) used in eLP. Finally, there are a number of design mistakes which are still part of the current eLP implementation which we chose not to expose here.

We expect that the next set of significant improvements in the implementation techniques for λProlog and related languages will come from a more economical representation of λ-terms [26] and the development of compilation technology [24].

We conclude with the remark that the complete Standard ML code for all versions of the interpreter discussed here including a modest front end are available via **ftp** over the Internet.[14]

References

[1] A. J. Bonner, L. T. McCarty, and K. Vadaparty. Expressing database queries with intuitionistic logic. In Ewing Lusk and Ross Overbeek, editors, *Proceedings of the North American Conference on Logic Programming*, pages 831–850, Cambridge, Massachusetts, 1989. MIT Press.

[2] M. Carlsson. On implementing Prolog in functional programming. *New Generation Computing*, 2(4):347–359, 1984.

[3] A. Church. A formulation of the simple theory of types. *Journal of Symbolic Logic*, 5:56–68, 1940.

[4] T. Coquand and G. Huet. The Calculus of Constructions. *Information and Computation*, 76(2/3):95–120, February/March 1988.

[5] N. G. de Bruijn. Lambda-calculus notation with nameless dummies: a tool for automatic formula manipulation with application to the Church-Rosser theorem. *Indag. Math.*, 34(5):381–392, 1972.

[6] C. Elliott. *Extensions and Applications of Higher-order Unification*. PhD thesis, Carnegie Mellon University, May 1990. Available as Technical Report CMU–CS–90–134, Carnegie Mellon University, Pittsburgh.

[7] C. Elliott. Higher-order unification with dependent types. In *Rewriting Techniques and Applications*, pages 121–136. Springer-Verlag LNCS 355, April 1989.

[8] C. Elliott and F. Pfenning. eLP: A Common Lisp implementation of Prolog in the Ergo Support System. Available via ftp over the Internet, October 1989. Send mail to elp-request@cs.cmu.edu on the Internet for further information.

---

[14]Please send mail to the second author at **fp@cs.cmu.edu** for more information.

[9] M. Felleisen. Transliterating Prolog into Scheme. Technical Report 182, Indiana University, Bloomington, Indiana, October 1985.

[10] A. Felty. *Specifying and Implementing Theorem Provers in a Higher-Order Logic Programming Language*. PhD thesis, Department of Computer and Information Science, University of Pennsylvania, July 1989.

[11] D. M. Gabbay. N-prolog: an extension of Prolog with hypothetical implications II. *Journal of Logic Programming*, 2(4):251–283, 1985.

[12] D. M. Gabbay and U. Reyle. N-prolog: an extension of Prolog with hypothetical implications I. *Journal of Logic Programming*, 1(4):319–355, 1985.

[13] M. J. Gordon, R. Milner, and C. P. Wadsworth. *Edinburgh LCF*. Springer-Verlag LNCS 78, 1979.

[14] R. Harper, F. Honsell, and G. Plotkin. A framework for defining logics. Submitted. A preliminary version appeared in *Symposium on Logic in Computer Science*, pages 194–204, June 1987, January 1989.

[15] R. Harper, R. Milner, K. Mitchell, N. Rothwell, and D. Sannella. Functional programming in Standard ML. Notes to a five day course given at the University of Edinburgh, April 1988.

[16] R. Harper and R. Pollack. Type checking, universe polymorphism, and typical ambiguity in the Calculus of Constructions. In *TAPSOFT '89, Proceedings of the International Joint Conference on Theory and Practice in Software Development, Barcelona, Spain*, pages 241–256. Springer-Verlag LNCS 352, March 1989.

[17] C. T. Haynes. Logic continuations. *Journal of Logic Programming*, 4(2):157–176, June 1987.

[18] G. Huet. A unification algorithm for typed -calculus. *Theoretical Computer Science*, 1:27–57, 1975.

[19] J. Jaffar and J. L. Lassez. Constraint logic programming. In *Proceedings of the Fourteenth Annual ACM Symposium on Principles of Programming Languages, Munich*, pages 111–119. ACM, January 1987.

[20] P. Lee, F. Pfenning, G. Rollins, and W. Scherlis. The Ergo Support System: An integrated set of tools for prototyping integrated environments. In Peter Henderson, editor, *Proceedings of the ACM SIGSOFT/SIGPLAN Software Engineering Symposium on Practical Software Development Environments*, pages 25–34. ACM Press, November 1988. Also available as Ergo Report 88–054, School of Computer Science, Carnegie Mellon University, Pittsburgh.

[21] D. Miller. A logical analysis of modules in logic programming. *Journal of Logic Programming*, 6(1-2):57–77, January 1989.

[22] D. Miller, G. Nadathur, F. Pfenning, and A. Scedrov. Uniform proofs as a foundation for logic programming. *Journal of Pure and Applied Logic*, 1988. To appear. Available as Ergo Report 88–055, School of Computer Science, Carnegie Mellon University, Pittsburgh.

[23] D. A. Miller. Unification under mixed prefixes. Unpublished manuscript, 1987.

[24] G. Nadathur and B. Jayaraman. Towards a WAM model for lambda Prolog. In *Proceedings of the 1989 North American Conference on Logic Programming*, pages 1180–1198. MIT Press, October 1989.

[25] G. Nadathur and D. Miller. An overview of Prolog. In Robert A. Kowalski and Kenneth A. Bowen, editors, *Logic Programming: Proceedings of the Fifth International Conference and Symposium, Volume 1*, pages 810–827, Cambridge, Massachusetts, August 1988. MIT Press.

[26] G. Nadathur and D. S. Wilson. A representation of lambda terms suitable for operations on their intensions. In *Proceedings of the 1990 Conference on Lisp and Functional Programming*. ACM Press, June 1990. To appear.

[27] L. Paulson. A higher-order implementation of rewriting. *Science of Computer Programing*, 3:119–149, 1983.

13 The Architecture of PRL: A Mathematical Medium

Joseph Bates

A trend in the design of programming languages is to extend their expressive power toward the ability to fully specify and explain code. An example of this trend is the inclusion of increasingly sophisticated type systems.

When programming languages begin to approach the expressive power of general mathematical language, the distinction between writing and checking program text fades. Programs start to resemble discussions of problems, and as with general mathematical discussions, one needs to omit unnecessary detail and write just enough to make checking the reasoning feasible. Thus checking and writing occur together, and this means that for machines to continue providing effective assistance as programming languages are enriched, existing compilers, type checkers, and other kinds of verifiers must evolve into tools that participate actively in the writing process.

PRL is an interactive environment that supports the language of constructive type theory, a very rich framework for presenting mathematical thought, including programs and their explanations. PRL includes facilities for creating new definitions, for stating and proving propositions and programs, for extracting programs from proofs, for defining new tools to help automate these activities, and for meta-level reasoning about the new tools. This chapter describes the PRL architecture, the major issues that arose in implementing PRL, the solutions chosen in the current system, and techniques for improving the architecture and implementation.

13.1 Introduction

PRL (pronounced "pearl") is the generic name for several interactive computer systems, developed at Cornell University starting in the late 70's, that are designed to provide a comfortable environment for mathematicians to use in creating, accumulating, and applying mathematical knowledge [11,29]. PRL includes within its domain not just the treatment of numbers, lists, sets, and vectors, but of essentially all the varied types of objects that people use in the study of mathematics, logic, and computer science. Particularly included is support for meta-mathematics, which is reasoning about mathematical texts and the process of constructing them.

The primary purpose of the PRL systems, which we shall henceforth refer to in the singular, was to let us explore the idea of the machine as a new medium [3,21,30,33]. Unlike paper, machines are able to act on the information that is expressed to and through them, and we wanted to explore the implications of taking seriously the idea of the machine as a new medium.

The secondary goal for the system was to accumulate knowledge and reasoning methods as one path toward building a competent, automated mathematician. Human mathematicians spend many years in school studying and accumulating mathematical knowledge as well as techniques for applying that knowledge and extending it. It struck us as unreasonable to imagine that a machine would be able to function as an effective automated mathematician without having access to those many years of collected human knowledge. Because PRL is an environment for editing and accumulating this knowledge, we believe it to be the right sort of foundation for automating mathematics [3].

A third goal, based on our view that programming and mathematics are deeply interwoven disciplines, was to use PRL as a programming environment [7]. Many mathematical discussions implicitly describe how to compute. For example, if you look in a book on the theory of context-free languages, you will find definitions and theorems about grammars, languages, parse trees, derivations, and so on, but little explicit code. Nonetheless, after reading the book you would expect to be able to turn those discussions into code. Thus, we wanted PRL to be able to extract code from the mathematical discussions it accumulated. In addition, since PRL needed to follow and assist with the increasingly high-level discussions recorded in its libraries, PRL had to be a programming environment, at least implicitly, so that it could be used to extend its functional abilities as its libraries grew. Thus, PRL needed to be a programming environment for development of both object-level and meta-level programs.

The PRL systems were developed out of work done at Cornell in the early and mid 1970's. Based on ideas from Robert Constable's PL/CV project [12,14] and on my experience with top-down programming, I completed a thesis in 1979 describing a system called PRL [2]. That system was based on a simple logic of numbers and finite sets. The main contribution was the presentation of a *refinement logic*, which embodied a top-down subgoaling proof structure, a constructive interpretation for proofs, and an algorithm to extract moderately efficient executable code from proofs.

In 1980, the implementation efforts of PL/CV were joined with the ideas in my thesis, and we started implementing the Lisp-based LambdaPRL system [29]. The main goal was to explore our ideas for a new system architecture based on refinement proofs, flexible definitions, and explicit meta-programs (the latter defined in the ML language of [16]). We knew the LambdaPRL logic was inadequate for doing real mathematics, but using such a simple logic let us build a system quickly, so that we could test our architectural ideas.

While building LambdaPRL, we were working on variations of Martin-Löf's constructive type theory [23]. The main task was to present that theory in a refinement style while extending it in certain ways to support the rich types we thought were needed. In 1984, the LambdaPRL implementation was finished. Subsequent experience with LambdaPRL suggested that the architecture was relatively successful, so we started building a successor system, NuPRL, which had the same system architecture but replaced the simple constructive predicate calculus with our new type theory [6]. That system was mostly operational by 1986 and at that point we began building libraries in NuPRL.

Work on PRL has continued, producing several Ph.D. theses [1,10,18,20,22,24,31] and a fairly widely distributed system. Some of the current work is in building libraries, some in continuing to extend the logic, and some in designing new system architectures. One such architecture is called MetaPRL, which removes the type theory and much of the structure of mathematics from the system design, leaving an abstracted "meta" system, and also revises the system implementation based on what we learned from experience with PRL [4,5].

PRL was developed at Cornell by a large, well-integrated group consisting of Robert Constable, Joseph Bates, and roughly 15 other students, staff, and faculty.

13.1.1   The Description of PRL

We will present PRL as having three primary components: the logic, the editing environment, and the mechanisms for expressing and using meta-knowledge.

The logic is the foundation for all mathematics expressed in PRL libraries. While LambdaPRL had a very simple logic, NuPRL is at the other extreme with a very rich logic. From brief inspection, the system design appears to be independent of the logic, but once one starts to consider meta-reasoning, especially reflection, the logic becomes part of the system. Thus, we will try to give the reader a sense of the NuPRL logic.

The editing environment includes the library mechanism, which holds a variety of structured objects, the editors that let people manipulate those objects, and the reasoners that help make manipulation of the objects practical.

The meta level allows existing PRL mechanisms, especially the editing environment, to be extended as the content of the library grows and changes. For example, as new proof methods are developed, the proof checkers must be able to recognize valid instances of the new forms. Without adequate extension facilities, PRL would become unusable as the library grows beyond the capabilities of any set of fixed tools.

13.2   The Mathematical Foundation of NuPRL

NuPRL is built on a constructive type theory that was developed at Cornell from earlier work by Scott, Martin-Löf, and others [23,32]. Roughly speaking, this theory is to constructive mathematics as classical logic and set theory are to classical mathematics. Thus, it is intended to be rich enough to express anything that one would want to say while doing mathematics and computer science. Although this clearly cannot be the case, since mathematics is known to be a creative and evolving activity, the theory does allow one to discuss and manipulate atoms, integers, tuples, functions, propositions, and types, defined directly or by recursion.

This means that one can talk about (that is, quantify over or manipulate in code) complex objects such as:

- real numbers, represented as infinite convergent sequences of rationals,

- context-free grammars and context-free languages,

- inference procedures that manipulate propositions and proofs.

One might use this power to state and prove that

$$\left(\forall G: \text{LL}(1) \text{ grammar}\right)\left(\exists P: \text{rec. descent parser}\right)$$
$$\left(\forall s: \mathcal{L}(G)\right)\left(P(s) \text{ is a parse tree in } G \text{ for } s\right).$$

From a proof of this proposition, NuPRL could automatically extract a parser generator for context free LL(1) grammars.

The NuPRL type theory is presented in [11] (and an earlier version in [6]). While it is an important part of NuPRL, we can present most of the PRL system architecture without knowing the specifics of the theory. Thus, in the remainder of this chapter, we will use familiar predicate calculus notation when we need to look at samples of mathematics.

13.3   The Library

PRL provides a very simple library mechanism: a library is a flat linear collection of objects. In certain contexts, objects can refer to other objects; however the surface structure is linear, and this is the way the library is presented to the user.

Richer structure, such as the hierarchical structure typically found in books, is desirable in a system like PRL. However, the simple linear structure we adopted was adequate to explore the other issues that interested us; it was easy to explain and use, and it was easy to implement.

A library object is a definition, a theorem and its proof, an extracted piece of code, or a meta-language expression. The PRL library window shows a contiguous subsequence of the library, with a few lines summarizing each object in the subsequence. The summary shows the object's name, kind, status, and a brief description. The name is used for referencing the object in commands or from other library objects. The kind indicates whether the object is a definition, theorem/proof, extracted code, or meta-language expression. The status tells whether the object (for instance, a proof) is well formed and complete, well formed but incomplete, or ill formed. The brief description varies with the kind of object, but is intended to summarize the content of the object. For instance, for a theorem/proof object it is a statement of the theorem.

Here is a sample library window showing two definitions and a theorem. The leading "∗" is the status indicator for "well formed and complete."

Library (cantor)
∗ imp   DEF $\langle proposition \rangle \Rightarrow \langle proposition \rangle$
∗ some   DEF $(\exists \langle var \rangle : \langle type \rangle) \langle proposition \rangle$
∗ *cantor*   THM $\rangle \rangle (\forall g{:}int \to (int \to int))(\exists d{:}int \to int)(\forall i{:}int)(d \neq g(i))$

Libraries must fit into the virtual memory space of the running PRL system. Thus, the PRL architecture is not suited to very large libraries. Some experiments with PRL have required Lisp images of over one hundred megabytes, and the libraries were not nearly as large as one would expect them eventually to become. Thus, a more appropriate architecture would be based on a persistent object system, with that object system in turn based on appropriate database technology to provide sharing, distributed storage, and reliability.

PRL libraries can be written from virtual memory to a file system, for permanent storage. Saved library files can be loaded into PRL, either replacing the previously active library or inserted into the active library. We found loading and saving to be a slow process, whether we saved the entire Lisp representation or whether we saved the minimal amount of information needed to reconstruct the remainder during loading. Both of these functions are provided in PRL. Neither is very pleasant. Again, a library mechanism based on a persistent object system should provide better function and better performance.

The PRL editing environment lets users edit or browse multiple views of one or more library objects at any given time. The system attempts to update all the views whenever editing operations occur in any view. Thus, it provides the viewing facilities standard in modern text editors, but on objects with highly structured underlying representations.

PRL's algorithms for producing displayed images from objects are somewhat complicated, as will be discussed below. Finding incremental display-update techniques for these algorithms was not easy. Indeed, one of the most complex parts of the system is the set of display algorithms. We believe it would have been better to unify the system's variety of object representations into a single representation, so that we could have spent more effort on a single efficient incremental display algorithm.

13.4   Definitions

One purpose of mathematical discussion is to develop new language for discussing new concepts. The clearest example of this is the *definition*. PRL definitions allow users to create new abstract entities as compositions of existing linguistic forms, and to declare notations for these compositions.

13.4.1   The Definition Facility

When designing PRL we wanted to provide a very general notation-extension facility, beyond what could be described using a precedence parser or LALR grammar. This was because mathematics uses many rich notations, two-dimensional forms, ambiguous forms, and so forth, and we thought these necessary for proofs to be readable, and thus for PRL to be used. We attempted to achieve this flexibility by using a structure editor with user-defined templates.

A PRL definition looks like

$$template == body,$$

where the template describes the form and parameters of the new notation and the body shows the meaning of the new notation in terms of already defined language. The most primitive expressions, from which all others are ultimately built, are simply individual characters.

Here are several example definitions:

len: $|\langle x \rangle| ==$ length($\langle x \rangle$)
sub: $\langle A \rangle [\langle i \rangle] ==$ select($\langle A \rangle, \langle i \rangle$)
inrange: $\langle a \rangle$ in $\langle b \rangle .. \langle c \rangle == \langle b \rangle \leq \langle a \rangle \wedge \langle a \rangle \leq \langle c \rangle$
sorted: $\langle x \rangle$ is sorted $== (\forall i$: integer)(i in $2..|\langle x \rangle| \Rightarrow \langle x \rangle [i - 1] \leq \langle x \rangle [i])$

For each of these definitions, the display form of an instance is constructed by taking the template, leaving the characters exactly as shown, but inserting the display forms for each of the arguments in place of the corresponding parameters. The parameters are the names enclosed in angle brackets. For example, an instance of the "len" definition looks like a vertical bar, followed by the display form of the argument to "len," followed by another vertical bar.

The last definition, "sorted," has as its body a form which is built almost exclusively from notation not present in the NuPRL base language. Thus, the $\forall$ quantifier, the "in" notation, the "len" notation, the $\Rightarrow$, the two uses of subscripting, and the $\leq$ symbol are all definitions expressed in a PRL library. Only the subtraction symbol, the parentheses, and the atom "integer" are built into NuPRL. This extensive use of defined notation is the norm in PRL libraries. Our experience suggests that an effective mathematics environment must provide a notation facility at least this rich.

The underlying structure manipulated by the definition editor is called a text tree or *Ttree*. A Ttree is defined as follows:

$$\text{Ttree} = (\text{char} + \text{defref})*$$
$$\text{defref} = \text{defname} \times \text{Ttree}*$$

Thus, a Ttree is a sequence of characters and definition references, where a definition reference is a definition name and a list of Ttrees that serve as actual parameters to substitute for the formal parameters of the definition. The standard editing operations on Ttrees include walking around in the tree, and inserting, deleting, and copying sequences of characters and definition references.

Ttrees and the Ttree editor are used in several places in PRL to allow attractive display forms for terms, propositions, proof rules, and meta-language. Thus, in addition to the sample definitions above, PRL libraries include definitions such as:

note: note that $\langle P$:proposition$\rangle$ == sequence $\langle P \rangle$
obv: $\langle T$:tactic$\rangle$ and so on... == $\langle T \rangle$ THEN ObviousReasoningTactic

which define a new proof rule and a meta-language expression, respectively.

These last examples show that each formal parameter of a definition can include a parameter description as well as a variable name. When a definition is instantiated, but before the parameter is filled in, it is the description that shows up on the display. If the description is missing, then the variable name is used. For example, when the "note" definition is instantiated, by typing the Instantiate-key, then "note," the display will show

note that $\langle$proposition$\rangle$

which can be then further extended by filling in the parameter with text, instantiations of other definitions, or a mixture of both.

Parameter descriptions are intended to suggest to the user what kind of linguistic entity should be inserted. However, they are not part of any formal language of types, and are not checked by the system. A disadvantage of this decision is that errors are not detected immediately as Ttrees are entered. An advantage is that definitions can be used to extend any of the languages used within PRL, without the definition editor having to understand them.

When a Ttree is used in some context in PRL, it eventually must be turned into some expression in the particular language expected in that context. For example, if a Ttree represents a formula, it must be parsed as a formula. If it represents a meta-language expression, it must be parsed and processed by the ML (meta-language) subsystem. Whenever one of PRL's language processors begins to read a Ttree, the Ttree is first expanded to a sequence of characters. The resulting text is then scanned and parsed in a way that depends on the context of use.

For example, according to our sample definitions, "A is sorted" expands to

$$(\forall i: \text{integer})(2 \leq i \wedge i \leq \text{length}(A) \Rightarrow \text{select}(A, i-1) \leq \text{select}(A, i)).$$

In the actual NuPRL library, since $\forall$, $\leq$, $\wedge$, and $\Rightarrow$ are themselves definitions, this form is further expanded to text and then parsed according to the underlying language of type theory.

13.4.2   Discussion of the Definition Facility

The PRL definition facility demonstrates several strengths and weaknesses which we believe deserve consideration in the design of future systems.

A primary strength is notational flexibility. Since we directly manipulate the Ttree structure with the editor, we never need to parse the displayed forms of user defined notations. We need only to generate display forms (and to macro expand for semantic processing). This means that notational extensions can be very rich, even ambiguous.

For example, if templates allowed operators to generate subscripts and superscripts, we could write

definite-integral: \integral \down ⟨low⟩ \up ⟨high⟩ ⟨body⟩ d⟨var⟩ == ...

which would display as

$$\int_{\langle \text{low} \rangle}^{\langle \text{high} \rangle} \langle \text{body} \rangle \text{d} \langle \text{var} \rangle.$$

In general we could imagine supporting notation such as provided by TeX or Postscript.

Since definitions are entered by their library names, which are unique, PRL has no problem handling a variety of different interpretations for a notation such as A[i]. This allows the normal freedom mathematicians enjoy to define new notations and then use context when reading to determine which meaning is intended.

Despite the notational flexibility of user defined templates, we were concerned in choosing this approach that a structure editor might be unpleasant to use. With this in mind, we were careful to choose the keyboard cursor motion operations to make the visible motion of the on-screen cursor as natural as possible. Thus, instead of assigning simple tree operations (previous-sibling, parent, first-child) to cursor motion keys, we chose, for example, to make the left-arrow key adjust the tree cursor as necessary to make the screen cursor move left one character position.

We feel that the PRL structure editor is tolerable to use, but that in its current form it is not acceptable for extended editing of large objects. Conceptually it is adequate, but the actual keystrokes needed to invoke definitions, move the cursor, and so forth, are inconvenient. However, we also feel that there may be easily implemented techniques to make entry and manipulation of templates far more natural. Examples of these techniques may be found in mathematics processors on modern personal computers, for instance the Milo system on the Apple Macintosh.

Given that one is using a structure editor with user defined-notations, there arises the problem of displaying the instantiated templates in real time WYSIWYG. Currently, PRL includes some mechanisms for incremental screen update, and because of this achieves adequate performance. However, the notational power is not as developed as one would like, so there remain interesting problems of how to incrementally update a screen in response to incremental changes in, say, PostScript code. We believe it would be useful to explore subsets of Postscript that support rich notation, yet are amenable to the kind of symbolic differentiation needed to do incremental display.

Probably the largest issue that arises in PRL's way of handling notation is the treatment of definitions as macros. When the system actively manipulates language specific parse trees, as it does whenever it works with the meanings of Ttrees, the question of how to preserve the attractive display forms arises.

For example, suppose one is trying to prove

$$\gg (\exists A)|A| = 0$$

by introducing the empty list for A. Upon suggesting that [] might work for A, we would like to see the subgoal $|[]| = 0$. However, the goal is parsed roughly as $(\exists A)\text{length}(A) = 0$ (it is actually worse than this since $\exists$ is a defined notation), so the easiest output to produce is $\text{length}([]) = 0$. Avoiding the potentially disastrous expansion of long chains of definitions, as this example suggests might happen, means that it must be possible to calculate "best" Ttrees from parse trees, even when those parse trees are modified by the system (e.g., by substitution).

The current PRL implementation does this by attaching a Ttree to each node of each parse tree. That Ttree represents the desired display form for the subtree rooted at the parse tree node. When operations are performed on the parse tree, these best Ttrees move along with the nodes. Thus, we can generate new display forms by recursively walking the parse tree, using the attached best Ttree for a node if there is one, and otherwise composing the Ttrees for children with the proper glue characters.

Thus when $|A|$ is expanded to length(A) and parsed, the nice form for A is attached to the appropriate subnode of the parse tree, and $|A|$ is attached to the top node. If the system needs the display form of the argument to length, it can grab the best Ttree easily by looking in the appropriate subnode.

This method fails if a substitution is done, because the entire set of Ttrees attached to nodes from the substitution point back along the path to the root must be destroyed when substitutions occur. For example, when A is replaced by [], $|A|$ is no longer a correct display form for length([]) and it is deleted. Thus, in our example, we would lose the $|\cdot|$ notation.

To avoid this problem, the PRL substitution algorithm uses a heuristic. Besides doing a correct mathematical substitution on the parse tree, in particular correctly handling the capture of bound variables, it does a heuristic substitution on the display form (Ttree) of the root node. Specifically, it looks for all instances of the identifiers to be replaced, and substitutes for them the Ttrees of the new expressions. The resulting Ttree may or may not correctly denote the parse tree resulting from the mathematical substitution, so PRL expands the Ttree produced by the heuristic, parses the result, and does an α-equality test on the resulting parse trees. If they are α-equal, then the heuristic produced a correct result, and it can be used as the attractive Ttree for the result of substitution. If the results are not α-equal, then we use the correct parse tree, and do our best to generate a Ttree using the recursive walk mentioned earlier.

If we look at our substitution example, by replacing A by [] in $|A| = 0$, we get a Ttree, $|[]|$, which when parsed produces the same parse tree as if we take the parse tree, length(A) = 0, and substitute [] for A. Thus, we can use the Ttree $|[]| = 0$ as the result instead of length([]) = 0.

We find this heuristic works well in practice. However, along with the costs of macro expansion, it is one of the primary causes of poor performance in PRL. In addition, when capture occurs, and also in certain more pathological situations, it fails.

The treatment of definitions as macros has benefits and disadvantages. The disadvantages are clear: a complex method is required to maintain acceptable display forms in the face of modifications to parse trees, a time consuming process of expansion and parse occurs very frequently in PRL (both when reading expressions and when substituting), and there is non-intuitive behavior of the definitions with respect to bound variables.

Advantages are that the same mechanism works all across PRL. So terms, goals, proof rules, and tactics can all be extended using definitions. The definition mechanism is modular, in that it need not anticipate which kind of parse trees it is dealing with. Parsers need not know about the facility. Thus, for instance, users can extend the meta-language without changing the ML implementation in any way. Also, of great importance, meta-language tactics which work on base language expressions automatically work on extended notations, since they see only the base language, never the Ttrees.

For example, in NuPRL we define predicate calculus in terms of type theory. In particular, implication $(A \Rightarrow B)$ is defined as function space construction $(A \rightarrow B)$. Treating definitions as macros allows the rules for reasoning about $\rightarrow$ (and related ML tactics, discussed below) to apply to $\Rightarrow$ without change. If we made new notations be genuinely new terms, then existing rules and tactics would have to be extended whenever we added notational variants of existing definitions.

This example shows that it is often beneficial that reasoners do not see uses of defined notations. However, this can cause serious problems for sophisticated reasoners. We conjecture that people depend heavily on defining new notations, becoming familiar with them, and then reasoning directly with those notations. That is, they do not always map expressions down to base language. So we believe that to develop increasingly powerful reasoners in a PRL-like system, one must choose to treat defined notations exactly as base language is treated, and then find ways to deal with the ensuing problems, particularly the extension of old reasoners to new definitions.

13.5   Proofs

PRL proofs are built by repeatedly refining goals into subgoals until the simplest subgoals are proved by axioms. Thus a proof is a tree of nodes, where each node has a goal and an associated proof rule (refinement rule). The goals of the children of a node are the result of applying the node's rule to the node's goal.

A goal in PRL is a sequent [15]: a collection of assumptions together with a conclusion that is claimed to follow from the assumptions. These sequents are written as A1, ..., An $\gg$ C. The symbol $\gg$ serves the same purpose as $\Rightarrow$ or $\vdash$.

Here is a sample proof:

$$A \wedge B \gg A \vee B \quad \text{by elim 1}$$
$$A, B \gg A \vee B \quad \text{by intro right}$$
$$A, B \gg B \quad \text{by hypothesis.}$$

We have displayed the tree in preorder, where the goal comes first, then a refinement rule, and finally the display forms for the children (subtrees) of the goal. This proof has a goal with one subgoal, which in turn has one subgoal, which has no subgoals.

The rules of PRL are organized in the style of natural deduction [8]. Many of the rules tell how to break an assumption or conclusion apart around its main operator (connective).

In the example, "elim 1" means to take the first assumption and break it apart. Since it is a conjunction, the rule produces a subgoal with the two appropriate assumptions in its place. The rule encodes the belief that if we can prove the single subgoal, then the goal is true.

The second rule used, an "intro" rule, breaks apart the conclusion. In this case the main connective is a disjunction, so we can prove it by proving either component. "intro right" means to produce a subgoal in which the right-hand disjunct is taken as the new conclusion.

The third proof rule is that of "hypothesis." When the conclusion is a member of the list of assumptions, the rule succeeds and produces no subgoals. If the conclusion is not found among the assumptions, then the rule is not applicable. Trying to apply it would generate an error and the tree could not be extended by this means.

PRL proofs are built by successive refinement. The initial goal is stated by the user and entered into the tree at the root. Then the user gets to enter only refinement rules. PRL generates subgoals automatically and the user provides rules for those new subgoals. This repeats until all the leaf goals are proved (that is, their rules generate no new leaves below them).

At any moment the proof display shows one goal, one proof rule, and the immediate subgoals of that goal. The contents of the proof trees (if any) for those subgoals are not shown. Here is an example of how proofs are displayed:

$$A, B \gg (\forall n : \mathcal{N})P(n) \quad \text{by induction}$$
$$A, B \gg P(0)$$
$$A, B, n : \mathcal{N}, P(n-1) \gg P(n)$$

The cursor motions in proofs are *up*, *down*, *in*, *out*, and *next unproven goal*. *Up* and *down* move to adjacent subgoals of a goal. Thus, they move up and down on a given view of the proof. *In*, when positioned on a subgoal, redraws the screen with that subgoal as the goal and its rule and subgoals shown. *Out* reverses this process, moving up to the parent and leaving the cursor positioned on the subgoal. *Next unproven goal* moves the cursor to the next unproven goal in the tree, in a preorder walk from the current node, and displays that goal at the top of the screen.

The status of every subtree is maintained by PRL and displayed. A node is *complete* if it has a valid proof rule and all its children are complete. A node is *bad* if it has a bad proof rule (there are no children in this case) or if any of its children are *bad*. A node is Incomplete if it is neither *complete* nor *bad*. This information is displayed as a *, –, or #, respectively.

While NuPRL has a rich and somewhat complex set of proof rules, LambdaPRL rules are mostly familiar from predicate calculus. They include *elim* to take apart assumptions, *intro* to take apart conclusions, *induction* to prove universally quantified propositions over integers and lists, *hyp* to prove a result by hypothesis, and *seq* to introduce an intermediate proposition into a proof. *Seq* is sometimes called a "cut" rule, or proof by sequencing. It allows one to prove $A \gg C$ by proving both $A \gg B$ and $A, B \gg C$.

There are several more complex and interesting rules. The Lemma rule allows a result from the library to serve as the justification for a goal. If the goal can be seen as a special case of the lemma, then no subgoals are generated and the goal is considered proved. A goal is a special case of a lemma if the assumptions of the goal are a superset of those of the lemma and the conclusion of the goal matches that of the lemma.

Sometimes goals can be easily seen correct, yet a complex calculation stands behind this process. PRL is intended to let people express proofs in terms natural to them, so we want the machine to have a sense of "easily seen" that matches people's sense. In LambdaPRL, mechanisms are provided by which the machine can recognize "obvious" results in equality reasoning, arithmetic reasoning, and simplification. LambdaPrl provides rules called Equality, Arith, and Simplification that use a congruence closure algorithm, a graph algorithm, and a recursive simplifier, respectively. We will say more about these in a moment.

The final class of proof rule is used to invoke an explicit procedural proof method defined in the ML programming language. These *tactics*, defined in PRL libraries, allow users to gradually build up collections of proving methods that are specific to the domains in which they are working. Examples include "obvious" logical reasoning (such as we carried out in the example proof above), simple inductions, and proving expressions well formed (as is necessary in the NuPRL type theory). If the user enters a proof rule that is not recognized as being from one of the built-in classes, then PRL assumes it must be an ML expression and tries to execute it as a user defined proving method.

13.6   Complex Reasoners

Proof steps are intended to capture clearly correct reasoning. Often this is a simple matter of checking whether the claimed proof step matches (for example, can be unified with) the structure of a proof rule. However, some obvious reasoning involves more complex manipulations, such as whether $2 * x + y > y + x - 3$ over the natural numbers.

In order to provide rapid recognition of certain sorts of obvious reasoning, LambdaPRL provides the rules of Simplification, Equality, and Arith.

13.6.1   Simplification

Simplification is the simplest form of obvious reasoning. The simplifier takes an expression involving arithmetic operators, function calls, constants, and variables, and tries to put it into sum-of-products form, folding constants and expanding certain function calls in the process (e.g., factorial($x + 1$) becomes $(x + 1) * $ factorial(x)). This is a very simple operation, but quite handy when compared to doing the individual simplification steps one by one using smaller proof rules.

The simplifier works well in LambdaPRL, but in NuPRL the type theory makes simplification a much more subtle process, so there is no built-in simplifier. However, user-written ML tactics can provide much of the effect of LambdaPRL's Lisp-coded simplifier.

13.6.2   Equality

The equality algorithm tries to prove a conclusion involving uninterpreted functions, lists, and equality from assumptions of the same form. It is useful for doing simple substitutions, and for reasoning by composing transitivity, reflexivity, and symmetry. The algorithm is a congruence closure algorithm, as described by Nelson and Oppen [28].

As with simplification, the equality algorithm is correct in the LambdaPRL predicate calculus. However, in type theory substitution is sufficiently subtle that we cannot directly apply the congruence closure algorithm. Again, tactics can provide much of the power, but at some cost in performance.

13.6.3   Arith

The arithmetic algorithm reasons about literals (equalities and inequalities) over integers, $+$, $-$, $*$, and uninterpreted functions. It embodies the ring axioms for $*$ and $+$, the transitivity of $<$ and $=$, knowledge that nothing lies between x and $x + 1$, and a trivial form of monotonicity of integers: that if $x < y$ then $x + c < y + c$ for any constant c.

The algorithm is strongly based on the work of Chan [9], though the implementation is new. The idea is to turn the set of assumptions and the conclusion into a question of whether a set of literals is consistent. Thus,

$$P1, P2, \ldots \gg (Q1 \lor Q2 \lor \ldots)$$

is provable just when $\{P1, P2, \ldots, \neg Q1, \neg Q2, \ldots\}$ is not satisfiable. Each literal is two arithmetic expressions connected by one of the six relations $=$, $\neq$, $<$, $\leq$, $>$, $\geq$. The last four can be turned into equivalent literals over $\leq$, by turning $x < y$ into $x + 1 \leq y$. $x = y$ can be turned into the two literals $x \leq y$ and $y \leq x$.

The result of this transformation is a set of literals involving only $\leq$ and $\neq$. Let us for the moment ignore the $\neq$ literals. To check the consistency of a set of $\leq$ literals, we build a directed graph with weighted edges. First, we take each literal $A \leq B$ and put

A and B into a canonical sum of products form. This uses properties of $+$, $-$, and $*$. A and B then have the form $P + c$, where c is an integer constant, and P is the part of the polynomial excluding the constant. We can put the constants on one side of the $\leq$, getting the literal into the form $P + d \leq Q$.

Now, for each unique constant free polynomial P or Q, we build a node labeled with that polynomial. For each literal $P + d \leq Q$, we place an arc from P to Q labeled with the edge weight d. If there is a cycle of positive weight w in this graph, then $P + w$ must be less than or equal to P. But this is impossible for any assignment of values to the variables of the literals. Thus, this indicates that the set of literals is unsatisfiable.

A careful analysis (see [9]) shows that a positive-weight cycle will occur exactly when the set of literals is provably unsatisfiable according to the reasoning rules mentioned at the beginning of this section. This means that the original sequent is provable by simple arithmetic. By checking that the literal set is unsatisfiable for each possible sense of any literals involving $\neq$, we obtain an algorithm that is provably complete, and fast in practice.[1]

13.6.4 Issues with complex reasoners

When we started building PRL, there were interesting theoretical and practical results being obtained on decision procedures for various mathematical domains [9,26,27]. It seemed prudent to take advantage of these results, and to build the system around a collection of fast decision procedures. In retrospect, I believe this was a conceptual error that derived from our mathematical leaning, and that a psychological or "AI" view would have served us better. There are two issues, consideration of which leads to this conclusion.

First, in a system designed to work closely with humans, it is of great importance to meet human expectations about the ability of the system to combine its knowledge sources. If the system knows about domains A and B, then it should be able to think about entities constructed of components drawn from both A and B. For example, knowing about arithmetic and the behavior of functions should allow one to realize that if $x \leq y$ and $y \leq x$ then $f(x) = f(y)$.

Nelson and Oppen demonstrated ways to combine certain reasoners to get provably complete reasoners for combined domains. LambdaPRL used heuristics to obtain practically effective combined reasoners for simplification, equality, and arithmetic.

The problem with these elegant "mathematical" approaches is the very thing that makes them mathematically delightful: they are clever solutions to narrowly defined problems.

---

[1]For each literal, $x \neq y$, we confirm that the literal set is unsatisfiable whether $x < y$ or $x > y$. In general this requires an exponential number of satisfiability calculations, but in practice there are seldom more than a few literals involving $\neq$.

However, as new provers (knowledge sources) are added to a system, they should be able to join in on a common communication protocol. If the existing provers use a powerful but very specialized protocol for sharing information, such as used by Nelson and Oppen or LambdaPRL, then the new provers may have difficulty providing their knowledge to the cooperating whole. Thus, we believe systems should be built on general notions of how agents communicate, instead of on provably efficient protocols for specific cases.

Just what such a protocol should look like is not clear to us. However, people seem to be able to mix new and old knowledge fairly easily, without learning specific techniques for each pair of domains. So perhaps there is reason to believe that some such protocol may exist.

Ease of incorporating new provers is one important criterion for a cooperating prover architecture. Another is the ability of individual and combined provers to explain their activities.

While decision procedures that succeed are rarely asked to explain how they succeeded, those that fail must be able to provide explanations, for otherwise they leave the user with little or no information about how to proceed with the proof. Users can benefit by seeing "how far" the prover got, where the "hard part" is, etc. Provers, such as Arith, that map from the linguistic domain of proofs into unfamiliar representations, such as weighted directed graphs, often provide little help in explaining how far they got and why they got stuck. Arith, for example, would say "no positive weight cycle was found."

Explanations are useful to recover from failure, to learn from failure, and to learn from success. People and machines have equal need to engage in these activities, and they need to communicate about them. So even if we can find very high-performance decision procedures for important problems, there is some reason to believe that these procedures should not be used. Instead, in a system that is intended to have human-like performance and to cooperate with humans, the greatest weight should be placed on mimicking human reasoning. Of course, this idea has been well understood in the AI community, particularly the knowledge-based systems community, for years. We suggest that it is also important to the automated-mathematics community.

13.7 Meta-Knowledge

As a mathematics book progresses, the nature of what constitutes meaningful mathematics changes. Partly this is a matter of new domain concepts being introduced, but it is also a result of the reader coming to accept new ways for describing objects and new techniques for proof. Thus, mathematical text conveys meta-knowledge of various sorts.

While mathematics books often convey this knowledge implicitly, simply by using new forms of definition and proof, PRL libraries contain explicit meta-level objects that describe how to build and manipulate PRL objects [13]. For example, methods for building proofs for certain kinds of propositions are extremely common in PRL libraries.

PRL meta-knowledge is expressed as code written in the ML programming language. ML was developed as the programming language component of the Edinburgh LCF system [16]. LCF is an implementation of a typed lambda calculus, together with an ML based framework for building proofs in the calculus. Thus, while ML has become a well known functional language [25], it was originally created for the very purpose to which it is put in PRL.

The NuPRL ML implementation is adapted from the Lisp-based Cambridge ML system. ML and PRL coexist within a single Lisp image, both maintaining state, and with control passing back and forth as necessary. Generally PRL is considered the top-level, with calls into ML eventually returning results to be used by PRL. However, ML may invoke PRL recursively, so the interaction can be complex.

ML can be used from PRL in several ways. First, ML expressions can be typed directly to the ML interpreter for evaluation. In this mode PRL simply functions as a read-eval-print loop. Second, a specified piece of ML code can be invoked to examine a PRL goal and attempt to construct a (partial) proof for the goal. In this *refinement* mode ML is used to provide extensions to the built-in PRL proof rules. Finally, ML code can look at a proof tree and construct another tree, for instance doing global editing operations or proof by analogy. In this *transformation* mode ML is used to extend the editing operations of the built-in proof editor.

In order to let ML manipulate PRL objects, the terms, formulas, goals, rules, and proofs of PRL are provided as new ML primitive data types. For example, the following functions are defined in PRL's ML implementation:

$$\text{Assumptions : Goal} \rightarrow \text{Formula List}$$
$$\text{Is\_conjunction : Formula} \rightarrow \text{Boolean}$$
$$\text{Rule\_of\_proof : Proof} \rightarrow \text{Rule}$$

The first and last are selectors (projections) that decompose structures. The second tests the type of a value, in this case examining a formula's main operator.

A refinement tactic is an ML term of type Goal → (partial) Proof. That is, a tactic is a function which takes the ML encoding of a PRL goal and returns the ML encoding of a PRL proof. The proof may not be complete, but it will be a tree that has the goal at the root and some number of PRL rules and subgoals forming the body. [2]

---

[2]The actual type of refinement tactics is somewhat more complicated, being Goal → (Goal List ×

Tactics, that is, functions that build proofs, use as their primitive building operation the built-in function Refine: rule → tactic. Refine takes as input the encoding of a PRL proof-rule name and returns a function which when applied to a goal attempts to apply the corresponding PRL proof rule to the goal.

An example of building a simple tactic using refine is "Refine AndIntro," which builds a tactic that maps goals whose conclusion is a conjunction into proof trees that have the same goal and have children that result from applying the "and intro" rule to the goal.

Tactics are intended to map goals (or proofs) to proofs. However, just as proof rules can fail to apply to a goal, tactics can similarly fail. ML provides a mechanism, similar to throw/catch in Lisp, for signaling and handling failure during function invocations. When a tactic is applied to a goal either the tactic will fail, causing a branch in control flow to a surrounding error handler, or else it will succeed, returning a proof and possibly generating some side-effects in the ML state. Tactics are generally written so that failures produce no side effects.

The most primitive one-step tactics are instances of "Refine." These tactics succeed or fail as the proof rule applies or does not apply to the input goal. All other tactics are ultimately built by composing these primitives. One can do this composition explicitly by invoking the primitive tactics on goals and then mapping other primitives across resulting lists of subgoals, but an easier way is provided using *tacticals*. Tacticals are to tactics as functionals are to functions. One can build a tactic by combining existing tactics using a tactical.

The basic tacticals are Then, ThenL, OrElse, and Repeat. "A Then B" is a tactic that when applied to a goal first applies tactic A and if it succeeds then applies tactic B to each of the leaves of the resulting proof tree. If A or B fail then "Then" fails. "A ThenL B" (ThenL means "then list") takes a tactic A and a list of tactics B. After applying A it makes sure the length of B is the same as the number of leaves in the proof tree produced by A, and then it applies each element of B to the corresponding leaf of the proof tree. "ThenL" fails if A or B fail. "A OrElse B" applies A, and if it fails then it applies B instead. If B also fails then the entire composed tactic fails. "Repeat A" applies the tactic A to the goal and repeatedly applies it to the leaves. It stops at each leaf on which A fails. This builds a maximal-sized tree with A as the proof rule at each internal node.

(Proof List → Proof)), which is similar to the way tactics are defined in LCF. A goal is mapped to a goal list, which is the list of unproven subgoals at the fringe of the proof tree, together with a function, called a *validation*, that takes proofs of those subgoals into a proof of the goal. Actually applying the validation is left until later, when the caller of the tactic actually needs the final proof. This mechanism makes it easier to backtrack during proving, because the underlying proof structures are not being modified, hence need not be restored upon backtracking.

13.7.1   Refinement Tactics

As mentioned earlier, tactics are used in two ways in PRL. The most common use is as refinement tactics, which extend the set of proof rules in the proof editor.

Imagine the screen is displaying an unproven goal in a proof. If the user enters a proof rule that is not recognized as a built-in rule, then the text of the rule is passed to the concurrently running ML interpreter along with the goal. The text is parsed as if it were an ML expression, and the expression is applied to the ML encoding of the PRL goal. Thus, the text should denote an ML object of type tactic.

After the tactic is applied to the goal, the resulting partial proof tree is packaged together with the proof-rule text and retained internally by PRL as the representation of the proof step. The unproven leaves of the tree, if any, are displayed as the children of the proof step. Thus, refinement tactics are like derived proof rules – they may succeed or fail, and they are used in exactly the same way as proof rules.

Refinement tactics never build invalid proofs. This is because of two aspects of the implementation. First, ML is a strongly typed language, so that any objects claimed to be of type proof are in fact assured to be of that type. Second, when Refine (actually, a validation produced by Refine) composes subproofs into a proof, it makes sure that the subproofs are not merely of type proof, but also that they have the correct subgoals as their roots. Since proofs in ML can be created only by use of Refine, together these constraints assure that all ML-built proofs are valid.

As examples of tactics and tacticals, we consider several tactics built in LambdaPRL that assist with simple predicate calculus over integers and lists.

The first example, called "Immediate," is built from instances of Refine using tacticals. Immediate is intended to capture a class of reasoning that one might consider especially trivial and obvious.

$$
\begin{array}{lll}
\text{Immediate} = \text{Repeat} & (& (\text{Refine AndIntro}) \\
& \text{OrElse} & (\text{Refine AndElim}) \\
& \vdots & \\
& \text{OrElse} & (\text{Refine Hyp}) \\
& \text{OrElse} & (\text{Refine Arith/Equality/Simplification}))
\end{array}
$$

Immediate reasoning repeatedly tries to apply simple proof rules that break apart assumptions and conclusions in simpler components, until the subgoals follow by hypothesis or the LambdaPRL cooperating decision procedure described earlier. This may succeed in completely proving a goal or may leave unproven subgoals.

An example to which Immediate would effectively apply is

$$x \text{ in } y..z \gg x \neq z \Rightarrow x < z \text{ by Immediate.}$$

Recall that "x in $y..z$" is a definition for a conjunction. In this case Immediate does AndElim on the hypothesis, then ImpliesIntro on the conclusion, and then the decision procedure shows that if $y \leq x$ and $x \leq z$ and $x \neq z$ then $x < z$ must follow. Thus, this proof is completed by the Immediate tactic without user assistance.

Immediate is so named because it is intended to capture reasoning that anyone familiar with elementary algebra and logic can see without significant thought. This is the kind of reasoning one prefers not even to see sketched – it is "immediate."

Other tactics have been defined that capture less obvious sorts of reasoning. One such is "Trivial," which extends Immediate by trying to reason from universally quantified formulas and trying to prove existentially quantified formulas. Trivial is based on heuristics that suggest choosing terms already present in the goal to instantiate the quantifiers. Trivial is capable of proving the associativity of append and that $|\text{append}(x, y)| = |x| + |y|$, once the user says that induction is to be used. Thus, in PRL one would say the associativity of append is a "trivial induction."

The tactic "Skolem t," removes a string of leading $\forall$ quantifiers from a conclusion, instantiates an $\exists$ using the term t, and then applies Trivial. The tactic "BackChain" looks in the goal for assumptions of the form $A1 \wedge A2 \wedge \ldots \wedge An \Rightarrow (B1 \vee B2 \vee \ldots \vee Bk)$ and does back-chaining through these assumptions.

13.7.2 Transformation Tactics

Besides being used to extend the set of proof rules recognized by the proof editor, tactics can be used to extend the set of proof-editing operations. The difference is that proof rules remain as visible steps in the proof, while editing operations are forgotten once they have completed a change to the proof structure.

The primary built-in editing operation on proofs is to change the refinement rule at some node. This deletes all the children of the node, including any substructure below those children. Thus, this kind of change is seldom desired once large subtrees have been developed below a node, because it destroys these subtrees. A more useful pair of extended editing operations would permit "cut" and "paste" on subtrees. Transformation tactics are the mechanism by which such operations can be defined.

Transformation tactics are proof $\rightarrow$ proof mappings. Typically they map their input proof to some other proof with more desirable structure. There is a single keystroke proof-editor operation, called transform, that may be invoked whenever the display shows the root of a subtree of a proof. Transform accepts the name of an ML tactic, passes the entire subtree rooted at the currently displayed node to that tactic, and then replaces the subtree with the result returned from the tactic. Thus, transformation tactics extend the proof-editing operations with user-defined mechanisms.

In order to assure that only well-formed proofs are built, the transform operation checks to make sure that the result of a transformation tactic has the same goal as its input. Since all tactics are known only to build proofs consistent with their goals, this goal check is sufficient to make sure that transformations do not introduce invalid steps into proofs.

The cut and paste operations mentioned above are implemented by two tactics, called Mark and Copy. Mark simply returns its input, thereby leaving the marked subtree unchanged, but has the side effect of recording a copy of the tree in a global ML variable. The copy persists until Mark is again invoked. Copy ignores its input, and returns the value of the variable previously set by Mark. Thus, if one Marks a tree, moves to a place with the same goal but no proof, and does Copy, then a copy of the marked tree will be inserted into the proof. If a genuine cut operation is desired, the original tree can be removed after marking simply by deleting its initial refinement rule.

There are richer versions of Copy, which attempt to use the marked proof as a guide to prove a similar, but not necessarily identical, goal. Simple variations allow the new goal to have additional assumptions, which requires Copy to modify the assumption numbers that are specified in proof rules of subtrees. Copy may also try invoking Immediate or other tactics on subgoals that are not successfully proved by the corresponding parts of the marked proof.

These extensions to Copy provide an elementary facility for proof by analogy. If one were so inclined, the transformation tactic framework could be used to build increasingly powerful mechanisms for building new proofs from old.

13.7.3   Discussion of Tactics

Tactics are exceptionally useful in PRL and form a large fraction of the contents of typical libraries. Without them, it would be infeasible for users to develop even relatively simple proofs. We conjecture that some means of collecting and applying meta-knowledge, at least as powerful as the PRL tactic mechanism, is necessary in any serious mathematics environment.

One of the disadvantages of PRL's approach to meta-knowledge is that users must invoke tactics explicitly, hence they must know the names of all the relevant tactics. This is a substantial burden which increases as libraries grow.

One technique we have used to limit the burden is called the *autotactic*. There is a global ML variable, changeable by the user, that generally holds a transformation tactic as its value. Each time a primitive proof step is completed in the proof editor, this transformation tactic is automatically applied to each of the subgoals of the step. This gives the system an opportunity to prove any easy subgoals automatically, before the user sees them.

The typical autotactic is similar to the Immediate tactic described earlier. It quickly tries a variety of different basic proof rules and fails completely if it does not succeed in producing a complete proof. In principle, one could imagine having an indexing scheme for tactics, so that the autotactic could automatically apply those tactics from the library which appear potentially applicable to the current goal. To the extent that such an indexing mechanism was successful, the autotactic mechanism would alleviate the need for users to remember and explicitly specify tactic names.

One of the general principles we learned from using ML in PRL is that the system's extension facilities should have access to everything granted human users. For example, if users can create library objects or view more than one object at a time, then some analogous facilities should be made available for use in tactics.

There are two reasons for this principle. First, if a mechanism is useful to a human attempting to build a proof, then there is good reason to believe that it will also be useful to a machine. Second, even if we can imagine mechanical provers that don't use human methods, in practice much of the system's meta-knowledge is developed by humans noticing patterns in their own activity and then recording the patterns in the form of tactics. Since the patterns are about the human's interaction with the mechanisms of the system, tactics must be able to perceive similar information and take similar actions.

This principle leads to a system that is reflective, in the sense that the system is one of the users of its own user interface.

13.8   Extraction

Once a domain is discussed in a PRL library, we want the system to be able to extract executable code from the discussion. This is facilitated in LambdaPRL by basing the system on a constructive predicate calculus, and in NuPRL by basing the system on a constructive type theory. While this does not assure that every discussion will have interesting executable content, it is natural in these languages to express computational discussions in an implicitly computational manner.

After one proves a theorem in PRL, code can be extracted from the proof. The function of the code is determined by the statement of the theorem, and in fact the theorem is a specification for the code. Each logical connective in the statement of the theorem corresponds to a particular aspect of the input/output behavior of the code.

The general interpretation of the constructive meaning of connectives together with mechanisms for extracting code from proofs can be found in [2] and [11], for predicate calculus and type theory, respectively. Here we present a few simple examples to give the flavor of the constructive interpretations.

If one proves a proposition of the form $(\forall x : A)(\exists y : B)P_{x,y}$ then one can extract a function $f : A \to B$ such that for any input, a in A, $f(a)$ is in B and $P_{a,f(a)}$ holds. Thus, the PRL library that concludes with

$$(\forall n : \mathcal{N})(\exists p : \text{prime-factorization})(\text{value}(p) = n)$$

allows one to extract a function which calculates prime factorizations of natural numbers. When running PRL, this function can be extracted and then executed on specific numerical inputs.

Other examples of extraction are:

$$\big(\forall G\text{: LL(1) grammar}\big)\big(\exists P\text{: rec. descent parser}\big)$$
$$\big(\forall s\text{:}\mathcal{L}(G)\big)\big(P(s) \text{ is a parse tree in } G \text{ for } s\big)$$

from which one can extract a function mapping LL(1) grammars to recursive descent parsers,

$$(\forall g\text{:int} \to (\text{int} \to \text{int}))(\exists d\text{:int} \to \text{int})(\forall i\text{:int})(d \neq g(i))$$

from which one can extract a function that returns a diagonal element from any supposed enumerator of the int $\to$ int functions, and

$$(\forall r : \mathcal{R})(\forall s : \mathcal{R})(\exists t : \mathcal{R})\dots$$

which is the beginning of a specification for functions that manipulate real numbers, perhaps representing those numbers are infinite convergent sequences of rationals.

Extraction itself is computationally cheap. The resulting code can be interpreted or compiled using familiar technology. This approach is adequate for an experimental system such as PRL. However, a more serious programming environment would require optimization of extracted code, which can be complex. Techniques for such optimizations are presented in [2] and [31].

While obtaining code from a completed theorem is sometimes a PRL user's motivating goal, most interaction with PRL goes into building libraries. People generally use PRL as a proving environment, rather than as a programming environment. These users do produce a substantial amount of ML code, but since ML is implemented as a separate programming language from the PRL executable language, tactics are built explicitly, rather than being extracted from discussions.

Thus, we have accumulated little direct evidence so far to support or refute our hypothesis that correct code can be produced most easily as a by-product of formal discussions of problems. A positive answer to this question can come from the creation of a production-quality system for mathematics and programming. A negative answer might come from discovering some serious and apparently insurmountable problem in this sort of system. Since we have built a system, learned a lot, and not come across insurmountable problems, we believe it is appropriate to further investigate this hypothesis by continuing work on PRL-like systems.

13.9   Conclusion

Users at Cornell and elsewhere have developed a variety of libraries in NuPRL. These include number theory up through unique prime factorization, automata theory to the pumping lemma for regular sets, elementary theory of sequential programs including a linear time saddleback array search [17], and work related to Girard's paradox, denotational semantics, parallel program semantics, and real analysis. Library building continues on a range of topics.

The NuPRL system has been distributed to a variety of research sites, including other parts of Cornell, MIT, Carnegie Mellon, University of Edinburgh, University of Texas, Cambridge University, INRIA, and to sites in Japan, Germany, Sweden, and elsewhere.

NuPRL is large and fairly slow, but it is reliable, reasonably portable, and very powerful. We believe the main idea of the system, that it is possible to build a new kind of active, knowledge-based medium, has proven itself. On this basis, we think a new "PRL-like" system should be constructed, based on what we learned from PRL. In particular, our experience has led us to formulate the following requirements for such a new system. These ideas are being incorporated into the design of MetaPRL.

Mathematics is a tremendously creative activity in which new language is constantly defined. For a particular mathematician, defined language gradually becomes as primitive as anything considered foundational by philosophers. Thus, a mathematics environment should make the least possible commitment to any particular language, mathematical foundation, or linguistic assumptions, thereby providing great flexibility to support the variety of mathematical language that already exists and will be invented.

This is not to say that tools for defining particular kinds of mathematical language, such as the Logical Framework [19], should be avoided, only that they should be in the library, not built into the system. Also, unlike the PRL macro-like definition facility, defined language should be able to be as primitive as any built-in language, and built-in language should be as analyzable as any defined language. Finally, it is especially clear that the system must support constant incremental language extension, and not depend on an iterative process of language specification and system recompilation.

The notion of what constitutes a proof is as fluid as the underlying language. We would hypothesize that any locally checkable set of structural constraints on the underlying linguistic forms could constitute a notion of proof. Thus, the system should support the accumulation of named collections of local linguistic constraints, to be applied according to the social needs of the user community. Typically, each portion of the library would be mechanically checked for consistency with some widely recognized constraint set, such as "Johnson's Elementary Algebra, Revised" or "Martin-Löf's 1980 type theory paper." Thus, in the domain of proof, two primary functions of the system are to maintain inviolable published versions of constraint sets and to check text for consistency with those publications.

Since the active behavior of the system must be extended as the content of libraries grows, and since libraries will be built using many hardware platforms, the system must include a fast, flexible, and widely supported symbolic programming language. Other executable languages will certainly be built on top of this language, so many users may not see the base language. If at all possible, the language should support many existing reasoning tools that have been developed by the automated reasoning and other AI communities. In our opinion, Common Lisp appears a suitable choice.

The system itself, including its definition, constraint, and execution mechanisms, should be expressed in the library. This will permit reflection on the basic processes of reasoning, once suitable mathematical notions are defined much higher up in the library. That this sort of reasoning will be circular, and therefore of curious validity, is appropriate. Most agents that think about themselves use their own minds to do it.

The system must be built for robustness and efficiency in the face of very large libraries. Earlier we mentioned the relevance of persistent object systems, constructed on appropriate database technology, to provide sharing, distributed storage, and reliability. Version control and flexible inter-object reference are also key concerns.

Within this linguistic universe, many different mathematical frameworks will be defined. Some will be called foundations by various parties, but people will argue about these claims. Results introduced at one point in the library will claim meta-mathematical properties of constructions defined elsewhere, for instance that one foundation is explainable in terms of another, or that some theory developed by another group is demonstrably false. In general, the library will grow with compatible and incompatible theories, and a great mess will be made. This is as it should be, and could be taken as a sign of success for a new medium.

Acknowledgments

The National Science Foundation provided substantial support for the PRL project through a series of grants over many years. Christine Bowker and Peter Lee provided similar support for this chapter.

References

[1] S. Allen. *A Non-Type-Theoretic Semantics for Type-Theoretic Language*. Doctoral Dissertation, Department of Computer Science, Cornell University, Ithaca, New York, 1987.

[2] J. Bates. *A Logic for Correct Program Development*. Doctoral Dissertation, Department of Computer Science, Cornell University, Ithaca, New York, 1979.

[3] J. Bates. *The PRL Mathematics Environment: A Knowledge Based Medium*. Technical report, Department of Computer Science, Cornell University, Ithaca, New York, 1986.

[4] J. Bates. *MetaPrl: A Framework for Knowledge Based Media*. Workshop on Meta-Languages and Tools, Carnegie Mellon University, November 1987.

[5] J. Bates. *MetaPrl: The Core of an Environment for (Programming) Knowledge*. Workshop on Advanced Environments, Berkeley, California, June 1988.

[6] J. Bates and R. Constable. *The Nearly Ultimate PRL*. Technical report TR-83-551, Department of Computer Science, Cornell University, Ithaca, New York, 1983.

[7] J. Bates and R. Constable. *Proofs as Programs*. ACM Transactions on Programming Languages and Systems, Vol 7, No 1, January 1985, pp. 113-136.

[8] J. Bell and M. Machover. *A Course in Mathematical Logic*. North-Holland, Amsterdam, 1977.

[9] T. Chan. *An Algorithm for Checking PL/CV Arithmetic Inferences*. Technical report TR-77-326, Department of Computer Science, Cornell University, Ithaca, New York, 1978.

[10] W. Cleaveland. *Type-theoretic Models of Concurrency*. Doctoral Dissertation, Department of Computer Science, Cornell University, Ithaca, New York, 1987.

[11] R. Constable, et al. *Implementing Mathematics with the NuPRL Proof Development System*. Prentice-Hall, Englewood Cliffs, New Jersey, 1986.

[12] R. Constable, S. Johnson, and C. Eichenlaub. *Introduction to the PL/CV2 Programming Logic*. Lecture Notes in Computer Science, Vol 135, Springer-Verlag, New York, 1982.

[13] R. Constable, T. Knoblock, and J. Bates. *Writing Programs That Construct Proofs*. Journal of Automated Reasoning, Vol 1, No 3, 1985, pp. 285-326.

[14] R. Constable and D. Zlatin. *The Type Theory of PL/CV3*. ACM Transactions on Programming Languages and Systems, Vol 6, No 1, 1984, pp. 94-117.

[15] G. Gentzen. *Investigations into Logical Deduction*. In *The collected papers of Gerhard Gentzen*, edited by M. Szabo, North-Holland, Amsterdam, 1969.

[16] M. Gordon, A. Milner, and C. Wadsworth. *Edinburgh LCF: A Mechanized Logic of Computation*. Lecture Notes in Computer Science, Vol 78, Springer-Verlag, New York, 1979.

[17] D. Gries. *The Science of Programming*. Springer-Verlag, New York, 1982.

[18] R. Harper. *Aspects of the Implementation of Type Theory*. Doctoral Dissertation, Department of Computer Science, Cornell University, Ithaca, New York, 1985.

[19] R. Harper, F. Honsell, and G. Plotkin. *A Framework for Defining Logics*. Second Annual Symposium on Logic in Computer Science, IEEE, 1987, revised version available as technical report CMU-CS-89-173, School of Computer Science, Carnegie Mellon University, 1989.

[20] D. Howe. *Automating Reasoning in an Implementation of Constructive Type Theory*. Doctoral Dissertation, Department of Computer Science, Cornell University, Ithaca, New York, 1988.

[21] A. Kay and A. Goldberg. *Personal Dynamic Media*. IEEE Computer, vol 31, March, 1977.

[22] T. Knoblock. *Metamathematical Extensibility in Type Theory*. Doctoral Dissertation, Department of Computer Science, Cornell University, Ithaca, New York, 1987.

[23] P. Martin-Löf. *Constructive Mathematics and Computer Programming*. In Sixth International Congress for Logic, Methodology, and Philosophy of Science, North-Holland, Amsterdam, 1982, pp. 73-118.

[24] P. Mendler. *Inductive Definition in Type Theory*. Doctoral Dissertation, Department of Computer Science, Cornell University, Ithaca, New York, 1987.

[25] R. Milner, M. Tofte, and R. Harper. *The Definition of Standard ML*. MIT Press, Cambridge, Massachusetts, 1990

[26] G. Nelson. *Techniques for Program Verification*. Technical report CSL-81-10, Xerox Palo Alto Research Center, Palo Alto, California, June 1981.

[27] G. Nelson and D. Oppen. *Simplification by Cooperating Decision Procedures*. ACM Transactions on Programming Languages and Systems, Vol 1, No 2, 1979, pp. 245-257.

[28] G. Nelson and D. Oppen. *Fast Decision Algorithms Based on Congruence Closure*. Journal of the ACM, Vol 27, No 2, April 1980, pp. 356-364.

[29] PRL Staff. *PRL Programmer's Manual (LambdaPRL VAX Version)*. Department of Computer Science, Cornell University, Ithaca, New York, 1983.

[30] H. Rheingold. *Tools for Thought: The People and Ideas Behind the Next Computer Revolution*. Simon and Schuster, New York, 1985.

[31] J. Sasaki. *The Extraction and Optimization of Programs from Constructive Proofs*. Doctoral Dissertation, Department of Computer Science, Cornell University, Ithaca, New York, 1985.

[32] D. Scott. *Constructive Validity*. Symposium on Automated Demonstration, Lecture Notes in Mathematics, Vol 125, Springer-Verlag, New York, 1970.

[33] M. Stefik. *The Next Knowledge Medium*. AI Magazine, Vol 7, No 1 (Spring 1986), pp. 34-46.

14 A Simple System for Object Storage in Common Lisp

Eugene J. Rollins

Spartan is a simple system for persistent object storage in Common Lisp engineered to meet some of the needs of program and proof development environments. It handles highly structured objects that may have structure sharing among their parts. Since one can save and restore regular Common Lisp data structures, using Spartan incurs no run-time overhead. For this reason, it is especially suitable for computation-intensive applications.

14.1 Introduction

Program and proof development environments can enable users to share work with each other through libraries of published objects (e.g., program components, results of program analysis, theorems, proof structures). Several characteristics of development systems distinguish them from traditional business database applications (e.g., airline reservation systems, automated teller machines). Development systems deal with more-highly structured objects. They often feature computation-intensive subsystems. Libraries for development environments are updated less frequently than business databases.

Spartan is a persistent object manager for Common Lisp engineered for implementing object libraries for development applications. Spartan enables one to save and restore regular Common Lisp data structures, for example, numbers, characters, symbols, conses, arrays, hash tables, and structures. Aside from actually saving and restoring objects, there is no overhead in computing with saved or restored data. Unlike many other object managers and database systems that interface to Common Lisp, Spartan does not require the use of an object-oriented programming system. This feature is important for computation-intensive subsystems, such as higher-order type inference, where one cannot afford the poor performance of method invocation on objects. Although there is no direct support for object-oriented programming yet, it is not precluded either. Common Lisp can be used as a query language because Spartan provides a function **scan** for applying a query function to all objects in a particular object store. Spartan is simple and portable; it runs in several Common Lisp implementations on Apple Macintoshes and Unix machines.

14.2   Programming Interface Overview

The programming interface of Spartan comprises functions and macros for managing individual stores, accessing data in those stores, initiating transactions, and describing properties of persistent data. The interface is outlined in this section and elaborated in the sections that follow.

The interface is adapted from PS-Algol [2]. In PS-Algol one can put the root of a heap-allocated data structure into a database. On *commit*, all the data reachable from that root is stored in the database. One can retrieve such a data structure from a database by loading its root. The rest of the data structure is loaded on demand as the data structure is traversed or accessed. To preserve structure sharing and to implement demand-driven retrieval PS-Algol has two kinds of pointers: (1) (memory) pointers, and (2) persistent identifiers (PIDs). When the root of a data structure is retrieved, any pointer fields in the root are represented by PIDs. When a PID is dereferenced the node it references is loaded, and the PID is replaced by a pointer.

Spartan differs from PS-Algol is several ways. First of all, by default when one loads the root of a data structure, everything reachable from the root is loaded at that time. Through declarations, the user can specify certain parts of data structures to be loaded on demand. Secondly, Spartan preserves structure sharing among a collection of data structures, but to improve performance it uses PIDs sparingly. This interface enables Spartan to deal with highly-structured objects.

Persistent data is kept in a *store*, which is a mapping from keys to values. One can **enter** (write) and **lookup** (read) values associated with keys. The arguments to **enter** are **store**, **key**, and **value**. The arguments to **lookup** are **store** and **key**.

```
(enter parts-data 'keyboard keyboard-record)
(setq the-cpu (lookup parts-data 'cpu))
```

The function **connect** allows one to find an existing store and make a connection to it. If the store does not exist it is created.

```
(setq parts-data (connect "Mac Parts"))
```

Spartan uses two mechanisms for synchronizing users: transactions and version control. Transactions provide exclusive locks on stores. The version control mechanism provides access to multiple versions of objects and exclusive locks on individual objects. Although transactions do not permit any concurrency, they can be short in duration since objects that are looked up are accessible between transactions. The combination of store and object locks affords a programmer a great deal of flexibility in engineering an application, without the complexity and overhead of fine-grained concurrency. The example in Section 14.6 features the function **new-part-addition**, which separates dialog with the user from the locking of the parts store during integrity checking and updating.

In applications where libraries are updated less frequently, synchronization can be optimistic. Transactions insure that the store is kept in a consistent state. But, object locks are optional. Conflicting object writes succeed and the new object values become siblings in the object's version tree.

The macro **with-transaction** takes three arguments: **store, io-direction**, and **body**. Evaluating the macro **with-transaction** starts a transaction on **store** by opening and locking it. After that **body** is evaluated. A transaction ends normally by completing the evaluation of **body**. Alternatively, a transaction may end if it is aborted in several ways described in Section 14.4.1. If a transaction is aborted, the contents of the store revert to what they were before the transaction was started.

```
(with-transaction (parts-data :output)
  (enter parts-data 'display display-record)
  (enter parts-data 'cpu cpu-record)
  (enter parts-data 'keyboard keyboard-record))

(with-transaction (parts-data :io)
  (let ((the-cpu (lookup parts-data 'cpu)))
    (change-cost the-cpu 3100)
    (enter parts-data 'cpu the-cpu)))
```

The **scan** function allows one to use Common Lisp as a query language. It takes three arguments: **store, env**, and **query**. **Scan** iterates over all entries in **store** applying the function **query** to each key/value pair. **Query** takes three arguments: **env, key**, and **value**. The argument **env** can be used to maintain some state during iteration over **store**. The **scan** iteration can be prematurely ended without aborting a transaction.

```
(defun print-all-expensive-parts ()
  "List all parts that cost more than $100."
  (with-transaction (parts-data :input)
    (scan parts-data nil #'print-expensive-part)))

(defun print-expensive-part (env key part)
  (if (> (get-cost part) 100)
      (format t "~S $~S~%" (get-name part) (get-cost part))))
```

Since Common Lisp is a computationally complete language, transitive closure queries are expressible. See the function **total-part-cost** in the example in Section 14.6.

14.3   Data Access

The data access functions enable one to read and write the contents of a store. The functions **enter** and **lookup** are described in the previous section. The optional arguments and return values of these functions, as well as the function **release-lock** are explained in Section 14.4.2 on version control. The function **count-entries** will return the total number of key/value pairs in the store.

Data Access Functions		
enter	store key value {get-lock}	-> branchp
lookup	store key {version} {get-lock}	-> value
release-lock	store key {version}	
scan	store env query	-> new-env
query	env key value	-> new-env
count-entries	store	-> integer

The **scan** function, introduced in Section 14.2, iterates over all entries in the store applying the function **query** (the third argument to **scan**) to each key/value pair. The first time **query** is called it is passed the second **scan** argument, **env**. On subsequent calls to **query**, it is passed the value produced by the preceding call to **query**.

```
(defun add-all-costs ()
  "Determine the total cost of buying one of each part."
  (multiple-value-bind (status total-costs)
      (with-transaction (parts-data :input)
        (scan parts-data 0 #'add-part-cost))
    total-costs))

(defun add-part-cost (total key part) (+ total (get-cost part)))
```

The function **query** may terminate the scan of the store at any time by throwing (raising the exception) **scan-exit**, which the **scan** function will catch.

```
(defun expensive-part-p ()
  "Is there any part that costs more than $100?"
  (multiple-value-bind (status result)
      (with-transaction (parts-data :input)
        (scan parts-data nil #'expensivep))
    result))

(defun expensivep (env key part)
  (if (> (get-cost part) 100)
      (throw 'scan-exit t)
      nil))
```

14.4 Access Synchronization

14.4.1 Transactions

One uses transactions for synchronization with other users who may want access to a store.

Transaction Macros			
`with-transaction`	`(store io-direction) form*`	`-> status, value`	
`abort-transaction`	`abort-value`		
`multiple-catch`	`(tag*) form*`	`-> status, value`	
`multiple-catch-1`	`(tag*) form*`	`-> status, value`	

The **io-direction** may be one of the following keywords: **:input**, **:output**, or **:io**. Currently, the lock limits access to only one user at a time. A future version may allow multiple readers, or one writer.

The macro **with-transaction** returns two (multiple) values. The first is a status, and the second is the value returned by the last **form**. If a transaction completes successfully it returns a status of **nil**. A transaction can be aborted, and the contents of the store will be reverted to what they were at the start of the transaction. An aborted transaction returns the symbol **transaction-aborted** for its status. The example below allows the user to retry aborted transactions. If the user declines a retry, the program halts. If the transaction commits, the loop exits and the program continues.

```
(loop
  (multiple-value-bind (status value)
      (with-transaction (parts-data :input)
        (read-the-store-contents parts-data)
        (if (predicate) (abort-transaction t))
        (read-more parts-data))
    (if status
      (unless (yes-or-no-p "Transaction aborted - Try again? ")
        (error "Can not continue; program aborted."))
      (return))))
```

A transaction is aborted if control is passed out of the body by any dynamic exit facility such as a **throw**, or by any lexical exit facility such as **return**. The **with-transaction** macro contains an **unwind-protect** to execute an abort in all such cases.

Consider the following piece of code.

```
(catch 'illegal-value
  (with-transaction (parts-data :input) (compute)))
```

There is no way to tell whether control passed to the catch form because of a **throw** or by completion of the transaction. To make handling this situation easier Spartan provides the macro **multiple-catch**. This macro serves as a target for transfer of control by **throw** in the same manner as **catch**. However, **multiple-catch** differs in three ways: (1) it serves as a target for several tags, (2) it does not evaluate the tags, and (3) it returns two (multiple) values: a status and a value. When a **multiple-catch** expression catches a **throw** to one of its **tags**, the status it returns is the tag of the **throw** and the value is the value of the **throw**.

The **multiple-catch** macro assumes the last form in its body also returns a status/value pair, and returns this pair if control flow passes to the **multiple-catch** expression normally (without a **throw**). The **multiple-catch-1** macro assumes the last **form** returns a single value. If control flow passes to the **multiple-catch-1** expression normally, it returns a status of **nil** and the value of the last form in its body.

```
(multiple-value-bind (status value)
    (multiple-catch (illegal-value)
      (with-transaction (parts-data :input) (compute)))
  (cond
    ((eq status 'transaction-aborted) (format t "Abort"))
    ((eq status 'illegal-value) (format t "Illegal value-Abort"))
    ((null status) (format t "Commit"))))
```

14.4.2   Version Control

Each key in a store maps to a tree of object versions. At first, each key in a store is uninitialized. A call of lookup with an uninitialized key returns the symbol **not-found**. A call of **enter** with an uninitialized key creates the root of a version tree for that key. The version identifier **1** indicates the version at the root of a version tree. The first new version appended to the root is identified as version **2**. If new versions are appended linearly in this fashion, their version identifiers will be successive integers. If a new version is appended to a version tree node that already has a child version node, its version identifier will be a list of integers (e.g., (**1 1 1**)). The sequence of versions that were appended to their parents first, starting from the root, is the *main branch* of the version tree. The last version of the main branch is called the *main leaf*.

The functions **lookup** and **enter** take a keyword (optional) argument **version**, which defaults to the main leaf. The **lookup** function will retrieve the version with version identifier **version**. The **enter** function inserts a new version node into the version tree by appending it onto the parent node identified by **version**. For each of these functions, if the keyword argument **get-lock** is not **nil**, an exclusive lock is obtained on the identified version node. Object locks persist across Lisp sessions. The

release-lock function removes a lock that the user has on the identified version node. Locks are automatically removed on the parent version when a new version is appended.

```
(with-transaction (parts-data :input)
  (setq the-display (lookup parts-data 'display :get-lock t)))
(change-cost the-display 280)
(with-transaction (parts-data :output)
  (enter parts-data 'display the-display))
```

For each user, and for each key, the *active* version is the one most recently entered or looked up by that user. Without the keyword argument **version**, a call to **enter** creates a tree edge from the active version to the new value. If the user does not obtain a version lock, another user may write a new version for that key between the first user's last access and current update. The first user's new value would be appended to his active version. The **enter** function returns **nil** if the new version was added to the main branch and returns **t** otherwise. With this information the user can take appropriate action.

The support for version control is not yet fully developed. The additional functionality needed includes functions for handling version identifiers, new optional arguments for the data access functions, and functions for rearranging and pruning version trees.

14.5   Defining Properties of Persistent Objects

In PS-Algol the granularity of *loadable* items is a data structure node. This means that PIDs are encountered and translated quite often. The system must somehow decide how much data to read from disk with no clues from the developer. The granularity of *savable* items is an entire data structure and all that is reachable from it. The developer cannot conveniently save the "main" part of a data structure representing an object, and ignore additional reachable data. In LISP systems data structures become intimately intertwined to the point where saving a single data structure could result in saving the entire heap.

In Spartan one can circumscribe the portion of a data structure that represents a single object through the use of additional declarations. For example, an abstract syntax tree (AST) could be represented by a structure with three fields: operator, arguments (a possibly empty list of ASTs), and an attribute set. AST object could be defined to be the operator and arguments and *not* the attribute set. The attribute set could be declared to be either (1) a separate object loaded on demand, or (2) a non-persistent field to be recomputed. The save and load granularity would be objects. Then PIDs would be encountered less often and larger amounts of data would be loaded at once.

The macro **defstructure** extends the Common Lisp macro **defstruct** to allow one to define object boundaries. Two additional slot options are recognized.

The option **:volatile** *x*, where *x* is not **nil**, specifies that the slot should not be saved when an instance of the structure is saved into a store. If *x* is **nil** this option has no effect. The argument form *x* is not evaluated.

The option **:demand** *x*, where *x* is not **nil**, specifies that the slot should not be read into memory when an instance of the structure is read into memory from a store. Instead, it should be read on demand, when the slot is accessed. If *x* is **nil** this option has no effect. The argument form *x* is not evaluated.

Examples of persistent structures are:

```
(defstructure ast
  (op nil :type operator)
  (args nil :type (or null (list ast)))
  (attr nil :volatile t))

(defstructure version-tree
  (version-id nil :type number)
  (author nil :type string)
  (program nil :type ast :demand t)
  (children nil :type (or null (list version-tree)))))
```

The macro **defstructure** defines a function **save-***structure-name* (e.g., **save-ast**) that is used to save the structure in a store. Note that any slot of a persistent structure that is of a non-persistent type (e.g., a stream, or a plain structure) will be volatile.

Spartan will preserve structure sharing between data structures entered into the same store during the same transaction. In order to preserve this substructure sharing, all memory pointers to shared substructure are converted to PIDs upon commitment of the transaction. Upon retrieval from a store, most PIDs are converted into memory pointers. Structure slots that have been declared with the option **:demand t** will remain PIDs and are converted to memory pointers on demand.

14.6 Full Example

The example given in this section is based upon the test case given in [1] for comparing database programming languages. The test case is an "illustrative *fragment* of a manufacturing company's parts database." Here the example is written in a client/server style, and is presented as a simple, but complete application that runs in Common Lisp. The test case comprises four tasks: the database description, and three queries. Task 2 (the first query) is to print the names of all parts that cost over $100. This query is easy to express in most database query languages. Task 3 is to print the total cost of a composite part by summing its components, and adding its cost increment. This requires a recursive traversal of the components hierarchy of the database, which cannot be expressed in many query languages. Task 4 is to add a new part to the database. It is used to examine how integrity checking and database updating can be separated from dialog with the user.

Parts Server.

```
(in-package 'parts)
(export '(new locate cost basep data
             scan-components scan-components-exit))
(deftype part-name () '(or null simple-string))
(deftype comp-list () '(or null (list (cons part-name number))))

(spartan:defstructure
    (partrec (:constructor make-part (name cost components)))
  (name       nil :type part-name)
  (cost       0   :type number)
  (components nil :type comp-list))

(defvar data nil)
(defparameter location "/usr/stores/mac")

(defun initialize ()
  (unless data (setq data
                     (spartan:connect "Mac Parts" location))))

(defun new (name cost &optional components)
  (spartan:enter data name (make-part name cost components)))
(defun locate (name)
  (let ((entry (spartan:lookup data name)))
    (if (eq entry 'cancelled) 'spartan:not-found entry)))
(defun cost (part) (partrec-cost part))
(defun basep (part) (null (partrec-components part)))

(defun reserve (name)
  (let ((entry (spartan:lookup data name :get-lock t)))
    (if (eq entry 'spartan:not-found)
        (progn
          (spartan:enter data name 'lock-holder :get-lock t)
          t)
        (progn
          (spartan:release-lock data name)
          nil))))
```

```lisp
(defun cancel-reservation (name)
  (spartan:enter data name 'cancelled))

(defun scan-components (part env query)
 ; query: env * part * amount -> env
 (let (effect complist comp abort-value)
    (setq effect env)
    (setq abort-value
          (catch 'scan-components-exit
            (setq complist (partrec-components part))
            (loop
             (unless complist (return))
             (setq comp (car complist))
             (setq effect
                (funcall query effect (locate (car comp))
                                      (cdr comp))))
             (pop complist)))))
    (if abort-value abort-value effect)))
```

Client Application.

```lisp
(defun price-list-editor ()
  "Prompt for a command, and dispatch to the appropriate action."
  (parts:initialize)
  (loop
   (case (aref (prompt-for-line "Parts:") 0)
     (#\e (all-expensive-parts)) ;;; Task 2
     (#\t (total-part-cost))     ;;; Task 3
     (#\n (new-part-addition))   ;;; Task 4
     (#\q (return))
     (t (format t "? Unknown command~%")))))

(defun prompt-for-line (prompt)
  (format t prompt) (read-line *query-io*))

(defun prompt-for-integer (prompt)
  (loop (format t prompt)
    (let ((result
            (parse-integer (read-line *query-io*) :junk-allowed t)))
      (when result (return-from prompt-for-integer result)))
    (format t "? The input is not an integer~%")))
```

Task 2.

```lisp
(defun all-expensive-parts ()
```

```
    (spartan:with-transaction (parts:data :input)
      (format t "Base parts costing more than $100:~%")
      (spartan:scan parts:data nil #'expensive-part)
      (fresh-line)))

(defun expensive-part (env name part)
  (when (and (parts:basep part) (> (parts:cost part) 100))
    (format t "~S " name)))
```

Task 3.

```
(defun total-part-cost ()
  (let ((name (prompt-for-line "Total cost of part:")))
    (spartan:with-transaction (parts:data :input)
      (let ((part (parts:locate name)))
        (if (eq part 'spartan:not-found)
            (format t "Part ~S not found.~%" name)
            (format t "Total cost is $~D.~%"
                (total-cost part)))))))

(defun total-cost (part)
  (parts:scan-components part (parts:cost part) #'cost-add))

(defun cost-add (sum part amount)
  (+ sum (* amount (total-cost part))))
```

Task 4.

```
(defun new-part-addition ()
  (let ((name (prompt-for-line "New part name:"))
        (cost (prompt-for-integer "Cost:"))
        component-names cname components)

    (spartan:with-transaction (parts:data :input)
      (unless (parts:reserve name)
        (format t "? Part ~S already exists~%" name)
        (return-from new-part-addition)))))

    (format t "Enter component names, one per line.~%")
    (setq component-names nil)
    (loop
     (setq cname (prompt-for-line
                    "Name (enter period when done):"))
     (if (equalp (aref cname 0) #\.) (return))
     (push cname component-names))
```

```
(spartan:with-transaction (parts:data :input)
  (dolist (cname component-names)
    (let ((entry (parts:locate cname)))
      (when (or (eq entry 'spartan:not-found))
        (format t "? Part ~S does not exist~%" cname)
        (parts:cancel-reservation name)
        (return-from new-part-addition)))))

(setq components nil)
(dolist (cname component-names)
  (format t "  ~S " cname)
  (setq quantity (prompt-for-integer "Quantity:"))
  (push (cons cname quantity) components))

(multiple-value-bind (status value)
    (spartan:with-transaction (parts:data :io)
      (parts:new name cost components))
  (if status
      (format t "? Transaction aborted; part not added~%")
      (format t "New part added.~%")))))
```

14.7 Implementation Notes

The current implementation of Spartan comprises about 1600 lines of Common Lisp. It works in several different Common Lisp implementations.

Spartan is implemented on top of the file system through standard Common Lisp functions. It works on UNIX as well as Apple Macintosh files. The Common Lisp data types that can be made persistent in this implementation is limited to numbers, characters, symbol names, arrays, lists, structures, and hash tables. Excluded are symbol property lists, readtables, packages, pathnames, streams, random states, and functions.

There is no performance overhead in using data structures saved or restored by Spartan, except in the case of demand structure slots. For demand slots, Spartan redefines the slot-accessor function to check if the slot value needs to be loaded from the store. In all other cases, saved or restored data structures and the functions that operate on them are defined by the Common Lisp implementation in the usual manner.

Spartan uses its own variant of the FASL (FASt Load) format to save data structures on disk. This is the format that many Common Lisp implementations use to save compiled programs. Since Spartan reads and writes FASL format files itself, Spartan stores written within one Common Lisp implementation can be read within another.

Measurements indicate that the input/output performance of Spartan is acceptable for the intended applications. One experiment compared the time required to parse a program into an abstract syntax tree (AST) with the time needed to save and restore that AST. The parser, which was implemented as tool-generated Common Lisp code, was for a subset of ML. The program consisted of 100 lines and 4569 characters. The AST for this program was composed of 3668 two-slot structs, 2018 conses, 1948 nils, 43 distinct symbols, and 52 integers. The print representation for this AST was over 100,000 characters. The AST is a much more verbose representation of the program than the source code. The Spartan FASL representation of this AST was only 21,539 bytes. The time to restore the AST from disk was about the same as the time it took to read the source program and parse it into the AST. The following table shows the average of 10 timing samples taken on a Sun-3/60.

Timing in Seconds		
Parse	6.9	(870 lines per minute)
Lookup	6.7	
Write	5.9	
Detect Sharing	2.8	
Commit	8.7	(Write + Detect Sharing)

The input/output performance could be improved for specific Common Lisp implementations by exploiting implementation dependent features such as some of their own internal functions for building data structures from FASL descriptions. More dramatic improvements could be obtained at the expense of portability and great effort by integrating data structure storage with the garbage collector. This avenue is being explored by Project Venari in the School of Computer Science at Carnegie Mellon.

14.8 Future Work and Conclusions

Several applications could be enhanced by the introduction of persistent data managed by Spartan. One of these is the implementation of LEAP [4], a functional language with an eval function and polymorphic strong typing. The LEAP implementation proceeds in two phases: (1) parsing, name binding, and type inference, and (2) interpretation. Since LEAP type inference is so expensive (requiring higher-order unification), it would be attractive to save the results of the first phase on disk to be reused for several runs of the LEAP program. It is important to preserve structure sharing within the data structures representing type information. LEAP is implemented in Lambda Prolog [3] (a higher-order logic programming language), which in turn is implemented in Common Lisp. Hence, we could build a persistent Lambda Prolog that allows one to save and restore Prolog facts.

This work does not address distributed systems in which the client application is running on a different machine than the data server. Since queries are expressed as

Common Lisp functions, these functions must be shipped from the client's machine to the server's machine, the query must be executed by the server process, and the result must be transmitted back to the client process. This method is known as *remote evaluation* and is being addressed by Project Venari (mentioned above).

Spartan is a simple object storage system for Common Lisp engineered for applications that manage highly-structured objects, have computation-intensive subsystems, feature low-frequency concurrency, and handle a low volume of data. Using Spartan incurs no runtime overhead. The current implementation of Spartan is simple and portable, and has acceptable input/output performance.

References

[1] M. P. Atkinson and O. P. Buneman. Types and persistence in database programming languages. *ACM Computing Surveys*, 19(2):105–190, June 1987.

[2] M. P. Atkinson, P. J. Bailey, K. J. Chisholm, P. W. Cockshott, and R. Morrison. An approach to persistent programming. *The Computer Journal*, 26(4):360–365, 1983.

[3] G. Nadathur and D. Miller. An overview of Prolog. In Robert A. Kowalski and Kenneth A. Bowen, editors, *Logic Programming: Proceedings of the Fifth International Conference and Symposium, Volume 1*, pages 810–827, MIT Press, Cambridge, Massachusetts, August 1988.

[4] F. Pfenning and P. Lee. *LEAP: A Language with Eval and Polymorphism*. Ergo Report 88–065, Carnegie Mellon University, Pittsburgh, Pennsylvania, July 1988.

15   Architectural Considerations for Combinator Graph Reduction

Philip Koopman, Jr. and Peter Lee

15.1   Introduction

Lazy functional programming languages, such as SASL [33] and Haskell [15], possess a number of theoretical properties that make them intriguing candidates for study. However, relatively little is known about how to implement these languages, despite the fact that implementation techniques have long been the subject of research. In 1979 Turner [34] described a technique for implementing lazy functional languages by a technique known as SK-combinator reduction. This idea is based on the well-known observation from combinatory logic that all of the variables in a functional program can be abstracted by transforming it into an applicative expression involving only *combinators*. A combinator is simply a closed λ-expression [5]. Three combinators of particular interest are called **S**, **K**, and **I**:

$$\mathbf{S} \quad = \quad \lambda f.\lambda g.\lambda x.(fx)(gx) \qquad (15.1)$$

$$\mathbf{K} \quad = \quad \lambda x.\lambda y.x \qquad (15.2)$$

$$\mathbf{I} \quad = \quad \lambda x.x \qquad (15.3)$$

The crucial property is that any λ-expression can be transformed into an expression consisting solely of these combinators, by a so-called "bracket abstraction" algorithm [35]. (Actually, only **S** and **K** are necessary, as **I** = **SKK**. In practice, a handful of other combinators, comprising what we shall refer to as the "Turner Set," are also used in order to reduce the size of the combinator expressions.) With all variables abstracted, the resulting expression is easily represented as a binary tree with combinators appearing at the leaves and the internal nodes representing application. As a further optimization, the tree can be transformed into a graph in which the sharing of subgraphs denotes the occurrence of common subexpressions in the combinator expression, cycles denote recursion, and combinator definitions correspond to graph-rewriting rules. For example, Figure 15.1 depicts the graph rewriting corresponding to the **S** combinator.

In this scheme, then, executing programs is a process of graph reduction. The left-most "spine" of the graph is traversed until a combinator is encountered, at which point the

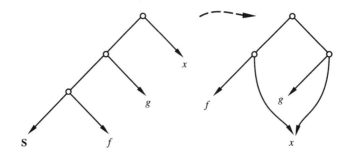

Figure 15.1: Graph rewrite corresponding to the **S** combinator.

graph is rewritten according to the corresponding rewrite rule. This process is consistently repeated on the new graphs until finally an irreducible graph is produced, at which point program execution is complete.

An advantage in efficiency is obtained from the sharing of subgraphs, so common subexpressions need be reduced only once. Also, the language implementation overall becomes much simpler by virtue of the fact that variable substitution is, in effect, encapsulated in a fixed set of simple rules for rewriting graphs. Indeed, a pure graph reducer can be implemented quite easily and will often exhibit better performance than implementations of lazy functional languages based on other approaches. Such simplicity also lends itself to direct hardware implementation, as in SKIM [32] and NORMA [28]. Still, normal-order evaluation (or, more precisely, lazy evaluation) of functional programs, even via combinator-graph reduction, is in practice much less efficient than applicative-order ("eager") evaluation. Lazy functional programming languages such as Haskell require lazy evaluation, so a great deal of research has been directed towards improving the efficiency of combinator-based techniques. One significant development along these lines, first proposed by Hughes [16], is the notion of *supercombinators*, in which the observation is made that any function can be made into a combinator by adding extra formal parameters corresponding to the free variables appearing in the function body. Supercombinator compilation produces a set of "tailor-made" combinators for each program, resulting in much larger-grain reduction steps and thus requiring fewer reductions for evaluation.

15.2 A Study of Architectural Considerations

In this chapter, we explore the effects of computer architecture features on the efficiency of graph reduction, and hence of lazy functional programming languages. In particular, we present the results of our experiments with an abstract machine for reducing combinator graphs. The abstract machine, which we have called TIGRE (the **T**hreaded **I**nterpretive **G**raph **R**eduction **E**ngine), treats combinator graphs as self-modifying threaded programs, in a manner similar to that described by Augusteijn and van der Hoeven [1]. We have found that this method seems to reduce combinator graphs at a rate that compares quite favorably with previously reported techniques on similar hardware. TIGRE maps remarkably easily and efficiently onto computer architectures that allow a restricted form of self-modifying code [19,20]. This provides some indication that the conventional "stored program" organization of computer systems (the so-called "von Neumann" architecture[1]) may be more appropriate for functional programming language implementations than previously thought [3].

This is not to say, however, that present-day computer systems are well-equipped to reduce combinator graphs. During our experimentation with TIGRE, the speed of graph reduction on different hardware platforms repeatedly surprised us, in some cases failing to meet expectations, and in other cases substantially exceeding predicted performance levels. For example, a VAX 8800 mainframe system [7] with a faster clock rate and wider system bus than the DECstation 3100 [10] performed only 355,000 reduction applications per second (RAPS), compared to the DECstation's 470,000 RAPS. Further experimentation with the VAX implementation led to the discovery that its reduction rate could be increased by 20% simply by making a small change to the code to partially compensate for the write-no-allocate cache-management strategy used by that machine.

It was this unexpected behavior that prompted us to undertake a detailed study of the architectural issues affecting the efficiency of graph reduction, in particular the effect of hardware-cache behavior. Our study begins with the simulation of a TIGRE graph reducer running on a reduced-instruction-set computer with the following hardware-cache parameters varied: cache size, cache organization, block size, associativity, memory update policy, and write-allocation policy. The simulation proceeds in two stages, the first stage being an exhaustive test of selected values for all combinations of parameters, and shows that there are no local extrema in cache miss behavior as a function of cache design choices. At this point we take the cache design of a real machine and simulate the performance sensitivity with respect to variations of individual parameters for several programs. As a check on the accuracy of our simulations, we compare the results with measured performance on real hardware. From the results of this simulation study, we can conclude that graph reduction in TIGRE depends on a write-allocate strategy for good performance, and exhibits high spatial and temporal locality. Finally, on the basis of our experiments, we examine possible architectural changes to the MIPS R2000

---

[1]Actually, credit for the notion of the stored program computer should be given to Eckert and Mauchly [12, pg. 23].

processor. The changes illustrate some of the differences between graph reduction and more conventional methods for executing programs.

Before proceeding with the description of our experiments and analysis, we will first briefly review the technique of combinator-graph reduction. This will then be followed by a description of the TIGRE abstract machine and its implementation, as well as a preliminary report on its performance. Throughout this chapter we will concentrate on SK-combinator reduction. The issues involved in SK-combinator reduction differ somewhat from those for supercombinator reduction. Of particular importance in super-combinator reduction is the interaction between compile-time analyses (such as strictness analysis and sharing analysis) and the reducer. Promising approaches to supercombinator reduction include TIM [11] and the "Spineless, Tagless, G-machine" [24]. The TIGRE approach described in this paper extends naturally to supercombinator reduction. However, like Norman [22], we desire to study first the effects of architecture on pure graph reduction, thereby isolating the effects of sophisticated compiler technology.

15.3   The TIGRE Abstract Machine

The major difficulties in performing graph reduction efficiently are in traversing the left spine of the graph (referred to as "stack unwinding") and in the analysis of graph-node tags. Reduction or elimination of these costs can greatly improve performance. In this section we shall begin by describing a straightforward mechanism for graph reduction (based on the Chalmers G-Machine as described by Peyton Jones [25]). Then we shall explain how self-modifying threaded code, as employed by TIGRE, is able to avoid certain inefficiencies present in the straightforward approach.

Figure 15.2 shows that graph nodes are typically represented by three one-word fields. The first field is a tag for the values in the application node. This tag value is selected so as to be an index value into an entry table containing addresses of action routines. Accessing a node requires a double-indirection operation through the tag and entry table. On a VAX architecture, unwinding a node while traversing the stack requires four instructions, including a double-indirect jump through the entry table [25]:

```
movl    Head(r0), r0
movl    r0, -(%EP)
movl    (r0), r1
jmp     *0_Unwind(r1)
```

One of the key points of TIGRE is the elimination of most of this overhead for traversing tree nodes during the stack unwinding process. This can best be accomplished simply by eliminating the need for tags, thereby eliminating the cost of tag interpretation. In the following presentation, we will eliminate the tags in several stages.

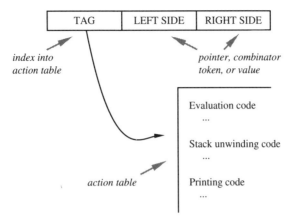

Figure 15.2: Simple scheme for graph-node tag analysis.

TAG	LEFT SIDE	TAG	RIGHT SIDE

Figure 15.3: Basic structure of a graph node.

Figure 15.3 shows a generalized node representation which has tags associated with both the left-hand and right-hand fields of the node. Figure 15.4 shows a tree for the expression `((+ 11) 22)`, where `+` is the addition combinator, which we shall use as a running example. The numbers next to the nodes serve as labels for our discussion. Although only three tag types are shown in the example, typically more tag types are used in actual implementations.

As a first step in eliminating tags, we shall replace the fields containing constant values by pointers to indirection nodes (i.e., nodes involving the application of the **I** combinator).

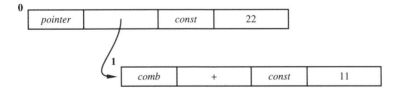

Figure 15.4: Sample graph for the expression `((+ 11) 22)`.

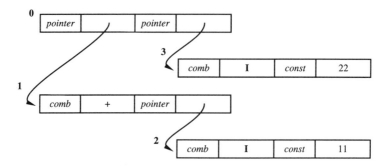

Figure 15.5: Sample graph using indirection nodes.

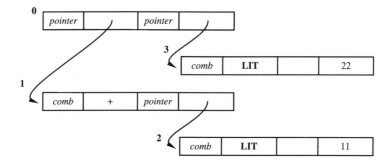

Figure 15.6: Sample graph using LIT nodes.

Figure 15.5 shows the result of this rewriting. Any graph can be rewritten so that constant values are placed in indirection nodes, and in fact this is a standard technique in graph rewriting [34]. For example, the + combinator, when executed, creates an indirection node with the sum. This allows the fields of the root node of the original graph to be overwritten by the result of the graph rewrite.

Now, constant values are only found as arguments to indirection combinators. If we rename the **I** combinators in the left-hand sides of constant nodes as **LIT** combinators (short for "literal value" combinators), as shown in Figure 15.6, the constant tag is no longer needed, since the **LIT** combinator implicitly identifies the argument as a constant value. All other special tags, including tags for other numeric types, can be eliminated by defining new combinators (e.g., **FLIT** for floating point constants) in a similar manner.

The graph shown in Figure 15.6 now only has two tag types: combinator and pointer. At this point, standard techniques can be used to reduce tag-checking costs. (See Chap-

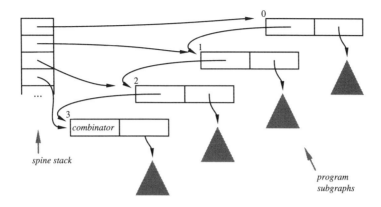

Figure 15.7: Sample graph with the spine stack.

ter 1 for a complete discussion of this point.) For instance, all nodes and therefore pointer values can be aligned on 4-byte boundaries. The lowest bit of a cell's contents can then be used as a one-bit tag. In this case, the tag analysis for numeric constants has been replaced by the need to reduce **LIT** combinators. However, the amount of tag checking on all other cells has been reduced. This is the representation used for interpreted implementations of TIGRE. For instance, in the C-based implementation, TIGRE loops while scanning the lowest order bit of left-hand side cells to unwind the stack. When a non-pointer value is found, TIGRE then uses a **case** statement to jump to the correct action code.

15.4 Self-modifying Threaded Code

There is a key insight which provides approximately a twofold speedup in the execution speed of TIGRE. This is gained by exploiting the hardware support for graph traversal that already exists in most conventional processors.

The generic graph shown in Figure 15.7 is executed by traversing the leftmost spine, placing pointers to ancestor nodes onto a stack (the so-called "spine stack"). When a combinator is encountered in the graph, some code to carry out the graph rewrite is executed. The data structure is controlling the execution of the program. Another, more insightful, way to view this is that the data structure is itself a program with two instruction types: pointer and combinator. Then graph reduction is essentially a process of interpreting a self-modifying threaded program that happens to reside in the node heap. In other words, the graph is a program that consists mainly of calls to subroutines. These subroutines then contain calls to other subroutines, and so on until, finally, some other executable code, which performs a graph rewrite, is found.

The key idea is that *the spine stack is actually a subroutine return stack* for the threaded program. As control flows from node 0 to node 1 to node 2 to node 3 in the graph of Figure 15.7, these nodes are stored on the spine stack. Eventually, a rewriting of the graph involving the right-hand side fields of these nodes will be performed. So, what is actually needed on the stack are pointers to the right-hand side fields of each node. If the left-hand sides of each node are viewed as subroutine call instructions, then the return addresses which would be automatically saved on the return stack would be the addresses of the right-hand fields of the spine of the graph, which is exactly the desired behavior.

Combinator nodes, such as node 3 in Figure 15.7, contain some sort of token value that invokes a combinator. At some point during program execution, this value will have to be resolved to an address for a piece of graph-rewriting code to be executed, so the actual code addresses of the combinator action routines can be stored instead of token values. In fact, a subroutine call to the combinator code can be stored, so that the address of the right-hand side of node 3 will be pushed onto the spine stack, and the combinator will have all its arguments pointed to by the spine stack (i.e., the subroutine return stack). A pleasant side effect of this scheme is that there is now only one type of data in the graph: the pointer. Hence there is only one type of node, and therefore *no conditional branching or case analysis is required at runtime*. All nodes contain either pointers to other nodes or pointers to combinator code. Figure 15.8 shows our running example of ((+ 11) 22) compiled using this scheme. Since all node values (except the right-hand sides of **LIT** nodes) are subroutine call instructions, we can simplify matters by saying that each field contains a pointer that is interpreted as a subroutine call by the TIGRE execution engine.

In the typical TIGRE implementation, graph nodes are represented by triples of 32-bit cells. The first cell of each triple contains a subroutine call instruction while the second and third cells of the triple contain the left-hand and right-hand sides of the node, respectively. The hardware's native subroutine calling mechanism is used to traverse the spine, using the subroutine return stack as the spine stack. Figure 15.9 shows the example graph as it appears in the VAX assembly-language implementation of TIGRE. (Note that the **jsb** is the fast VAX subroutine call instruction which only pushes the program counter onto the return address stack, as opposed to the slower function call instructions which automatically allocate stack frames.) Thus, threaded code interpretation [6] is performed by the C version of TIGRE.

Evaluation of a program graph is initiated by doing a subroutine call to the **jsb** node of the root of a graph. The machine's program counter then traverses the left spine of the graph structure by executing the **jsb** instructions of the nodes following the leftmost spine. When a node points to a combinator, the VAX simply begins executing

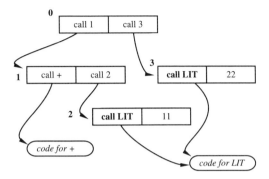

Figure 15.8: A TIGRE graph with only subroutine call nodes.

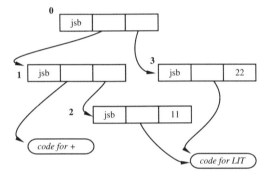

Figure 15.9: The VAX representation of a TIGRE graph.

the combinator code, with the return address stack providing addresses of the right-hand sides of parent nodes for the combinator argument values. When graph nodes are rewritten, only the pointer values (which are 32 bits in size on a VAX) need be rewritten. The **jsb** opcode is initialized upon acquisition of heap space and thereafter never modified.

TIGRE performs subroutine call operations down the left spine of the graph. When combinators are reached, they pop their arguments from the return stack, perform graph rewrites, and then jump to the new subgraph to continue traversing the new left spine. The use of the return stack for graph reduction is different than for "normal" subroutines in that subroutine returns are never performed on the pointers to the combinator arguments but rather, the addresses are consumed from the return stack by the combinators. (This seems to be a characteristic of other combinator reducers as well.)

```
DO_S:                          DO_I:                          DO_LIT:
need2(r8,r7)                   movl *(sp),r6                  movl *(sp)+,r11
movl *(sp)+,r6                 movab 4(sp),sp                 rsb
movl r6,(r8)                   jmp (r6)
movl *(sp),(r7)
movl 4(sp),r10                                                DO_PLUS:
movl (r10),4(r7)               DO_IF:                         movl *(sp)+,r6
movl (r10),4(r8)               movl *(sp)+,r6                 jsb (r6)
movab -2(r8),-4(r10)           jsb (r6)                       movl *(sp),r6
movab -2(r7),(r10)             movl 4(sp),r10                 pushl r11
movab 4(r8),(sp)               tstl r11                       jsb (r6)
jmp (r6)                       jeql L39                       addl2 (sp)+,r11
                               movl *(sp),(r10)               movl (sp)+,r9
                               L39: $DO_I,-4(r10)             movl $DO_LIT,-4(r9)
DO_K:                          movl (r10),r6                  movl r11,(r9)
movl *(sp),r6                  addl2 $8,sp                    rsb
movab 8(sp),sp                 jmp (r6)
jmp (r6)
```

Figure 15.10: VAX code listings for some TIGRE combinators.

The processor is in no sense interpreting the graph. It is *directly executing* the data structure, using the hardware-provided subroutine call instructions to do the stack unwinding. In our experiments, we have found that this technique exhibits performance that compares favorably with other approaches described in the literature.

15.5 Implementing TIGRE

The availability of a fast subroutine-call instruction on most modern architectures makes the TIGRE technique applicable, in theory, to most computers. In practice, however, there are issues having to do with modifying the instruction stream that make the approach difficult to implement on many machines. These problems can be viewed as the result of inappropriate tradeoffs (for the application of graph reduction) in system design, and not the result of any inherent limitation of truly general-purpose CPUs. Inasmuch as graph reduction is a self-modifying process, it is not surprising that a highly efficient graph reduction implementation makes use of self-modifying techniques.

Figure 15.10 gives a sketch of the VAX-assembler implementation of the combinators for the SKI combinator set. This code is a simple version written for clarity. The VAX implementation actually in use has various small optimizations to eliminate redundant memory reads and better exploit the pipeline of high-end VAX mainframe systems.

In TIGRE, traversing the left spine is typically less expensive than rewriting the graph. This leads to some novel design decisions, one of which affects the implementation of "projection" combinators such as **I** and **K**. The implementations of these combinators as shown in Figure 15.10 do not modify the graph at all, but rather redirect the flow of control of the graph evaluation, popping elements from the return stack as they execute. **K** and **I** are two instances of the set of projection combinators which simply drop a number of parent nodes while performing an indirection operation on the topmost node on the spine stack. This optimization may degrade memory usage by, for example, leaving subtrees attached to a **K** node when they would have otherwise been abandoned, but our experience thus far has been that the speedup realized by avoiding graph rewrites more than makes up for this inefficiency.

Another aspect of the TIGRE implementation is that it uses the same primitive operations over and over again to implement combinators. Only a few primitives such as "fetch the right-hand value of the parent node" are needed to implement the standard Turner Set of combinators. An assembly language of similar primitives can be used to defined supercombinators for TIGRE, even on a special purpose hardware version, with only a minimal set of machine operations.

15.6   TIGRE performance

TIGRE has been implemented in C, VAX assembler, and MIPS R2000 assembler. (An initial exploration was carried out in Forth, a language noted for its support of threaded code.) The C version uses a threaded interpretation as previously discussed. The VAX assembler version uses the `jsb` instruction to perform subroutine-threaded execution of the graph. The MIPS R2000 version uses a carefully written threaded interpretive loop, because the architecture does not have a subroutine call instruction.

Figure 15.11 gives some performance figures for TIGRE. Simple stop-and-copy garbage collection is used. The allocated heap space is small enough to force several dozen garbage collection cycles in each benchmark. No sharing analysis or other optimizations are used. The assembler versions show significant improvements over versions compiled with an optimizing C compiler. The Fib benchmark program is the standard recursive Fibonacci function. The Nfib program is the commonly reported benchmark that tallies the number of recursions used in computing a Fibonacci function. Tak, NthPrime, and 8Queens are lazy functional versions of other well-known benchmarks.

The DECstation 3100 is a 16.7 MHz MIPS R2000-based workstation. The VAX 8800 is a 22 MHz mainframe. The Cray Y-MP [26] is a vectorized supercomputer that has a fast scalar processing unit. The Sun 3/75 system is a 16 MHz 68020 workstation with no cache memory. For the C implementation on the Sun 3/75 workstation, the

Platform	Language	Combinators	Benchmark	Time (sec)	Speed (NRAPS)
DECstation 3100 (16.7 MHz)	assembler	SKI	Fib(23)	2.20	495000
		Turner	Fib(23)	1.58	470000
			NFib(23)	2.68	484000
			Tak	12.58	420000
			NthPrime(300)	2.60	364000
			8Queens(20)	5.63	433000
		supercombinators	Fib(23)	0.36	2046000
			NFib(23)	0.80	1626000
VAX 8800 (22 MHz)	assembler	SKI	Fib(23)	2.82	387000
		Turner	Fib(23)	2.10	355000
			NFib(23)	3.55	366000
			Tak	16.07	329000
			NthPrime(300)	3.91	242000
			8Queens(20)	8.33	293000
		supercombinators	Fib(23)	1.22	611000
			NFib(23)	0.97	1339000
Cray Y-MP (167 MHz)	C	SKI	Fib(23)	3.09	352000
		Turner	Fib(23)	2.40	310000
			NFib(23)	4.25	305000
			Tak	14.69	360000
			NthPrime(300)	3.40	277000
Sun 3/75 (16 MHz)	C	SKI	Fib(23)	14.62	75000
		Turner	Fib(23)	12.75	58000
			NFib(23)	22.02	59000

Figure 15.11: Some TIGRE performance results.

GNU C compiler [31] was used with the optimization switch turned on. Reduction-rate figures for supercombinator implementations were normalized to approximate Turner Set measurements as follows. First, we measured the speedup of the supercombinator version over a Turner Set version on the same platform. Next, this speedup was used to scale the Turner Set reduction rate to arrive at the normalized supercombinator reduction rate (NRAPS).

The reduction rates measured for TIGRE compare quite favorably with those reported for other approaches to graph reduction, including Hyperlazy evaluation [22], the G-Machine [2,17,25], the Spineless, Tagless G-machine [24], TIM [11,36], and NORMA [28]. Due to differences in hardware platforms and compiling technology, direct comparisons are difficult to make. The most direct comparison can be made with NORMA, which is a special-purpose computer dedicated to Turner-set combinator reduction. The reported reduction rate for NORMA is 250,000 RAPS.

15.7 The basis for the architectural study

During the implementation and performance measurements of TIGRE, we noted unexpected results on different platforms. We conjectured that the unexpected performance variations observed among TIGRE implementations were caused by hardware differences among platforms, especially with regard to cache organization and management. In order to better understand the operation of TIGRE, a set of cache simulations was run to measure TIGRE's use of cache memory.

Since our measurements on several hardware platforms have shown the DECstation 3100 to be the fastest available TIGRE implementation (despite the need for an interpretive threading loop), we used this machine's cache configuration as our starting point. This approach gives a starting point based on a real system. From this starting point, we examined how variations in cache organization affect program performance. (A study of cache behavior based on exhaustive search simulation techniques is described by Koopman et al. [21]).

The DECstation 3100 has a split instruction and data cache. During combinator-graph reduction execution, the instruction cache holds code to execute primitives of an abstract machine. The data cache contains the actual combinator graph, which is the abstract machine program being executed. Since the kernel of code required for graph reduction is small, previous simulations showed that the instruction cache on this machine experiences essentially a 100% hit ratio after the cache becomes filled with combinator code. Therefore, we concentrated our simulation efforts on the data cache performance.

Since graph reduction may be thought of as an interpretive process of executing a program expressed as a data structure, the data cache is actually the cache of prime importance. In this situation, the instruction cache is acting as a kind of microcode memory for storing code to execute primitive operations, and the data cache actually contains both the interpreted code (the program graph) and the program data. The approach of studying only the data cache has the added advantage of largely decoupling the particulars of the abstract-machine implementation (which affect instruction cache access) from the mechanics of graph reduction (which appears as accesses to the data cache).

In order to carry out the simulations, memory-access traces from TIGRE were used as input to the DineroIII trace-driven cache-simulator program [13]. In the first phase of the experimentation, an exhaustive exploration of a number of cache design parameters were tried in order to find the best combinations. An exhaustive search was performed in order to avoid the pitfalls of hill-climbing strategies that may become trapped at local extrema.

	Fib	NthPrime	8Queens	Real	Tak
cache miss ratio	0.1434	0.1768	0.1554	0.1595	0.1912
bus traffic ratio	0.5854	0.6262	0.5942	0.5971	0.6478

Figure 15.12: Cache performance for the baseline organization: 64K data cache, 4-byte block size, direct-mapping, write-through, and write-allocate.

On the basis of this exploration, and on the basis of DECstation 3100 characteristics, we arrived at the following "optimum" cache design parameter values: split I- and D-cache organization (with only the D-cache simulated), 64K byte data cache size, 4-byte block size, direct-mapped organization, write-through memory updates, and allocation on cache write miss. Kabakibo et al. [18] and Smith [30] provide more information on cache management strategies and terminology.

15.8   Parametric analysis

For the second phase of the experimentation, individual parameters were altered, one at a time across a wide range to observe performance trends. The benchmark programs run were: Fib (recursive Fibonacci calculation), NthPrime (a prime number generator), 8Queens (the 8-queens problem), Real (infinite precision real arithmetic), and Tak (a program that tests recursive function calls). In all cases, between one and two million data memory accesses were simulated, with accesses to a heap space at least 320K bytes in size.

   Figure 15.12 summarizes the results of simulating the baseline cache configuration. Two important characteristics emerge from the simulation. The cache miss ratio (percentage of cache accesses experiencing a cache miss) is a relatively high 14% to 19% for all the programs. Furthermore, the bus traffic ratio (the average number of 4-byte words transferred on the memory bus per cache access) is between 0.58 and 0.65. As a result, graph-reduction programs generate memory references in excess of DECstation 3100 available bus bandwidth (this is discussed in detail in a later section). We shall show that varying the cache parameters can decrease both the cache miss ratio and the bus traffic ratio dramatically.

15.8.1   Write allocation: The importance of a write-allocate strategy

A cache is said to perform write allocation when a memory write that generates a cache miss copies the data being written into a newly allocated cache block (allowing subse-

Allocation strategy	Fib	NthPrime	8Queens	Real	Tak
write-allocate	0.1434	0.1768	0.1554	0.1595	0.1912
write-no-allocate	0.2405	0.3099	0.2669	0.2848	0.3271

Figure 15.13: Cache miss ratios with varying write-allocation strategy.

quent reads and writes to that address to achieve cache hits). A write-no-allocate policy does not write the data to cache, but instead transfers the data directly to memory.

Figure 15.13 shows the results of varying the write allocation policy. We have found that this design parameter is more important by far than any of the other parameters, with cache miss ratios almost doubling when a write-no-allocate policy is used.

The reason for the extreme sensitivity to write-allocation policy lies with the use of heap nodes. Graph reduction allocates nodes from a garbage-collected heap frequently during program execution. As heap nodes are allocated, the addresses of the new cells are generated without accessing heap memory (when using a many current garbage collection algorithms). After heap nodes are allocated, graph data is first written to the heap, then read back from it for further reduction operations. The first time the node is written, a cache miss is generated. A write-allocate strategy will load the node into the cache, while a write-no-allocate strategy will simply write the node value into main memory. The problem comes on the subsequent read of this node. A write-no-allocate policy will experience a second cache miss, while a write-allocate policy will often get a cache hit on the previously written element (as long as no intervening memory reference has bumped the node out of cache). This second cache miss with a write-no-allocate policy significantly degrades performance. The effect becomes even more pronounced when a long sequence of writes (each generating a cache miss) is performed in succession before the first read, as can happen when performing a sequence of graph rewrites on a small portion of the program graph.

As an example of the importance of this range of cache performances, the VAX 8800 mainframe uses a write-no-allocate strategy in managing its cache. This strategy is commonly used to simplify the cache control logic on machines with large cache block sizes. This strategy, combined with the longer latency for a cache miss than that found on the DECstation 3100, accounts for most of the performance difference between the two machines. In order to increase the VAX 8800's speed, our graph reduction code performs a dummy memory read (i.e. a memory read, the results of which are discarded) each time a group of heap cells is allocated. This forces allocation of a cache line before the initial write to the heap cell, and can increases overall performance by 20% despite the overhead of executing extra instructions to perform the memory reads.

Graph reduction makes extremely heavy use of a garbage-collected heap, so the effectiveness of write-allocation on cache miss ratios is quite pronounced. However, the need for a write-allocate cache policy when using garbage-collected heaps probably extends beyond the graph reduction domain. Since a heap, by its very nature, is used in a write-followed-by-read manner, a write-allocate cache policy is likely to be important to support any system that uses a heap.

15.8.2   Block size: Strong spatial locality means larger block size

Figure 15.14 shows the results of varying block size (the number of bytes in the smallest allocated unit of memory in the cache) over a range of 4 bytes to 2K bytes. The cache miss ratio for all programs decreases up to a cache size of 256 bytes. This suggests very strong spatial locality. This spatial locality is probably due to the fact that heap nodes are allocated from the heap space in sequential memory locations.

One could, at first glance, decide to build a machine with a 256 byte cache block size based on the miss ratios alone. For conventional programs, this decision could be unwise, because the bus traffic ratio (the number of words of data moved by the system bus) often increases dramatically with an increased block size. This heavy traffic can slow a system down by greatly increasing the time required to refill a cache block after a miss. With combinator-graph reduction, this effect is much less pronounced. The traffic ratio does not increase appreciably until the block size is between 128 and 256 bytes in size. So, a machine with a 128 byte cache block size appears to be entirely reasonable for this application.

Large block sizes are seldom seen in practice, because most conventional programs do not have enough spatial locality to justify very large block sizes. But, the significant performance increases possible with this application give strong incentive to consider large block size. Even a block size of 16 elements brings dramatic reductions in the miss ratio.

15.8.3   Write through policy

A write-through cache transmits modified data to system memory every time the processor performs a store operation. A copy-back cache buffers the data in cache until it must be flushed to make the cache block available for another address. If multiple writes are performed to a single address, a copy-back cache eliminates the requirement to use memory bus bandwidth for all but the ultimate write.

Figure 15.15 shows the traffic ratio for a write-through versus copy-back management

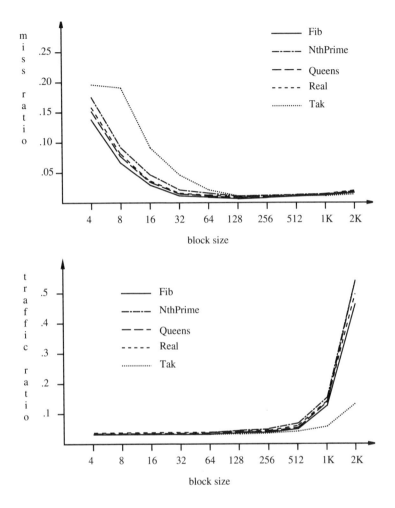

Figure 15.14: Cache performance with varying block size

Memory update	Fib	NthPrime	8Queens	Real	Tak
write-through	0.5854	0.6262	0.5942	0.5971	0.6478
copy-back	0.2863	0.3507	0.3063	0.3123	0.3769

Figure 15.15: Cache traffic ratios with varying write-through strategy.

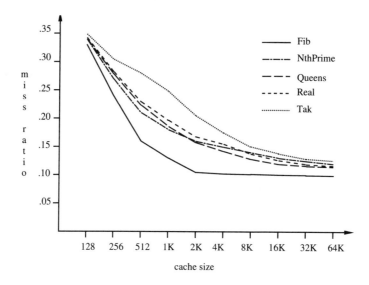

Figure 15.16: Cache performance with varying cache size

policy. The cache miss ratios are the same since this policy does not affect whether misses occur. However, the bus traffic generated for the write-through method is significantly higher than for copy-back. This is caused by the fact that a very high percentage of memory accesses are memory writes (between 44% and 46% of memory references were writes on the programs simulated). This can cause severe problems with system performance by causing memory bus saturation.

Since one of the promises of combinator-graph reduction is simple parallel program execution, and since many multiprocessors are built with a common memory bus, bus traffic is a prime consideration in predicting the limits to parallel processing performance. Since graph reduction causes a high number of memory writes, use of copy-back cache is highly desirable to avoid bus saturation for a multiprocessor system. However, even with copy-back cache the bus traffic is reduced by less than a factor of two, indicating that a multiprocessor using a common data bus could have a severe bus bandwidth bottleneck.

15.8.4 Cache size

Figure 15.16 shows the results of varying cache size over a range of 128 bytes to 64K bytes. While different programs show different degrees of temporal locality, the curves suggest that increases in cache size beyond 64K will not significantly change the miss

Associativity	Fib	NthPrime	8Queens	Real	Tak
direct-mapped	0.1434	0.1768	0.1544	0.1595	0.1912
2-way set	0.1425	0.1724	0.1515	0.1530	0.1858
4-way set	0.1425	0.1724	0.1514	0.1530	0.1857
8-way set	0.1425	0.1724	0.1513	0.1530	0.1857

Figure 15.17: Cache miss ratios with varying associativity.

ratio. So, conventional hardware platforms which typically have more than 16K bytes of cache seem to be adequate with respect to cache size.

15.8.5 *Associativity*

Figure 15.17 shows the results of varying the associativity of the cache from direct mapped (1-way associative) to 8-way associative. 2-way set associative seems to bring a slight performance improvement, but beyond that there is little or no advantage to adding cache sets.

Many systems use direct mapped caches because they are simpler to build and can be more easily made to run at high speeds [27]. The miss ratio penalty of using such a direct mapped cache over a set associative cache is quite small, so the performance tradeoff of using direct mapped caches seems desirable.

15.8.6 *Comparison with actual measurements*

Cache simulation results are an important architectural design tool. However, there is always the question of whether the results of such simulations correspond to the "real world." In order to establish some confidence in the simulation results, a comparison was made between the results of a simulation of the DECstation 3100 and the results of actual program execution.

Simulation indicates that for Fib, the R2000 processor executes 27.82 instructions per combinator reduction application (on average). The R2000 also performs 33.95 memory reads (including both instruction reads and data reads) per combinator reduction application, which when multiplied by a combined instruction and data cache simulated miss ratio of 0.0097, gives 0.33 cache read misses per combinator reduction. The DECstation 3100 has a cache read miss latency of 5 clock cycles, resulting in a cost of 1.65 clock cycles per combinator because of cache misses. This, when added to the 27.82 cycle instruction execution cost (27.82 instructions at one instruction per clock cycle), yields an execution time of 29.47 clock cycles per combinator.

The DECstation 3100 has a cost of zero clock cycles for a cache write miss, so long as the write buffer does not overflow. With an average of 4.74 writes (at 6 clock cycles per write using the write-through memory updating policy) plus 0.33 cache miss reads (at 5 clock cycles per read) per combinator, a total of at least 30.09 clock cycles is needed per combinator to provide adequate memory bandwidth for the write-through strategy. This is somewhat longer than the 29.47 clock cycle instruction execution speed, leading to the conclusion that the DECstation 3100 implementation of TIGRE is constrained by memory bandwidth.

As a result of this analysis, we calculate the simulated execution speed of the DEC-station 3100 to be 30.09 clock cycles per combinator. At 16.67 MHz, this translates into a speed of 554000 RAPS between garbage collections.

When actually executing the Skifib benchmark, the DECstation 3100 performed approximately 475000 reduction applications per second (RAPS) including garbage collection time. Garbage collection overhead was measured at approximately 1%. This rather low cost is attributed to the fact that a small number of nodes are actually in use at any given time, so a copying garbage collector must typically copy just a few hundred nodes for each collection cycle on the benchmark used. Virtual memory overhead can be computed based on a 0.0091 miss ratio for a block size of 4K bytes, with 6.67 data access per combinator, giving a computed virtual memory miss ratio of 0.00136 per combinator. Assuming 13 clock cycles overhead per TLB miss (based on an 800 ns TLB miss overhead for a MIPS R2000 with a 16 MHz clock as reported by Siewiorek and Koopman [29]), and noting that an average combinator takes 30.09 clocks, this gives a penalty of:

$$0.00136 * 13/30.09 \text{ (clocks per combinator)}$$

$$= 0.06\%$$

Together with the 1% garbage collection overhead, this 1.06% overhead predicts a raw reduction rate of:

$$475000 * 1.0106 = 480000 \text{ RAPS}$$

This rate is 15% slower than the 554000 RAPS predicted raw reduction rate. Some of this 15% discrepancy is due to the overhead of cache cold starts on a multiprogrammed operating system. The rest of the discrepancy is probably caused by bursts of traffic to the write buffer, which stalls the processor when full. The simulators available to us did not permit exploring the behavior of a write buffer, but an examination of the code shows that write buffer stalls are likely.

15.9 The potential of special-purpose hardware

15.9.1 DECstation 3100 as a baseline

We have described various implementation methods and performance data for TIGRE. This section uses those data points to propose architecture and implementation features which could be used to speed up the execution of TIGRE. The reason for examining such features is to determine the feasibility of constructing special-purpose hardware, or, if construction of special-purpose hardware is not attractive, the features that should be selected when choosing standard hardware to execute TIGRE.

Since the best measured performance for TIGRE was for the MIPS R2000 assembly language implementation, the approach used for examining processor features to support TIGRE will be made in terms of incremental modifications to the MIPS R2000 processor. This approach will give a rough estimate for the potential performance improvement, while maintaining some basis in reality. While it is understood that adding complexity to a RISC architecture may be undesirable (because, for example, it may reduce the maximum clock frequency for existing instructions), this is a way to obtain an approximation of potential benefits.

Since TIGRE has been shown to have some unusual cache access behavior, the first area for improvement that will be considered is changing the arrangement of cache memory. Then, improvements in the architecture of the R2000 will be considered. For the purposes of the following performance analysis, the characteristics of the SKI implementation of the Fib benchmark executing on the DECstation 3100 shall be used.

15.10 Improvements in cache management

15.10.1 Copy-back cache

The most obvious limitation of the DECstation 3100 cache is that it uses a write-through cache. This caused the limiting performance factor to be bus bandwidth for memory write accesses, instead of instruction read or data read miss ratios. A simple improvement, then, is to employ a copy-back cache. A cache simulation of Fib for the DECstation 3100 shows that this reduces the data cache traffic ratio from 0.5461 to 0.2078, removing the bus bandwidth as the limiting factor to performance. This reduces the execution time of an average combinator from 30.09 clock cycles (the bus bandwidth-limited performance) to 29.47 clock cycles (the cache hit ratio-limited performance).

15.10.2   Increased block size

A second parameter of the cache that could be improved is the block size. TIGRE executes well with a large block size, so increasing the cache-block size from 4 bytes to, say 128 bytes, should dramatically decrease the cache miss ratio, but would suffer from the limited width of the memory bus. Using a wide bus-write buffer with a 4 byte cache-block size can capture many of the benefits of a large block size, and reduce bus traffic. A write buffer width of 8 bytes (one full graph node) could probably be utilized efficiently by a supercombinator compiler to get a high percentage of paired 4-byte writes to the left-and right-hand sides of cells when updating the graph.

However, even if a very sophisticated cache mechanism were used to reduce cache misses to the theoretical minimum (ideally, 0.0000 miss ratio), the speedup possibilities are somewhat small. This is because only 1.65 clock cycles of the 29.47 clock cycles per combinator are spent on cache misses to begin with.

15.11   Improvements in CPU architecture

The opportunities for improvement by changing the architecture of the R2000 are somewhat more promising than those possible by modifying the cache management strategy. In particular, it is possible to significantly increase the speed of stack unwinding and performing indirections through the stack elements.

15.11.1   Stack unwinding support

The one serious drawback of the R2000 architecture for executing TIGRE is the lack of a subroutine call instruction. The current TIGRE implementation on the R2000 uses a five-instruction interpretive loop for performing threading (i.e. stack unwinding). Since 1.37 stack unwind operations are performed per combinator, this represents 6.85 instructions which, assuming no cache misses, execute in 6.85 clock cycles.

But, there is a further penalty for performing the threading operation through graphs with the R2000. A seven-instruction overhead is used for each combinator to perform a preliminary test for threading, and to access a jump table to jump to the combinator code when threading is completed. (One of these instructions increments a counter used for performance measurement. It can be removed for production code, as long as measuring the number of combinators executed is not important.) This imposes an additional 7.00 clock cycle penalty on each combinator.

So, the total time spent on threading is 13.85 clock cycles per combinator. It takes three clock cycles to simulate a subroutine call on the R2000:

```
# store current return address
sw      $31, 0($sp)
# subroutine call
jal     subr_address
# branch delay slot instruction follows
# decrement stack pointer
addu    $sp, $sp, -4
```

So, it is reasonable to assume that a hardware-implemented subroutine call instruction could be made to operate in three clock cycles. Thus, if the instruction cache were made to track writes to memory (permitting the use of self-modifying code), a savings of 10.85 clock cycles is possible. One important change to the instruction set would be necessary to allow the use of subroutine call instructions.[2]

An alternate way to implement a subroutine call with a modifiable address field is to define an indirect subroutine call that reads its target address through the data cache, eliminating the need to keep the instruction cache in synch with bus writes. This implementation is likely to be more desirable for split-cache systems.

15.11.2   Stack access support

An important aspect of TIGRE's operation is that it makes frequent reference to the top elements on the spine stack. In fact, 4.61 accesses to the spine stack are performed per average combinator. Most of the load and store instructions that perform these stack accesses can be eliminated by the use of on-CPU stack buffers that are pushed and popped as a side effect of other instructions.

For spine-stack unwinding, two of the three instructions used to perform a subroutine call could be eliminated with the use of hardware stack support, leaving just a single **jal** instruction to perform the threading operation at each node. Of course, the R2000 requires the use of delayed branches, so it probably not the case that the actual time for the threading operation could be reduced to less than two clock cycles. But, the second clock cycle could be used to allow writing a potential stack buffer overflow element to memory.

Of the 4.61 instructions that access the spine stack, the threading technique just described may be used to eliminate the effect of 1.37 of the instructions per combinator. The remaining 3.24 instructions can also be eliminated by introducing an indirect-through-spine-stack addressing mode to the R2000. All that would be required is to access the top, second, and third element of a spine-stack buffer as the source of an address instead

---

[2]The subroutine call instruction would have to be defined to have all zero bits in the opcode field so that the instruction could be used as a pointer to memory as well.

cumulative optimizations	clock cycles per combinator
current implementation	30.09
copy-back cache	29.47
100% cache hit ratio	27.82
subroutine call + self-modifying code	16.97
hardware stack indirect addressing	12.36
8-byte store instructions	11.47

Figure 15.18: Possible performance improvements to the MIPS R2000 for TIGRE.

of a register. A simple implementation method could map the top of stack buffer registers into the 32 registers already available on the R2000. This gives a potential savings of 3.24 clock cycles, since explicit load instructions from the spine stack need not be executed when performing indirection operations.

15.11.3 Double-word stores

TIGRE is often able to write cells in pairs, with both the left-and right-hand cells of a single node written at approximately the same point in the code for a particular combinator. Thus, it becomes attractive to define a "double store" instruction format. Such an instruction would take two source register operands (for example, an even/odd register pair), and store them into a 64-bit memory double-word. If the processor were designed with a 64-bit memory bus, such a "double store" could take place in a single clock cycle instead of as a two-clock sequence. The savings of using 64-bit stores is 0.895 clock cycles per combinator for the SKI implementations of Fib, and 1.192 clock cycles per combinator for the Turner set implementation of Fib (measured by instrumenting TIGRE code to count the opportunities for these stores as the benchmark program is executed). Support of 64-bit memory stores would speed up supercombinator definitions even more, since the body of supercombinators often contains long sequences of node creations. For example, the supercombinator implementation of Fib can make use of 1.33 64-bit stores per combinator.

Figure 15.18 summarizes the efficiency improvements that may be gained through the cache and processor architecture changes just discussed. Nearly a three-fold speed improvement is possible over the R2000 processor with just a few architectural changes. This is a significant speedup, but probably does not justify the production of a special CPU for uniprocessor implementations. Rather, the results should indicate desirable architectural features that should be sought when selecting a standard RISC platform for combinator-graph reduction.

15.12   Results

We have described an abstract machine for combinator-graph reduction, and shown that it has good performance compared to other graph reducers and closure reducers. Using TIGRE, we have performed architectural simulations that show it has unusual execution characteristics, including: a very strong dependence on a write-allocate strategy for efficient execution, a high degree of spatial locality, and a high proportion of memory writes to total memory accesses. Thus, a system which will execute these programs efficiently should ideally have a write-allocate cache with copy-back memory updating, and a relatively large block size of at least 16 or 32 bytes. Since the combination of copy-back updating with write-allocation requires additional complexity in control logic, this combination is not likely to appear without evidence to suggest that it is useful for some applications. This study is a piece of evidence in that vein.

The results of this research should help users of combinator-graph reduction select commercial machines which will perform efficiently. They may also influence the course of design of special-purpose graph reduction hardware in the future.

15.13   Further work

Our simulated programs are restricted to small benchmarks. The measurements of TIGRE behavior are limited by a lack of extensive software support. Additionally, large lazy functional programs are difficult to find and we have been hampered by a lack of extensive compiler support. Therefore, we plan to repeat the experiments on TIGRE when a larger software base is available. Also, it would be revealing to compare TIGRE against other abstract machines using a comprehensive benchmark suite with comparable implementations and compilers. This would not only improve understanding of the strengths and weaknesses of TIGRE, but also of common architectural requirements for combinator reduction techniques in general.

A problem with parallel graph reduction in the past has been one of practicality. If individual graph reduction processors do not execute within a factor of 100 times the speed of a uniprocessor running an imperative language, there seems little point in building a 100-processor system. TIGRE and other fast combinator reducers (such as TIM) make it feasible to consider the design of a parallel graph reduction engine that can potentially run programs more quickly than a uniprocessor using imperative languages. While TIM makes parallel closure reduction machines such as the Grip project

[23] practical, TIGRE may make parallel pure graph reduction viable. Graph reduction appears to be a more obvious program manipulation technique than other methods, and therefore *may* allow better insight into parallel execution issues.

References

[1] A. Augusteijn and G. van der Hoeven. (1984) Combinatorgraphs as self-reducing programs.

[2] L. Augustsson. (1984) A compiler for lazy ML. In *Proceedings of the ACM Symposium on Lisp and Functional Programming, Austin*, pp. 218-27, August.

[3] J. Backus. (1978) Can programming be liberated from the von Neumann style? A functional style and its algebra of programs. *Comm. of the ACM*, August 1978, **21**(8) 613-641

[4] H. Baker. (1978) List processing in real time on a serial computer. *Communications of the ACM*, 21(4) 280-294, June.

[5] H. P. Barendregt. (1981) *The Lambda Calculus: Its Syntax and Semantics*, Elsevier, New York.

[6] J. Bell. (1973) Threaded code. *Communications of the ACM*, 16(6) 370-372, June.

[7] R. Burley. (1987) An overview of the four systems in the VAX 8800 family. *Digital Technical Journal*, 4:10-19, February.

[8] G. Burn, S. Peyton Jones, and J. Robson. (1988) The spineless G-Machine. In: *Proceedings of the 1988 ACM Conference on Lisp and Functional Programming*, Snowbird UT, July 25-27.

[9] H. B. Curry and R. Feys. (1968) *Combinatory Logic, Volume 1*, North-Holland.

[10] Digital Equipment Corporation (1989) *DECstation 3100 Technical Overview (EZ-J4052-28)*, Digital Equipment Corporation, Maynard MA.

[11] J. Fairbairn and S. Wray. (1987) TIM: A simple, lazy abstract machine to execute supercombinators. In Kahn, G. (ed.), *Proceedings of the Conference on Functional Programming and Computer Architecture, Portland*, pp. 34-45, Springer Verlag, 1987.

[12] J. Hennessy and D. Patterson. (1990) *Computer Architecture: a quantitative approach*, Morgan Kaufmann Publishers, San Mateo, CA.

[13] M. D. Hill. (1984) Experimental evaluation of on-chip microprocessor cache memories, *Proc. Eleventh Int. Symp. on Computer Architecture*, Ann Arbor, June.

[14] P. Hudak and B. Goldberg. (1985) Serial combinators: "optimal grains of parallelism. In *Conference on Functional Programming Languages and Computer Architecture, Nancy*, Springer Verlag, pages 382-399.

[15] P. Hudak, P. Wadler, et al. (1990) *Report on the Programming Language Haskell, Version 1.0*, Research Report YALEU/DCS/RR-777, April.

[16] R. J. Hughes. (1982) Supercombinators: a new implementation method for applicative languages. In *Proceedings of the 1982 ACM Symposium on Lisp and Functional Programming, Pittsburgh*, ACM, August 1982.

[17] T. Johnsson. (1984) Efficient compilation of lazy evaluation. In *Proceedings of the ACM Conference on Compiler Construction, Montreal*, pp. 58-69, June.

[18] A. Kabakibo, V. Milutinovic, A. Silbey, and B. Furht. (1987) A survey of cache memory in modern microcomputer and minicomputer systems. In: Gajski, D., Milutinovic, V., Siegel, H. and Furht, B. (eds.) *Tutorial: Computer Architecture*, IEEE Computer Society Press, pp. 210-227.

[19] P. Koopman. (1990) *An Architecture for Combinator Graph Reduction*, Academic Press, Boston.

[20] P. Koopman and P. Lee. (1989) A Fresh Look at Combinator Graph Reduction. In *Proceedings of SIGPLAN '89 Conference on Programming Language Design and Implementation, Portland OR, June 21-23, SIGPLAN Notices,* **24**(7), July 1989, 110-119.

[21] P. Koopman, P. Lee, and D. Siewiorek. (1990) "Cache Performance of Combinator Graph Reduction". In: *1990 International Conference on Computer Languages,* March 12-15, 39-48.

[22] A. C. Norman. (1988) Faster combinator reduction using stock hardware. In *Proceedings of the 1988 ACM Conference on Lisp and Functional Programming, Snowbird Utah,* pp. 235-243, ACM, July.

[23] S. L. Peyton Jones, C. Clack, J. Salkild, and M. Hardie. (1987) GRIP - a high-performance architecture for parallel graph reduction. In: Kahn, G. (ed.) *Functional Programming Languages and Computer Architecture, Portland OR, September 14-16,* Springer-Verlag, 98-112

[24] S. L. Peyton Jones and J. Salkild. (1989) The spineless tagless G-machine. In *The Fourth International Conference on Functional Programming Languages and Computer Architecture, London,* pp. 184-201, September.

[25] S. L. Peyton Jones. (1987) *The Implementation of Functional Programming Languages,* Prentice-Hall, London.

[26] Pittsburgh Supercomputer Center (1989) *Facilities and Services Guide,* Pittsburgh PA.

[27] S. Przybylski, M. Horowitz, and J. Hennessy. (1988) Performance tradeoffs in cache design. In *The 15th Annual International Symposium on Computer Architecture, Honolulu, Hawaii, 30 May - 2 June,* IEEE Computer Society Press, pp. 290-298

[28] M. Scheevel. (1986) NORMA: A graph reduction processor. In *Proceedings of the 1986 ACM Conference on Lisp and Functional Programming, Cambridge Massachusetts,* pp. 212-219, ACM, August.

[29] D. Siewiorek and P. Koopman. (1989) *A Case Study of a Parallel, Vector Workstation: the Titan Architecture,* Academic Press, Boston. In Press.

[30] A. J. Smith. (1982) Cache memories, *ACM Computing Surveys,* 14(3):473-530, September.

[31] R. Stallman. (1988) GNU Project C Compiler. In *UNIX Programmer's Manual,* on-line system documentation, Unix version 4.3.

[32] W. Stoye. (1984) *The Implementation of Functional Languages using Custom Hardware,* Technical Report No. 81, University of Cambridge Computer Laboratory.

[33] D. A. Turner. (1976) *SASL Reference Manual,* University of St. Andrews.

[34] D. A. Turner. (1979a) A new implementation technique for applicative languages. *Software - Practice and Experience,* **9**(1):31-49, January.

[35] D. A. Turner. (1979b) Another algorithm for bracket abstraction. *Journal of Symbolic Logic,* 44(2) 67-270.

[36] S. C. Wray and J. Fairbairn. (1988) Non-strict languages (197) programming and implementation (draft) October 16, 1988.

[37] S. C. Wray. (1988) Private communication, October 24.

Index

The MIT Press, with Peter Denning as general consulting editor, publishes computer science books in the following series:

ACM Doctoral Dissertation Award and Distinguished Dissertation Series

Artificial Intelligence
Patrick Winston, founding editor
J. Michael Brady, Daniel G. Bobrow, and Randall Davis, editors

Charles Babbage Institute Reprint Series for the History of Computing
Martin Campbell-Kelly, editor

Computer Systems
Herb Schwetman, editor

Explorations with Logo
E. Paul Goldenberg, editor

Foundations of Computing
Michael Garey and Albert Meyer, editors

History of Computing
I. Bernard Cohen and William Aspray, editors

Information Systems
Michael Lesk, editor

Logic Programming
Ehud Shapiro, editor; Koichi Furukawa, Jean-Lois Lassez, Fernando Pereira, and David H. D. Warren, associate editors

The MIT Press Electrical Engineering and Computer Science Series

Research Monographs in Parallel and Distributed Processing
Christopher Jesshope and David Klappholz, editors

Scientific and Engineering Computation
Janusz Kowalik, editor

Technical Communication
Ed Barrett, editor